THE knitting machine BOOK

HAZEL RATCLIFFE

knitting machine DIGEST

COLLINS

Standard abbreviations used in the patterns:

alt	alternate	grms	grammes	rept	repeat
altog	altogether	H/P	holding position	RHS	right hand side
beg	beginning	inc	increase	RT	rib tension
carr	carriage	k	knit	rem	remaining
cms	centimetres	l	left	S/S	stitch size
col	colour	LHS	left hand side	st	stitch
COL	carriage on left	MT	main tension	sts	stitches
con	contrast	N(s)	needles	T	tension
COR	carriage on right	NWP	non working position	tog	together
dec	decrease			UWP	upper working position
DK	double knit	patt	pattern		
ev	every	pos	position	WP	working position
Ff	fully fashioned	r	right	WY	waste yarn
foll	following	RC	row counter		

Figures in brackets refer to larger sizes.

First published in 1984 by
Wm. Collins Sons & Co. Ltd.,
London . Glasgow . Sydney . Auckland
Toronto . Johannesburg

This book was designed and produced by
The Oregon Press Ltd.,
Faraday House, 8 Charing Cross Road,
London WC2H 0HG

Most of this material first published
in the magazine *Knitting Machine Digest*
© Hazel Ratcliffe 1984

ISBN 0 00 411726 3

Printed by Acanthus Press Ltd.,
The Trading Estate, Wellington, Somerset TA21 8ST
Bound by Robin Hartnell, Bodmin, Cornwall.

Lady's twin set

Lady's Fair Isle cardigan and sweater

Lady's Jacquard waistcoat

Lady's tennis jumper

Contents

1. Jumpers, cardigans and sweaters

2. Dresses, suits and skirts

Lady's Fair Isle sweater knitted sideways

Tracksuit

A Silverknit design

Lady's jumper and skirt

Unisex yoke sweater

Contents

Round neck sweater/saddle shoulders

Quilted jerkin

Mother and daughter sweaters

Man's cable T-shirt

Mother and daughter top

Mother and daughter snowmen sweaters

Specials for school

Toddler size three-piece outfit

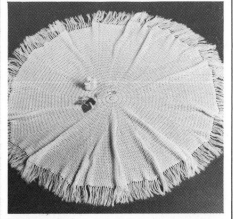

For your little treasure

Christening Day cape

Snuggle

Contents

Cassie caterpillar

Lady's gloves

Baby doll sleeping bag

Doll's outfit

Dear Readers,

When I bought my first knitting machine, 13 years ago, I had many questions to ask — where do I find easy to follow patterns that are reliable and straightforward and also fashionable? How do I know which yarns are suitable for my machine? And, most important of all, after the instruction book, where to next? I wish that such a book as this had been available at that time as it would have saved me many a false start and many hours of searching for the right pattern, the most suitable yarn, and wondering whether or not it could be knitted on my machine. Well, they do say that if you want anything doing . . . do it yourself. So I have, and here it is.

This collection of patterns from *Knitting Machine Digest Magazine* has many advantages over other machine knitting patterns. They are all tried and tested and have all proved popular with our early subscribers. They are all made in yarns that are readily available, if not locally to you they can easily be purchased by mail order. There is also sufficient information in each pattern for you to be able to substitute another yarn should you not be able to obtain the one recommended.

The patterns can be knitted on all the Japanese punchcard machines and where a pattern is for a specific machine such as a chunky knitter or a fine gauge, then it is clearly indicated on the pattern. Plain, classic garments can be knitted on any machine and where pattern is used you are free to use the scope of your own machine to produce the required effect. Knitting machine patterns should not be restricted by yarn brands or machine makes and models. Where instructions are given for ribbed welts and bands, owners of single bed machines can substitute mock ribs.

A special word to the new knitter. Before you launch yourself into your first garment spend an hour or two reading your machine instruction book and familiarise yourself with the knobs and levers and their terminology. The best way to learn is to knit a garment. Choose a light coloured, coned yarn, a soft 4 ply in acrylic or an acrylic wool mixture is ideal. Avoid too much nylon content and don't dabble with the 'hairies' and 'knobblies' until you are more familiar with your machine. Look through this book and try something simple. I would suggest the *Summer vest top,* opposite, the *Lady's classic sweater* on page 25, the *Lady's two piece evening outfit* on page 54, the *Gent's classic* on page 89, the *Specials for school* on page 105, or any of the toy or dolls' clothes patterns. There should be plenty there for you to choose from.

A knitting machine is an expensive item, but if it is put to good use it will be an invaluable investment. Not only will it save you money by producing the family wardrobe at a fraction of the cost of buying knitteds, but it can also be a source of income earned enjoyably in your own home.

We cannot compete with the chain store prices for everyday garments, but we can produce that exclusive sweater with the team name on it or the picture of the latest children's cartoon character. The versatility of the home knitting machine today is endless.

Where the instruction book finishes, this book begins, and the wealth of hints and tips contained within these pages are a tribute to all the wonderful people that I have met and the friends that I have made from all over the world because I once bought a knitting machine.

This book will not prevent you from dropping stitches but it will help you to pick them up again and 'Carry on Knitting'.

My thanks to everyone who has helped to make this book possible and my best wishes to you, the reader.

Hazel Ratcliffe

Summer vest top

Our summer top is another easy knit from Singer. An attractive yarn and simple design usually produces worthwhile results and this is no exception.

To suit most makes and models of machine.

MATERIALS

Phildar Pure Cotton 324 Perlé No. 50. 5 (6) x 40 grms balls col.1 (beige), 1 x 40 grms ball col.2 (white), 1 x 40 grms ball col.3 (turquoise)

MEASUREMENTS

To fit 81-86 (86-91) cms., 32-34 (34-36) ins. Figures in brackets refer to larger sizes.

TENSION

16 sts. and 24 rows to 5 cms (2 ins.) measured over stocking stitch. (Approx. tension 5.)
Check tension before starting garment.

BACK

Cast on 138 (154) sts. in col. 1 MT. knit 5 rows. *Knit 20 rows in col. 1, 2 rows in col. 2, 2 rows in col. 3*. Repeat from *to* throughout. Knit straight to R.C.220 (235)**.

Shape armholes

Dec. 5 sts. at beg. next 2 rows. Dec. 2 sts. at beg. next 4 (6) rows. Dec. 1 st. at beg. foll. 16 (18) rows. Continue straight to R.C.288 (320). [104 (118) sts.].

Shape neck

Carr. at right. Put 59 (68) Ns. at left into H/P. ***Knit 1 row. Cast off 5 (7) sts. at neck edge. Knit 1 row. Dec. 1 st. at neck edge, every foll. 22 (25) rows. Continue straight to R.C.322 (348). Cast of rem. 16 (18) sts. Rejoin yarn. Cast off centre 16 (18) sts. Knit 1 row. Repeat from *** reversing shaping.

FRONT

Knit as back to **.

Shape armholes

Cast off 6 sts. at beg. next 2 (2) rows. Cast off 3 sts. at beg. next 4 (4) rows. Cast off 2 sts. at beg. next 2 (4) rows. Dec. 1 st. at beg. foll. 16 (16) rows. 94 (106) sts. remain.

Shape neckline

Bring 51 (58) Ns. at left into H/P ****carr. at right. Knit 1 row. At neck edge cast off 2 sts. every alt. row 6 times. [31 (36) sts.] Dec. 1 st. every alt. row 10 (12) times. Dec. 1 st. every 4th row 5 (6) times. 16 (18) sts. remain. Continue straight to R.C.322 (348). Cast off rem. sts.

Rejoin yarn.

Cast off centre 8 sts. Knit 1 row. Repeat from **** reversing shapings.

TO MAKE UP

Press front and back according to ball band. Join shoulder seams. Join side seams to within 10 cms of bottom edge. Turn in all edges 1 cm, mitering corners of side splits. Press all turning.

NOTE:
Seams can be done by hand or on a sewing machine using a small straight stitch and the * Even Feed Foot available at Singer shops. Fits most machines.

Lady's Intarsia sweater

For Knitmaster Machines with Intarsia Carriage

MEASUREMENTS

To fit 81-106 cms/32-42 inch bust or chest; completed length from top of shoulder 75.5(76.5,76.5,77.5,77.5,78.5) cms; sleeve seam 42(42,41,41,40,40) cms.

MATERIALS

Sirdar Wash'n'Wear 4-ply. 9(9, 10,10,11,11) 20g balls in col 1 (red); 7(7,8,8,9,9) 20 grm balls in col 2 (yellow); 4(4,4,5,5,5) 20 grm balls in col 3 (white); 2(2,3,3,3,4) 20 grm balls in col 4 (green); 2(2,2,3,3,3) 20 grm balls in col 5 (blue); 2 20 grm balls in col 6 (black).

TENSIONS

32 sts and 46 rows to 10 cms (4 ins), using intarsia carr (see notes). Tension Dial at approx (5.); 32 sts and 46 rows to 10 cms (4 ins), using main carr. Tension Dial at approx (6).

NOTES

For tension using intarsia carr, work in 3 cols i.e. 32 sts in col 1, 6 sts in col 6 and 32 sts in col 2. Figures in brackets refer to the larger sizes respectively.

BACK

Using waste yarn, cast on 158 (166,174,182,190,198) sts and knit several rows ending with carr at left. Break off waste yarn. Remove main carr and place intarsia carr at left of machine. Take carr to right. (Ns are in C pos). Row Counter 000. Tension Dial at (5.). Lay col 5 across 47(51,55,59,63,67) Ns, col 6 across 6 Ns, col 3 across 52 Ns, col 6 across 6 Ns and col 4 across rem 47(51,55,59,63,67) Ns. Pass carr across. Continuing in this col sequence, knit 66 rows. Row Counter 067. Carr at left. Lay col 4 across 47(51,55,59,63,67) Ns, col 6 across 6 Ns, col 3 across 52 Ns and col 6 across rem 53(57,61,65,69,73) Ns. Pass carr across. Continuing in this col sequence, knit 9 rows. Row Counter 077. Carr at left. Lay col 4 across 47(51,55,59,63,67) Ns, col 6 across 6 Ns, col 3 across 52 Ns, col 6 across 6 Ns, and col 3 across rem 47(51,55,59,63,67) Ns. Pass carr across. Continuing in this col sequence, knit 24 rows. Row Counter 102. Carr at right. Lay col 3 across 47(51,55,59,63,67) Ns and col 6 across rem 111(115,119,123,127,131) Ns. Pass carr across. Continuing in this col sequence, knit 9 rows. Row Counter 112. Carr at right. Lay col 3 across 47(51,55,59,63,67) Ns, col 6 across 6 Ns and col 1 across rem 105(109, 113,117,121,125) Ns. Pass carr across. Continuing in this col sequence, knit 84 rows. Row Counter 197. Carr at left. Place a marker at each end of last row knitted. Lay col 1 across 105(109,113, 117,121,125) Ns and col 6 across rem 53(57,61,65,69,73) Ns. Pass carr across. Continuing in this col sequence, knit 9 rows. Row Counter 207. Carr at left. Lay col 1 across 105(109,113,117,121,125) Ns, col 6 across 6 Ns and col 2 across rem 47(51,55,59,63,67) Ns. Pass carr across*. Continuing in this col sequence, knit 96(100,100,104,104,110) rows. Row Counter 304(308,308,312,312,318). Carr at right.

Shape Shoulders

Cast off 6(6,7,7,7,8) sts beg of next 6(8,2,8,8,6) rows and 5(6,6,7,7,7) sts beg of next 4(2,8,2,2,4) rows.

Shape Back Neck

Using a length of col 1, cast off centre 36 sts. Push 33(35,38,38,42,43) Ns at left to D pos.

Knit Right Part as Folls:-
Cast off 5(6,6,6,7,7) sts beg of next row and 2 sts beg of next row. Rept the last 2 rows once more. Cast off 5(5,6,6,7,7) sts beg of next row and 2 sts beg of next row. Rept the last 2 rows once more. Cast off rem 5(5,6,6,6,7) sts. Carr at right. Push Ns at left back to C pos. Using col 1, knit 1 row. Now knit left part as for right part. Remove intarsia carr and replace main carr.

FRONT

Work as given for Back to *. Continuing in this col sequence, knit 86(90,90, 94,94,100) rows. Row Counter 294(298, 298,302,302,308). Carr at right.

Shape Neck

Using a length of col 1, cast off centre 20 sts. Push 69(73,77,81,85,89) Ns at left to D pos.

Knit Right Part as Folls:-
Knit 1 row. Cast off 4 sts beg of next row, knit 1 row. Cast off 3 sts beg of next row, knit 1 row. Cast off 2 sts beg of next and foll alt row, knit 1 row. Dec 1 st beg of next row.

Shape Shoulder

Cast off 6(6,7,7,7,8) sts beg of next row, dec 1 st beg of next row. Cast off 6(6,

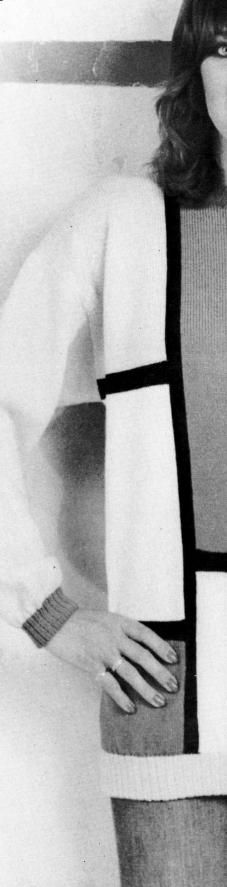

See colour plate opposite page 16

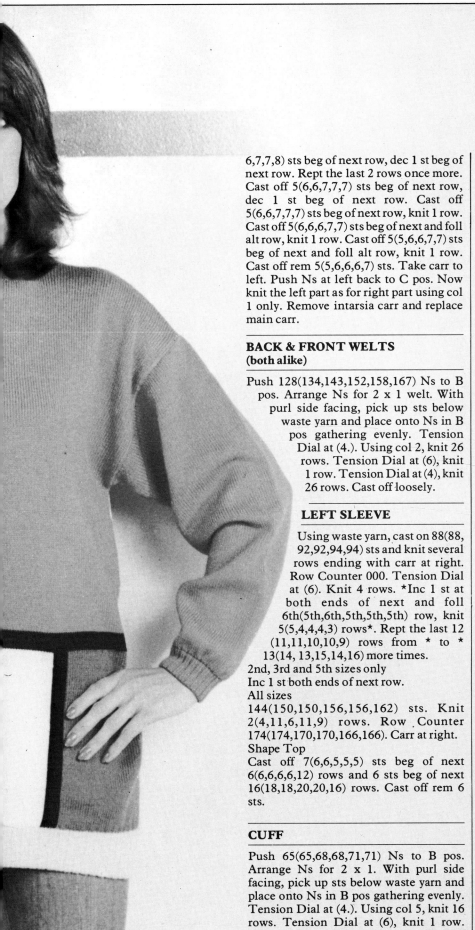

6,7,7,8) sts beg of next row, dec 1 st beg of next row. Rept the last 2 rows once more. Cast off 5(6,6,7,7,7) sts beg of next row, dec 1 st beg of next row. Cast off 5(6,6,7,7,7) sts beg of next row, knit 1 row. Cast off 5(6,6,6,7,7) sts beg of next and foll alt row, knit 1 row. Cast off 5(5,6,6,7,7) sts beg of next and foll alt row, knit 1 row. Cast off rem 5(5,6,6,6,7) sts. Take carr to left. Push Ns at left back to C pos. Now knit the left part as for right part using col 1 only. Remove intarsia carr and replace main carr.

BACK & FRONT WELTS
(both alike)

Push 128(134,143,152,158,167) Ns to B pos. Arrange Ns for 2 x 1 welt. With purl side facing, pick up sts below waste yarn and place onto Ns in B pos gathering evenly. Tension Dial at (4.). Using col 2, knit 26 rows. Tension Dial at (6), knit 1 row. Tension Dial at (4), knit 26 rows. Cast off loosely.

LEFT SLEEVE

Using waste yarn, cast on 88(88, 92,92,94,94) sts and knit several rows ending with carr at right. Row Counter 000. Tension Dial at (6). Knit 4 rows. *Inc 1 st at both ends of next and foll 6th(5th,6th,5th,5th,5th) row, knit 5(5,4,4,4,3) rows*. Rept the last 12 (11,11,10,10,9) rows from * to * 13(14, 13,15,14,16) more times.
2nd, 3rd and 5th sizes only
Inc 1 st both ends of next row.
All sizes
144(150,150,156,156,162) sts. Knit 2(4,11,6,11,9) rows. Row Counter 174(174,170,170,166,166). Carr at right.
Shape Top
Cast off 7(6,6,5,5,5) sts beg of next 6(6,6,6,6,12) rows and 6 sts beg of next 16(18,18,20,20,16) rows. Cast off rem 6 sts.

CUFF

Push 65(65,68,68,71,71) Ns to B pos. Arrange Ns for 2 x 1. With purl side facing, pick up sts below waste yarn and place onto Ns in B pos gathering evenly. Tension Dial at (4.). Using col 5, knit 16 rows. Tension Dial at (6), knit 1 row. Tension Dial at (4.), knit 16 rows. Cast off loosely.

RIGHT SLEEVE

Work as given for left sleeve but use col 2 in place of col 1.

NECKBAND

Join left shoulder seam. Push 137 Ns to B pos. With plain side facing, pick up sts evenly around neck edge and place onto Ns. Tension Dial at (5). Using col 5, knit 1 row. Transfer ev 3rd st onto its adjacent N for 2 x 1. Tension Dial at (4.), knit 11 rows. Tension Dial at (6) knit 1 row. Tension Dial at (4.), knit 12 rows. Push empty Ns to B pos. Pick up loop from the row below and place onto empty Ns. Knit 1 row. Using waste yarn, knit several rows and release from machine.

TO MAKE UP

Pin out each piece and press with a warm iron over a damp cloth. Join shoulder and neckband seams. Set in sleeves between marked points. Join side and sleeve seams. Fold cuffs and lower welts in half and catch down on the inside. Fold neckband in half pin into pos. and backstitch through open loops of last row knitted in col 5. Unravel waste yarn. Give final light press.

HINTS & TIPS

A TIP FOR THE CHARTING DEVICES

When you move the row scale on your charting device you MUST use the clutch lever to disengage it before you move the dial. If you are not sure, go back to the instruction book and READ it. You will damage your charting device and you will certainly get a false reading if you just force the row scale round without using the clutch.

RIBBER RULE

This tip is especially for ribber owners. Take note next time you use your ribber. Where do you put the hand that is not pushing the carriage along? If you lean on the ribber with it . . . DON'T. Leaning on the ribber as you knit can push it out of line and cause unnecessary strain on it.

Lady's twin set

MACHINES

For Knitmaster Punchcard and SK500 Electronic Machines. Suitable for all punchcard machines with a 24 stitch pattern repeat.

MEASUREMENTS

To fit 86-112 cms/34-44 inch bust. Slipover: Completed length from top of shoulder 59(60,61,62,63,63) cms. Cardigan: Completed length from top of shoulder 65(66,67,68,69,69) cms. Completed sleeve seam 44 cms.

MATERIALS

3 Suisse's Suizetta. Slipover 3(4,4,4,5,5) 50 grm balls in col 1; 2(3,3,3,4,4) 50 grm balls in col 2. Cardigan: 7(7,8,8,8,9) 50 grm balls in col 1; 1(1,2,2,2,2) 50 grm balls in col 2; 6 buttons. Punchcard 267 from series 55-56.

TENSIONS

31 sts and 41 rows to 10 cms (4 ins), measured over pattern. 31 sts and 4 rows to 10 cms (4 ins) measured over stockinet. Tension Dial at approx (6).

ABBREVIATIONS

Alt	Alternate	Carr	Carriage
Beg	Beginning	Cm(s)	Centimetre(s)
Col	Colour	Patt	Pattern
Dec	Decrease	Pos	Position
Ev	Every	Rept	Repeat
Foll	Following	Rem	Remaining
Grms	Grammes	St	Stitch
Inc	Increase	Sts	Stitches
N(s)	Needle(s)	Tog	Together

NOTE:
Figures in brackets refer to the larger sizes respectively.

SLIPOVER

BACK

Push 71(75,79,83,87,91) Ns at left and 72(74,79,84,86,91) Ns at right of centre O to B pos. [143(149,158,167,173,182) Ns altog.].
Punchcard Machines
Insert card into machine and lock on row 23.
Electronic Machines
Inspection button on. Insert card and set to row 23. Pattern width indicator 24. Needle 1 cam 12 at right of centre 0. Point cams at edge of knitting. Buttons 1(left) and 2(left).
All Machines
Arrange Ns for 2x1 welt. Using waste yarn cast on and knit several rows ending with carr at right. Tension Dial at 4. Using col 1, knit 26 rows. Tension Dial at

(6) knit 1 row. Tension Dial at (4) knit 6 rows. Using col 2, knit 2 rows. Using col 1, knit 10 rows. Using col 2, knit 2 rows. Using col 1, knit 6 rows. Turn up a hem, knit 1 row. Carr at right.
1st, 2nd, 4th & 5th Sizes Only
Dec(inc,dec,inc) 1 st at right edge.
All Sizes
142(150,158,166,174,182) Ns. Row Counter 000. Tension Dial at (6).
Punchcard Machines
Release card.
Electronic Machines
Inspection button off.
All Machines
Insert yarn separators. Set carr for fairisle. With col 1 in feeder 1 and col 2 in feeder 2, knit 124 rows. Carr at right*.
Shape Armholes
Cast off 4(4,5,5,5,5) sts beg next 2 rows, 3 sts beg next 4(6,6,6,8,8) rows, 2 sts beg next 6(4,4,6,4,4) rows. Dec 1 st both ends next and ev foll alt row 3(3,3,2,2,4) times in all, knit 3 rows. Dec 1 st both ends next and ev foll 4th row 5(5,5,5,5,4) times in all. 94(100,106,112,118,124) sts. Knit 49(53,57,61,65,65) rows without shaping. Row Counter 210(214,218,222,226,226). Carr at right.
Shape Shoulders
Cast off 5(6,7,7,8,8) sts beg next 2 rows, 5(6,6,7,8,8) sts beg next 2 rows.
Shape Back Neck
Using length of col 1, cast off centre 36 sts. Using nylon cord knit 19(20, 22,24,25,28) sts at left by hand taking Ns back to A pos.
Punchcard Machines
Take note of row number showing on patt panel.
Electronic Machines
Inspection button on. Take note of row number showing on patt panel. Inspection button off.
All Machines
Knit Right Part as folls:-
Cast off 5(6,6,7,7,8) sts beg next row, 2 sts beg next row, 5(5,6,7,7,8) sts beg next row, 2 sts beg next row. Cast off rem 5(5,6,6,7,8) sts.
Punchcard Machines
Carr at right. Reset card to number previously noted and lock. Take carr to left. Release card.
Electronic Machines
Carr at right. Inspection button on. Reset card to number previously noted. Take carr to left. Inspection button off.
All Machines
Unravel nylon cord bringing Ns back to B pos. Knit left part as for right part.

FRONT

Foll instructions for Back to ★.

Shape Neck and Armhole

Using nylon cord knit 71(75,79,83,87,91) sts at left by hand taking Ns back to A pos.

Punchcard Machines

Take note of row number showing on patt panel.

Electronic Machines

Inspection button on. Take note of row number showing on patt panel. Inspection button off.

All Machines

Knit Right Part as follows:-

Dec-ing 1 st at left edge on the next (next,5th,5th,5th,5th) and ev foll 4th row, AT THE SAME TIME cast off 4(4,5,5,5,5) sts beg next row, knit 1 row. Cast off 3 sts beg next and ev foll alt row 2(3,3,3,4,4) times in all, knit 1 row. Cast off 2 sts beg next and ev foll alt row 3(2,2,3,2,2) times in all, knit 1 row. Dec 1 st beg next and ev foll alt row 3(3,3,2,2,4) times in all, knit 3 rows. Dec 1 st beg next and ev foll 4th row 5(5,5,5,5,4) times in all. 37(40,44,47,50,53) sts. Keeping right edge straight dec 1 st at left edge on the 4th and ev foll 4th row 12(12,13,13,13,13) times in all. Knit 1(5,5,9,13,13) rows without shaping. Row Counter 210(214,218,222,226,226). Carr at right.

Shape Shoulder

Cast off 5(6,7,7,8,8) sts beg next row, knit 1 row. Cast off 5(6,7,7,8,8) sts beg next row, knit 1 row. Cast off 5(6,6,7,7,8) sts beg next row, knit 1 row. Cast off 5(5,6,7,7,8) sts beg next row, knit 1 row. Cast off rem 5(5,6,6,7,8) sts.

Punchcard Machines

Carr at right. Reset card to number previously noted and lock. Take carr to left. Release card.

Electronic Machines

Inspection button on. Reset card to number previously noted. Take carr to left. Inspection button off.

All Machines

Unravel nylon cord bringing Ns back to B pos. Knit left part as for right part but read right for left and vice versa. Remove card.

NECKBAND (2 pieces alike)

Join shoulder seams. Push 110(113, 116,119,122,122) Ns to B pos. Arrange Ns for 2x1. With plain side facing pick up sts from centre front to centre back and place onto Ns in B pos at both ends. Set carr for stockinet. Tension Dial at (4). Using col 1, knit 1 row. Dec 1 st at centre front on next 5 rows. Tension Dial at (6) knit 1 row. Tension Dial at (4). Inc1 st at centre front on next 2 rows. Using col 2. Inc 1 st at centre front on next 2 rows. Using col1. Inc 1 st at centre front on next row, knit 1 row. Push empty Ns to B pos. Pick up a loop from the row below and place onto empty Ns, knit 1 row. Using

waste yarn, knit 8 rows and release from machine.

ARMHOLE BANDS (both alike)

Push 158(161,164,167,170,170) Ns to B pos. Arrange Ns for 2x1. With plain side facing pick up sts evenly around armhole edge and place onto Ns in B pos. Tension Dial at (4). Using col 1, knit 1 row. Dec 1 st both ends next 5 rows. Tension Dial at (6) knit 1 row. Tension Dial at (4). Inc 1 st both ends next 2 rows. Using col 2. Inc 1 st both ends next 2 rows. Using col 1. Inc 1 st both ends next row, knit 1 row. Push empty Ns to B pos. Pick up a loop from the row below and place onto empty Ns, knit 1 row. Using waste yarn, knit 8 rows and release from machine.

TO MAKE UP

Pin out and steam carefully with a warm iron over a damp cloth. Join side and band seams. Fold bands in half onto the outside. Pin into pos and backstitch through open loops of last row knitted in col 1. Unravel waste yarn. Give final light steam.

ELECTRONIC CHART

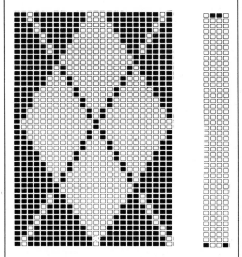

CARDIGAN

BACK

Push 75(79,83,87,91,95) Ns at left and 74(79,84,86,91,96) Ns at right of centre O to B pos. [149(158,167,173,182,191) Ns altog].

★Punchcard Machines

Insert card into machine and lock on row 23.

Electronic Machines

Inspection button on. Insert card and set to row 23. Pattern width indicator 24. Needle 1 cam 12 at right of centre 0 (left of centre 0 on Left Front). Point cams at edge of knitting. Buttons 1 (left) and 2(left).

All Machines

Arrange Ns for 2x1 welt. Using waste yarn cast on and knit several rows ending with carr at right. Tension Dial at (4). Using col 1, knit 26 rows. Tension Dial at (6) knit 1 row. Tension Dial at (4) knit 6 rows. Using col 2, knit 2 rows. Using col 1, knit 10 rows. Using col 2, knit 2 rows. Using col 1, knit 6 rows. Turn up a hem, knit 1 row. Carr at right★.

1st, 3rd, 4th & 6th Sizes Only

Inc(dec,inc,dec) 1 st at right edge.

All Sizes

150(158,166,174,182,190) sts. Row Counter 000. Tension Dial at (6).

Punchcard Machines

Release card

Electronic Machines

Inspection button off.

All Machines

Insert yarn separators. Set carr for fairisle. With col 1 in feeder 1 and col 2 in feeder 2, knit 46 rows. Remove card and yarn separators. Set carr for stockinet. Using col 1, knit 38 rows. Dec 1 st both ends next and foll 40th row. 146(154,162, 170,178,186) sts. Knit 39 rows without shaping. Row Counter 164. Carr at right.

Shape Armholes

Cast off 5 sts beg next 2 rows, 3 sts beg next 2(2,4,4,4,6) rows, 2 sts beg next 4(6,4,4,6,4) rows. Dec 1 st both ends next and ev foll alt row 3(2,2,3,2,2) times in all, knit 3 rows. Dec 1 st both ends next and ev foll 4th row 5 times in all. 106(112, 118,124,130,136) sts. Knit 51(55,59, 61,67,67) rows without shaping. Row Counter 248(252,256,260,266,266). Carr at right.

Shape Shoulders

Always taking yarn round first inside Ns in D pos, push 6(6,7,7,8,8) Ns at opposite end to carr to D pos on next 2 rows and 5(6,6,7,7,8) Ns on next 4 rows.

Shape Back Neck

Using length of col 1, cast off centre 36 sts. Using nylon cord knit 19(20, 22,23,25,26) sts in B pos at left by hand taking Ns back to A pos.

Knit Right Part as folls:-

Knit 1 row. Cast off 2 sts at beg and push 5(6,6,7,7,8) Ns at opposite end to carr to D pos on next row, knit 1 row. Cast off 2 sts at beg and push 5(5,6,6,7,7) Ns at opposite end to carr to D pos on next row, knit 1 row. 5(5,6,6,7,7) Ns rem in B pos. Push Ns at right from D pos back to C pos, knit 1 row. Using waste yarn, knit 8 rows and release from machine. Take carr to left. Unravel nylon cord bringing Ns back to B pos. Knit left part as for right part but read left for right.

RIGHT FRONT

Push 74(80,83,86,92,95) Ns at right of centre 0 to B pos. Foll instructions for Back from ★to★.

1st, 2nd, 4th & 5th Sizes Only

Inc (dec,inc,dec) 1 st at right edge.

All Sizes

75(79,83,87,91,95) sts. Row Counter 000. Tension Dial at (6).

Punchcard Machines

Release card.

Electronic Machines

Inspection button off.

All Machines

Insert yarn separators. Set carr for fairisle. With col 1 in feeder 1 and col 2 in feeder 2, knit 46 rows. Remove card and yarn separators. Set carr for stockinet. Using col 1, knit 38 rows. Dec 1 st at right edge on next and foll 40th row. 73(77,81,85,89, 93) sts. Knit 18(18,23,23,28,28) rows without shaping. Row Counter 143 (143,148,148,153,153).

Shape Front Edge

Dec 1 st at left edge on next and ev foll 5th row 5(5,4,4,3,3) times in all. Row Counter 164. Carr at right.

Shape Armhole

Dec-ing 1 st at left edge on the 5th and ev foll 5th row. AT THE SAME TIME cast off 5 sts beg next row, knit 1 row.

1st & 2nd Sizes only

Cast off 3 sts beg next row, knit 1 row.

3rd, 4th, 5th & 6th Sizes Only

Cast off 3 sts beg next and ev foll alt row (2,2,2,3) times in all, knit 1 row.

All Sizes

Cast off 2 sts beg next and ev foll alt row 2(3,2,2,3,2) times in all, knit 1 row. Dec 1 st beg next and ev foll alt row 3(2,2,3,2,2) times in all, knit 3 rows. Dec 1 st beg next and ev foll 4th row 5 times in all. 42(45,49,51,55,58) sts. Keeping right edge straight, dec 1 st at left edge on the 2nd(2nd,2nd,5th,5th,5th) and ev foll 5th row 11(11,12,11,12,12) times in all. 31(34,37,40,43,46) sts. Knit 0(4,3,7,8,8) rows. Row Counter 249(253,257, 261,267,267). Carr at left.

Shape Shoulder

Always taking yarn round first inside N in D pos, push 6(6,7,8,8,8) Ns at opposite end to carr to D pos on next row, knit 1 row, 5(6,6,7,7,8) Ns on next and ev foll alt row 3 times in all, knit 1 row, 5(5,6,6,7,7) Ns on next row, knit 1 row. 5(5,6,6,7,7) Ns rem in B pos. Push Ns in D pos back to C pos, knit 1 row. Using waste yarn, knit 8 rows and release from machine.

LEFT FRONT

Work as given for Right Front but reverse the shapings by reading left for right and vice versa throughout. (Do not reverse pos of buttons on Electronic machines).

SLEEVES (both alike)

Push 47(47,47,50,50,50) Ns at left and right of centre 0 to B pos. [94(94, 94,100,100,100) Ns altog].

Punchcard Machines

Insert card into machine and lock on row 23.

Electronic Machines

Inspection button on. Insert card and set to row 23. Pattern width indicator 24. Needle 1 cam 12 at right of centre 0. Point cams edge of knitting. Buttons 1(left) and 2(left).

All Machines

Using waste yarn, cast on and knit several rows ending with carr at left. Tension Dial at (6). Using col 1, knit 1 row. Carr at right. Row Counter 000.

Punchcard Machines

Release card.

Electronic Machines

Inspection button off.

All Machines

Insert yarn separators. Set carr for fairisle. With col 1 in feeder 1 and col 2 in feeder 2, knit 46 rows. Remove card and yarn separators. Set carr for stockinet. Using col 1, knit 3(7,4,4,5,5) rows. Inc 1 st both ends next and ev foll 20th(12th, 9th,9th,7th,7th) row 6(9,12,12,15,15) times in all. 106(112,118,124,130,130) sts. Knit 14 rows without shaping. Row Counter 164. Carr at right.

Shape Top

Cast off 5 sts beg next 2 rows, 3 sts beg next 4(6,6,6,6,6) rows, 2 sts beg next 4(2,4,6,6,6) rows. Dec 1 st both ends next and ev foll 5th row 8(9,9,9,9,9) times in all, knit 4(1,1,1,1,1) rows. Cast off 2 sts beg next 4(2,2,2,2,2) rows, 3 sts beg next 4(6,4,4,6,6) rows, 4 sts beg next 4(4,6,4,4,4) rows.

4th, 5th & 6th Sizes Only

Cast off 5 sts beg next 2 rows.

All Sizes

Row Counter 226(228,230,232,234,234). Cast off rem 24 sts.

CUFFS (both alike)

Push 62(62,62,68,68,68) Ns to B pos. Arrange Ns for 2x1. With purl side of sleeve facing, pick up sts from below waste yarn and place onto Ns in B pos gathering evenly. Unravel waste yarn. Row Counter 000. Tension Dial at (4). Using col 1, knit 6 rows. Using col 2, knit 2 rows. Using col 1, knit 10 rows. Using col 2, knit 2 rows. Using col 1, knit 6 rows. Tension dial at (6) knit 1 row. Tension Dial at (4) knit 26 rows. Push empty Ns back to B pos. Turn up a hem by placing the loops of first row of cuff onto the 1st and 3rd and ev foll 2nd and 3rd N. Cast off loosely.

BACK NECK BAND

Push 59 Ns to B pos. Arrange Ns for 2x1. With plain side facing, pick up sts across back neck and place onto Ns in B pos. Tension Dial at (4). Using col 1, knit 6 rows. Tension Dial at (6) knit 1 row. Tension Dial at (4), knit 2 rows. Using col 2, knit 2 rows. Using col 1, knit 2 rows. Push empty Ns to B pos, pick up a loop from the row below and place onto empty Ns, knit 1 row. Using waste yarn, knit 8 rows and release from machine.

BUTTONHOLE BAND

Push 185(188,191,194,197,197) Ns to B pos. Arrange Ns for 2x1. With plain side of right front facing pick up sts evenly along front edge and place onto Ns in B pos. *Tension Dial at (4). Using col 1, knit 3 rows. Counting from the lower (right) edge to the first front dec, make 6 buttonholes evenly spaced over 3 Ns. Knit 3 rows. Tension Dial at (6) knit 1 row. Tension Dial at (4) knit 2 rows. Using col 2, knit 1 row. Make buttonholes over same Ns as before, knit 1 row. Using col 1, knit 2 rows. Push empty Ns to B pos. Pick up a loop from the row below and place onto empty Ns, knit 1 row. Using waste yarn, knit 8 rows and release from machine.

BUTTON BAND

Push 185(188,191,194,197,197) Ns to B pos. Arrange Ns for 2xl. With plain side of left front facing pick up sts evenly along front edge and place onto Ns in B pos. Work as given for buttonhole band from *to end but omit buttonholes.

TO MAKE UP

Pin out and steam carefully with a warm iron over a damp cloth. Join shoulder, side, band and sleeve seams. Set in sleeves. Fold bands in half onto the outside. Pin into pos and backstitch through open loops of last row knitted in col 1. Unravel waste yarn. Finish buttonholes and sew on buttons to correspond.

HINTS & TIPS

INSIDE OUT

If you have knitted garments that tend to 'pill' in the wash and emerge covered in little woolly balls, mostly this applies to the acrylics, try turning the garment inside out before you put it in the wash and then all the pilling will be on the inside of the garment. I am told that this is a very old tip but I had not heard it before and I can assure you that it works.

INTERESTING FIND

We have found a scarf that has the same design on it as one of the Knit-master punchcards and we have seen material with a similar design on it. Our plan is to knit a sweater with the same design and then add the scarf to complete the outfit. The material had already been made into a blouse and the lady in question had made a jacket and waistcoat to wear with the blouse and had used the punchcard to make Fair Isle borders on the knitted garments . . . result something very smart and definitely not available in the shops.

Lady's punch pile jacket

For Knitmaster Punchcard and Electronic Machines with SRP50 ribbing attachment.

SIZES

To fit 81-107 cms./32-42 inch bust.

MATERIALS

2 (2, 3, 3, 3, 3) 200 grm. cones Silverknit Dakota in col. 1; 2 (2, 3, 3, 3, 3) small cones 30's cotton in col. 2; 2 large press studs. Both yarns available from Silverknit, Dept. K, The Old Mill, Epperstone-By-Pass, Woodborough, Notts.

TENSION

39 sts (on ribber) and 60 rows to 10 cms (4 ins) measured over punch pile. 33 sts (on ribber) and 59 rows to 10 cms (4 ins) measured over plain pile. Tension dials at approx 3.

NOTES:

Figures in brackets refer to the larger sizes respectively. When casting off or decreasing, cast off or decrease on ribber and push corresponding Ns. on knitter to A pos. When increasing, increase on ribber and push corresponding Ns. on knitter to B pos.

UPPER BACK (A)

With ribbing attachment in pos., set half pitch lever to H and swing indicator to 5.
Needle Arrangement 1 1 1 1
                1 1 1 1
Carr. at right. Arrange 53 (55, 55, 57, 57, 58) Ns. at left and right of centre 0 in B pos. on knitter and arrange 107 (111, 111, 115, 115, 117) Ns. in B pos. on ribber for double rib.
Punchcard machines
Insert special card and lock on row 1.
Electronic machines
Inspection button on. Set point cams to width of knitting and needle 1 cam at centre of machine. Take carr. across twice.
All machines
**Set knitter and ribber as shown in line 1 of cast on for pile knitting. Tension dials at 3. Using col. 1, cast on. Carr. at left. R.C. 000. Suspend cast-on comb. Transfer knitter sts. to ribber, leaving empty Ns. in B pos. Suspend weights. Set cam lever to slip and auxiliary yarn feeder lever to P.

Depress drop levers to middle pos. Thread col. 2 in auto-tension and auxiliary yarn feeder. Restore ribber to upper pos. Depress pile levers★★.
Punchcard machines
Release card.
Electronic machines
Insert special card and set to first row. Pattern width indicator 24. Buttons 1 (left) and 2 (left). Inspection button off.
All machines ★ and ★★★
Counting from left edge, mark st. 71 on ribber with waste yarn. Work in punch pile knitting throughout, knit 258 (276, 288, 306, 324, 342) rows. Counting from left edge, mark st. 71 on ribber with waste yarn. Cast off.

LOWER BACK (B)

With ribbing attachment in pos., set half pitch lever to H and swing indicator to 5.
Needle arrangement   1 1 1 1
　　　　　　　　　　1 1 1 1 1
Carr. at right. Arrange 57 Ns. at left and right of centre 0 in B pos. on knitter and arrange 115 Ns. in B pos. on ribber for double rib. Work as given for Upper Back from ★ to ★. ★★★. Push 12 Ns. on knitter at left to A pos. Work in punch pile knitting throughout. Knit 294 (312, 324, 342, 360, 378) rows. Cast off.

LOWER RIGHT FRONT (C)

Work as for Lower Back to ★★★. Push 12 Ns. on knitter at left to A pos. (right on Lower Left Front). Work in punch pile knitting throughout. Knit 190 (198, 206, 214, 222, 232) rows. Cast off.

LOWER LEFT FRONT (C)

Work as for Lower Right Front, noting following alterations:
Punchcard machines
Insert card back to front.
Electronic machines
Use button 2 (right) not left.

UPPER RIGHT FRONT (D)

Work as for Upper Back to ★★★. Counting from left edge, mark st. 71 on ribber with waste yarn (right edge on Upper Left Front). Work in punch pile knitting throughout. Knit 105 (113, 119, 129, 137, 147) rows. Knit 1 row extra for Upper Left Front. Carr. at right (left on Upper Left Front).
Shape front edge (see notes)
Cast off 3 sts. (on ribber) at beg. of next and ev. foll. alt. row 20 (24, 24, 28, 28, 30) times in all, knit 1 row. Cast off 2 sts. (on ribber) at beg. of next and ev. foll. alt. row 14 (10, 10, 6, 6, 4) times in all. 19 sts. on ribber. Cast off.

UPPER LEFT FRONT (D)

Work as for Upper Right Front, noting alteration in number of rows worked, reversing shapings and noting following alterations:
Punchcard machines
Insert card back to front.
Electronic machines
Use button 2 (right) not left.

SLEEVES (both alike) (E)

With ribbing attachment in pos., set half pitch lever to H and swing indicator to 5.
Needle arrangement   1 1 1 1
　　　　　　　　　　1 1 1 1 1
Carr. at right. Arrange 50 (54, 54, 58, 58, 62) Ns. at left and right of centre 0 in B pos. on knitter and arrange 101 (109, 109, 117, 117, 125) Ns. in B pos. on ribber for double rib. Work as given for Upper Back from ★ to ★. Work in punch pile knitting throughout. Knit 18 rows. Inc. 1 st. (on ribber – see notes) at beg. of next 2 rows and ev. foll. 11th and 12th rows 18 times in all. 137 (145, 145, 153, 153, 161) sts. on ribber. Knit 10 (10, 8, 4, 4, 4) rows. R.C. 234 (234, 232, 228, 228, 228). Carr. at left.
Shape top (see notes)
Cast off 4 (4, 5, 6, 6, 6) sts. (on ribber) at beg. of next 18 (10, 10, 20, 20, 12) rows and 5 (5, 5, 7, 7, 7) sts. (on ribber) at beg. of next 12 (20, 18, 4, 4, 12) rows. 5 sts. on ribber. Cast off.

FRONT WAISTBANDS
(both alike) (F)

Electronic machines
Inspection button on, insert card 13 pattern 39. Pattern width indicator 1. Point cams at width of knitting. Needle 1 cam centre of machine. Buttons 1 (left) and 2 (left).
All machines
With ribbing attachment in pos., set half pitch lever to H and swing indicator to 5.
Needle arrangement   1 1 1 1
　　　　　　　　　　1 1 1 1
Carr. at right★. Arrange 81 (86, 89, 94, 99, 104) Ns. in B pos. on knitter and 82 (87, 90, 95, 100, 105) Ns. in B pos. on ribber for double rib. ★★Work as given for Upper Back from ★★ to ★★.
Electronic machines
Inspection button off.
All machines
Work in plain pile knitting throughout, knit 18 rows. Cast off.

BACK WAISTBAND (G)

Work as given for Front Waistbands to ★. Arrange 116 (126, 132, 142, 152, 162) Ns. in B pos. on knitter and 117 (127, 133, 143, 153, 163) Ns. in B pos. on ribber for double rib. Work as given for Front Waistbands from ★★ to end.

RIGHT FRONT YOKE (H)

Work as given for Front Waistband to ★. Arrange 57 (62, 66, 71, 76, 81) Ns. in B pos. on knitter and 58 (63, 67, 72, 77, 82) Ns. in B pos. on ribber for double rib. Work as given for Upper Back from ★★ to ★★.
Electronic machines
Inspection button off.
All machines
Work in plain pile knitting throughout. Knit 4 rows. Knit 1 row extra for Left Front Yoke. Dec. 1 st. (on ribber – see notes) at beg. of next and ev. foll. 4th row 10 times in all. 48 (53, 57, 62, 67, 72) sts. on ribber. Knit 14 rows. R.C. 55 (56 on Left Front Yoke). Carr. at right (left on Left Front Yoke).
Shape shoulder (see notes)
Cast off 4 (5, 5, 5, 6, 6) sts. (on ribber) at beg. of next row, knit 1 row. Cast off 4 (4,

PUNCHCARD MACHINES

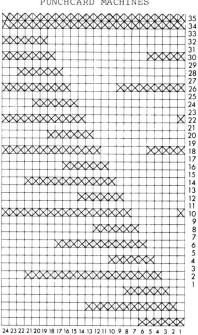

ELECTRONIC MACHINES

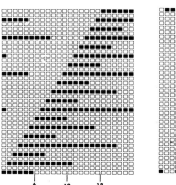

5, 5, 6, 6) sts. (on ribber) at beg. of next row, knit 1 row. Cast off 4 (4, 5, 5, 5, 6) sts. (on ribber) at beg. of next and ev. foll. alt. row 7 (7, 3, 8, 5, 5) times in all, knit 1 row. Cast off 3 (4, 4, 4, 5, 5) sts. (on ribber) at beg. of next and ev. foll. alt. row 3 (3, 7, 2, 5, 5) times in all, knit 1 row. 3 (4, 4, 4, 5, 5) sts. on ribber. Cast off.

LEFT FRONT YOKE (H)

Work as for Right Front Yoke, noting alteration in number of rows worked and reversing shapings. Do not reverse pos. of buttons on Electronic machines.

LEFT BACK YOKE (I)

Work as given for Front Waistbands to ⋆. Arrange 70 (75, 79, 84, 89, 94) Ns. in B pos. on knitter and 71 (76, 80, 85, 90, 95) Ns. in B pos. on ribber for double rib. Work as given for Upper Back from ⋆⋆ to ⋆⋆.
Electronic machines
Inspection button off.

All machines
Work in plain pile knitting throughout. Knit 55 rows. Knit 1 row extra for Right Back Yoke. Carr. at right (left on Right Back Yoke).
Shape shoulder (see notes)
Cast off 4 (5, 5, 5, 6, 6) sts. (on ribber) at beg. of next row, knit 1 row. Cast off 4 (4, 5, 5, 6, 6) sts. (on ribber) at beg. of next row, knit 1 row. Cast of 4 (4, 5, 5, 5, 6) sts. (on ribber) at beg. of next and ev. foll. alt. row 3 (3, 3, 3, 3, 5) times in all, knit 1 row. Cast off 4 (4, 4, 5, 5, 5) sts. (on ribber) at beg. of next and ev. foll. alt. row 4 (4, 4, 4, 2) times in all.
Shape neck (see notes)
Cast off 20 sts. (on ribber) at beg. of next row, 3 (4, 4, 5, 5, 5) sts. (on ribber) at beg. of next row, 1 st. (on ribber) at beg. of next row, 3 (4, 4, 4, 5, 5) sts. (on ribber) at beg. of next row, 1 st. (on ribber) at beg. of next row, 3 (4, 4, 4, 5, 5) sts. (on ribber) at beg. of next row and 1 st (on ribber) at beg. of next row. 3 (4, 4, 4, 5, 5) sts. on ribber. Cast off.

RIGHT BACK YOKE (I)

Work as for Left Back Yoke, noting alteration in number of rows worked and reversing shapings. Do not reverse pos. of buttons on Electronic machines.

FRONT BANDS

Using waste yarn, cast on 12 sts. on knitter only. Knit several rows ending with carr. at right. R.C. 000. Tension dial at 1. Knit approx. 748 (760, 760, 772, 772, 784) rows. Using waste yarn, knit 8 rows and release from machine.

TO MAKE UP

Join centre back yoke seam. Join shoulder seams. Join upper back and upper fronts to yoke. Gather lower edge of upper back and upper fronts and join to waistbands. Gather upper edge of lower back and lower fronts and join to waistband. Sew top of sleeves into pos. between marked sts. Join side and sleeve seams. Turn up 12 rows at lower edge and catch down on inside. Sew front band to front and neck edges and catch down on the inside. Neaten ends. Sew press studs into inside and outside edges of waistband overlap.

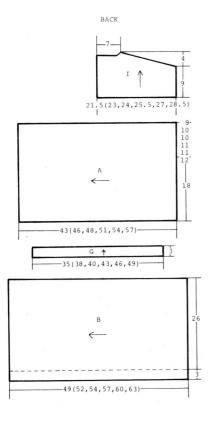

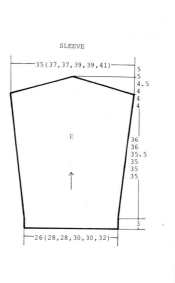

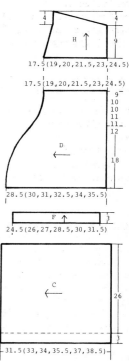

Diagram of finished measurements in centimetres

Have you ever tried lace?

Perhaps you are new to machine knitting or perhaps you have a new lace making machine or you have had a lace carriage for a long time and never got round to using it, well now is the time to have a go. This pattern was written for us by Joan Godfrey from our Eastbourne School and although it is written with the beginner in mind, it is a pattern we can all enjoy knitting and it will make a useful addition to any wardrobe.

CUT AND SEW

If you are new to cut and sew then before you complete this garment read our cut and sew article in this issue and then proceed . . .

LACE TWO PLY JUMPER

The jumper was knitted on a Knitmaster 360 but can be knitted on any machine with a lace carriage. Punch lace could also be substituted provided that the correct tension is obtained.

TENSION

8 sts nd 12 rows to one inch measured over the pattern. This pattern is for a finished measurement of 97 cms (38 ins) bust. Add 8 sts for every extra inch required and adjust the length by knitting 12 extra rows for every extra inch required.

FRONT

Cast on 150 sts. in 1 x 1 rib and knit 30 rows T. 1/1.
Transfer sts. to main bed.
Insert card and set pattern (pattern used was card 1 from basic lace pack).
T. (4) R.C. 000. In pattern knit 136 rows.
Put a marker thread at each edge to mark for armhole.
Knit in pattern till row 90. Set machine for stocking stitch and shape shoulders.
Hold 10 sts. at each end until 40 sts. are in the holding position leaving 70 sts. in the centre.
Knit 1 row on all sts. including those that were in hold.
Run off on waste yarn.

BACK

Cast on 150 sts. in 1 x 1 rib and knit 30 rows T. 1/1.
Transfer sts. to main bed.
Insert card and set pattern (pattern used was card 1 from basic lace pack).
T. (4) R.C. 000. In pattern knit 136 rows.
Put a marker thread at each edge to mark for armhole.
Knit in pattern till row 90. Set machine for stocking stitch and shape shoulders.
Hold 10 sts. at each end until 40 sts. are in the holding position leaving 70 sts. in the centre.
Knit 1 row on all sts. including those that were in hold.
Run off on waste yarn.

CUT AND SEW NECKLINE

When shoulders are joined (either by grafting or on the machine) fold the front in half and measure down three inches and graduate up to the shoulders, on the back measure down about ½ an inch.
Do 2 rows of zig zag on a sewing machine, or 2 rows of backstitching before cutting.

NECKBAND

Cast on 150 sts. 1 x 1 rib T. 1/1 knit 44 rows.
Change to T. 3/3 knit 16 rows tubular and run off on waste yarn. Join sides of neckband, press waste yarn. Fit band carefully round neck of jumper, backstitch on the right side and catch down on the inside. Fold band in half and catch down on the inside.

ARMBANDS

Cast on 124 sts. 1 x 1 rib. T. 1/1. Knit 30 rows. Put sts. onto main bed and with wrong side of work facing you, pick up sts. between the markers, knit one row at T. 9 and cast off.
To finish sew up side seams with mattress stitch.

Opposite: **Lady's Intarsia sweater** (see pattern on page 8)

Lady's Fair Isle cardigan and sweater

A design by Argyll Wools

Opposite: **Bow jumper** (see pattern on page 20)

Above: **See colour plate on front cover** 17

SIZES

Cardigan and sweater to fit 82 (87, 92, 97) cms, 32 (34, 36, 38) ins bust.
Length to shoulder: Cardigan, 59 (60, 61, 62) cms, 23 (23½, 24, 24½) ins.
Sweater, 55 (56, 57, 58) cms, 21½ (22, 22½, 23) ins.
Sleeve seam, 43.5 cms, 17 ins.

MATERIALS

Argyll Starlite on 340 grm cone. 1 cone each Nimbus 269 (M), Aquarius 267 (A), Aries 268 (B), Scorpio 266 (C), Gemini 265 (D).
6 Buttons.

TENSION

30 sts and 37 rows to 10 cm (4 ins) measured over Fair Isle on MT (approx T8). Tensions must be matched exactly before starting to knit.

NOTES:
Punchcard machines
Punch a card as shown before starting to knit. (Refer to instructions for your machine and colour sequence). When working Fair Isle pattern, read 2 colour pattern rows as follows:— Thread first colour stated into feeder 1/A and second colour stated into feeder 2/B (eg k 3 rows M/A means k 3 rows with M in feeder 1/A and A in feeder 2/B.
Fair Isle pattern
K 3 rows M/B, 3 rows M/C, 3 rows M/D, 3 rows M/A.
These 12 rows form pattern.

CARDIGAN

BACK

Punchcard machines
Insert card and lock on row 1.
All machines
Push 134 (141, 149, 156) Ns to WP. * Push every 3rd N back to NWP. Using MT and WY, cast on and k a few rows ending with carriage at right. Set RC at 000. Using MT 3 and A, k 55 rows. Push Ns from NWP to WP and make a hem by placing loops of first row worked in A evenly along the row. Unravel WY when work is completed *. Inc 1 (0, 0, 1) st. 135 (141, 149, 157) sts. Set RC at 000. Using MT and M, k 1 row. ***
Punchcard machines
Release card. Set machine for Fair Isle and work in Fair Isle pattern as given in Note.
All other machines
Work from Fair Isle chart.
All machines
K 126 rows. Work measures 40 cms, 15¾ ins.
Shape armholes
Cast off 4 sts at beg of next 2 rows. Dec 1 st at each end of every row until 119 (125, 129, 133) sts rem, then on every alt row until 103 (107, 111, 115) sts rem. K 48 (50, 52, 54) rows. RC shows 197 (201, 205, 209) and work measures 59 (60, 61, 62) cms, 23 (23½, 24, 24½) ins.

Shape shoulders
Cast off 10 (10, 10, 11) sts at beg of next 4 rows and 9 (10, 11, 10) sts at beg of foll 2 rows. Cast off rem 45 (47, 49, 51) sts.

RIGHT FRONT

Punchcard machines
Lock card on row 1.
All machines
Push 68 (71, 75, 78) Ns to WP. Work as for back from * to *. Inc 0 (0, 0, 1) st. 68 (71, 75, 79) sts. Set RC at 000. Using MT and M, k 1 row.
Punchcard machines
Release card. Set machine for Fair Isle and work in Fair Isle pattern as given in Note.
All other machines
Work from Fair Isle chart.
All machines
K 126 rows. Work measures 40 cms, 15¾ ins.
Shape armhole
Cast off 4 sts at beg of next row. K 1 row. Dec 1 st at armhole edge on every row until 60 (63, 65, 67) sts rem, then on every alt row until 52 (54, 56, 58) sts rem. K 25 (27, 29, 31) rows. RC shows 174 (178, 182, 186).
Shape neck
Cast off 10 (11, 12, 13) sts at beg of next row. K 1 row. Dec 1 st at neck edge on every row until 29 (30, 31, 32) sts rem. K 8 rows. RC shows 197 (201, 205, 209).
Shape shoulder
Cast off 10 (10, 10, 11) sts at beg of next and foll alt row. K 1 row. Cast off rem 9 (10, 11, 10) sts.

LEFT FRONT

Work as for right front reversing shapings and reading right for left and left for right.

SLEEVES (both alike)

Punchcard machines
Lock card on row 1.
All machines
Push 83 (87, 91, 95) Ns to WP. Using MT and WY, cast on and k a few rows ending with carriage at left. Set RC at 000. Using M, k 1 row.
Punchcard machines
Release card. Set machine for Fair Isle and work in Fair Isle pattern as given in Note.
All other machines
Work from Fair Isle chart.
All machines
Shape sides by inc 1 st at each end of every 13th row until there are 103 (107, 111, 115) sts. K 8 rows. RC shows 139 and work measures 37.5 cms, 14¾ ins.
Shape top
Cast off 4 sts at beg of next 2 rows. Dec 1 st at each end of every alt row until 49 sts rem, then on every row until 31 sts rem. Cast off.

CUFFS (both alike)

Push 59 (61, 63, 65) Ns to WP. With purl side facing, pick up 83 (87, 91, 95) sts from lower edge of sleeve and place onto Ns as

follows:— 1 st onto each of the first 6 (5, 4, 3) Ns, * 1 st onto next N, 2 sts tog onto next N; rep from * along the row ending with 1 st onto each of last 5 (4, 3, 2) Ns. Unravel WY. Set RC at 000. Using MT and A, k 1 row. Transfer every 3rd st onto adjacent N and push empty Ns to NWP. Using MT 3, k 54 rows. Cast off.

BUTTONHOLE BAND

Using A, cast on 19 sts by hand. Set RC at 000. Using MT 2, k 6 rows. * Counting from each end, make buttonholes over 5th, 6th and 7th sts, k 38 rows; rep from * 4 times more. Make buttonholes over same sts as before. (6 sets of buttonholes). K 6 rows. Cast off.

BUTTON BAND

Using A, cast on 19 sts by hand. Set RC at 000. Using MT 2, k 202 rows. Cast off.

NECKBAND

Join shoulder seams. Push 126 (130, 134, 138) Ns to WP. Push every 3rd N back to NWP. Using MT and WY, cast on and k a few rows. Set RC at 000. MT 3 and A, k 24 rows. Push Ns from NWP to WP and place loop from row below adjacent st onto empty N. K 1 row. Make a hem by placing loops of first row worked in A evenly along the row. Purl side of garment facing, replace sts at neck edge onto Ns evenly along the row. K 1 row and cast off loosely.

TO MAKE UP

Sew side and sleeve seams. Set in sleeves. Fold cuffs in half to inside and catch down. Fold buttonhole and button band in half, neaten short ends then sew in position with buttonholes on right front. Finish buttonholes. Sew on buttons.

SWEATER

BACK

Punchcard machines
Insert card and lock on row 1.
All machines
Push 134 (141, 149, 156) Ns to WP. Work as for cardigan back from * to ***.
Punchcard machines
Release card. Set machine for Fair Isle and work in Fair Isle pattern as given in Note.
All other machines
Work from Fair Isle chart.
All machines
K 114 rows. Work measures 31 cms, 12¼ ins.
Shape armholes
Cast off 4 sts at beg of next 2 rows. Dec 1 st at each end of every row until 119 (125, 129, 133) sts rem, then on every alt row until 101 (105, 109, 113) sts rem.****. K 44 (46, 48, 50) rows. RC shows 183 (187, 191, 195) and work measures 55 (56, 57, 58) cms, 21½ (22, 22½, 23) ins.

Shape shoulders
Cast off 10 (10, 10, 11) sts at beg of next 4 rows and 9 (10, 11, 10) sts at beg of foll 2 rows. Cast off rem 43 (45, 47, 49) sts.

FRONT

Work as for back to ★★★★. K 22 (24, 26, 28) rows. 22 rows less have been worked to shoulder than on back.
Shape neck
Cast off centre 15 (17, 19, 21) sts. Push 43 (44, 45, 46) Ns at right to H/P and cont on rem sts at left for first side. K 1 row. Dec 1 st at neck edge on every row until 29 (30, 31, 32) sts rem. K 7 rows.
Shape shoulder
Cast off 10 (10, 10, 11) sts at beg of next and foll alt row, K 1 row. Cast off rem 9 (10, 11, 10) sts. With carriage at right, push Ns from H/P to WP and finish to correspond with first side, reversing shapings.

SLEEVES (Both alike)

Punchcard machines
Lock card on row 1.
All machines
Push 59 (61, 63, 65) Ns to WP. Work as for cardigan back from ★ to ★. Set RC at 000. Using MT and M, k 1 row.
Punchcard machines
Release card. Set machine for Fair Isle and work in Fair Isle pattern as given in Note.
All other machines
Work from Fair Isle chart.
All machines
Shape sides by inc 1 st at each end of every 7th (7th, 6th, 6th) row until there are 95 (99, 103, 107) sts. K 12 (5, 18 12) rows. RC shows 139 and work measures 37.5 cms, 17 ins.
Shape top
Cast off 4 sts at beg of next 2 rows. Dec 1 st at each end of every alt row until 51 sts rem, then on every row until 31 sts rem. Cast off.

NECKBAND

Join right shoulder seam. Push 124 (128, 132, 136) Ns to WP. Push every 3rd N back to NWP. Using MT and WY, cast on and k a few rows. Set RC at 000. MT3 and A, k 24 rows. Push Ns from NWP to WP and place loop from row below adjacent st onto empty N. K 1 row. Make a hem by placing loops of first row worked in A evenly along the row. Purl side of garment facing, replace sts at neck edge onto Ns evenly along the row. K 1 row and cast off loosely.

TO MAKE UP

Join left shoulder seam. Sew side and sleeve seams. Set in sleeves. Sew neckband seam.

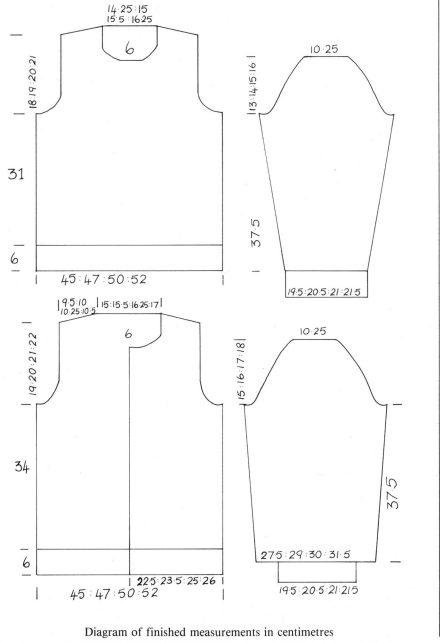

Diagram of finished measurements in centimetres

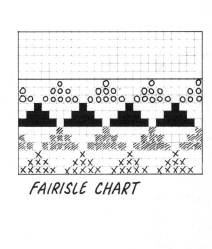

FAIRISLE CHART

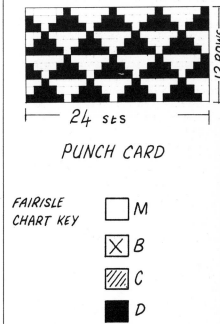

24 sts

PUNCH CARD

FAIRISLE CHART KEY

☐ M

☒ B

▨ C

■ D

◯ A

See colour plate opposite page 17

Bow jumper

A design from Singer

Knitted on Singer model Memo II 600. Suitable for most machines.

SIZE

To fit 81-86 (86-91, 91-96) cms, 32-34 (34-36, 36-38) ins bust.

MATERIALS

Agryll Sportsday 4 ply 1x340 gm Cone. Twilleys Goldfingering 5x50g balls.

TENSION

MT 29 sts and 42 rows to 10 cms (4 ins) measured over bow pattern. (Approximately tension 7). RT – approximately tension 3. Check tension before starting.

BACK

Cast on 131 (143, 153) sts in 1x1 rib using main yarn. RT RC 000 knit 20 rows rib. RC 000. Transfer to stocking stitch. Carriage at left. Change to contrast yarn MT knit 1 row. Carriage at right. Programme design into design board. Set carriage for Fair Isle. Continue in pattern using contrast yarn to end of jumper back. Knit 140 rows straight. RC 000. Cast off 4 (5, 6) sts at beginning next 2 rows. Dec 1 st each end of every row 5 (5, 6) times. Decrease 1 st each end of every 2nd row 6 (10, 10) times. There are now 101 (103, 109) sts.* Knit straight to RC 82 (88, 90). Shape shoulder – at beg of next 8 (8, 10) rows cast off 8 (8, 7) sts. Cast off rem 37 (39, 39) sts.

FRONT

Knit as jumper back to *. Knit straight to RC 56 (60, 62). Work 40 (41, 44) sts nearest carriage. Place rem sts on to waste yarn and remove from machine.
Shape neck
At neck edge decrease 1 st every 2nd row 8 (9, 9) times. There are now 32 (32, 35) sts. Knit straight to RC 82 (88, 90).
Shape shoulder
At beg of every 2nd row at armhole edge, decrease 8 (8, 7) sts 4 (4, 5) times. Put sts on waste yarn back on to machine. Cast off centre 21 (21, 21) sts. Work 2nd side to match the 1st reversing shapings.

SLEEVES

Cast on 63 (65, 69) sts in 1x1 rib using main yarn. RT RC 000. Knit 20 rows rib. RC 000. Transfer to st st, carriage at left. Change to contrast yarn MT. Knit 1 row. Carriage at right. Change to main yarn. Continue in pattern with contrast yarn, knit 2 rows. Inc 1 st each end of this and every following 8 (8, 8) rows. Inc 18 (18, 19) times altogether. There are now 99 (101, 107) sts. Knit straight to RC 160 (160, 160).
Shape sleeve cap
RC 000. At beg of next 2 rows cast off 4 (5, 6) sts. Decrease 1 st each end every 2nd row 10 (11, 16) times. Decrease 1 st each end every row 28 (26, 22) times. RC 50 (50, 56). Cast off rem 15 (17, 19) sts. Knit another sleeve the same.

NECKBAND

Using main yarn cast on 125 (133, 137) sts for 1x1 rib. RT. Knit 30 rows. Knit a few rows in waste yarn – remove from machine.

NOTE:
When attached, neckband is folded in half.

TO MAKE UP

Join shoulder and side seams. Join sleeve seams and set sleeves into jumper. Using back stitch attach neckband around neck edge unravelling waste yarn as you go. Turn neckband in half to inside and slipstitch down.

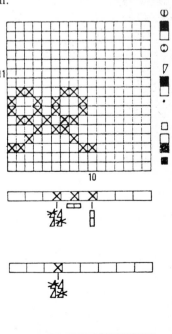

This design can be easily transferred to a punchcard or electronic design card.

Aran jumper jacket and hat

This super outfit was knitted on the
Corona Jumbo knitter. It is a simple tuck
pattern and can be knitted on any chunky
knit machine.

SIZES

Finished measurements 36 (38, 40, 42,
44) ins., 92 (97, 102, 107, 112) cms.

MATERIALS

One 1000 grm. cone Throstle Aran Yarn,
100% pure wool spun by Edmondson
Bros., Croft Mill, Cowling Nr. Keighley,
West Yorkshire.

TENSION

Stocking stitch 4½ sts. and 6¼ rows per
inch. Tuck stitch 4 sts. and 7½ rows per
inch. Main tension throughout T.(7).

NOTES:

Sleeves are reverse stocking stitch. Back
and two fronts are tuck stitch as follows:-
Counting from the right, select every 4th
needle to tuck for 3 rows. Row 4 knit all
sts. Row 5 select every 4th needle counting from the 2nd N. from the right to tuck
for 4 rows. Row 8 knit all sts.
These 8 rows form the pattern.

See colour plate opposite page 32

JUMPER JACKET

BACK

Cast on with waste yarn 72 (76, 80, 84, 88) sts. Knit a few rows and change to main yarn. MT. Working in pattern R.C. 000. Knit 124 rows all sizes.

Shape armholes
R.C. 000. Cast off 7 (7, 8, 9, 9) sts. at beg. of next 2 rows.
Knit straight to row 62 (66, 70, 72, 76).

Shape shoulders
Change to stocking stitch.
Cast off 6 (6, 7, 7, 7) sts. at beg. of next 2 rows.
Cast off 6 (6, 6, 6, 7) sts. at beg. of next 2 rows.
Cast off 5(6, 6, 6, 7) sts. at beg. of next 2 rows.
Run remaining sts. 24 (26, 26, 28, 28) off on waste yarn.

RIGHT FRONT

Cast on with waste yarn 36 (38, 40, 42, 44) sts. Knit a few rows and change to main yarn. MT. Knitting in pattern R.C. 000. knit 124 rows straight.

Shape armholes
R.C. 000. Cast off 7 (7, 8, 9, 9) sts. at beg. of next row, knit straight to row 46 (50, 54, 56, 60).

Shape neck
At neck edge cast off 6 sts. at beg. of next row, knit 1 row.
Dec. 1 st. at neck edge on the next and every row 6 (7, 7, 8, 8) times altog.
Knit to row 62 (66, 70, 72, 76).

Shape shoulder
Change to stocking stitch. Carriage on right.
Cast off 6 (6, 7, 7, 7) sts. at beg. of next row. Knit 1 row.
Cast off 6 (6, 6, 6, 7) sts. at beg. of next row. Knit 1 row.
Cast off the remaining 5 (6, 6, 6, 7) sts.

LEFT FRONT

Knit as for right front, reversing the shapings.

SLEEVES (both alike)

Cast on with waste yarn 74 (78, 84, 86, 90) sts. Knit a few rows. Change to main yarn. R.C. 000. MT. stocking stitch, knit 118 (124, 126, 126, 126) rows. Cast off loosely.

HEMS

Front bottom hems
Pick up the stitches from the waste yarn with the pattern (purl) side facing you. Inc. 1 st. at the front edge. MT. knit 6 rows. T.(10) knit 1 row. MT. knit 6 rows. Run off on waste yarn.
Knit hem for second front in the same way.
Back bottom hem
Knit as for front hems but omit the increase stitch.

SLEEVE CUFFS

With purl side facing you pick up 50 sts. decreasing evenly along the row from the cast on edge. Remove the waste yarn. Knit 10 rows MT. Knit 1 row T.(10). Knit 10 rows MT. Run off on waste yarn.

TO FINISH HEMS

Turn all edges and pin down on right side of garment (purl side). Backstitch into position through open loops of last row knitted. Carefully remove waste yarn.

FRONT EDGES (both alike)

With pattern side (purl side) facing you pick up sts. evenly along front edges and knit as for bottom edge. Backstitch into place as for hems.

COLLAR

With pattern side facing you pick up sts. evenly round neck edge.
T.(6) knit 2 rows. Inc. 1 st. at beg. of every row 10 times altog. Knit 6 rows. Knit 1 row T.(10). Dec. 1 st. at each end of alt. rows 10 times altog. Knit 2 rows. Run off on waste yarn. Backstitch down onto right side of garment.
Neaten collar edge with mattress stitch.

TO MAKE UP

Press sleeves, hems and edges only. Do NOT press tuck stitch.
Set in sleeves, join side and sleeve seams.

FRONT FASTENING

Pin front edges together edge to edge and mattress stitch together ⅔ of the way up. Make a lace with a contrast yarn (we crocheted ours with some shiny, dark brown yarn). Lace the cord through the knitting as follows:-
Start about 1 inch up from the bottom and take the lace through the back of the knitting, up and over the two front bands and back into the knitting, as for starting the lace on a shoe. Then continue and lace it through in crosses as per diagram. See diagram of finished measurements.

HAT

Cast on by hand 70 sts. T.(2) knit 30 rows. Drop down alt. sts. and latch up for 1 x 1 rib.
R.C. 000. MT. working in pattern knit 48 rows.
Change to stocking stitch and knit 2 rows. Transfer every alt. st. to its adjacent needle and leave the empty needles in N.W.P.
T.(2) knit 3 rows.

Knit 1 row T.(10) and remove from machine with a wool needle threading the yarn through the sts. Draw up and sew side seam.

BUTTON FOR TOP OF HAT

Ours is crocheted as follows:-
6 mm crochet hook.
Make 5 ch, join with a slip stitch.
Make 8 dc into ring. Join with slip stitch.
1 dc 1 ch into each dc. Join with slip stitch. Continue in this way until 5 rounds are completed. Join with slip stitch, run thread through, stuff with small oddment of yarn and sew to hat.
This could be substituted by a button or pom pom as you choose.

ADDITIONAL NOTES:
We found it easier to cast off for the armholes, both edges at the same time, so we cast off with the main yarn on the carriage side and a piece of waste yarn on the other side.
On some sizes it is useful to add an extra stitch at the front edge to make the pattern repeat complete.

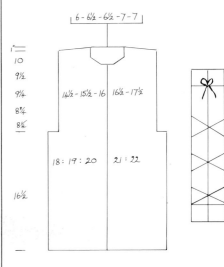

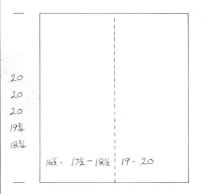

Diagram of finished measurements in inches

Lady's classic sweater

This garment is a classic with a special touch...it can be knitted on any machine.

SIZES

Finished measurements 81 (86, 92, 97, 102, 107) cms, 32 (34, 36, 38, 40, 42) ins bust.

MATERIALS

6 (6, 6, 7, 7, 8) 50 grm. balls Robin Aurora 4 ply. 64% acrylic, 21% wool, 15% nylon.

TENSION

6¾ sts and 9½ rows per 2.5 cm (1 inch) measured over stocking stitch. Tension dial approx (8).

NOTE:
Wrong or purl side is used as the right side throughout.

BACK

Cast on 108 (114, 122, 128, 136, 142) sts. for 1 x 1 rib. S/S 4/4.

Ribbers and double bed machines knit 28 rows rib, transfer sts. to main bed.
Single bed machines knit 56 rows 1 x 1 mock rib T.(4). Turn up hem.
Main T.(8) knit 96 (114, 114, 124, 124, 134) rows straight.★
Shape armholes
R.C. 000.
Cast off 4 sts. at beg. of next 2 rows.
Cast off 3 sts. at beg. of next 2 rows.
Cast off 2 sts. at beg. of next 2 rows.
Dec. 1 st. at each end of the next and every foll. alt. row 4 (5, 6, 7, 8, 9) times altog. 82 (86, 92, 96, 102, 106) sts. remain.
Knit straight to row 60 (62, 68, 74, 78, 80).
Shape back neck and shoulders
Put the centre 28 (30, 32, 34, 36, 38) Ns. into the H/P and all Ns. to the left into H/P. Work on right hand set of Ns. only.
Dec. 1 st. at neck edge on the next and every foll. alt. row 4 times altog.
AT THE SAME TIME
Shape shoulders
Cast off 6 (6, 7, 7, 8, 8) sts. at right edge. Knit 1 row.
Cast off 6 (6, 7, 7, 7, 8) sts. at right edge. Knit 1 row.
Cast off 6 (6, 6, 7, 7, 7) sts. at right edge. Knit 1 row.
Cast off 6 (6, 6, 6, 6, 7) remaining sts.
Leave centre 28 (30, 32, 34, 36, 38) Ns. in H/P in centre and put left hand Ns. back to WP. and work left half to match right reversing the shapings.
Run centre sts. off on waste yarn.

FRONT

Knit as for back as far as ★.
Shape armholes
R.C. 000.
Cast off 4 sts. at beg. of next 2 rows.
Cast off 3 sts. at beg. of next 2 rows.
Cast off 2 sts. at beg. of next 2 rows.
Dec. 1 st. at each end of next and every foll. alt. row 4 (5, 6, 7, 8, 9) times altog.
Knit straight to row 34 (36, 42, 44, 48, 50).
Shape neck
Put centre 20 Ns. and all Ns. to the left of these into the H/P.
Work on right hand set of Ns. only.
Dec. 1 st. at neck edge on next and every foll. alt. row 8 (9, 10, 11, 12, 13) times altog.
Knit straight to row 60 (62, 68, 74, 78, 80).
Shape shoulder
Cast off 6 (6, 7, 7, 8, 8) sts. at right side. Knit 1 row.

Cast off 6 (6, 7, 7, 7, 8) sts. at right side. Knit 1 row.
Cast off 6 (6, 6, 7, 7, 7) sts. at right side. Knit 1 row.
Cast off 6 (6, 6, 6, 6, 7) remaining sts. Leave centre 20 sts. in H/P. Return left hand set of Ns. to WP. and knit left half to match the right reversing the shapings. Run centre sts. off on waste yarn.

SLEEVES (two alike)

Cast on 54 (58, 60, 62, 64, 66) sts. for 1 x 1 rib.
Double bed machines and ribbers knit 28 rows 1 x 1 rib S/S 4/4. Transfer all sts. to main bed.
Single bed machines knit 56 rows 1 x 1 mock rib T.(4) and turn up hem.
Main T.(8) inc. 1 st. at each end of every 8th (10th, 8th, 8th, 7th, 7th) row 14 (13, 16, 18, 19, 19) times altog. 82 (84, 92, 98, 102, 104) sts.
Knit straight to row 124 (142, 142, 152, 152, 152).
Shape sleeve cap
Cast off 4 sts. at beg. of next 2 rows. Dec. 1 st. at each end of the next and every foll. alt. row 14 (15, 17, 19, 20, 21) times altog.
Cast off 5 (5, 4, 4, 5, 4) sts. at beg. of next 2 rows.
Cast off 4 (4, 4, 4, 4, 3) sts. at beg. of next 2 rows.
Cast off 4 (4, 4, 4, 4, 3) sts. at beg. of next 2 rows. Cast off rem. sts.

NECK TIE

Cast on by hand 6 sts. over 7 Ns. (. . .3 sts, 1 empty N. . . . 3 sts.) T.(8) Inc. 1 st. at opposite end to carr. every row until you have 20 sts.
Knit to row 420.
Dec. 1 st. at opposite end to carr. every row until 6 sts. remain. Cast off.

NECKBAND

Join one shoulder seam. With 'knit' side facing you pick up sts. evenly round the neck edge. K.1 row T.(8), 6 rows T.(7), 1 row T.(8).
Pick up alt. sts. from first row knitted and put onto alt. Ns. K.1 row T.(10).
Cast off.

TO MAKE UP

Join 2nd shoulder seam.
Sew on tie so that the knit side is the right side to give a contrast to the rest of the garment. Arrange the tie so that one end is longer than the other and pin it round the neckband with the knit side down and the edge along the neckband edge. Slip stitch into place. Now roll the tie into a sausage so that the wide row caused by the missing N. is on the inside edge of the neckband. Catch down with a slip stitch. Join side of tie and tie as preferred.
Join side and sleeve seams. No pressing required.

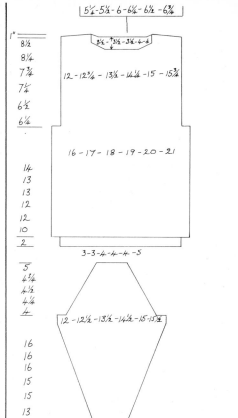

Diagram of finished measurements in inches

HINTS & TIPS

KEEP IT CLEAN

In spite of being in constant use knitting machines do still tend to gather dust, and if they are left uncovered for even a few hours the dust settles on the oiled parts in particular and makes both the knitting and the cleaning of the machine harder.
An inexpensive way of making yourself a plastic machine cover is to buy a plastic tablecloth, cut it in half and sew the ends up. One cloth makes two covers sufficient for a machine plus ribber.

HAND KNIT PATTERNS

New machine knitters often start off with hand knit patterns, and providing that the tension is correct they can often be used quite successfully, but I had a letter from a knitter who had met a problem . . . The instructions said knit 2 together right across the row . . . It's quite easy. Run the knitting off on waste yarn, adjust the number of needles in working position and then replace the stitches 2 to every needle. Knitting patterns involving yokes are usually dealt with in this way, also tight cuffs etc.

A TIP FROM SINGER

This tip is from a Singer owner for beginners who want to try their first tuck stitch garment. Use any of the small tuck stitch cards and set your machine so that it knits one row and tucks one row. This is easy on the Singer punchcard machines because there is a knob for each direction. The pattern is still interesting and textured but is softer than an all tuck pattern and has the added advantage for beginners in that if you do make a mistake it is easy to unpick to the knitted row and see that you have all your stitches safely on the needles. Any machine where the tuck has to be set for both directions can do this.

MAGICTAPE

There is a white Sellotape on sale in the larger stationery shops which is very useful. The surface can be written on and the back is sticky. When you knit your tension swatches you need not cast off, just run off on waste thread and stick a bit of the tape on the last row, this will stop it from unravelling in your workbasket and you can write tension details and any other information needed on the tape.

HERE COMES ANOTHER HEM

Next time you knit a panelled skirt try this hem. Cast on a 1 x 1 rib using your ribber and knit about 4 rows rib at the usual rib tension. Transfer to the top bed and continue knitting. When the garment is pressed, press the rib flat, turn the rib section up and stitch down, just lightly catching it into place. This makes a neat invisible hem and does not flare out.

A FIRM CAST ON EDGE

This tip is for ribber owners and is useful when you are knitting a piece which does not require a hem or a rib at the bottom. Cast on for 1 x 1 rib, that is knitting one zig zag row, one row across the main bed and one row across the ribber and then one more row both beds. The tension should be at 0 for these rows and it is not necessary to use any weights. Transfer the stitches from the ribber to the main bed, pull all the needles out to the holding position for a couple of rows until the work gets going and then continue as normal. This gives a nice firm edge which does not curl.

Lady's Jacquard waistcoat

If you have not tried Jacquard knitting then this is the ideal garment for you to make your first attempt. The design is simple and the pattern gives an interesting 3D effect. The punchcard is given in single bed form. If you are not sure how to punch out your card for Jacquard see Knitting Machine Digest issue number 2.

This garment was designed and knitted on the Singer electronic 2310 machine and is also suitable for the Superba S48. The pattern used for the Jacquard is No. 4 from sheet 13. We knitted the garment in pale green and white, green in feeder one, white in feeder two.

OTHER MACHINES

The pattern for the Jacquard is a 12 stitch repeat and can be punched out as a Jacquard punchcard or drawn for electronic machines. The diagram of finished measurements and details of the punchcard in single bed form are given and this garment can be knitted on any punchcard machine and ribber capable of producing a 12 stitch repeat.

SIZES

Finished measurements 92 (97, 102) cms, 36 (38, 40) ins bust.
Underarm length 33 (36, 38) cms, 13 (14, 15) ins adjustable.

MATERIALS

Any soft 3 ply. Approx. 100 (100, 120) grms. colour one. 80 (90, 100) grms. colour two.

TENSION

6½ sts. and 8½ rows to one inch measured over the pattern.
Jacquard setting for the front carriage is knit key only. S/S 5/7. 2 x 1 ribs S/S 2/2. Stocking stitch for bands T.(4).

NOTES:
Weights
Use three medium weights on all pieces until the armhole shapings. On the back, continue with 2 weights on the fronts, one weight in the centre is sufficient.
When you start shaping, adjust the cursor stop as soon as you have finished your decreases to ensure that you pass the cursor each time.
Button bands
No weights are necessary, flow combs opposite, front bed in upper position, spacing on 6 and just hold the knitting underneath with your hand.

BACK

Cast on for 2 x 1 rib 118 (124, 130) sts.
S/S. 2/2 knit 23 rows. Carriage on left.
Bring up all Ns. to WP. Knit 2 rows circular. Change to S/S. 5/7 knit 1 row rib. Carriage on right.
Thread up colour 2, insert pattern sheet and set cursor.
Carriage settings are:-
Back carriage: Knit key and Jacquard key, needle return buttons in the upper position.
Front carriage: Knit key only. S/S 5/7 throughout.
R.C. 000. Knit 90 (98, 106) rows.*
Shape armholes
R.C. 000. Cast off 10 sts. at the beg. of the next 2 rows. (To cast off transfer the stitches to the back bed and then cast off).
Dec. 1 st. at each end of the next and ev. foll. alt. row 9 (10, 10) times altog. 80 (84, 90) sts. Knit straight to row 70 (74, 78).
Stop pattern, transfer all sts. to back bed, knit 1 row T.(12). Cast off.

RIGHT FRONT

Cast on 59 (63, 65) sts. at the right of centre 0. Knit as for back as far as *.
Shape armholes
R.C. 000. Carriage on right. Cast off 10 sts. at the beg. of the next row, knit 1 row.
Dec 1 st. at the armhole edge on the next and every foll. alt. row 9 (10, 10) times altog. 40 (44, 45) sts.
Knit straight to row 40.
Shape neck
Knit to the left, cast off 12 sts. at the neck edge, knit 1 row.
Dec. 1 st. at the neck edge on the next and

every foll. alt. row 10 (11, 12) times altog. Knit straight to row 70 (74, 78).
Stop pattern, transfer all sts. to back bed, knit 1 row T.(12). Cast off.

LEFT FRONT

Knit as for right front but cast sts. on to the left of centre 0 and reverse the shapings.

NECKBAND

Cast on 110 (120, 126) sts. for 2 x 1 rib. S/S. 2/2 knit 24 rows. Transfer all sts. to back bed. T.(4) knit 3 rows stocking stitch, run off on waste yarn.

ARMBANDS (two alike)

Cast on 120 (130, 136) sts. for 2 x 1 rib.
Knit as for neckband.
Join shoulder seams.
Attach neck and armbands by pinning to right side of work and backstitching through open loops of the last row knitted in the main yarn. Carefully remove the waste yarn.
Turn edge of band onto the inside edge of the garment and catch down.

BUTTONHOLE BAND

With right side of knitting facing you pick up the front edge of the garment including the neckband. Pick up as many sts. as you can comfortably get on without stretching the garment. Inc. 1 st. at each end of the first row. T.(4) knit 4 rows. Make 4 buttonholes as follows: first buttonhole over Ns. 5, 6 and 7 counting from the right, miss out 4 Ns. and then make another buttonhole over 3 Ns. and so on for 4 buttonholes.
Knit 4 rows. Knit 1 row T.(8). Knit 4 rows T.(4). Make another set of buttonholes as before. Knit 4 rows T.(4). Knit 1 row T.(5). Run off on waste yarn.
Turn to the right side and pin down, backstitch into place.

BUTTON BAND

Knit as for the buttonhole band omitting buttonholes.

TO MAKE UP

Neaten the edges of the bands. Sew side seams. You may need to carefully press the button bands. No other pressing is necessary.

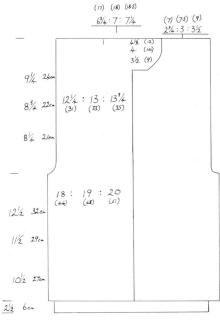

Diagram of finished measurements.

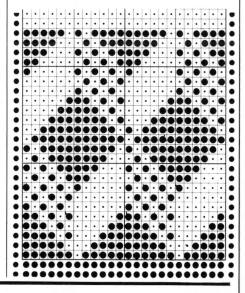

HINTS & TIPS

TAKE A SEAT

This sounds silly, but next time you have to press a garment arrange things so that you can sit down to the job — you will find that you make a better job of it. This tip applies to the everyday ironing as well, and it is kinder on the legs.

USEFUL READING

All knitters, take your instruction book

and pretend that it is the latest novel. Read it from cover to cover, no knitting, just reading. Please try it and you will be surprised at what you have missed before.

Take a red pen and underline important pieces of information for easy reference in the future.

If you have a ribbing attachment or colour changer, try the same experiment with the instruction books for them.

Lady's tennis jumper

A design from Knitmaster

rows to 10 cms (4 ins) measured over stockinet. Tension dial at approximately 6. 48 rows to 10 cms (4 ins) measured over knit 2 purl 2 rib. Tension dials at approx 4.

BACK

Push 83 (88, 92, 96) Ns at left and right of centre 0 to B pos. 166 (176, 184, 192) Ns altog. Push corresponding Ns on ribber to B pos. Arrange Ns for knit 2 purl 2 rib. Using col 1, cast on. RC 000. Tension dials at 4, knit 19 rows. Carr at right. Transfer sts to main bed. RC 000. Tension dial at 6. Knit 6 rows. * Counting from the right edge, drop the 4th and 11th (5th & 12th; 5th & 12th; 5th & 12th) and ev foll 12th & 19th (13th & 20th; 14th & 21st; 15th & 22nd) sts, leave empty Ns in B pos.
Cables are worked over the 6 sts between empty Ns. Using 2 treble transfer tools cross each set of 3 sts, knit 12 rows*. Rept from * to * 8 more times. Knit 4 rows stockinet. RC 118. Latch tool up all dropped sts either side of cables.
Using waste yarn knit 8 rows and release from machine. Push 152 (160, 168, 176) Ns to B pos. With purl side facing pick up sts from below waste yarn and place onto Ns in B pos gathering evenly. Reset RC to 118. * Knit 2 rows col 3, 2 rows col 1, 2 rows col 3, 2 rows col 1, 4 rows col 2, 4 rows col 1, 2 rows col 3 *. Mark both ends with waste yarn. Continue in col 1 **. Knit 114 (120, 124, 130) rows. RC 250 (256, 260, 266). Carr at right.
Shape shoulders
Cast off 8 (8, 9, 10) sts beg next 4 rows.
Shape back neck
Cast off centre 56 sts. Using nylon cord knit 32 (36, 38, 40) sts at left by hand taking Ns back to A pos.
Knit right part as Follows:—
Cast off 7 (8, 9, 9) sts beg next row, 2 sts beg next row. Rept the last 2 rows once more. Cast off 7 (8, 8, 9) sts beg next row, knit 1 row. Cast off remaining 7 (8, 8, 9) sts. Take carr to left. Unravel nylon cord bringing Ns back to correct pos. Knit left part as for right part.

POCKET

Insert special card into machine and lock on row 1. Push 15 Ns at left and right of centre 0 to B pos. 30 Ns altog. Using waste yarn cast on and knit several rows ending with carr at right. RC 000. Tension dial at 6. Using col 1, knit 4 rows. Release card. Set carr for single motif knitting. With col 1 in feeder 1 and col 2 in feeder 2, knit 33 rows. Knit 3 rows

For Knitmaster 260/360 machines with ribbing attachment.
For stockists write to Knitmaster Ltd., 30/40 Elcho St., London SW11.

SIZES

To fit 81-96 cms, 32-38 ins bust.

MATERIALS

Emu Mix'n'Match 4-ply. 11 (11, 12, 12) 50 grm balls in col 1; 1 50 grm ball in cols 2 and 3.

TENSIONS

35 sts and 47 rows to 10 cms (4 ins) measured over cable pattern. 32 sts and 48

stockinet col 1. Hem – Tension dial at 9, knit 1 row. Tension dial at 5, knit 6 rows. Tension dial at 9, knit 1 row. Tension dial at 4, knit 6 rows. Pick up first row of hem and place onto corresponding Ns. Tension dial at 10, knit 1 row. Cast off loosely.

FRONT

Work as given for back to ★★. Knit 40 rows. Counting from the right of centre 0. Put sts 33 to 62 inclusive onto waste yarn and release from machine. With plain side of pocket facing pick up sts from below waste yarn at lower edge and place onto empty Ns. Replace sts taken off onto waste yarn back onto Ns in front of pocket sts. Unravel waste yarn. Knit 56 (62, 66, 72) rows. RC 232 (238, 242, 248). Carr at right.

Shape neck
Cast off centre 32 sts. Using nylon cord knit 60 (64, 68, 72) sts at left by hand taking Ns back to A pos.
Knit right part as Follows:—
Knit 1 row. Cast off 4 sts beg next row, Knit 1 row. Cast off 3 sts beg next and foll alt row, knit 1 row. Cast off 2 sts beg next row, knit 1 row. Dec 1 st beg next and ev foll alt row 4 times in all, knit 2 rows. RC 250 (256, 260, 266). Carr at right.

Shape shoulder
Cast off 8 (8, 9, 10) sts beg next and foll alt row, knit 1 row. Cast off 7 (8, 9, 9) sts beg next and foll alt row, knit 1 row. Cast off 7 (8, 8, 9) sts beg next row, knit 1 row. Cast off remaining 7 (8, 8, 9) sts. Take carr to left. Unravel nylon cord bringing Ns back to correct pos. Knit left part as for right part but read left for right.

SLEEVES

Push 41 (45, 48, 52) Ns at left and right of centre 0 to B pos. 82 (90, 96, 104) Ns altog. Using waste yarn cast on and knit several rows ending with carr at right. RC 000. Tension dial at 6. Using col 1, knit 5 rows. Inc 1 st both ends of the next and ev foll 5th row 26 (20, 20, 14) times in all, knit 5 rows. Inc 1 st both ends of the next and ev foll 6th row 10 (15, 15, 20) times in all. 154 (160, 166, 172) sts. Knit 5 rows without shaping. RC 196. Carr at right.

Shape top
Set carr for partial knitting. Always taking yarn round first inside N in D pos, push 9 (9, 10, 10) Ns at opposite end to carr to D pos on the next 2 rows, 9 (9, 9, 10) Ns on the next 2 rows, 8 (9, 9, 10) Ns on the next 4 rows, 8 (9, 9, 9) Ns on the next 2 rows, 8 (8, 9, 9) Ns on the next 4 rows. 38 Ns rem in B pos. Break off yarn. Using a transfer tool bring Ns in D pos back to B pos. Knit stripes as given on back from ★ to ★. Knit 2 rows col 1. Tension dial at 8, knit 1 row. Cast off.

CUFFS

Push 58 (62, 66, 70) Ns to B pos. Push corresponding Ns on ribber to B pos. Arrange Ns for knit 2 purl 2 rib. Using col 1, cast on.
Tension dials at 4, knit 19 rows. Tension dials at 6, knit 1 row. Tension dials at 4, knit 19 rows. Transfer sts to main bed. With purl side of sleeve facing pick up sts from below waste yarn and place onto Ns gathering evenly. Tension dial at 10, knit 1 row. Cast off loosely.

NECKBAND

Join one shoulder seam. Push 140 Ns to B pos. With plain side facing pick up sts around neckedge and place onto Ns in B pos. Tension dial at 4. Using col 1, knit 10 rows. Tension dial at 8, knit 1 row. Tension dial at 4, knit 11 rows. Using waste yarn knit 8 rows and release from machine.

TO MAKE UP

Pin out to size and press carefully with a warm iron over a damp cloth. Join remaining shoulder and neckband seam. Set in sleeves between marked points. Join side and sleeve seams. Fold neckband in half onto the outside and backstitch into pos. Sew sides of pocket into pos. Fold cuffs in half onto the outside. Give final light press.

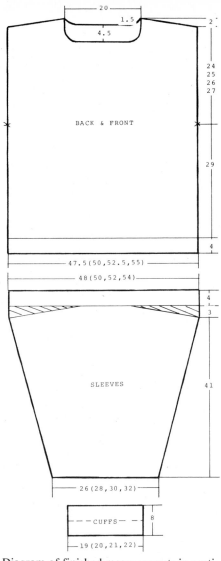

Diagram of finished measurements in centimetres

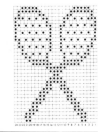

HINTS & TIPS

BUSY BEES

Shetland yarn and lambswool and other very soft yarns do present a sewing up problem because the yarn breaks after a few stitches and it is not always easy to find a matching thread in another type of yarn. A tip from a friend in Eastbourne is to use beeswax and wax the thread before you sew with it and you will have no problems. We have tried it and it works very well.

WE NEVER GIVE UP

I must get more suggestions on pressing acrylics than any other subject except perhaps tension swatches . . .

The latest is to put greaseproof paper over the garment (pin and block the garment out first) and then put brown paper over it and press as normal with a warm iron. This tip was from a lady who has knitted for years and says that it how she was taught when synthetic yarns first appeared on the market.

FINALLY

A small point but one which has caused many a headache and dropped stitch . . . if your ribber is not knitting as it should, check that your pile levers are up and not down as for pile knitting (Knitmaster ribbers only). If they are down you need to lower the ribber and push them up and then raise the ribber again to the knitting position. They are easily lowered accidentally as you raise and lower the ribber. Check with your instruction book if you are not sure which are your pile levers.

Lady's Fair Isle sweater knitted sideways

Pattern card is from page 130 of 'A Resource Book for Machine Knitters' by Kathleen Kinder.
Punchcard reproduced here by kind permission of Kathleen Kinder.

MATERIALS

1 (2, 2, 2) cones main col and small amounts for Fair Isle of 4 ply Superwash wool available on 400 grm cones from Woolscope, The Buttermarket, North Street, Chichester, West Sussex PO19 1LQ.

TENSION

6½ sts and 10½ rows to 2.5 cm (1 inch) measured over stocking stitch. Tension dial approx T(6), stocking stitch increased to T(6) for Fair Isle.

NOTE:
Sweater is knitted sideways in 2 pieces with ribs and cuffs attached separately.

BACK

Cast on with waste yarn 68 (72, 76, 78) sts. Knit a few rows. Change to main yarn.
RC 000. MT. Knit 158 (168, 168, 168) rows.
Carriage on right. Inc 1 st at right every row 22 times altog. 90 (94, 98, 98) sts RC 180 (190, 190, 190).
Carriage on right. Cast on 60 (60, 64, 68) sts at right. 150 (154, 162, 166) sts.
RC 000. Knit 132 (142, 152, 162) rows.
Start Fair Isle. Tension dial up two dots.
Knit Fair Isle as follows:

Feeder 1	Feeder 2	
White	Empty	4 rows – start card
White	Navy	4 rows
White	Empty	4 rows
White	Red	18 rows
White	Empty	4 rows
White	Navy	4 rows
White	Empty	4 rows

Navy only. Tension dial back to stocking stitch tension. K 16 rows.
RC 000. Carriage on right. Cast off 60 (60, 64, 68) sts and dec 1 st at right every row 22 times altog. 68 (72, 76, 78) sts.
Knit to row 180 (190, 190, 190). Run off on waste yarn.

FRONT

Cast on with waste yarn 68 (72, 76, 78) sts. Knit a few rows. Change to main yarn.
RC 000. MT. Carriage on right. Knit 158 (168, 168, 168) rows.
Carriage on right. Inc 1 st at right every row 22 times altog. 90 (94, 98, 98) sts. RC 180 (190, 190, 190).
Carriage on right. Cast on 60 (60, 64, 68) sts at right. 150 (154, 162, 166) sts.
RC 000. Knit 16 rows.

SIZES

Finished measurements 92 (97, 102, 107) cms, 36 (38, 40, 42) ins bust.

Start Fair Isle and knit Fair Isle sequence as for back. Remember to put tension dial up 2 dots.

Change to navy and main stocking stitch tension.

K 9 (11, 13, 19) rows. Carriage on left.

Shape neck

Cast off 10 (10, 8, 6) sts at left. K 2 rows. Dec 1 st next and every foll alt row 12 (12, 14, 15) times altog. K 10 (16, 14, 10) rows straight.

Carriage on left. Inc 1 st on left on next and ev foll alt row 12 (12, 14, 15) times altog.

Cast on 10 (10, 8, 6) sts at left. Knit to the right. Knit to row 190 (200, 210, 220).

Cast off 60 (60, 64, 68) sts.

RC 000. Dec 1 st at right every row 22 times altog. 68 (72, 76, 78) sts.

Knit to row 180 (190, 190, 190). Run off on waste yarn.

Press according to yarn. Join top sleeve seams to neck openings.

NECKBAND (knitted in two pieces)

Front

With right side of knitting facing pick up approx 64 sts along front neck edge.

T(5..) k 10 rows white.

Start pattern card and with white in feeder 1 and navy in feeder 2 knit 4 rows Fair Isle. Stop card. Knit 4 rows white. Run off on waste yarn.

Back

With right side facing pick up approx 52 sts along back neck edge and knit as for front band.

Pin neckbands into place on right side of garment and backstitch through open loops of last row knitted in white.

Carefully remove waste yarn.

CUFFS (both alike)

Cast on 68 (72, 72, 74) sts in 2 x 1 rib using red colour. T(4) knit 4 rows red, 4 rows white, 2 rows red, 4 rows white, 12 rows navy.

Transfer all sts to main bed. Knit 1 row T(6). With wrong side of knitting facing pick up edge of cuff onto sts, decreasing evenly along the edge.

K 1 row T(10). Cast off.

RIBS (front and back alike)

Cast on 136 (142, 150, 158) sts in 2 x 1 rib using red colour. Knit as for cuffs.

With wrong side facing, pick up sts from front edge evenly onto needles (pick up the sts from the very edge). Knit 1 row T(10) (2 rows if it is tight) and cast off.

TO MAKE UP

Join side and sleeve seams and give final press.

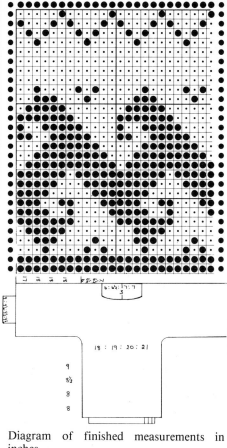

Diagram of finished measurements in inches

HINTS & TIPS

ADD AN ACCESSORY

Next time you knit yourself a plain sweater and you have a few ounces of yarn left over, instead of putting it in the waste yarn bin knit a scarf to wear with the sweater. It could be a small square one if the yarn is fine or it could be a long, narrow scarf in Fisherman's rib. The same applies with such things as a child's Fair Isle jumper. Use up the oddments left over and knit a hat. This extra effort produces an outfit as opposed to just a garment and you will be surprised at the difference it makes when things are worn and noticed by others. Be prepared for lots of orders . . .

INTARSIA KNITTING

Learning to use intarsia carriages, feeders or whatever or just doing intarsia knitting on the older machines is not in itself difficult. The difficulties arise when you are faced with numerous balls of yarn of varying colours and sizes all dangling in front of your machine and getting in a tangle each time you knit across the row. For fairly small amounts of yarn I found this method easy. I cut out 'H' shaped pieces of cardboard and wrapped as much yarn of each colour round the centre of the shape as I thought I would need to complete the pattern. Next I threaded an empty cotton reel on to the end of the yarn so that as I used the yarn it ran through the cotton reel up to the machine.

As I knitted I passed each thread over the next one in turn. The H shapes kept the yarn tidy and the cotton reels added a little bit of weight, which made it easy to cross them over.

There must be other solutions to this problem, many of which will originate as this one does, from hand knitting.

KNITTING WITH THE RIBBER ARM

If you have been knitting with the ribber and have transferred all the stitches to the main bed, it may be that you need to knit just a few rows of stocking stitch; perhaps the work needs to be run off on waste yarn. Whatever the reason it saves time if you do not have to disconnect the ribber arm and replace it with the knitting brush assembly. Some ribbers have side clips which can be attached to ensure that the edge stitches knit correctly, and these work well. But to ensure that the knitting knits OK all you need to do is bring the needles out to the holding position each row and the ribber arm will knit happily. Leave the comb and the weights on while you are knitting in this way.

ALL WASHED UP

I saw this tip on the club notice board at the Littlehampton knitting club and made a mental note to pass it on.

Zips tend to shrink in the wash, so if you wash them before putting them into the garment you will have a better fitting zip.

Zips do seem to cause problems from time to time. Usually the length that we need for our garment falls between two standard zip measurements, so we are left hovering in the shop trying to make a decision as to whether to buy the zip a bit to long or a bit too short — we usually favour the bit too long one.

Zips should be pinned into place and preferably tacked before the final sewing and it is important not to stretch the knitting as you insert the zip or you will end up with unsightly puckers.

Opposite: **Aran jumper, jacket and hat** (see pattern on page 22)

Fair Isle jacket and camisole

For KNITMASTER SK560 Machines. For Stockists write to Knitmaster Ltd., 30/40 Elcho St., London, S.W.11.

SIZES

To fit 81-97 cms (32-38) ins bust.

MATERIALS

Silverknit Jupiter. Complete Set. 1(1, 1, 2) 200 grm cones in col 1 (shade 2717); 1(1, 1, 2) 200 grm cones in col 2 (shade 2740); 4 buttons, 2 press studs.
Yarn available from Silverknit, Dept K, The Old Mill, Epperstone-By-Pass, Woodborough, Notts.

TENSION

Jacket: 36 sts and 41 rows to 10 cms (4 ins) measured over Fair Isle. Tension dial at approximately 4. 36 sts and 60 rows to 10 cms (4 ins) measured over stockinet. Tension dial at approximately 2.
Camisole: 37 sts and 57 rows to 10 cms measured over stockinet. Tension dial at approximately 2.

JACKET

BACK

Push 86 (90, 95, 99) Ns at left and right of centre 0 to B pos. 172 (180, 190, 198) Ns altog. *Using waste yarn cast on and knit several rows ending with carr at left. Inspection button on. Insert special card and set to first row. Pattern width indicator at 40. Point cams at edge of knitting. Needle 1 cam centre of machine. Buttons 1 (left) and 2 (left). RC 000. Tension dial at 3. Using col 1, knit 4 rows. Tension dial at 5, knit 1 row. Tension dial at 3, knit 4 rows. Turn up a hem. Carr at right. RC 000. Tension dial at 4. Inspection button off. Set carr for Fair Isle*. With col 1 in feeder 1 and col 2 in feeder 2, knit 104 rows. Carr at right. Mark both edges with waste yarn.
Shape armholes
Cast off 14 (14, 16, 16) sts at beg of next 2 rows. 144 (152, 158, 166) sts. Knit 80 (84, 88, 92) rows. Row Counter 186 (190, 194, 198). Carr at right.
Shape shoulders
Set carr for partial knitting. Always taking yarn round first inside N in D pos, push 7 (8, 8, 9) Ns at opposite end to carr to D pos on next 4 rows and 7 (7, 8, 8) Ns on next 2 rows.
Shape back neck
Using a length of col 1, cast off centre 44 sts. Using nylon cord knit 29 (31, 33, 35) sts at left by hand taking Ns down to A pos. Inspection button on. Note row number showing on pattern panel. Inspection button off.
Knit right part as follows:
Knit 1 row. **Push 7 (7, 8, 8) Ns at opposite end to carr to D pos and dec 1 st at beg of next row, knit 1 row. Push 7 (7, 8, 8) Ns at opposite end to carr to D pos and dec 1 st at beg of next row, knit 1 row. Push 6 (7, 7, 8) Ns at opposite end to carr to D pos and dec 1 st at beg of next row, knit 1 row. 6 (7, 7, 8) Ns rem in B pos. Break off yarn. Using a transfer tool push Ns in D pos at right back to B pos. Set carr for stockinet. Using waste yarn, knit 8 rows and release from machine**. Carr at right. Inspection button on. Set card to number previously noted. Inspection button off. Set carr for Fair Isle. Unravel nylon cord bringing Ns back to correct pos. Knit left part as for right part from **to** but read left for right.

RIGHT FRONT

Push 29 Ns at left and 86 (90, 95, 99) Ns at right of centre 0 to B pos. 115 (119, 124, 128) Ns altog. Work as given for back to *to*. With col 1 in feeder 1 and col 2 in feeder 2, knit 15 rows. Counting from the left edge, make a buttonhole over Ns 5, 6, 7, 8 and 9. Knit 35 rows. Make a buttonhole over the same Ns as before. Knit 2 rows.

Opposite: **Tamarisk lady's jacket** (see pattern on page 36)

Shape front edge

Dec 1 st at left edge on next and ev foll alt row 22 (18, 14, 10) times in all, knit 2 rows. Dec 1 st at left edge on next and ev foll 3rd row 3 (5, 8, 11) times in all. 90 (96, 102, 107) sts. Knit 0 (2, 1, 0) rows. RC 104. Carr at right. Mark right edge with waste yarn.

Shape armhole

Dec 0 (1, 0, 0) st at left edge and cast off 14 (14, 16, 16) sts at beg of next row, knit 1 (2, 0, 1) rows. Dec 1 st at left edge on next and ev foll 3rd row 27 (28, 30, 31) times in all. 49 (53, 56, 60) sts. Knit 2 rows. Carr at left.

Shape shoulder

Set carr for partial knitting. Always taking yarn round first inside N in D pos, push 7 (8, 8, 9) Ns at opposite end to carr to D pos and dec 1 st at beg of next row, knit 1 row. Push 7 (8, 8, 9) Ns at opposite end to carr to D pos on next row. Dec 1 st at left edge on next row. Push 7 (7, 8, 8) Ns at opposite end to carr to D pos on next and ev foll alt row 3 times in all, knit 1 row. Push 6 (7, 7, 8) Ns at opposite end to carr to D pos on next row, knit 1 row. 6 (7, 7, 8) Ns rem in B pos. Break off yarn. Using a transfer tool push Ns in D pos back to B pos. Set carr for stockinet. Using waste yarn, knit 8 rows and release from machine.

LEFT FRONT

Work as given for right front but reverse the shapings by reading left for right and vice versa and omitting buttonholes. Do not alter buttons 1 and 2.

SLEEVES

Push 36 (36, 36, 40) Ns at left and right of centre 0 to B pos. 72 (72, 72, 80) Ns altog. Work as given for back from *to*. With col 1 in feeder 1 and col 2 in feeder 2, inc 1 st at both ends of next and ev foll 7th (6th, 6th, 6th) row 16 (29, 11, 16) times in all, knit 5 (4, 4, 4) rows. Inc 1 st at both ends of next and ev foll 6th (5th, 5th, 5th) row 16 (6, 28, 22) times in all. 136 (142, 150, 156) sts. Knit 0 (3, 1, 1) rows. RC 202. Mark both edges with waste yarn. Knit 5 (1, 3, 3) rows. Inc 1 st at both ends of next and ev foll 6th (5th, 5th, 5th) row 2 (3, 3, 3) times in all. 140 (148, 156, 162) sts. Knit 5 rows.

Shape top

Set carr for partial knitting. Always taking yarn round first inside N in D pos, push 7 (8, 8, 9) Ns at opposite end to carr to D pos on next 8 (8, 6, 6) rows and 8 (8, 9, 9) Ns on next 6 (6, 8, 8) rows. 36 Ns rem in B pos. Mark centre with waste yarn. Break off yarn. Using a transfer tool, push Ns in D pos back to B pos. Using col 1, cast off. Set carr for stockinet.

RIGHT FRONT FACING

Push 26 Ns to B pos. Using waste yarn cast on and knit several rows ending with carr at right. RC 000. Tension dial at 1. Using col 1, knit 6 rows. Tension dial at 3, knit 1 row. Tension dial at 1, knit 6 rows. Turn up a hem. Carr at left. RC 000. Tension dial at 2, knit 21 rows. Counting from right edge,

make a buttonhole over Ns 12, 13, 14, 15 and 16. Knit 51 rows. Make a buttonhole over same Ns as before. Inc 1 st at left edge on next and foll 3rd row, knit 2 rows.

1st, 2nd and 3rd sizes only

Inc 1 st at left edge and dec 1 st at right edge on next and ev foll 3rd row 16 (10, 4) times in all, knit 2 rows. Inc 1 st at left edge on next row. Dec 1 st at right edge on next row, knit 1 row. Inc 1 st at left edge on next row, knit 1 row. Dec 1 st at right edge on next row. Inc 1 st at left edge on next row, knit 2 rows. Inc 1 st at left edge and dec 1 st at right edge on next row, knit 3 rows. Inc 1 st at left edge and dec 1 st at right edge on next and ev foll 4th row 32 (38, 44) times in all.

4th size only

Inc 1 st at left edge and dec 1 st at right edge on next row, knit 2 rows. Inc 1 st at left edge on next row. *Dec 1 st at right edge on next row, knit 2 rows. Inc 1 st at left edge on next row*. Rept from *to* 49 times more.

All sizes

Knit 3 (3, 3, 1) rows. Dec 1 st at right edge on next and ev foll 4th (4th, 4th, 5th) row 3 times in all. 26 sts. Knit 2 rows. Carr at left.

Shape shoulder

Cast off 5 sts at beg of next and foll alt row, knit 1 row. Cast off 4 sts at beg of next and ev foll alt row 3 times in all, knit 1 row. Cast off rem 4 sts.

LEFT FRONT FACING

Work as given for right front facing but reverse the shapings by reading left for right and vice versa and omitting buttonholes.

BACK NECK FACING

Using col 1, cast on 44 sts by hand. RC 000. Tension dial at 2, knit 1 row. Cast on 4 sts at beg of next 4 rows, 3 sts at beg of next 6 rows and 2 sts at beg of next 4 rows. Inc 1 st at both ends of next and ev foll alt row 3 times in all, knit 3 rows. Inc 1 st at both ends of next and ev foll 4th row 5 times in all. 102 sts. Knit 2 rows. RC 42. Carr at right.

Shape neck

Using a length of col 1, cast off centre 44 sts. Using nylon cord, knit 29 sts at left by hand taking Ns down to A pos.

Knit right part as follows:

Cast off 5 sts at beg of next row. Dec 1 st at beg of next row. Cast off 5 sts at beg of next row, knit 1 row. Cast off 4 sts at beg of next row. Dec 1 st at beg of next row. Cast off 4 sts at beg of next and foll alt row. Dec 1 st at beg of next row. Cast off rem 4 sts. Carr at left. Unravel nylon cord bringing Ns back to correct pos. Knit left part as for right part.

TO MAKE UP

Pin out each piece to size and press carefully with a warm iron over a damp cloth. Graft shoulders. Join shoulder seams of facings. Join side and sleeve seams to markers. Set in sleeves matching markers. With right sides tog, sew facings into pos. Turn facings to inside, matching buttonholes and leaving a narrow edging on right side. Catch down facings on inside. Finish buttonholes and sew

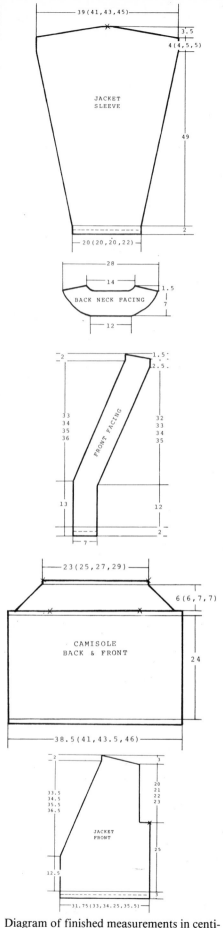

Diagram of finished measurements in centimetres

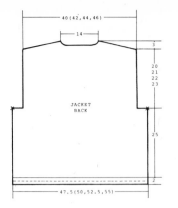

Diagram of finished measurements in centimetres

on buttons to correspond. Sew press studs to inside and sew on buttons as shown.

CAMISOLE

BACK

Push 144 (152, 162, 172) Ns to B pos. Using waste yarn cast on and knit several rows ending with carr at left. RC 000. Tension dial at 1. Using col 2, knit 6 rows. Tension dial at 3, knit 1 row. Tension dial at 1, knit 6 rows. Turn up a hem. Carr at right. RC 000. Tension dial at 2, knit 138 rows★. Counting from both edges, mark st 36 (37, 38, 39) with waste yarn. ★★Tension dial at 1, knit 6 rows. Tension dial at 3, knit 1 row. Tension dial at 1, knit 6 rows. Pick up loops from first row above marked row and place onto Ns. Cast off★★.

FRONT

Foll instructions for back to★.
Shape top
Set carr for partial knitting. Always taking yarn round first inside N in D pos, push 8 Ns at opposite end to carr to D pos on next 2 rows, 1 N on next 22 (20, 30, 28) rows and 2 Ns on next 10 (12, 8, 10) rows. 86 (92, 100, 108) Ns rem in B pos. Mark end sts in B pos with waste yarn. Break off yarn. Push Ns from D pos back to C pos. Work as given for back from ★★to★★.

SHOULDER STRAPS (both alike)

Using col 2, cast on 3 sts by hand. Tension dial at 2, knit 300 rows in circular cord knitting as given in instruction book. Cast off.

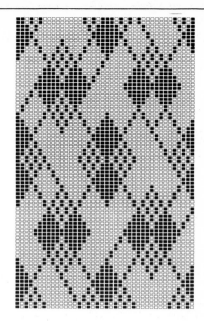

TO MAKE UP

Pin out each piece to size and press carefully with a warm iron over a damp cloth. Join side seams. Sew shoulder straps to marked sts.

HINTS & TIPS

A NEAT 'V'

'V' necks often cause trouble by dragging at the 'V' and distorting the neckline. There are alternatives to shaping the 'V'. The band can be knitted straight and the two ends overlapped or they can be knitted straight and then a mitre can be shaped by sewing. This technique is often used industrially. Fully fashioned shapings have a tendency to tighten the edges and so again the neat effect can be spoilt by the tight edge dragging the 'V' shape. This pulling or dragging shows up even more when there is patterning or striping involved.

One of my readers telephoned me (Mrs G. from Swansea) and told me to try the holding method instead of decreasing. I think that this is the nicest 'V' shape I have seen, try it:

Use a fully fashioned decrease when you shape your 'V' neck as this gives a much better edge to pick up on for the band.

THE BAND. With the inside (wrong side) of the knitting facing you, pick up sts. evenly along the neck edge . . . make sure that you pick up well into the 'V'. Main tension minus one whole number knit one row increasing one stitch at the neck edge. Knit one more row.

Set the carriage to hold sts. and put one needle at the neck edge into the holding position every row 8 times altogether. Knit one row at a looser tension (for the fold line). Back to the band tension, return one needle at the neck edge to the working position every row until all needles are back in the working position.

NOTE. When you are returning a needle to the working position with the carriage at the same side as the needle to be returned, wrap the yarn round the needle to be returned (as in dart shapings). When the carriage is at the opposite end just push the needle back to the working position. Pick up alternate sts. from the 'pick up edge' at the start of the band. Knit one row tension 10 and cast off with the latch tool. Repeat for left hand band and then join the mitre neatly on the inside.

CHUNKY TIPS

This tip was first of all recommended to us for Jacquard knitting but it is also a great help on chunky knits.

When you are required to cast off stitches at, for example, the beginning of the armhole shaping, instead of casting off the given number of stitches at one side and then knitting across and repeating the procedure, cast off at the right with the usual method and then take a piece of spare yarn and cast off the same number of stitches at the left. This keeps the work even and is especially useful in keeping the pattern exactly matching.

CHUNKY TIP TWO

I have had various suggestions for knitting ribs on the chunky machines and the latest is as follows: Using the rib tension knit the rib rows on alternate needles as for a mock rib. When you have knitted sufficient rows use the latch tool to latch up the bar between the knitted stitches and then transfer it to the empty needle (now brought forward to the working position). Turn up the tension and carry on . . . it's great.

A PRESSING ENGAGEMENT

Next time you have to take your courage in your hands and press an acrylic, try pressing carefully with a wet cloth on top of a dry cloth. Garment is wrong side up on the pressing board, dry cloth next and then the wet cloth. Keep to the usual rules of lifting the iron up and putting it down again, NOT ironing back and forth.

MARKING THE COMBS

Quite a number of ribber and double bed machine owners will have already find out how useful it is to have the centre tooth of the cast on comb marked with something like nail varnish or Tippex to make it easier to hang the comb centrally. Now we have a sequel to the tale for the owners of Singer electronic and Superba machines. Mark the centre flow comb (this is the equivalent to the sinker pins for the benefit of other machine owners) with nail varnish or the like, and then you can easily hang the comb centrally.

Tamarisk lady's jacket

SIZES

To fit 86/91 (97/102) cms, 34/36 (38/40) ins bust. 51 cms, 20 ins sleeve seam. 74 cms, 29 ins length.

MATERIALS

Lister Lee Tamarisk 25 grm balls. 15 (16) Almond (A), 1 Smoked Lilac (L), 1 Crushed Raspberry (R), 1 Shocking Pink.

TENSION

11 sts and 14 rows to 5 cms (2 ins). Using alternate needles approx tension dial 7. Always check your tension before commencing.

NOTES:
Unless otherwise stated all welts can be knitted using a ribbing attachment. Cast on in 1 x 1 rib T 4/4 and knit half the amount of rows.

BACK 1

With waste yarn cast on 60 (63) sts as 1 x 1 mock rib. Knit a few rows. Carriage at right RC 000 change to col A. RT knit 15 rows, T10 knit one row, RT knit 15 rows. Make a hem, do not fill in all empty needles, and knit the row *. RC 000 MT col A knit 4 rows. Change to col R knit 4 rows, change to col A knit 4 rows. Dec one st on left hand side of next and every foll 20 rows 5 times. ** Continue in A to row 110. Change to col S, knit 8 rows S 20 rows A, 4 rows R, 10 rows A, 4 rows L, 10 rows A, 4 rows S, change to col A. *** Knit to row 190, cast off.

BACK 2

Knit as back 1 to *. RC 000, col A knit 8 rows. At right hand side of next and every foll 20th row dec one st 5 times, whilst patterning as follows. ** Knit A to RC 30. **** Change to col L, knit 8 rows, col A 20 rows, S 4 rows, A 10 rows, R 4 rows, A 10 rows, L 4 rows. Change to col A ***. Knit to row 190, cast off.

FRONT 1

With waste yarn cast on 80 (83) sts as 1 x 1 mock rib. Knit a few rows. Carr at right RC 000 change to col A. RT knit 15 rows, T10 one row, RT knit 15 rows, make a hem, do not fill in all empty Ns * and knit the row. RC 000 MT col A knit one row. Carr at left hand side cast on 5 sts. Knit 3 rows, change to col R knit 4 rows, change to col A knit 4 rows. Dec one st on right hand side of next and every foll 20th row 5 times. Knit as back 1 from ** to ***. Knit col A to row 170. Put 15 sts on left hand side on hold. Knit one row, cast off 20 sts, knit the row. At neck edge of next and every foll alt row dec one st for 18 rows. Cast off rem 35 (38) sts. Take sts on left hand side off hold. Dec one st at neck edge of next and every foll alt row for 10 rows, dec one st at either end of next and every foll alt row for 10 rows. 2 sts rem, cast off.

FRONT 2

Knit as front 1 to *. RC 000 cast on 5 sts, col A knit 8 rows. At left hand side of next and every foll 20th row dec one st 5 times whilst patterning as follows. Knit as back 2 from ** to ***. Knit to row 170. Shape neck as for front 1 reversing all shapings.

NECKBANDS (two alike)

With wrong side of work facing and beg at right side pick up 20 sts across back of neck, 40 sts across front. Place on machine as 1 x 1 mock rib. Carr at right RC 000 RT col A, knit 7 rows, T10 knit 1 row, RT knit 8 rows, cast off.

SLEEVE 1

With waste yarn cast on 40 (44) sts, as 1 x 1 mock rib. Knit a few rows. Carr at right RC 000 change to col A. RT knit 19 rows, T10 knit one row, RT knit 19 rows. Make a hem, do not fill in all empty Ns and knit the row. RC 000 MT col A, at each end of next and every foll 4th row inc one st to 90 sts, whilst patterning as follows. * Knit 20 rows A, 8 rows R, 20 rows A, 4 rows L, 10 rows A, 4 rows S, 10 rows A, 4 rows R, change to col A, knit to row 120, cast off.

SLEEVE 2

Knit as sleeve 1 to *. Knit 50 rows A, pattern as back 2 from **** to ***. Knit straight to row 120, cast off.

SCARF

Using col A cast on 40 sts as 1 x 1 mock rib. Knit 30 rows A, 10 rows R, 30 rows A, 10 rows L, 30 rows A, 10 rows S. Repeat this patterning to row 470, cast off.

TO MAKE UP

With right side of work facing sew down centre back. Sew down neckbands. Turn in 5 sts on centre fronts and sew down. Place centre of sleeves to shoulder seam and sew along top of sleeves. Sew sleeve and side seams. Attach scarf to back of neck. Sew 6 buttons down front and crochet loops to match. Sew one button on right hand side of neck and make buttonhole to match.

See colour plate opposite page 33

Woven jacket

For Knitmaster Chunky 120 machines with weaving attachment.

SIZES

To fit 81-86 (91-96, 101-106) cms, 32-34 (36-38, 40-42) ins bust.

MATERIALS

3 Suisses in 50 grm balls. 10 (11, 12) balls Suizy in col 1, 6 (6, 7) balls Lesley in col 2.

TENSION

19 sts and 28 rows to 10 cms (4 ins) measured over weaving pattern, 20 sts and 28 rows to 10 cms (4 ins) measured over stockinet. Tension dial at approx 4.

NOTES:
Using 3 x 1 needle pusher. * Push the 1st and ev foll 4th N to E pos, weave 1 row col 2. Using col 1, knit 2 rows. Push the 3rd and ev foll 4th N to E pos, weave 1 row col 2. Using col 1, knit 2 rows **. Rept from * to ** throughout.

BACK

Push 50 (54, 59) Ns at left and right of centre 0 to B pos. 100 (108, 118) Ns altog. Using col 1 cast on by hand. Tension dial at 4, knit 2 rows. Using col 2, knit 2 rows. Using col 1, knit 2 rows. RC 000. Working in pattern as given in notes, knit 34 rows. Mark both edges with waste yarn for bottom of pocket pos. Knit 44 rows. Mark both edges with waste yarn for top of pocket pos. Knit 56 rows. Mark both edges with waste yarn for armhole pos. Knit 50 (56, 62) rows. RC 184 (190, 196). Using col 2, knit 2 rows. Tension dial at 8, knit 1 row. Cast off with a latchet tool.

LEFT FRONT

Push 50 (54, 59) Ns at right of centre 0 to B pos. Carr at left. Using col 1 cast on by hand. Tension dial at 4, knit 2 rows. Using col 2, knit 2 rows. Using col 1, knit 2 rows. RC 000. Working in pattern as given in notes, knit 34 rows. Mark right edge with waste yarn for bottom of pocket pos. Knit 16 rows. Mark left edge with

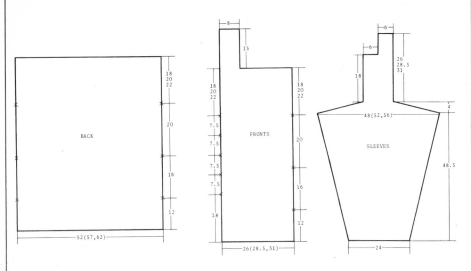

Diagram of finished measurements in centimetres

waste yarn. Knit 21 rows. Mark left edge with waste yarn. Knit 7 rows. Mark right edge with waste yarn for top of pocket pos. Knit 14 rows. Mark left edge with waste yarn. Knit 21 rows. Mark left edge with waste yarn. Knit 21 rows. Mark left edge with waste yarn and right edge with waste yarn for armhole pos. Knit 50 (56, 62) rows. RC 184 (190, 196). Using col 2, knit 2 rows. Tension dial at 8, knit 1 row. Carr at right. Using a latchet tool cast off 34 (38, 43) sts. 16 sts rem. Keeping pattern correct knit 42 rows. Using waste yarn knit 8 rows and release from machine.

RIGHT FRONT

Work as given for left front but reverse the shapings by reading right for left and vice versa.

LEFT SLEEVE

Push 23 Ns at left and right of centre 0 to B pos (46 Ns altog). Carr at right. Using col 1 cast on by hand. Tension dial at 4, knit 2 rows. Using col 2, knit 2 rows. Using col 1, knit 2 rows. RC 000. Working in pattern as given in notes, knit 2 (3, 10) rows. Keeping pattern correct, inc 1 st both ends next and ev foll 6th (5th, 4th) row 23 (27, 30) times in all. 92 (100, 106) sts. Knit 1 (2, 9) rows without shaping. RC 136. Carr at right.
Shape top
Cast off 6 (7, 7) sts beg next 6 rows, 6 (6, 7) sts beg next 4 rows and 5 (6, 7) sts beg next 2 rows. 22 sts. Knit 51 rows without shaping. Carr at left. Cast off 11 sts beg next row. 11 sts rem. Knit 20 (27, 34) rows without shaping. RC 220 (227, 234). Using waste yarn knit 8 rows and release from machine.

RIGHT SLEEVE

Knit as for left but reverse the shaping by reading left for right and vice versa.

COLLAR (two pieces)

Push 6 Ns at right and 2 Ns at left of centre 0 to B pos (8 Ns altog). Carr at right. Using col 1 cast on by hand. RC 000. Tension dial at 4. Working in pattern as given in notes knit 2 (8, 6) rows. Inc 1 st at right edge on the next and foll 8th (8th, 9th) row, knit 6 (0, 1) rows. Mark left edge with waste yarn. Knit 1 (7, 7) rows. Inc 1 st at right edge on the next and ev foll 8th (8th, 9th) row 7 times in all. 17 sts. Knit 42 rows without shaping. RC 109 (115, 121). Using waste yarn knit 8 rows and release from machine. Knit another piece in the same way but reverse the shapings by reading left for right and vice versa throughout.

POCKETS (two alike)

Push 24 Ns at right of centre 0 to B pos. Carr at right. Using col 1 cast on by hand. RC 000. Tension dial at 4. Knit 20 rows. Mark left edge with waste yarn, knit 8 rows. Dec 1 st at right edge on the next and ev foll 3rd row 6 times in all, knit 1 row. Dec 1 st at right edge on the next and ev foll alt row 4 times in all. Dec 1 st at right edge on the next 13 rows. RC 65. Fasten off rem st. Knit another piece in the same way but reverse the shapings by reading left for right and vice versa. Work second pocket as first.

COLLAR BANDS (two alike)

Push 56 (60, 64) Ns to B pos. With plain side of one collar piece facing pick up sts evenly along straight edge from marker to edge and place onto Ns in B pos. With purl side of front facing pick up sts from top marker to edge and place onto the same Ns. Tension dial at 4. Using col 1, knit 3 rows. Using col 2, knit 2 rows. Using col 1, knit 4 rows. Using waste yarn knit 8 rows and release from machine. Repeat for other side.

BUTTONHOLE BAND

Turn up plain rows along lower edge and slip stitch into pos. Push 80 Ns to B pos. With plain side of right front facing pick up 80 sts from lower edge to top marker (including remaining pieces of collar) and place onto Ns in B pos. Inc 1 st at both ends. 82 sts. Tension dial at 4. Using col 1, knit 1 row. Make 5 buttonholes over 2 Ns using markers as a guide, knit 2 rows. Using col 2, knit 2 rows. Using col 1, knit 2 rows. Make buttonholes over the same Ns as before, knit 2 rows. Using waste yarn knit 8 rows and release from machine.

BUTTONBAND

Work as given for buttonhole band omitting buttonholes and reading left for right.

TO MAKE UP

Graft back collar seam. Graft back of saddle shoulder tog. Set in sleeves between markers, joining lower edge of back saddle shoulder to back and lower edge of front saddle shoulders to fronts. Join pairs of pockets tog along shaped edge and up to marked point. Sew pockets into pos between markers. Join side and sleeve seams. Turn up plain rows along lower edge of sleeves and slip stitch into pos. Finish buttonholes and sew on buttons to correspond.

HINTS & TIPS

CASTING OFF AGAIN

If the knitting pattern tells you to cast off 5 stitches, for example at the beginning of the next row, try this: cast off 4 sts., take the last but one stitch and put it on to the outside stitch and then bring both stitches back in again to the empty needle. This gives a neat edge and does not leave a hole where you have finished casting off.

EVEN DECREASES

Sometimes a pattern tells you to decrease stitches evenly across a row. It may be that the knitting has been run off on waste yarn, perhaps for a sleeve, and then it has to be replaced on the machine on to less needles, probably for the cuff. The pattern does not always give you specific instructions such as put two sts. on to every needle, it will just say decrease evenly along the row. To do this put a couple of sts. on at each end, a couple in the middle of the work and then one opposite each number on the machine bed. This makes it easy to see at a glance how many stitches you have to decrease as you go along, and the decreases will be even.

Mohair cardigan

For Knitmaster 260 and 360 machines with lace carriage.

SIZES

To fit 81/86 (91/97, 101/107) cms, 32/34 (36/38, 40/42) ins bust.

MATERIALS

19 (20, 21) 25 grm balls in col 1 Lister Lee Tamarisk; 9 buttons; 3.3 (3.4, 3.5) metres 13 mm wide ribbon; 5 metres 6 mm wide ribbon.

TENSION

24 sts and 38 rows to 10 cms (4 ins) measured over lace pattern. Tension dial at approx 6.

BACK

Push Ns 46 to 89 (48 to 91, 50 to 93) inclusive at right of centre 0 to B pos. 44 Ns. Insert card 3L and lock on row 1. Side levers forward. With carr at right and using col 1, cast on by hand. RC 000. Tension dial at 6, knit 2 rows. Set edge pins. Release card. Side levers back. Knit 23 rows. Mark left edge with waste yarn. Knit 8 (6, 4) rows. Inc 1 st at beg of next and foll 8th row, knit 5 rows. Inc 1 st at beg of next and ev foll 6th row 5 (4, 3) times in all, knit 3 rows. Inc 1 st at beg of next and ev foll 4th row 4 (5, 6) times in all, knit 2 rows. Inc 1 st at left edge of next and ev foll 3rd row 14 (12, 10) times in all, knit 1 row. Inc 1 st at beg of next and ev foll alt row 27 (25, 23) times in all, knit 1 row. Cast on 2 sts at beg of next and ev foll alt row 10 times in all, knit 1 row. Cast on 4 sts at beg of next and ev foll alt row 2 (4, 6) times in all, knit 1 row. Cast on 6 (7, 8) sts at beg of next row, knit 1 row. Cast on 48 sts at beg of next row. 178 (183, 188) sts. Knit 76 (86, 96) rows without shaping. RC 288. Carr at right*.

Shape neck

Dec 1 st at beg of next and ev foll alt row 4 times in all. 174 (179, 184) sts. Knit 61 rows without shaping. Inc 1 st at beg of next and ev foll alt row 4 times in all. 178 (183, 188) sts. Carr at left. **Knit 76 (86, 96) rows without shaping. Cast off 48 sts at beg of next row, knit 1 row. Cast off 6 (7, 8) sts at beg of next row, knit 1 row. Cast off 4 sts at beg of next and ev foll alt row 2 (4, 6) times in all, knit 1 row. Cast off 2 sts at beg of next and ev foll alt row 10 times in all, knit 1 row. Dec 1 st at beg of next and ev foll 3rd row 14 (12, 10) times in all, knit 2 rows. Dec 1 st at beg of next and ev foll 4th row 4 (5, 6) times in all, knit 3 rows. Dec 1 st at beg of next and ev foll 6th row 5 (4, 3) times in all, knit 5 rows. Dec 1 st at beg of next and foll 8th row. 44 sts. Knit 7 (5, 3) rows without shaping. Mark left edge with waste yarn. Knit 25 rows. Cast off.

RIGHT FRONT

Work as for back to*.
Shape neck
Cast off 6 sts at beg of next row, knit 1 row. Cast off 3 sts at beg of next row, knit 1 row. Cast off 2 sts at beg of next and foll alt row, knit 1 row. Dec 1 st at beg of next and ev foll alt row 4 times in all, knit 3 rows. Dec 1 st at beg of next and ev foll 4th row 3 times in all. 158 (163, 168) sts. Knit 11 rows without shaping. RC 326. Carr at right. Side levers forward. Using waste yarn, knit 8 rows and release from machine, but leave Ns in B pos for left front.

LEFT FRONT

Lock card on row 1. Using waste yarn, cast on and knit several rows ending with carr at right. RC 000. Tension dial at 6. Using col 1, knit 2 rows. Release card. Side levers back. Knit 10 rows. Inc 1 st at beg of next and ev foll 4th row 3 times in all, knit 3 rows. Inc 1 st at beg of next and ev foll alt row 4 times in all, knit 1 row. Cast on 2 sts at beg of next and foll alt row, knit 1 row. Cast on 3 sts at beg of next row, knit 1 row. Cast on 6 sts at beg of next row. 178 (183, 188) sts. Carr at left. Work as for back from ** to end. Remove edge pins.

COLLAR FRILL

Push 28 Ns at right of centre 0 to B pos. Lock card on row 1. Side levers forward. Using waste yarn, cast on and knit several rows ending with carr at left. Tension dial at 8. Using col 1, knit 1 row. RC 000. Tension dial at 6. Knit 2 rows. Set edge pins. Release card. Side levers back. Knit 394 rows. RC 396. Remove card and edge pins. Side levers forward. Tension dial at 8, knit 1 row. Cast off with a linker or latchet tool.

BUTTONHOLE BAND

Push 158 (163, 168) Ns to B pos. With plain side of right front facing, replace 158 (163, 168) sts from below waste yarn onto Ns. RC 000. Tension dial at 6. Using col 1, knit 2 rows. Counting from neck edge, make buttonholes over 4th, 5th and 6th Ns and ev foll 15th, 16th and 17th (16th, 17th and 18th, 16th, 17th and 18th) Ns 9 times in all. Knit 4 rows. Tension dial at 8, knit 1 row. Tension dial at 6, knit 4 rows. Make buttonholes over same Ns as before. Knit 3 rows. Using waste yarn, knit 8 rows. Release from machine.

BUTTONBAND

Work as for buttonhole band reading left for right and omitting buttonholes.

TO MAKE UP

Using a latch tool, cast off first row of collar. Pin out each piece to size and press lightly with a warm iron over a damp cloth. Press collar frill to measure 104 cms long and 12 cms wide. Join shoulder, side and sleeve seams. Fold bands in half to right side, pin into pos and backstitch through open loops of last row knitted in col 1. Unravel waste yarn. Finish buttonholes and sew on buttons to correspond. Bind collar frill, lower edge of sleeves and garment with 13 mm ribbon. Gather collar frill and sew into pos. Thread 6 mm ribbon through collar frill to gather and tie in front. Thread 6 mm ribbon through sleeves using marked points as a guide. Thread 6 mm ribbon through lower edge to tie in front.

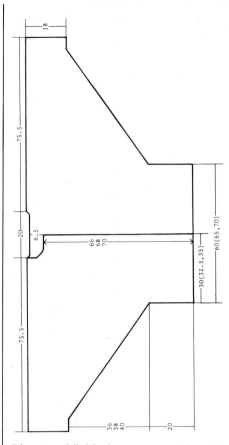

Diagram of finished measurements in centimetres

HINTS & TIPS

THE EASY WAY

If you are one of those people who like to get the difficult bit over with first so that the rest of the knitting is plain sailing . . . have a rethink. If you knit all the easy bits first and all goes well you gain confidence, get used to the technique, if it is something you have not done before, and by the time it comes to tackling the round neck shaping having done the back and sleeves first you will sail through with no bother . . . try it next time.

MATCHING STRIPES

If you are knitting a striped garment, or perhaps adding stripes to a plain jumper pattern, always work the stripe sequences out from the beginning of the armhole shaping so that the front and back match up with the sleeves and any extra length is added to the bottom and the stripe sequence is not thrown out.

SIDE WEIGHTS FOR DOUBLE BED KNITTING

Owners of double bed machines as opposed to ribbing attachments could make good use of one of the ribber accessories. The small side weights that are part of most ribber kits have wire holders shaped like a letter Z with a hook on the bottom for hanging the small weight on. These hooks are invaluable if you are having trouble with the edge stitches not knitting. They can be purchased from most machine knitting shops if they are not part of your standard equipment and I am reliably informed that they are easily made with strong wire. The top of the Z shape sits on the knitting between the two beds and the weight is hung on the hook. Make sure that the piece sitting on the knitting is lying flat and not sticking up in the way of the carriage. Knit across and carry on knitting, moving the weights up every 20 rows or so. These are especially useful when you are increasing.

RIBS RIBS RIBS

It is well worth a few minutes' effort involved in knitting a tension swatch for your ribs and cuffs, especially when they are done on the double bed. We all (if we are being good) do the necessary tension swatches for the main part of the garment, but how often do we bother to do a sample piece for the ribs. It is not always necessary to work out the tension in stitches and rows unless you are calculating for a band or a piece which needs to be a certain length. What is important is that the rib looks nice and is the right stitch size to give the correct degree of elasticity. It only takes a few minutes to knit a sample or two in the rib that you are going to use on the garment and it may well make all the difference to the finished article.

NOT SO MUCH A TIP AS A POINT TO PONDER ON

All machine knitters are weak willed when it comes to buying yarn, we all see rows of coned yarns and we buy as much as we can carry and afford in one go. To a certain extent it is a good thing because it is useful to have a range of plies and colours etc. to choose from, but beware, how often have you knitted a navy blue sweater when you really wanted a black one but had loads of navy in stock and it needed using up? It is worth thinking about. Next time you know that your will power is going to be taxed at the sight of lots of lovely yarns it would be well worth going armed with a list of what you plan to knit and buy those colours first, then you can fritter away the rest of your cash with a clear conscience . . . well, almost clear!

Batwing top

A design from Argyll

These instructions are written for chunky machines with ribbing attachment. We used a Knitmaster 120.

SIZES

To fit 82/87 (92/97) cm bust. Completed length, 47 (50) cm.

MATERIALS

Argyll Finesse (78% mohair/13% wool/9% nylon).

12 (14) x 25g balls in Chinchilla Gold 113. For best results you should use the specified yarn. If you have any difficulty in obtaining this yarn, please write to Argyll Wools Ltd., P.O. Box 15, Priestley Mills, Pudsey, West Yorkshire LS28 9LT.

TENSION

16 stitches and 20 rows to 10 cm (4 ins) measured over stocking stitch (tension dial approx 7). Tension must be matched exactly before starting the garment.

NOTE:
Knit side is used as right side. When shaping in H/P, always take yarn round first inside N in H/P to prevent a hole forming.

MAIN PART

Push 64 (69) Ns to WP. Using MT and WY, cast on and k a few rows ending with carriage at left. Set RC at 000. *Using main yarn, k 1 row. Push 13 Ns at left to H/P on next and foll 3 alt rows, k 1 row. Push 52 Ns at left from H/P to UWP. K 2 (4) rows. Push 52 Ns at left to H/P. K 2 rows. Push 13 inside Ns at left from H/P to UWP on next and foll 3 alt rows *. Rep from * to * once more. Place marker at right edge. ** K 1 row. Push 13 Ns at left to H/P on next and foll 3 alt rows, k 1 row. Push 52 Ns at left from H/P to UWP. K 2 rows. Push 52 Ns at left to H/P. K 2 rows. Push 13 inside Ns at left from H/P to UWP on next and foll 3 alt rows **. Rep from ** to ** 4 times more.
Place marker at right edge for cuff position.
Rep from ** to ** 5 times more. Place marker at right edge.
Rep from * to * 4 times more. Place marker at right edge.
Rep from ** to ** 5 times more.
Place marker at right edge for cuff position.
Rep from ** to ** 5 times more. Place marker at right edge.
Rep from * to * twice more.
Using WY, k a few rows and release from machine.

NECKBAND

Push 90 (98) Ns to WP. With k side facing, pick up 90 (98) sts around neck edge and place on to Ns. Set RC at 000. Using MT and main yarn, k 1 row. With ribbing attachment in position, transfer sts for 1x1 rib. Using MT−1, k 2 rows. Using MT−2, k 7 rows. Using MT−1, k 1 row. Transfer sts for stocking stitch. Using MT, k 2 rows. Using WY, k a few rows and release from machine.

CUFFS

Push 40 Ns to WP. With k side facing, pick up 20 sts each side of marker and place on to

NS. * Set RC at 000. Using MT and main yarn, k 1 row. With ribbing attachment in position, transfer sts for 1x1 rib. Using MT−2, k 26 rows. Transfer sts for stocking stitch. Using MT, k 2 rows. Using WY, k a few rows and release from machine *.

TO JOIN CENTRE BACK SEAM

Graft sts of first and last rows worked in main yarn to give an invisible seam. Alternatively, work as follows:- Push 64 (69) Ns to WP. With k side of main part facing, pick up 64 (69) sts from first row worked in main yarn and place on to Ns. With p side of main part facing, pick up 64 (69) sts from last row worked in main yarn and place on to Ns. Unravel WY. Using main yarn, cast off both sets of sts tog.

WELTS

Push 64 (72) Ns to WP. With k side facing, pick up 64 (72) sts along lower edge between second set of markers and place on to Ns. Work as for cuffs from * to *

TO MAKE UP

Join neckband, welt, sleeve and cuff seams. Fold neckband, welts and cuffs in half to right side and pin in position. Unravelling WY as required, backstitch through open loops of last row worked in main yarn. Brush lightly to restore pile.

HINTS & TIPS

INTARSIA KNITTING

In a recent issue of Knitting Machine Digest we discussed ways of keeping the balls of yarn tangle free when using the intarsia carriage or doing intarsia knitting on any machine and Mrs Leslie from Wakefield, Yorks., has sent us a useful suggestion. She says: 'Lyon's pure coffee is marketed in 8oz tins which have a spare plastic lid to be used after the tin is opened. When the tin is empty, I press down the jagged edges with some pliers and, using my punch card punch, I make a hole in the centre of the plastic lid. The wool goes in the tin and is threaded through the hole in the lid. This works very nicely.'

THE LONG AND SHORT OF IT

It is quite a simple matter to alter the number of rows required if, for example, your tension swatch gives you 11 rows per inch instead of 10 rows as indicated by the pattern.
All you have to do is knit 1 extra row for every inch knitted but DON'T FORGET as well as lengthening the body of the garment and sleeve depth you MUST also lengthen the sleeve cap by the same number of rows or your

sleeve head will be too small. Share the extra rows out evenly along the shaping, don't just add them at the beginning or end of the shaping.
The same applies to raglan shapings. If you have to fit in 10 extra rows and the decreases are alternate rows, then you can decrease every 4th row for the first 5 decreases. This will give you the 10 extra rows required and you will then need to do the same on all the pieces and it will be OK.

TRY THIS BUTTON BAND

You can knit this band on the ribber and then transfer the stitches to the main bed and then attach the garment to the band.
Cast on for 2 x 2 rib in the usual way and then knit 2 rows normal knitting and 2 rows circular. Repeat, 2 rows knit, 2 rows circular for as many rows as you require for the band. The buttonholes must be worked on the two knit rows.
This gives a really smart band and does not pull in too tightly; suitable for 'V' necks too.

BUTTONHOLES ON THE RIBBER

For a 2 x 1 (2 needles knitting 1 needle missing) or a 2 x 2 (2 needles knitting 2 needles missing) rib, the buttonholes when they are worked over two needles can be worked as follows. Transfer the stitches for the buttonhole using stitches on the MAIN bed, transfer one stitch to the right (down to the ribber) and one stitch to the left (down to the ribber). This leaves you with 2 empty needles on the main bed. Leave the needles in the working position and knit 2 rows and then pick up the loop formed under these two needles and put it on to one of the two needles, it does not really matter which one, and continue knitting. The buttonhole will be positioned neatly on a knit section of the rib and the rib will not be distorted.

WOOL WINDING

Most of us hate winding wool. This tip was passed to me in the school playground by my friend Nora (we do talk about other things as well . . .).
Thread the yarn that you are going to wind through the tension unit of your machine and then attach it to the wool winder. Doing this gives you a nice firm, even ball of wool and also stops you from burning your finger ends as the wool goes through them. We have tried it and it works a treat.
Nora's children and several other little souls have appeared at school wearing lovely warm hats knitted in Fair Isle, twice the required length and then

pulled through to make them double, gathered at the top and turned up at the bottom. These are all sporting penguins and teddy bears but they could be in school uniform colours, all over Fair Isle or just plain.

A NEAT NECK

A tip from Mrs Olive Jarvis, Surrey. This is a super method for a really neat round neck finish.
Method: Knit neck band of choice and complete on four rows of stocking stitch. Knit one row with buttonhole thread and finish with waste yarn.
Tack ribbing into place. Tack waste knitting into position. Break the rules and press the four plain rows, buttonhole thread and waste knitting on the right side.
Join the second shoulder and the neckband. With buttonhole thread and waste knitting till tacked in position back stitch through the open loops in the normal way but just above the buttonhole thread.
Remove the buttonhole thread. This may need to be cut in places to release it at first but comes out whole after practice.
Result: The back stitches sit at the top of the stitch, slightly proud, and are far more even.
Note: Do not use nylon cord as this fills up the stitches to be back stitched too much.

THE ROUGH AND THE SMOOTH

Fine industrial yarns are very popular among machine knitters and there are some very interesting yarns to be found, but sometimes they do present us with a problem or two along the way. Bobbly or knobbly yarns do make nice fabrics on the machine and the yarn itself is sufficient to produce a fashion garment from a very simple design. The fact that the yarns are so fine often means that it is necessary to run more than one strand to produce a fabric thick enough for a garment. Two strands of knobbly yarn is sometimes too knobbly or too thick, and the answer is to run a fine, smooth yarn with the knobbly one and you will still have a textured fabric but it will be easy to knit and not too heavy. A strand of bright courtelle is ideal because it also adds a shine to the fabric and when the two are pressed you have a fabric that is textured, shiny and has lots of movement in it, and it works out very economical too. Some of the knobbly yarns have several colours in them and it is easy to match one of the colours with a smooth yarn, which results in the one colour being highlighted and changes the look of the fabric completely.

Fine knit jacket skirt and vest

For Knitmaster 270/370 machines. For stockists write to Knitmaster Ltd., 30/40 Elcho St., London, S.W.11.

SIZES

To fit 81-101 cms, 32-40 ins bust.

MATERIALS

Jacket: 140 (160, 180, 200, 200) grms 1/15's in col 1, 20 (20, 20, 30, 30) grms 2/30's in cols 2, 3, & 4.
Skirt: 250 (250, 275, 275, 300) grms 1/15's in col 1, small amount of 2/30's in col 2, elastic to fit waist.
Vest: 70 (70, 80, 90, 100) grms 1/15's in col 1; small amount of 2/30's in cols 2, 3 & 4; crochet hook.

TENSION

Jacket: 46 sts and 55 rows to 10 cms (4 ins) measured over Fair Isle. Tension dial at approximately 1.
Skirt: 46 sts and 64 rows to 10 cms (4 ins) measured over tuck st and stockinet. Tension dial at approximately 2.
Vest: 45 sts and 60 rows to 10 cms (4 ins) measured over stripe pattern.
Tension dial at approximately 1 and 5.

NOTE:
Fair Isle pattern
With col 1 in feeder 1 and col 2 in feeder 2, knit 26 rows. Knit 4 rows col 1 only. With col 1 in feeder 1 and col 3 in feeder 2, knit 26 rows. Knit 4 rows col 1 only. With col 1 in feeder 1 and col 4 in feeder 2, knit 26 rows. Knit 4 rows col 1 only. The last 90 rows form pattern.
Stripe pattern
Tension dial at 1. Using col 1, knit 19 (20, 21, 22, 23) rows. Tension dial at 5. Using col 2, knit 1 row. Using carr release, take carr to opposite end. Tension dial at 1. Using col 1, knit 19 (20, 21, 22, 23) rows. Tension dial at 5. Using col 3, knit 1 row. Using carr release take carr to opposite end. Tension dial at 1. Using col 1, knit 19 (20, 21, 22, 23) rows. Tension dial at 5. Using col 4, knit 1 row. Using carr release, take carr to opposite end. The last 60 (63, 66, 69, 72) rows form pattern.

JACKET

BACK (1st, 2nd & 3rd sizes)

Insert special card 1 into machine and lock on row 1. Push 110 (115, 121) Ns at left and right of centre 0 to B pos. 220 (230, 242) Ns altog. Using col 1, cast on by hand. Tension dial at 1, knit 18 rows. Row counter 000. Release card. Set carr for Fair Isle. Working in Fair Isle pattern as given in notes, knit 240 rows. Mark both edges with waste yarn. Knit 132 (138, 144) rows. Row counter 372 (378, 384). Carr at right.
Shape shoulders
Set carr for partial knitting. Always taking yarn round first inside N in D pos, push 8 (8, 9) Ns at opposite end to carr to D pos on next 2 rows and 7 (8, 8) Ns on next 6 rows.
Shape back neck
Mark centre with waste yarn. Using a length of col 1, cast off centre 46 sts. Using nylon cord, knit 58 (60, 65) sts at left by hand taking Ns down to A pos. Note row number showing on pattern panel. Knit Right Part as Follows:—
Knit 1 row. *Push 7 (8, 8) Ns at opposite end to carr to D pos, cast off 2 sts at beg of next row, knit 1 row. Rept last 2 rows once more. Push 7 (7, 8) Ns at opposite end to carr to D pos, cast off 2 sts at beg of next row, knit 1 row. Push 7 (7, 8) Ns at opposite end to carr to D pos, dec 1 st at beg of next row, knit 1 row. Rept last 2 rows 2 more times. 7 (7, 8)

Ns rem in B pos. Using a transfer tool bring Ns in D pos at right back to B pos. Cast off*. With carr at left, set card at number previously noted and lock. Take carr to right. Release card. Unravel nylon cord bringing Ns back to correct pos. Knit left part as for right part from * to * but read left for right.

LEFT BACK (4th & 5th Sizes)

Insert special card 1 into the machine and lock on row 1. Push 31 Ns at left and (97, 103) Ns at right of centre 0 to B pos. (128, 134) Ns altog. With carr at right and using col 1, cast on by hand. Tension dial at 1, knit 18 rows. Row counter 000. Release card. Set carr for Fair Isle. Working in Fair Isle pattern as given in notes, knit 240 rows. Mark right edge with waste yarn. Knit (149, 155) rows. Row counter (389, 395). Carr at left.

Shape shoulder
Set carr for partial knitting. Always taking yarn round first inside N in D pos, push (9, 10) Ns at opposite end to carr to D pos on next and foll alt row, knit 1 row. Push 9 Ns at opposite end to carr to D pos on next and foll alt row, knit 1 row.

Shape back neck
Push 9 Ns at opposite end to carr to D pos, cast off 26 sts at beg of next row, knit 1 row. Push 9 Ns at opposite end to carr to D pos, cast off 2 sts at beg of next row, knit 1 row. Rept last 2 rows once more. Push (8, 9) Ns at opposite end to carr to D pos, dec 1 st at beg of next row, knit 1 row. Rept last 2 rows 2 more times. (8, 9) Ns rem in B pos. Using a transfer tool, bring Ns in D pos back to B pos. Cast off.

RIGHT BACK (4th & 5th Sizes)

Foll instructions for left back but reverse the shapings by reading left for right and vice versa.

RIGHT FRONT

Lock card on row 1.
Push 0 (0, 0, 30, 30) Ns at left and 110 (115, 121, 97, 103) Ns at right of centre 0 to B pos. 110 (115, 121, 127, 133) Ns altog. With carr at right and using col 1, cast on by hand. Tension dial at 1, knit 18 rows. Row counter 000. Counting from right edge, mark st 88 with waste yarn. Release card. Set carr for Fair Isle. Working in Fair Isle pattern as given in notes, knit 116 rows. Counting from right edge, mark edge and st 88 with waste yarn. Knit 117 (123, 124, 124, 124) rows.

3rd, 4th & 5th sizes only
Mark right edge with waste yarn, knit (5, 9, 15) rows.

All sizes
Shape front edge

1st size only
Dec 1 st (2 sts in) at left edge on the next and foll 4th row, knit 2 rows. Mark right edge with waste yarn, knit 1 row.

2nd size only
Dec 1 st (2 sts in) at left edge on the next row. Mark right edge with waste yarn, knit 3 rows.

All sizes
Dec 1 st (2 sts in) at left edge on the next and ev foll 4th row 6 (7, 8, 8, 8) times in all, knit 4 rows. Dec 1 st (2 sts in) at left edge on the next and ev foll 5th row 22 times in all, knit 1 row. Row counter 373 (379, 385, 389, 395). Carr at left.
Shape shoulder
Set carr for partial knitting. Always taking yarn round first inside N in D pos, push 8 (8, 9, 9, 10) Ns at opposite end to carr to D pos on next row, knit 1 row. Push 7 (8, 8, 9, 10) Ns at opposite end to carr to D pos on next row. Dec 1 st (2 sts in) at left edge on the next row. Push 7 (8, 8, 9, 9) Ns at opposite end to carr to D pos on next and foll alt row, knit 1 row. Push 7 (8, 8, 9, 9) Ns at opposite end to carr to D pos, dec 1 st (2 sts in) at left edge on the next row, knit 1 row. Push 7 (8, 8, 9, 9) Ns at opposite end to carr to D pos on next row, knit 1 row. Push 7 (7, 8, 9, 9) Ns at opposite end to carr to D pos on next row, knit 1 row. Push 7 (7, 8, 8, 9) Ns at opposite end to carr to D pos on next and ev foll alt row 3 times in all, knit 1 row. 7 (7, 8, 8, 9) Ns rem in B pos. Using a transfer tool, bring Ns in D pos back to B pos. Cast off.

LEFT FRONT

Foll instructions for right front but reverse the shapings by reading left for right and vice versa.

SLEEVES (both alike)

Lock card on row 1. Push 56 (56, 56, 60, 60) Ns at left and right of centre 0 to B pos. 112 (112, 112, 120, 120) Ns altog. Using col 1, cast on by hand. Tension dial at 1, knit 12 rows. Row counter 000. Release card. Set carr for Fair Isle. Working in Fair Isle pattern as given in notes, knit 12 rows. Inc 1 st at both ends of next and ev foll 6th (6th, 5th, 5th, 5th) row 15 (50, 20, 26, 56) times in all, knit 6 (6, 5, 5, 5) rows. Inc 1 st at both ends of next and ev foll 7th (7th, 6th, 6th, 6th) row 35 (5, 39, 34, 9) times in all. 212 (222, 230, 240, 250) sts. Knit 6 rows without shaping. Row counter 348. Carr at right.
Shape top
Set carr for partial knitting. Always taking yarn round first inside N in D pos, push 4 Ns at opposite end to carr to D pos on next 6 (6, 18, 18, 28) rows and 5 Ns on next 30 (32, 24, 26, 20) rows. 38 Ns rem in B pos. Break yarn. Mark centre with waste yarn. Using a transfer tool, bring Ns in D pos back to B pos. Cast off.

RIGHT POCKET

Lock card on row 1. Push Ns 23 to 110 (28 to 115, 34 to 121, 10 to 97, 16 to 103) inclusive at right of centre 0 to B pos. (88 Ns). Take carr across. Using col 1, cast on by hand. Row counter 000. Tension dial at 1. Release card. Set carr for Fair Isle. Working in Fair Isle pattern as given in notes, knit 116 rows. Change to stockinet. Using col 1, knit 17 rows. Cast off.

LEFT POCKET

Foll instructions for right pocket but read left for right. Remove card.

FRONT FACINGS (both alike)

Using col 1, cast on 8 sts by hand. Tension dial at 1, knit 81 (82, 83, 84, 85) cms. Cast off.

TO MAKE UP

Pin out to size and press carefully with a warm iron over a damp cloth.
4th & 5th sizes only
Join centre back seam.
All sizes
Turn in 17 rows at top of pockets and catch down on wrong side. Sew pockets onto marked pos. Join shoulder seams. Set in sleeves between markers. Join side and sleeve seams. Turn up hems at lower and sleeve edges and catch down on the inside. Sew facings into pos. Give final light press.

SKIRT

TO KNIT 4 (5, 5, 5, 5) panels alike

Insert special card 2 into machine and lock on row 1. Push 100 Ns at left and 111 Ns at right of centre 0 to B pos. (211 Ns altog). *Arrange Ns as follows:—

IIIII|0|IIIIIIIIIIIIIIX|IIIIIIIIII·IIII0|IIIIIIIIIIIIX|IIIIIII
‿‿‿‿‿‿
REPEAT

Using col 2, cast on by hand. Row counter 000. Tension dial at 2, knit 1 row. Release card. Set carr for tuck st. Using col 1, knit 384 rows. Cast off*.
1 (0, 1, 1, 1) panel
Lock card on row 1. Push 70 (40, 70, 100) Ns at left and 81 (21, 51, 81) Ns at right of centre 0 to B pos. 151 (61, 121, 181) Ns altog. Work as for first set of panels from * to *.

TO MAKE UP

Pin out to size and press carefully with a warm iron over a damp cloth. Join panels tog leaving one seam open. Press into pleats. Baste top edge of pleats.

YOKES (both alike)

Using col 1, cast on 192 (204, 214, 226, 238) sts by hand. Row counter 000. Tension dial at 2, knit 1 row. Always taking yarn round first inside N in D pos, push 28 Ns at opposite end to carr to D pos on next 2 rows. Push 6 inside Ns at opposite end to carr from D pos to C pos on next 8 rows. Push rem 4 Ns at opposite end to carr from D pos to C pos on next 2 rows. Dec 1 st at both ends of next and ev foll 3rd row 7 times in all, knit 1 row. Dec 1 st at both ends of next and ev foll alt row 16 times in all. 146 (158, 168, 180, 192) sts. Row counter 064. Mark both edges with waste yarn. Knit 26 rows. Cast off.

TO MAKE UP

Pin out to size and press carefully with a warm iron over a damp cloth. Sew yokes to skirt panels. Join side seams of yoke and remaining skirt seam. Fold waistband in half and catch down on the inside. Insert elastic and join ends. Give final light press.

VEST

MAIN PART

Push 72 Ns at left and 59 (63, 68, 72, 77) Ns at right of centre 0 to B pos. (131 (135, 140, 144, 149) Ns altog). Using waste yarn, knit several rows ending with carr at left. Using col 1, cast on 36 sts at left by hand. 167 (171, 176, 180, 185) sts. Row counter 000. Working in stripe pattern as given in notes, knit 17 (18, 19, 20, 21) rows.

1st size only
Cast on 2 sts at beg of next row. Inc 1 st at right edge on the next 2 rows. Cast on 2 sts at beg of next row and inc 1 st at right edge on the next row. Rept the last 2 rows 5 more times.

2nd size only
Inc 1 st at right edge on the next row. Cast on 2 sts at beg of next row. Inc 1 st at right edge on the next 2 rows. Cast on 2 sts at beg of next row and inc 1 st at right edge on the next row. Rept last 2 rows 2 more times.

3rd size only
Cast on 2 sts at beg of next row. Inc 1 st at right edge on the next 2 rows. Cast on 2 sts at beg of next row.

4th size only
Inc 1 st at right edge on the next row, knit 1 row.

5th size only
Inc 1 st at right edge on the next and ev foll alt row 3 times in all, knit 1 row.

All sizes
Inc 1 st at right edge on the next 23 (31, 39, 44, 42) rows. 212 (216, 221, 225, 230) sts. Knit 5 rows without shaping. Dec 1 st at right edge on the next 3 rows, knit 1 row. Dec 1 st at right edge on the next and ev foll alt row 29 times in all. 180 (184, 189, 193, 198) sts. Knit 17 (23, 29, 35, 41) rows without shaping. Inc 1 st at right edge on the next and ev foll alt row 29 times in all, knit 1 row. Inc 1 st at right edge on the next 3 rows. 212 (216, 221, 225, 230) sts. Knit 5 rows without shaping. Dec 1 st at right edge on the next 23 (31, 39, 44, 42) rows.

1st size only
Dec 1 st at right edge on the next row and cast off 2 sts at beg of next row. Rept last 2 rows 5 more times. Dec 1 st at right edge on the next 2 rows. Cast off 2 sts at beg of next row.

2nd size only
Dec 1 st at right edge on the next row and cast off 2 sts at beg of next row. Rept last 2 rows 2 more times. Dec 1 st at right edge on the next 2 rows. Cast off 2 sts at beg of next row. Dec 1 st at right edge on the next row.

3rd size only
Cast off 2 sts at beg of next row. Dec 1 st at right edge on the next 2 rows. Cast off 2 sts at

beg of next row.

4th size only
Knit 1 row. Dec 1 st at right edge on the next row.

5th size only
Knit 1 row. Dec 1 st at right edge on the next and ev foll alt row 3 times in all.

All sizes
167 (171, 176, 180, 185) sts. Knit 17 (17, 19, 19, 21) rows without shaping. Carr at right (left, right, left, right).

1st, 3rd & 5th sizes only
Using a length of col 1, cast off 36 sts at left edge, knit 1 row (col 2 of sequence). Using same length of col 1, cast on 36 sts at left edge.

2nd & 4th sizes only
Using col 1, cast off 36 sts at left edge. Knit 1 row (col 2 of sequence). Using col 1, cast on 36 sts at left edge.

All sizes
Knit 17 (18, 19, 20, 21) rows without shaping. Inc 1 st at right edge on the next 16 (13, 11, 8, 6) rows. Knit 1 row. Inc 1 st at right edge on the next and ev foll alt row (11 14, 16, 19, 21) times in all. 194 (198, 203, 207, 212) sts. Knit 5 rows without shaping. Dec 1 st at right edge on the next and ev foll 4th row 5 times in all, knit 1 row. Dec 1 st at right edge on the next and ev foll alt row 22 times in all. 167 (171, 176, 180, 185) sts. Knit 17 (23, 29, 35, 41) rows without shaping. Inc 1 st at right edge on the next and ev foll alt row 22 times in all, knit 1 row. Inc 1 st at right edge on the next and ev foll 4th row 5 times in all. 194 (198, 203, 207, 212) sts. Knit 5 rows without shaping. Dec 1 st at right edge on the next and ev foll alt row 11 (14, 16, 19, 21) times in all, knit 1 row. Dec 1 st at right edge on the next 16 (13, 11, 8, 6) rows. 167 (171, 176, 180, 185) sts. Knit 17 (17, 19, 19, 21) rows without shaping. Carr at left. Using col 1, cast off 36 sts at left edge. 131 (135, 140, 144, 149) sts. Using waste yarn, knit 8 rows. Release from machine.

SHOULDER STRAPS (both alike)

Tension dial at 0. Using col 1, make a cord over 4 Ns as given in instruction book for circular cord knitting. Knit 35 cms. Fasten off.

TO MAKE UP

Pin out to size and press carefully with a warm iron over a damp cloth. Using col 1, graft side seam. Using col 1, work 1 row of double crochet around all edges. Sew on shoulder straps. Give final light press.

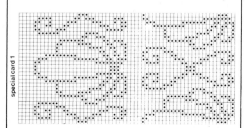

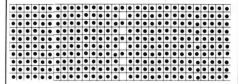

repeat throughout card

special card 2

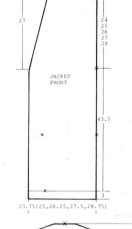

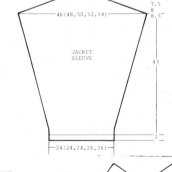

Diagram of finished measurements in centimetres.

A suit for the spring

Take a talented lady, a lovely yarn, leave them together with a knitting machine and the chances are that together they will create an outfit such as this – we put Silverknit Jupiter into the hands of Georgina and we watched as each garment emerged like a spring flower.

SIZES

To fit 81-92 cms (32-36 ins) bust.

MATERIALS

2 Cones of Jupiter (2 ply) by Silverknit in dark green. No 2704.
2 Cones of light green No. 2745.
Using 30s cotton in colours to match.
Optional, glitter thread was mixed with the light green.
1 in wide elastic for skirt waistband.
1 small button.

TENSION

28 stitches to 40 rows to 10 cms (4 ins). This garment was knitted on a Toyota 901 T(6), but can be knitted on any machine capable of tuck stitch.
The tuck card used was No. 276 from punchcard pattern book Vol. 3.

NOTES:
Tuck stitch sequence
Contrast Yarn [light green] 10 rows. RC 010.
Main yarn [dark green] 10 rows. RC 020.
Contrast yarn 6 rows. RC 026.
Main yarn 10 rows. RC 036.
Contrast yarn 10 rows. RC 046.

SKIRT (Knitted sideways)

TO KNIT

Using WY cast on 180 sts. Knit a few rows T6. RC 000. Change to main yarn. K 4 rows. Change to contrast yarn. K 4 rows.
The whole skirt is knitted by changing colour every 4 rows. Knit 4 rows – Carriage on the right. ** Bring 60 needles at the left to H/P. K 2 rows (make sure you keep the stripes going). * Put 5 inside needles from H/P to WP. (Always taking your yarn round the inside needle in D position) k 2 rows.*
Repeat from * to * 12 times altogether.
All needles now in WP. **
RC 000. Carry on in stripes until RC 240. Carriage on right. Repeat from ** to **. RC 000. Work in stripes until RC 180. Pick up first row from WY onto machine. Knit one row T10 and cast off or – Run off on WY and graft sides together.

WAISTBAND (Knitted in two pieces)

T(4). Cast on with WY 100 sts.
Knit a few rows. Main yarn knit 16 rows. T6. Knit 1 row. T4 knit 16 rows. Turn up the hem. K 1 row.
With knit side facing you hang the top of the skirt (half of it) onto the waistband.
Knit 1 loose row. Cast off. Repeat for second half.

DRESS (Tunic)

TO KNIT

T6. Using WY cast on 200 sts. Knit a few rows.
Change to main yarn. Knit 2 rows. *. Carriage on right. Bring 90 needles into H/P at left. K 2 rows. Bring 10 needles into H/P at left. K 2 rows. Repeat 9 times in all – 20 needles rem in WP. Then push back 10 needles – 9 times in all. Push all needles back to WP. K 1 row. Engage pattern card. K 1 row.** Carriage at the right. Using contrast yarn, start your tuck stitch sequence.***
Start the short rows from * to ** then continue from ** to *** 3 times in all. Using main yarn k 1 row. Carriage at left. Bring into H/P 130 needles on the right. K 2 rows.
Bring into H/P 10 needles. K 2 rows.
Repeat 4 times in all. Push back 10 needles to WP. K 2 rows. Repeat 4 times in all. Push all needles back to WP. Carriage on right.
Using contrast yarn start your tuck stitch sequence working from ** to *** using main yarn continue from * to **. Then from ** to *** and so on until you have 9 tuck sequences from the beginning.
Using main yarn k 1 row. Carriage on the left. Bring into H/P 130 needles at the right. Knit 2 rows. Bring 10 needles into H/P. K 2 rows. Repeat 4 times in all. Push back 10 needles into WP. K 2 rows. Repeat 4 times in all. Push back all the needles into WP. K 1 row. Carriage on the right. Bring 90 needles at the left into H/P and work from * to ** then from ** to *** until you have 12 tuck sequences

from the beginning.
Pick up the first row and join by knitting one row and casting off loosely.
For armholes
Cut 23 cms (10 ins) down both sides.
For front neckline
Cut 15 cms (6 ins) across and 7.5 cms (3 ins) down. Cut it out round.
Join the shoulders
Crochet the edges of the armholes and necklines. Make a loop on the left edge of the back and sew the button on the right.
For back neckline
Slit centre back 10 cms (4 ins) down. Then 4 cms (1½ ins) down each edge and 7.5 cms (3 ins) across.
Machine the edges of the armholes and necklines. Overlock them from the edges inside and blind stitch them flat.

BELT

TO KNIT

Make a corded belt using both colours. Make 2 loops at the side of the dress to hold the belt, crochet round the edge of the hem. Press lightly.

SCARF

TO KNIT

Using WY cast on 60 sts. K a few rows. Using main yarn cast on by hand. K 4 rows. Change to contrast yarn. Knit 4 rows. Continue in stripes until work measures 102 cms (40 ins). Cast off. Crochet all round.

TO MAKE UP

Using a steam iron press the garment lightly on the wrong side. Now you have to use some cut and sew. You will notice that after the 3rd tuck sequence from the beginning at the top you have more dark green showing – this is the centre front. Also if you count 6 tuck sequences from the centre front we have the centre back. Fold into 2 matching the centre front with the centre back.

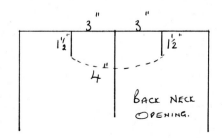

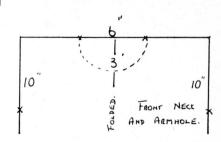

Diagram of finished measurements in inches

Jogging suit

For Knitmaster Punchcard & Electronic machines.

MEASUREMENTS

Top: to fit 81-107 cms/32-42 inch bust. Length 65.5 (66.5, 67.5, 68.5, 69.5, 70.5) cms; sleeve seam 54 cms.
Trousers: To fit hips 86-112 cms/34-44 inch. Outside leg length 111.5 (112, 112.5, 113, 113.5, 114) cms; inside leg length 85cms.

MATERIALS

Top: 2 (2, 3, 3, 3, 4) 200 grm. cones Silverknit Spaniel in col. 1; 1 200 grm. cone Silverknit Adah in cols. 2 and 3; elastic. A substitute yarn can be used providing the correct tension is obtained.
Trousers: 2 (2, 3, 3, 3, 4) 200 grm. cones Silverknit Spaniel in col. 1; small amount Silverknit Adah in cols. 2 and 3; elastic.
Both yarns available from Silverknit, Dept. K, The Old Mill, Epperstone-By-Pass, Woodborough, Notts.

TENSION

34 sts and 48 rows to 10 cms (4 ins) measured over stockinet. Tension dial at approx 3. 35 sts and 47 rows to 10 cms (4 ins) measured over Fair Isle on 'V' insert. Tension dial at approx 2.
NOTES:
Figures in brackets refer to the larger sizes respectively. Purl side of stockinet is used as right side.

'V' INSERT FAIR ISLE

Knit 2 rows col. 1, 2 rows col. 2 and 2 rows col. 1.
Punchchard machines
Release card.
Electronic machines
Inspection button off.
All machines
Set machine for Fair Isle. *With col. 2 in feeder 1 and col. 3 in feeder 2, knit 9 rows. Knit 2 rows col. 1, 2 rows col. 2 and 2 rows col. 1*. Rept. from * to * throughout.

TOP

BACK

Using waste yarn cast on 162 (170, 178, 188, 196, 200) sts. Tension dial at 3, knit several rows ending with carr. at left. Using col. 1, knit 10 rows. Turn up hem. Carr. at right. Row counter 000.
1st, 2nd, 3rd, 4th & 5th sizes only
Knit 19 rows. Dec. 1 st. at both ends of next and ev. foll. 76th row 3 times in all.
6th size only
Knit 171 rows. Dec. 1 st. at both ends of next row.

All sizes
156 (164, 172, 182, 190, 198) sts. Knit 20 rows. Row counter 192. Carr. at right.
Shape raglan armholes
Cast off 14 sts. at beg. of next 2 rows.
5th & 6th sizes only
Dec. 1 st. at both ends of next (2, 4) rows.
All sizes
Dec. 1 st. at both ends of next and ev. foll. alt. row 2 (14, 26, 39, 43, 45) times in all, knit 1 (1, 1, 1, 0, 0) row. *Dec. 1 st. at both ends of next row, knit 2 rows. Dec. 1 st. at both ends of next row, knit 1 row*. Rept. from * to * 20 (16, 12, 8, 7, 7) times more. Dec. 1 st. at both ends of next row, knit 2 rows. Using waste yarn, knit 8 rows over remaining 38 sts. Release from machine.

FRONT

Push 81 (85, 89, 94, 98, 100) Ns. at right of centre 0 to B pos. *Using waste yarn, cast on. Tension dial at 3, knit several rows ending with carr. at left. Using col. 1, knit 10 rows*. Break off yarn. Push Ns. to D pos. Push 81 (85, 89, 94, 98, 100) Ns. at left of centre 0 to B pos. Foll. instructions from * to *. Push Ns. from D pos. to C pos. 162 (170, 178, 188, 196, 200) sts. Tension dial at 5, knit 1 row. Tension dial at 3, knit 10 rows. Turn up a hem. Carr. at right. Row counter 000.
1st, 2nd, 3rd, 4th & 5th sizes only
Knit 19 rows. Dec. 1 st. at both ends of next and foll. 76th row, knit 56 rows.
6th size only
Knit 152 rows.
All sizes
158 (166, 174, 184, 192, 200) sts.
Shape neck
Using nylon cord, knit 79 (83, 87, 92, 96, 100) sts. at left by hand taking Ns. down into A pos.
Knit right part as folls:-
Dec. 1 st. at neck edge on next and ev. foll. 3rd row 14 times in all, AT THE SAME TIME, knit 19 rows. Dec. 1 st. at right edge of next row, knit 20 rows. 64 (68, 72, 77, 81, 85) sts. Carr. at right.
Shape raglan armhole
Dec. 1 st. at neck edge on 3rd (3rd, 3rd, 4th, 4th, 4th) and ev. foll. 3rd (3rd, 3rd, 4th, 4th, 4th) row 21 times in all, AT THE SAME TIME, cast off 14 sts. at beg. of next row, knit 1 row.
5th & 6th sizes only
Dec. 1 st. at raglan edge of next (2, 4) rows.
All sizes
Dec. 1 st at raglan edge of next and ev. foll. alt. row 2 (14, 26, 39, 43, 45) times in all, knit 1 (1, 1, 1, 0, 0) row.
1st, 2nd, 3rd & 4th sizes only
*Dec. 1 st. at raglan edge of next row, knit

2 rows. Dec. 1 st. at raglan edge of next row, knit 1 row*. Rept. from * to * 12 (8, 4, 0) times more.
All sizes
Fasten off rem. st. With carr. at left. Unravel nylon cord bringing Ns. to B pos. Knit left part as for right part but reverse the shapings by reading left for right.

RIGHT FRONT SLEEVE

Using waste yarn, cast on 46 sts. Tension dial at 3, knit several rows ending with carr. at right. Using col. 1, knit 10 rows. Tension dial at 5, knit 1 row. Tension dial at 3, knit 10 rows. Turn up a hem. Carr. at left. Row counter 000. Knit 10 rows. Inc. 1 st. at right edge of next and ev. foll. 7th (6th, 5th, 5th, 5th, 4th) row 4 (20, 43, 24, 8, 49) times in all, knit 5 (4, 4, 3, 3, 2) rows. Inc. 1 st. at right edge of next and ev. foll. 6th (5th, 4th, 4th, 4th, 3rd) row 33 (21, 2, 26, 46, 9) times in all. 83 (87, 91, 96, 100, 104) sts. Knit 19 rows. Row counter 249. Carr. at right.
Shape raglan top
Cast off 14 sts. at beg. of next row, knit 1 row. Dec. 1 st. at raglan edge of next 10 (14, 18, 20, 24, 22) rows. *Knit 1 row. Dec. 1 st. at raglan edge of next 3 rows*. ***. Rept. from * to * 7 (7, 7, 8, 8, 10) times more. Knit 1 row. 35 sts. Carr. at left.
Shape neck edge
Dec. 1 st. at raglan edge and cast off 5 sts. at beg. of next row. Dec. 1 st. at raglan edge of next row. Dec. 1 st. at raglan edge and cast off 5 sts. at beg. of next row, knit 1 row. Rept. from ** to ** once more. Dec. 1 st. at raglan edge and cast off 5 sts. at beg. of next row. Cast off rem. 3 sts.

LEFT FRONT SLEEVE

Foll. instructions for right front sleeve but reverse the shapings by reading left for right and vice versa.

LEFT BACK SLEEVE

Foll. instructions for right front sleeve to ***. Rept. from * to * 16 (16, 16, 17, 17, 19) times more, knit 1 row. Dec. 1 st. at raglan edge of next 2 rows. 6 sts. Carr. at left. Dec. 1 st. at both ends of next row, knit 1 row. Dec. 1 st. at raglan edge of next 3 rows. Fasten off rem. st.

RIGHT BACK SLEEVE

Foll. instructions for left back sleeve but reverse the shapings by reading left for right and vice versa.

 See colour plate opposite page 81

RIGHT 'V' INSERT

Join front raglan seams. Push 61 Ns. at left and 58 (62, 65, 69, 72, 76) Ns. at right of centre 0 to B pos. With carr. at left and plain side facing, pick up 119 (123, 126, 130, 133, 137) sts. along right neck edge and place onto Ns. Inc. 1 st. at left edge. 120 (124, 127, 131, 134, 138) sts.
Punchcard machines
Insert card for 'V' insert and lock on row 1.
Electronic machines
Inspection button on. Insert card for 'V' insert and set to first row. Pattern width indicator at 12. Point cams to all over Fair Isle. Needle 1 cam at centre 0. Buttons 1 (left) and 2 (left).
All machines
Row counter 000. Tension dial at 2. Work in patt. as given in notes, knit 2 rows. Dec. 1 st. at right edge on 5th and ev. foll. 5th row 6 times in all, AT THE SAME TIME, cast off 4 sts. at beg. of next and ev. foll. alt. row 9 times in all, knit 1 row. Cast off 3 sts. at beg. of next and ev. foll. alt. row 8 times in all, knit 1 row. 54 (58, 61, 65, 68, 72) sts.
Punchard machines
Lock card.
Electronic machines
Inspection button on.
All machines
Set machine for stockinet. Using waste yarn, knit 8 rows and release from machine.

LEFT 'V' INSERT

Foll. instructions for right 'V' insert but reverse the shapings by reading left for right and vice versa. Do not reverse buttons on electronic machines.

BRAID INSERT (2 pieces)

First piece
Push 13 Ns. at right of centre 0 to B pos.
Punchcard machines
Insert card for braid and lock on row 1.
Electronic machines
Inspection button on. Insert card for braid and set to first row. Pattern width indicator at 13. Point cams to all over Fair Isle. Needle 1 cam at centre 0. Buttons 1 (left) and 2 (left).
All machines
*Using waste yarn, cast on. Tension dial at 3, knit several rows ending with carr. at left. Using col. 2, knit 10 rows. Tension dial at 5, knit 1 row. Row counter 000. Tension dial at 3.
Punchcard machines
Release card.
Electronic machines
Inspection button off.
All machines
Set machine for Fair Isle. With col. 2 in feeder 1 and col. 3 in feeder 2, knit 10 rows. Turn up a hem. Carr. at right. Knit

329 (333, 337, 343, 347, 353) rows.
Punchcard machines
Lock card.
Electronic machines
Inspection button on.
All machines
Set machine for stockinet. Knit 1 row col. 2. Using waste yarn knit 8 rows and release from machine.
Second piece
Punchcard machines
Push 13 Ns. at left of centre 0 to B pos. Turn punchcard around and insert into machine. Lock on row 1. Foll. instructions for first piece from * to end.
Electronic machines
Foll. instructions for first piece, but set button 2 (right) NOT left.

WRIST CORDS (4 alike)

Using col. 1, make a cord over 4 Ns. as shown in instruction book for circular cord knitting. Knit until approx. 20 cms. long. Fasten off.

WAIST CORDS (2 alike)

Foll. instructions for wrist cords until approx. 25 cms. long. Fasten off.

TO MAKE UP

Pin out each piece to size and press carefully with a cool iron over a dry cloth. Pin out braid to measure 71 (72, 73, 74, 75, 76) cms. and press. Join back raglan seams. Insert braid between both halves of sleeves, leaving a small opening in hem at both sides of braid.

RIGHT NECKBAND

Push 90 (94, 97, 101, 104, 108) Ns. to B pos. With plain side of Fair Isle facing, pick up 54 (58, 61, 65, 68, 72) sts. along right 'V' insert, 13 sts. from braid, 4 sts. from back sleeve and 19 sts. from half of back neck and place onto Ns. Inc. 1 st. at back of neck. 91 (95, 98, 102, 105, 109) sts. Row counter 000. Tension dial at 3. Using col. 1, knit 1 row. Dec. 1 st. at right edge on next 4 rows. Tension dial at 5, knit 1 row. Tension dial at 3, inc. 1 st. at right edge on next 5 rows. Knit 1 row. Using waste yarn knit 8 rows and release from machine.

LEFT NECKBAND

Foll. instructions for right neckband but reverse the shapings by reading left for right.

TO MAKE UP

Join side, sleeve, 'V' insert and neckband seams. Fold neckband in half to right side and pin into pos. Backstitch through open loops of last row knitted in col. 1. Cut elastic to fit wrists and waist and insert into hems. Join cords to ends of elastic.

TROUSERS

RIGHT FRONT

Using waste yarn, cast on 63 (67, 71, 75, 80, 84) sts. *Tension dial at 3, knit several rows ending with carr. at left. Using col. 1, knit 10 rows. Tension dial at 5, knit 1 row. Tension dial at 3, knit 10 rows. Turn up a hem. Carr. at right*. Row counter 000. Knit 2 rows. Inc. 1 st. at beg. of next and ev. foll. 4th row 4 times in all, knit 5 rows. Inc. 1 st. at beg. of next and ev. foll. 6th row 5 times in all, knit 7 rows. Inc. 1 st. at beg. of next and ev. foll. 14th row 3 times in all. 75 (79, 83, 87, 92, 96) sts. Knit 16 (18, 20, 22, 26, 28) rows. Carr. at left. Inc. 1 st. at beg. of next and foll. 6th row, knit 1 row. Inc. 1 st. at beg. of next and ev. foll. alt. row 5 times in all, knit 1 row. Cast on 2 sts. at beg. of next and foll. alt. row, knit 1 row. Cast on 3 sts. at beg. of next row. 89 (93, 97, 101, 106, 110) sts. Row counter 120 (122, 124, 126, 130, 132). Carr. at right.
Shape leg
Dec. 1 st. at right edge on ev. 133rd (79th, 57th, 44th, 33rd, 28th) row 2 (4, 6, 8, 11, 13) times in all, AT THE SAME TIME, dec. 1 st. at left edge on ev. 40th (33rd, 28th, 25th, 22nd, 20th) row 9 (11, 13, 15, 17, 19) times in all, knit 38 (35, 34, 23, 24, 18) rows. 78 sts. Row counter 518 (520, 522, 524, 528, 530). Knit 10 rows. Tension dial at 5, knit 1 row. Tension dial at 3, knit 10 rows. Cast off.

LEFT FRONT

Foll. instructions for right front but reverse the shapings by reading left for right and vice versa.

LEFT BACK

Using waste yarn, cast on 61 (65, 69, 74, 78, 82) sts. Foll. instructions for right front from * to *. Row counter 000. Knit 1 row. Carr. at left.
Shape back
Always taking yarn round first inside N. in D pos., push 56 (56, 63, 63, 70, 70) Ns. at opposite end to carr. to D pos., knit 2 rows. Inc. 1 st. at left edge on the 3rd and foll. 10th row, AT THE SAME TIME, push 8 (8, 9, 9, 10, 10) inside Ns. at opposite end to carr. from D pos. down into C pos. on next and ev. foll. alt. row 7 times in all. Inc. 1 st. at left edge on ev. 10th row 8 times in all, AT THE SAME TIME, inc. 1 st. at beg. of next and foll. 4th row, knit 5 rows. Inc. 1 st. at beg. of next and ev. foll. 6th row 3 times in all, knit 7 rows. Inc. 1 st. at beg. of next and foll. 10th row, knit 13 rows. Inc. 1 st. at beg. of next and foll. 14th row, knit 11 rows. 80 (84, 88, 93, 97, 101) sts. Carr. at right. Dec. 1 st. at right edge on 2nd (4th, 3rd, 5th, 3rd, 5th) and ev. foll. 11th (11th,

12th, 12th, 14th, 14th) row 4 times in all, AT THE SAME TIME, knit 2 (2, 3, 3, 4, 4) rows. Inc. 1 st. at left edge of next and ev. foll. 3rd (3rd, 3rd, 4th, 4th, 4th) row 2 (2, 2, 2, 4, 5) times in all, knit 1 (2, 2, 2, 2, 2) rows. Inc. 1 st. at left edge of next and ev. foll. 2nd (3rd, 3rd, 3rd, 3rd, 3rd) row 2 (2, 3, 4, 3, 3) times in all, knit 1 row. Inc. 1 st. at beg. of next and ev. foll. alt. row 7 (7, 6, 5, 4, 3) times in all, knit 1 row. Cast on 2 sts. at beg. of next and ev. foll. alt. row 3 times in all, knit 1 row. Cast on 3 sts. at beg. of next and ev. foll. alt. row 3 times in all, knit 1 row. Cast on 7 sts. at beg. of next row. 109 (113, 117, 122, 126, 130) sts. Row counter 134 (136, 138, 140, 144, 146). Carr. at right.

Shape leg

Dec. 1 st. at right edge on ev. 25th (22nd, 20th, 17th, 16th, 15th) row 15 (17, 19, 22, 24, 26) times in all, AT THE SAME TIME, knit 2 rows. Dec 1 st. at left edge on next and ev. foll. 3rd row 4 times in all, knit 3 rows. Dec. 1 st. at left edge of next and foll. 4th row, knit 5 rows. Dec. 1 st. at left edge of next and ev. foll. 6th row 4 times in all, knit 7 rows. Dec. 1 st. at left edge of next and foll. 8th row, knit 17 rows. Dec. 1 st. at left edge of next and ev. foll. 100th (60th, 43rd, 33rd, 27th, 23rd) row 4 (6, 8, 10, 12, 14) times in all, knit 20 (20, 19, 23, 23, 21) rows. 78 sts. Row counter 532 (534, 536, 538, 542, 544). Knit 10 rows. Tension dial at 5, knit 1 row. Tension dial at 3, knit 10 rows. Cast off.

RIGHT BACK

Foll. instructions for left back but reverse the shapings by reading left for right and vice versa.

BRAID INSERT (2 pieces)

First piece
Push 13 Ns. at right of centre 0 to B pos.
Punchcard machines
Insert card for braid and lock on row 1.
Electronic machines
Inspection button on. Insert card for braid and set to first row. Pattern width indicator at 13. Point cams to all over Fair Isle. Needle 1 cam at centre 0. Buttons 1 (left) and 2 (left).
All machines
*Using waste yarn, cast on. Tension dial at 3, knit several rows ending with carr. at left. Using col. 2, knit 10 rows. Tension dial at 5, knit 1 row. Row counter 000. Tension dial at 3.
Punchcard machines
Release card.
Electronic machines
Inspection button off.
All machines
Set the machine for Fair Isle. With col. 2 in feeder 1 and col. 3 in feeder 2, knit 10 rows. Turn up a hem. Carr. at right. Knit 528 (530, 532, 534, 538, 540) rows.
Punchcard machines
Lock card.

Electronic machines
Inspection button on.
All machines
Set machine for stockinet. Change to col. 2 only. Tension dial at 5, knit 1 row. Tension dial at 3, knit 10 rows. Cast off.
Second piece
Punchcard machines
Push 13 Ns. at left of centre 0 to B pos. Turn punchcard around and insert into machine. Lock card on row 1. Foll. instructions for first piece from * to end.
Electronic machines
Foll. instructions for first piece, but set button 2 (right) NOT left.

ANKLE CORDS (4 alike)

Foll. instructions for wrist cords on Top until approx. 20 cms. long. Fasten off.

TO MAKE UP

Pin out each piece to size and press carefully with a cool iron over a dry cloth. Join crutch and inside leg seams. Insert braid between back and front legs, leaving a small opening in top of ankle hem at both sides of braid. Turn up hems at lower edge and catch down on inside. Insert 61 (64, 69, 74, 79, 84) cms. of elastic in waist hem and join ends. Cut elastic to fit ankles and insert into hems. Join cords to ends of elastic.

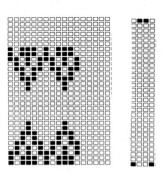

Electronic chart for 'V' insert

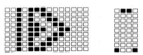

Electronic chart for braid

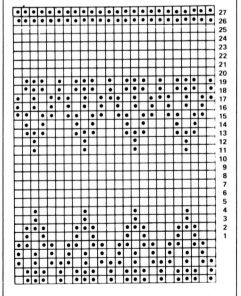

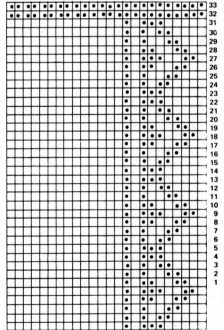

Punchcard chart for braid

Lady's two piece evening outfit

Designed and knitted by Fashion Adviser, Jackie Burchall on a Singer Memo-Matic knitting machine

MEASUREMENTS

Skirt:
To fit hip sizes 34(36,38,40) ins; 86.5 (91.5,96.5,101.5) cms.
Length to waistband – 40 ins(101.5cms).
Top:
To fit bust sizes 32-34(36-38) ins; 81-86.5(91.5-96.5) cms.

MATERIALS

Skirt:
13(14,16,17) 25-gm balls of 3 Suisses Soiree colour 1.
Elastic to fit waist.
Top:
4(5) 25-gm balls of 3 Suisses Soiree Colour 1.
1(2) 25-gm balls of 3 Suisses Soiree Colour 2.
Elastic to fit waist.
For your nearest 3 Suisses stockist write to:- Filature de l'Espierres, Saffron Way, Leicester. LE2 6UP.

TENSION

34 sts and 42 rows = 10 cms(4 ins) measured over stocking stitch with all needles in W.P.
Use same tension dial number as found correct over stocking stitch for 4 x 1 pattern stitch.
Approx tension 6. (Check tension first to ensure accuracy).

ABBREVIATIONS

Alt	Alternate	MT	Main tension
Beg	Beginning	WP	Working position
Cms	Centimetres	N.WP	Non-working position
Dec	Decrease	HP	Holding position
Inc	Increase	Gm	Grammes
Ins	Inches		
RC	Row Counter		
RC 000	Return RC to 000		
St	Stitch		
Sts	Stitches		
T	Tension		

SKIRT

Bring 175(181,187,193) needles to HP having extra needle to right of centre, cast on using handwind cast on method. Knit 1 row returning needles to WP. Transfer every 5th st on to its adjacent needle and return empty needles to N.WP. Needles should be as follows:- ||||•||||•||||•||||
Needles in N.WP. •
Needles in WP. |
RC 000 tension 2 numbers looser than MT.
* Knit 6 rows. Dec 1 st at each end. Repeat from * 5 more times. Change tension to 1 number tighter. Repeat last 36 rows (changing tension as before after each repeat) 5 more times.
RC 216.
Continue on MT. Dec 1 st at each end of every following 6th row, 24 times. 55(61,67,73) sts remain. Knit to 366 rows.

WAISTBAND

Transfer sts to 2 x 1 mock rib. Change tension to 1 number tighter than main. Knit 24 rows. Bring empty needles to WP. Knit 1 row at loosest tension and chain cast off.

Knit 3 more panels the same.

TO MAKE UP

Join panels together. Turn 4 rows at lower edge to wrong side and slip stitch in place.
Cut elastic to fit waist and join ends. Fold waistband over elastic to inside and slip-stitch in place.

TOP

BACK

Bring 124(166) needles to HP cast on using hand wind cast on method. Knit 1 row returning needles to WP.
Transfer every 3rd stitch to its adjacent needle for 2 x 1 mock rib. Return empty needles to N.WP tension 1 number tighter than main. Knit 24 rows. Transfer every 5th stitch on to its adjacent needle and return empty needles to N.WP.
Needles should be as follows:-
||||•||||•||||•||||
Needles in N.WP •
Needles in WP. |
RC 000 MT Knit 176(195) rows. Bring 104 needles at side opposite carriage to HP. Work on remaining 20 stitches at side of carriage.
Bring needles in N.WP back to WP and continue in stocking stitch.
Knit

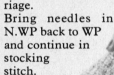

See colour plate opposite page 96

20 rows * dec 1 st at inside edge every alt row until 1 st remains. Cast off. Return 20 sts at opposite side to WP. Bring needles in N.WP back to WP. Knit as for other side reversing shapings.

RC 000. Bring centre 84 sts to WP. Arrange needles for 2 x 1 mock rib. MT knit 13 rows. Return needles in N.WP to WP. Knit 1 row on loosest T. Chain cast off.

FRONT

Knit as back to *. Change to 2nd colour. Dec 1 st at inside edge every alt row until 1 st remains. Cast off.

Return 20 sts at opposite side to WP. Bring needles in N.WP back to WP. Knit as for right side, reversing shapings.

RC 000. Bring centre

84 sts to WP. Arrange needles for 2 x 1 mock rib. MT transfer to main colour. Knit 13 rows.

Return needles in N.WP to WP. Knit 1 row on loosest tension. Chain cast off.

SIDE PANELS (Knit 2)

Bring 35 needles to holding position. With 2nd colour cast on using handwind cast on method. Knit 1 row returning needles to WP.

Transfer stitches for 2 x 1 mock rib. Tension 1 number tighter than MT. Knit 24 rows. Bring needles in N.WP to WP. Continue in plain stocking stitch. Knit 126(145) rows straight.

Bring 22 stitches at side opposite carriage to HP work on remaining 13 sts. Knit 1 row. Dec 1 st at inside edge every row until 1 st remains. Cast off. Cast off centre 10 stitches. Knit other side the same, reversing shapings.

TO MAKE UP

Join side panels to side seams. Turn back neck rib at back and front and slip stitch in place.

Cut elastic to fit waist and join ends. Fold waistband over elastic to inside and slip stitch in place.

Work a single row of crochet or blanket stitch around sleeve edges using main colour. Press lightly using a warm iron over a damp cloth.

Fair Isle jumper, skirt and hat

Suitable for any 24 pattern repeat machine.

SIZES

To fit 86 (91, 97) cms, 34 (36, 38) ins bust. 63.5 (64.25, 64.75) cms, 25 (25¼, 25½) ins length. 47.5 (47.75, 48) cms, 18¾ (18¾, 18¾, 19) ins sleeve seam. 62.25 cms, 24½ ins skirt length.

MATERIALS

Lister-Lee Thermo-Knit M/K cones. 2 cones Powder Blue 643 (main colour), 1 cone Midnight Blue 630 (1st con), 1 cone Burgundy 635 (2nd con). Elastic to fit waist.

TENSION

15 sts and 18 rows to 5 cm (2 ins) measured over Fair Isle (approx T 7). 15 sts and 20 rows to 5 cm (2 ins) measured over stocking stitch (approx T 6).

NOTES:

All welts may be knitted as 1 x 1 or 2 x 1 mock rib. Knit twice the number of rows stated and make a hem.

Colour sequence

1st con remains in A feeder throughout knitting Fair Isle. Colour changes occur as follows:
Row 1-7, main colour in B feeder.
Row 8, 1st con.
Row 9, 2nd con in B feeder.
Row 10, 1st con.
Row 11-17, main colour in B feeder.
Row 18, 1st con.
Row 19, 2nd con in B feeder.
Row 20, 1st con.
Row 21-23, main colour in B feeder.
Row 24-27, 2nd con in B feeder.
Row 28, 1st con.
Row 29-51, main colour in B feeder.
Row 52-55, 2nd con in B feeder.
Row 56, 1st con.
Repeat this colour sequence throughout knitting Fair Isle, unless otherwise stated.

JUMPER

BACK

Insert card and lock on row 1. With 2nd con cast on 146 (154, 162) sts as 1 x 1 rib. T 4/4. Work 29 rows in rib. Transfer sts on to main bed. Carriage on left. T 7. Set machine for Fair Isle. Knit the row. RC 000. Release card. Work in Fair Isle foll col sequence (see notes), to RC 120.
Shape armhole
Carriage on right. RC 000. Cast off 6 (7, 8) sts at beg of next 2 rows. 134 (140, 146) sts.★ Work straight to RC 76 (78, 80).
Shape shoulders
Cast off 10 (11, 11) sts at the beg of next and foll alt rows 4 times in all. Work one row. Cast off 4 (2, 4) sts. Knit in WY on rem 46 (48, 50) sts and release from machine.

FRONT

Knit as back to ★. Work to RC 54 (56, 58).
Shape neck
Carriage on right. Note position of card. Push 78 (82, 86) sts at left to H/P. Work on rem 56 (58, 60) sts for first side. Dec one st at neck edge on next 12 rows. Work straight to RC 76 (78, 80).
Shape shoulders
Cast off 10 (11, 11) sts at beg of next and foll alt rows 4 times in all. Work one row. Cast off rem 4 (2, 4) sts. Return 22 (24, 26) sts at right from H/P to WP. Knit in WY and release from machine. Return rem 56 (58, 60) sts to WP. Reset card and complete to correspond with first side, reversing all shapings.

NECKBAND

Join right shoulder seams. With 2nd con cast on 124 (128, 132) sts as 1 x 1 rib. Work 30 rows in rib. Transfer sts on to main bed. Wrong side facing, pick up 124 (128, 132) sts at neck edge and evenly place on to Ns. With 2nd con knit one row. Cast off loosely.

SLEEVES

Reset card and lock on row 1. With 2nd con cast on 60 (64, 68) sts as 1 x 1 rib. T 4/4. Work 29 rows in rib. Transfer sts on to main bed. Carriage on left. T 7. Set machine for Fair Isle. Knit the row. RC 000. Release card and work in Fair Isle, inc one st at each end every foll 4th row 34 times in all. 128 (132, 136) sts. Work straight to RC 142 (144, 146). Cast off.

SKIRT

PANELS (knit 6 alike)

Reset card and lock on row 1. Carriage on right. With 2nd con cast on by hand 125 (130, 135) sts. T 6 knit 6 rows. T 8 knit one row. T 6 knit 6 rows. Turn up hem. Carriage on left. T 7. Set machine for Fair Isle and knit the row. RC 000. Release card and work In Fair Isle to RC 28. Set machine for stocking stitch. T 6. With main colour work in stocking stitch to RC 180. Change to WY. Knit several rows and release from machine.

YOKE

Join side seams of 3 panels. Main bed push 150 (156, 162) Ns to WP. Wrong side facing, replace sts of 3 skirt panels to Ns as follows: 3 sts on to first N and 2 sts on to next N. Repeat along the row. Carriage on right. RC 000. T 6. With main colour work in stocking stitch, dec one st at each end of every foll 10th row 5 times in all. 140 (146, 152) sts rem. T 10 knit one row. Work 19 rows for waistband. Cast off. Join side seams of other 3 panels and complete to correspond with first side.

HAT

TO KNIT

With 2nd con cast on 152 sts as 1 x 1 rib. T 4/4 work 30 rows in rib. Transfer sts to main bed. Carriage on right. T 6 work 8 rows. Change to 1st con. Work 4 rows. Change to main colour. Work 20 rows. Push 114 sts at left to H/P. Work on rem 38 sts at right for 1st section. Knit 1 row. Using a 2 prong transfer tool, dec one st at each end 18 times in all. One st rem. Work one row and cast off. Return 38 sts at right from H/P to WP. Complete 2nd section to correspond with 1st section. Complete 3rd and 4th sections to correspond with 1st and 2nd sections.

TO MAKE UP

Jumper
Join left shoulder and neckband seam. Set in sleeves, and join sleeve and side seams.
Skirt
Join side seams. Turn waistband in half to the inside and catch down along loose row, leaving one inner waist hem seam open. Thread elastic through hem and join. Close seam.
Hat
Turn rib in half to the inside and catch down to the first row of stocking stitch. Join sections and side seams.

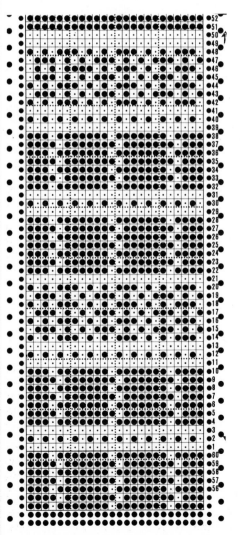

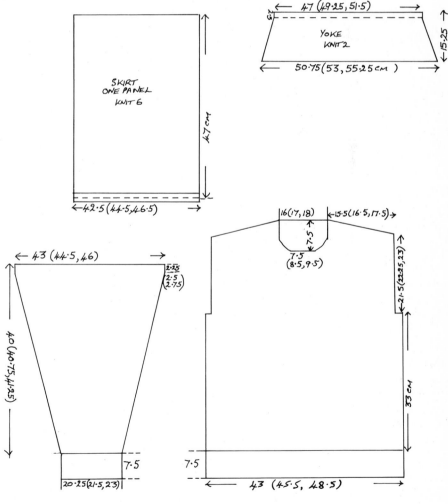

Diagram of finished measurements in centimetres

Spider's web dress

For Knitmaster SK560 machines.

Shape V

Using nylon cord hold 74 (78, 82, 86) sts at left. Knit right part as follows:—
At left, dec 1 st on the next and ev foll 4th row 7 times in all, knit 1 row. Row counter 238. Mark right edge with waste yarn for armhole position. Knit 2 rows. Dec 1 st at left edge on the next and ev foll 4th row 25 (29, 29, 29) times in all, knit 3 rows. Dec 1 st at left edge on the next and ev foll 3rd (3rd, 4th, 4th) row 10 (6, 6, 6) times in all. 32 (36, 40, 44) sts rem. Knit 2 (2, 1, 5) rows without shaping. Row counter 370 (374, 378, 382). Using waste yarn knit 8 rows and release from machine. Take carr to left. Reset row counter to 212. Knit left part as for right part but read right for left and vice versa.

FRONT

Knit as given for back to *. Knit 26 (30, 34, 38) rows. Inspection button on. Insert special card into machine and set to first row. Pattern width indicator 60. Point cams 60 at left and right of centre 0. Needle 1 cam 60 at right of centre 0. Buttons 1 (left), 2 (left), 3 & 5. Take carr across twice without knitting. Inspection button off. Set carr for Fair Isle. With col 1 in feeder 1 and col 2 in feeder 2, knit 68 (64, 60, 56) rows. Mark both ends with waste yarn for armhole pos. Knit 132 (136, 140, 144) rows. Row counter 370 (374, 378, 382). Remove card. Set carr for stockinet. Push 116 (120, 124, 128) Ns at left to D pos. Using waste yarn knit 8 rows over rem 32 (36, 40, 44) Ns at right and release from machine. Take carr to left. Bring first 32 (36, 40, 44) Ns back to B pos using a transfer tool. Using waste yarn knit 8 rows and release from machine. Bring remaining 84 Ns back to B pos. Tension dial at 8. Using col 1, knit 1 row. Tension dial at 6, knit 7 rows. Cast off.

RIGHT SLEEVE

Push 3 Ns at right of centre 0 to B pos. Carr at right. Using col 1, cast on by hand. Row counter 000. Tension dial at 6, knit 3 rows. At right, inc 1 st on the next and ev foll 3rd row (4, 8, 10, 14) times in all, knit 1 row. Inc 1 st at right edge on the next and ev foll alt row 17 (13, 11, 7) times in all, knit 1 row. Cast on 2 sts at beg of next and ev foll alt row 19 times in all, knit 1 row. Cast on 3 sts beg next and foll alt row, knit 1 row. Row counter 90 (94, 96, 100). Carr at right. Cast on 19 sts. 87 sts altog. Knit 43 (43, 45, 45) rows without shaping. Mark left edge with waste yarn, knit

SIZES

To fit 81-96 cms, 32-38 inch bust.

MATERIALS

Bramwell – Fine 4-ply 100% acrylic. 1 500 grm cone in col 1 (black); small amount lurex type yarn in col 2 (gold).

TENSION

31 sts and 36 rows to 10 cms (4 ins) measured over stockinet. Tension dial at approx 6.

BACK

Push 64 (68, 72, 76) Ns at left and right of centre 0 to B pos. 128 (136, 144, 152) Ns altog. Carr at right. Using col 1, cast on by hand. Tension dial at 5, knit 13 rows. Tension dial at 8, knit 1 row. Row counter 000. Tension dial at 6, knit 14 rows. Inc 1 st both ends next and ev foll 14th row 10 times in all. 148 (156, 164, 172) sts. Knit 3 rows. Row counter 144. Mark both ends with waste yarn*. Knit 68 rows. Row counter 212. Carr at right.

43 (43, 45, 45) rows. Row counter 176 (180, 186, 190). Carr at right. Cast off 19 sts beg next row, knit 1 row. Cast off 3 sts beg next and foll alt row, knit 1 row. Cast off 2 sts beg next and ev foll alt row 19 times in all, knit 1 row. Dec 1 st at right edge on next and ev foll alt row 17 (13, 11, 7) times in all, knit 1 row. Dec 1 st at right edge on the next and ev foll 3rd row 4 (8, 10, 14) times in all, knit 2 rows. Row counter 266 (274, 282, 290). Cast off rem 3 sts.

LEFT SLEEVE

Knit as given for right sleeve but reverse the shapings by reading left for right and vice versa throughout.

BANDS FOR V

Push 134 Ns to B pos. With purl side facing pick up along one edge of V and place onto Ns. Tension dial at 4. Using col 2, knit 6 rows. Pick up first row of band and place onto corresponding Ns. Tension dial at 10, knit 1 row. Cast off with a latch tool.

TO MAKE UP

Pin out to size and press. Fold plain rows at neckedge on front to the inside and catch down into pos. Graft shoulder seams. Set in sleeves between marked points and matching marker on sleeve to shoulder seam. Join side and sleeve seams. Turn up rows at lower edge and catch down on the inside. Give final light press.

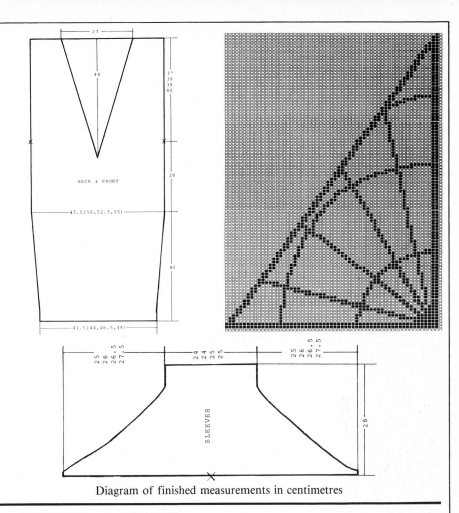

Diagram of finished measurements in centimetres

HINTS & TIPS

DROPPED LACE

This stitch could catch on, but is rather open — we saw some lace knitted on the Knitmaster 360 machine and there were rather more holes than our knitter had planned. Close investigation soon revealed the cause of the trouble. When you're knitting lace on the 260 or 360 and you have a ribbing attachment you need to have the knitting hanging in front of the ribber and with the weights attached. The ribber guards which you can buy to cover your ribber while it is not in use are invaluable when you are knitting lace, they keep the work off the ribber and prevent tangles with the ribber needles and dirty marks from the oil.

As soon as the knitting is long enough to do so, bring it IN FRONT of the ribber and attach the weights provided.

WASTE YARN

This 'golden oldie' is all about waste yarn — we must use yards and yards of it in the course of our knitting. For the benefit of any new knitters waste yarn is one method of removing the knitting from the machine without having to cast off — usually because we are going to rehang the stitches back on the machine, perhaps for the neckband. A few rows are knitted in an oddment of yarn after the knitting is finished and then the knitting is just removed from the machine and the waste yarn holds the knitting safely until you need to use that piece again. However, waste yarn can present some snags if no thought is given to it. Here are a few rules which we have come up with that we think are worth bearing in mind.

1. Always use a good contrast colour from your main yarn.
2. Make sure that the waste yarn is as thick or thicker than your main yarn, otherwise the stitches will close up over the waste yarn and you will have difficulty when it comes to picking the stitches up again.
3. Choose a smooth, strong yarn. Anything very soft such, as Shetland, will break easily and could cause complications, either when you are picking the stitches up or when you are trying to remove the waste yarn.
4. Don't use a knobbly or fluffy yarn, it will be difficult to remove.
5. Although you need to use a good contrasting colour, avoid using any-

thing very dark on white or very light yarns because the yarn will leave a light trace of fluff behind it when you remove it, resulting in a dark line.

MORE COMB HANGING

It is a tricky procedure to rehang a comb when the knitting has reached the floor. Often you can wind the work round the comb and improvise to rehang the weights, but if you want to do it properly and without snagging your knitting, here is how to do it. Remove the comb and weights, use a ruler or another comb to hold the butts of the ribber (front bed) needles down in the knitting position while you carefully push the main (back) bed needles forwards for about half an inch. Now place the teeth of the comb between the needles of the back bed. DON'T put them through the knitting, just between the needles. Thread in the wire and before you lower the comb push each back bed needle back into the working position. Now you can rehang the weights and continue knitting. It's easy and prevents any risk of snagging the knitting. Make sure that you hang the comb in the centre, otherwise it may tip.

Tracksuit

Suitable for any Machine with a ribber attachment.

SIZES

To fit all sizes: 81 (87, 91, 96) cm, 32 (34, 36, 38) ins.
Length: 63.5 (63.5, 64.75, 64.75) cm, 25 (25, 25½, 25½) ins.
Sleeve seam with cuff turned down: 51 cm, 20 ins.
Trousers to fit sizes: 87 (91, 97, 102) cms, 34 (36, 38, 40) ins.
Outside leg below waistband: 100.25 (101, 101.75, 102.5) cm, 39½ (39¾, 40, 40¼) ins.

MATERIALS

Lister-Lee Thermo-Knit 4 ply machine knitting cones.
2 (2, 3, 3) cones scarlet 634 (M).
1 cone sunshine white 640 (1st col).
Elastic for waist.

TENSION

32 sts and 61 rows to 10 cm (4 ins) measured over blister st (approx T.9/5).
30 sts and 40 rows to 10 cm (4 ins) measured over stocking st.

NOTES:
Sweater front/back bodice
Set racking indicator to '5'. Arrange Ns as follows:

MB
|||||||||||||||||||||||||||||||||||||||||||||||||||||||

RA
.....||||.....|H||...°.||||.....||||.....

Set half pitch lever to 'H'.
Racking sequence
⅛ Work 4 rows main bed. Rack to '2'. Work 1 row both beds.
  Work 4 rows main bed. Rack to '5'. Work 1 row both beds.
  Work 4 rows main bed. Rack to '8'. Work 1 row both beds.
  Work 4 rows main bed. Rack to '5'. Work 1 row both beds.*
These 20 rows form pattern. Rep from * to * throughout knitting blister stitch.
Colour sequence is as follows:
Rows 1-14, M in Feeder A.

Row 15, 1st col in Feeder A.
Repeat this col sequence throughout knitting blister stitch on front/back bodice.

SLEEVES and FRONT/BACK YOKE

Set Racking indicator to '5'. The arrangement of Ns and racking sequence is the same as front/back bodice. Set half pitch lever to 'H'.
Colour sequence is as follows:
Rows 1-4, 1st col in feeder A.
Row 5, M in feeder A.
Repeat this col sequence throughout knitting blister stitch on sleeves and yokes.

NOTES:
When arranging Ns for front/back bodice, push 1 N at each end on RA to WP for size 91 cm (36 ins). When shaping armhole, push 1 N at each end on RA to WP, for sizes 87 cm (34 ins) and 91 cm (36 ins). When inc on sleeve, continue to follow N arrangement, and where necessary push corresponding Ns on RA to WP.

SWEATER

BACK

With M cast on 148 (156, 164, 172) sts as 1 x 1 rib. T2/2. Work 31 rows in rib. COL. Trans sts to main bed. Arrange Ns (see notes) T9/5. Work 1 row both beds. RC 000. Work in blister stitch (see racking and col sequence) to RC 200.
Shape armholes
Cast off 8 (8, 9, 9) sts at beg of next 2 rows. 132 (140, 144, 152) sts rem. Work to RC 264 (264, 269, 269).★★
Yoke
With 1st col work 1 row both beds. Continue to work in blister stitch (see yoke col sequence) to RC 330 (330, 335, 335).
Shape shoulder
Cast off 12 (12, 13, 13) sts at beg of next and foll alt rows 3 times in all. Work 1 row and cast off 7 (10, 8, 11) sts. With WY work several rows over rem 46 (48, 50, 52) sts.

FRONT

Knit as back to ★★.
Front yoke
With 1st col work 1 row both beds. Continue to work in blister stitch (see yoke col sequence) to RC 300 (300, 305, 305).
Front neck
COR. Cast off centre 28 sts. Note position of racking indicator and N arrangement. With WY knit in several rows over 52 (56, 58, 62)

sts at left and release from machine. Work on rem 52 (56, 58, 62) sts at right for first side. Dec one st at neck edge on next and foll alt rows 9 (10, 11, 12) times in all. Work 12 (10, 8, 6) rows. RC reads 330 (330, 335, 335).

Shape shoulder

Cast off 12 (12, 13, 13) sts at beg of next and foll alt rows 3 times in all. Work 1 row and cast off rem 7 (10, 8, 11) sts.

Return 52 (56, 58, 62) sts at left onto Ns. Rejoin yarn at neck edge and complete to correspond with first side, reversing all shapings.

SLEEVES

With M cast on 68 (68, 72, 72) sts as 1 x 1 rib. T2/2. Work 31 rows in rib. Transfer sts to main bed. Arrange Ns (see notes). T9/5. Work 1 row both beds. RC 000. Work in blister stitch, inc one st at each end of every foll 7th row 34 times in all. 136 (136, 140, 140) sts. Work 22 rows. RC reads 260. Cast off.

NECKBAND

Join right shoulder seam.

With M cast on 122 (126, 130, 134) sts as 1 x 1 rib. T2/2. Work 30 rows in rib. Transfer sts to main bed. Wrong side of garment facing, pick up sts at neck edge and evenly place onto Ns. T10. Work 1 row. Cast off loosely.

TO MAKE UP

Join left shoulder and neckband seam. Set in sleeves. Join sleeve and bodice side seams. Fold neckband in half and catch down to inside.

TROUSERS

RIGHT FRONT

With WY cast on 52 (56, 60, 64) sts. Knit several rows ending with COR. RC 000. T6. With M work in stocking st, inc one st at left edge on every foll 8th row 30 times in all.★★ 82 (86, 90, 94) sts. Work 25 rows. RC reads 265.

Shape crutch

Cast off 8 sts at beg of next row. Dec one st on next 10 rows 64 (68, 72, 76) sts rem. Now dec one st at right edge on every foll 6th row 10 times in all, until 54 (58, 62, 66) sts rem. Work 5 (7, 9, 11) rows. RC reads 340 (342, 344, 346).

Yoke

Change to 1st col and work 25 rows. Knit several rows in WY and release from machine.

LEFT FRONT

Complete to correspond with right front, reversing all shapings.

LEFT BACK

With WY cast on 60 (64, 68, 72) sts. Work as right front to ★★ 90 (94, 98, 102) sts. Work 25

rows. RC reads 265.

Shape crutch

Cast off 10 sts at beg of next row. Dec one st on next 10 rows 70 (74, 78, 82) sts rem. Now dec one st at right edge on every foll 6th row 10 times in all, until 60 (64, 68, 72) sts rem. Work 5 (7, 9, 11) rows. RC reads 340 (342, 344, 346).

Yoke

Change to 1st col and work 25 rows.

Shape top

Push 14 Ns at right to H/P on next and foll alt rows 4 times in all. Work 1 row. Return Ns from H/P to UWP. Knit several rows in WY and release from machine.

RIGHT BACK

Complete to correspond with left back, reversing all shapings.

WAISTBAND

Join front crutch seam. Join back crutch seam.

Push 108 (116, 124, 132) Ns to WP. Wrong side of front facing, pick up sts and evenly place on to Ns T6. With 1st col work 20 rows. Cast off. Push 120 (128, 136, 144) Ns to WP. Wrong side of back facing, pick up sts and evenly place on to Ns T6. With 1st col work 21 rows. Cast off.

ANKLE CUFFS

Join outside leg seams. With 1st col. Cast on 80 (82, 84, 86) sts as 1 x 1 rib. T2/2. Work 30

rows in rib. Transfer sts to main bed. Wrong side of trouser leg facing, place on to Ns, distributing sts evenly along the row. T10. Work 1 row. Cast off.

TO MAKE UP

Join inside leg seams. Fold waistband in half and catch down to the inside. Cut elastic to fit waist, thread through waistband and join ends.

NOTE:

Passap Duomatic owners can do exactly the same stitch with the racking sequence thus:- 5 rows with the indicator at 0, 5 rows at 3 left, 5 at 0, 5 at 3 right. Total 20.

However, because the colour changer works at the right only, in order to acheive the single row of contrast every fifteenth row which gives the fabric its splashes of colour, the contast has to be removed from the lock on row 15 and left at the left-hand side and the lock must be set to GX/GX in order to return for the main colour. Then the row counter must be set back by one number. Repeat to RC 29, put down the main and return at GX/GX for the contrast. Knit the row and reset the row counter by one. It will now read 30, which is correct.

Perhaps this may seem a little tedious, but if you really WANT to do it, you will.

As an alternative try a six row repeat working rows 5 AND 6 in contrast. See also the stitch on page 62 in the Duo 80/Duo S stitch book (p.13 in the old stitch book) and the Model on page 9 in book 31.

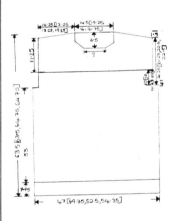

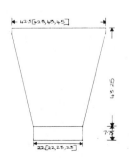

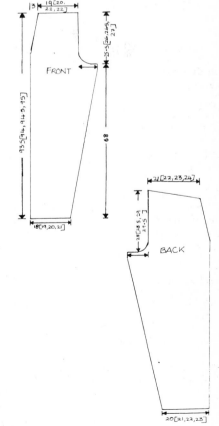

Diagram of finished measurements in centimetres

A Silverknit design

Skirt and Top in Adah and Ideal.
All punchcard machines.

SIZES

81 (86, 91, 96) cms, 32 (34, 36, 38) ins.

MATERIALS

Yarn 1 2 (2, 3, 3) cones of Silverknit Adah 5749.
Yarn 2 2 (2, 3, 3) cones of Silverknit Ideal 1720.

TENSION

54 rows and 39 sts to 10 cms (4 ins) measured over stockinet. T approx 2 rows and 39 sts to 10 cm (4 ins) measured over Fair Isle. T at MT + 1 whole number.

NOTES:
1. K 3 rows yarn 1, k 1 row yarn 2.
2. K 1 row yarn 2, k 19 rows yarn 1.

TOP (2 pieces)

Push up 162 (172, 182, 192) Ns to WP. * K several rows WY. MT. RC 000, stripe as Note 1 for 30 rows. Turn hem. * Begin striping at Note 2 throughout. Dec 1 st at each end of next and ev foll 4th row 8 times in all. 146 (156, 166, 176) sts. K to RC 63 (65, 68, 71).
Inc 1 st at each end of next and ev foll 10th row 12 times in all 170 (180, 190, 200) sts. RC 174 (176, 179, 182). K to RC 185 (189, 195, 201).
Cast off 4 sts at beg of next 4 rows. Cast off 2 sts at beg of next 4 (6, 8, 10) rows. Dec 1 st at each end of next and ev foll alt row 5 (5, 6, 6) times in all. K to RC 282 (288, 296, 304). K as for Note 1 to RC 312 (316, 324, 332). K several rows WY, release from machine.

SLEEVE

Push up 113 (117, 121, 125) Ns to WP. K as for top from * to * Begin striping as Note 2 throughout. Inc 1 st at each end of next and ev foll alt row 15 times in all. K to RC 80 (82, 25, 88) 143 (147, 151, 155) sts. Cast off 4 sts at beg of next 2 rows. Cast off 2 sts at beg of next 16 rows. RC 98 (100, 103, 106) 103, 107, 111, 115) sts. Dec 1 st at each end of next and ev foll 5th row 12 times in all. K 4 rows. Dec 1 st at each end of next and ev foll alt row 12 times in all. K 1 row. Cast off 2 sts at beg of next 2 (4, 8, 12) rows. Cast off rem.

SKIRT (3 Pieces)

Push up 173 (180, 187, 194) Ns to WP. K as for top from * to *. Set punchcard and k 1 row to prime. Using yarn 1 as main yarn, MT + 1, k to RC 259 (263, 267, 301). K several rows WY and release from machine. Sew up

2 seams, matching carefully. Push up 188 (192, 196, 200) Ns to WP. Place sts from last row of 3 skirt panels evenly on Ns and unravel WY. MT, yarn 1, k 36 rows. K several rows WY. Release from machine.

BELT

Cast on 2 sts by hand, MT, main yarn. Inc 1 st at each end of next and ev foll alt row 20 times in all. K to RC 400. Dec 1 st at each end of next and ev foll alt row 20 times in all. Cast off 2 rem sts.

TO MAKE UP

Top
Backstitch through last row of shoulder/neck edge. Lap back shoulder over front shoulder by 5 cms and catch down. Sew armhole seam, gathering evenly from 10 cms to each side of the central shoulder line (halfway between the two lapped shoulder edges). Sew under-arm and side seams.

Skirt
Backstitch through last row of waistband and unravel WY. Sew up skirt seam and insert elastic.

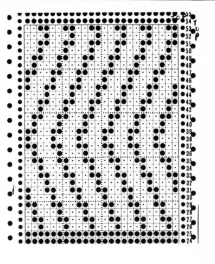

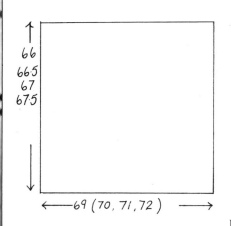

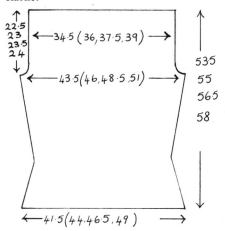

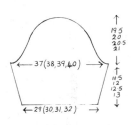

Diagram of finished measurements in centimetres

HINTS & TIPS

KNITTING FROM A WRITTEN PATTERN

There is a definite art in working from a written knitting pattern, especially if it is in several sizes. The first thing to do is to read the whole of the pattern through. How many of us have started decreasing at the armhole every other row to row 50, only to realise that we should have been shaping the 'V' neck at the same time . . . If you are knitting from a pattern that has lots of sizes, go through the pattern and in pencil ring the size that applies to you. If you have to decrease every 7th row and at the same time you are counting stripes or colour changes, or something equally challenging, then make out a card with the row numbers on it and work with your row counter so that when the number row appears on your row counter you know to decrease or what-ever. You can clip the card with the row numbers on to the yarn brake. Always make any alterations to the pattern before you start knitting. Don't start improvising mid-stream; it leads to disaster more often than not.

STRAIGHT SLEEVES

Dropped shoulder sweaters and sweaters with straight sleeves are always popular, especially with new knitters or if you are trying out a new or tricky stitch pattern, but do remember that if you decide to knit the sleeve straight and then gather it on to a cuff you will need to knit two or three extra inches to allow for the gathering of the sleeve on to the cuff. If you must knit the sleeve the usual length and then gather it on to a cuff you will find that your sleeve is too short.

SHINE ON

If you are the owner of a Knit Radar or a Pattern driver or Forma, you may at some time meet this problem: the paper in the roller is missing an odd row now and again. The roller has become very shiny from constant use and so the paper slips on the shine, especially at the very beginning and the very end of the sheet. A quick wipe over with a cloth and a little methylated spirit soon takes the shine off the roller and solves the problem.
If you are ever in doubt as to the accuracy of your charting device there is an easy test you can make to check it. Draw a line 10cm (4in) long on a piece of charting paper, or the plastic sheet if it is a Knit Leader, Knit Copy or Tracer, set the rows to 40 and then start at the bottom of the line and click the device through by hand. It should take 40 clicks to reach the top of the line and you can check to see if it is OK.
Anything interfering with the free roll of the paper will also result in misses, so make sure that the paper is free to roll through the device without any obstructions.

NO CHEATING!

We all kid ourselves a little from time to time when it comes to measuring the tension squares. If we know it should be 7 sts. and 10 rows per inch we tend to give it a hand to become so — a push here and a pull there. For com-plete accuracy, and no kidding, measure your swatch and see what it is and THEN look at the pattern to see what it SHOULD be.

OWNERS OF THE NEW KNITMASTER 360 or 260

I think that this machine is super but I hit a snag that was really my own fault. Because the pattern panel is now at the left of the centre and not exactly in the centre of the machine I found that when I had only got a few stitches on I tended not to clear the pattern panel . . . result — mistakes in the pattern. Once I was aware of what I was doing I kept my mind on the job and all was well.

Lacy top and skirt

For Knitmaster SK560 machine with Knitmaster SRP50 ribbing attachment. For stockists write to Knitmaster Ltd., 30/40 Elcho St., London SW11.

SIZE

To fit 81-101 cms, 32-40 ins bust.

MATERIALS

11 (11, 12, 13, 14) 50 grm balls in col 1 of Phildar Anouchka. 2 50 grm balls in col 2; 2 50 grm balls in col 3; elastic to fit waist; 6 buttons.

TENSION

30 sts and 40 rows to 10 cms (4 ins) measured over lace pattern. 34 sts and 40 rows to 10 cms (4 ins) measured over stockinet. Tension dial at approx 5.

Colour sequence
Knit 2 rows col 2, 30 rows col 1, 2 rows col 3 and 30 rows col 1. Repeat throughout.

When knitting back and front of top 2nd size start col sequence as given above. 1st, 3rd, 4th and 5th sizes start col sequence with 28 (4, 8, 12) rows col 1 and then work in sequence as given above. Card is designed to bleep when col 2 or 3 are used.

NOTE:

When increasing and decreasing on sleeve, only adjust the point cams at the opposite end to the carriage.

SKIRT

PANELS (knit 3 alike)

Push 79 (82, 84, 87, 90) Ns at left and right of centre 0 to B pos. 158 (164, 168, 174, 180) Ns altog. Using waste yarn cast on and knit several rows ending with carr at left. Inspection button on. Insert special card into machine and set to row 29. Pattern width indicator 54. Point cams 69 at each side of centre 0. Needle 1 cam between Ns 15 and 16 at left of centre 0. Buttons 1 (left) and 2 (right). Tension dial at 4. Using col 1, knit 4 rows. Tension dial at 6, knit 1 row. Tension dial at 4·· , knit 4 rows. Turn up a hem. Carr at right. RC 000. Tension dial at 5. Inspection button off. Set carr for plain lace. Working in col sequence as given in notes, 208 rows. Mark centre with waste yarn. Set carr for stockinet. Using waste yarn knit 8 rows and release from machine. Pin out pieces to size and steam carefully with a warm iron over a damp cloth.

BASQUE (knit 3 alike)

Push 51 (54, 56, 59, 62) Ns at left and right of centre 0 to B pos. 102 (108, 112, 118, 124) Ns altog. With purl side of one panel facing pick up sts from below waste yarn and place onto Ns in B pos gathering evenly and matching marked point to centre. RC 000. Tension dial at 5. Set carr for stockinet. Using col 1, knit 3 rows. Dec 1 st both ends next and ev foll 3rd row 13 times in all. 76 (82, 86, 92, 98) sts. RC 40. Mark both ends and centre with waste yarn. Knit 8 rows. Tension dial at 7, knit 1 row. Tension dial at 5, knit 8 rows. Pick up marked row and place onto Ns in B pos. Cast off loosely.

TO MAKE UP

Pin out basque and steam carefully with a warm iron over a damp cloth. Join 3 panels tog. Insert elastic into waistband and join ends. Using 3 strands of yarn fold in half and thread through holes made by pattern as shown, using 2 and 3 in turn. Give final light steam.

TOP

PEPLUM (knit 2 alike)

Push 83 (87, 91, 95, 98) Ns at left and right of centre 0 to B pos. 166 (174, 182, 190, 196) Ns altog. Using waste yarn cast on and knit several rows ending with carr at left. Inspection button on. Insert special card into machine and set to row 29. Pattern width indicator 27. Point cams 81 (85, 88, 92, 94) at each side of centre 0. Needle 1 cam between Ns 12 and 13 at right of centre 0. Buttons 1 (left) and 2 (right). Tension dail at 4. Using col 1, knit 4 rows. Tension dial at 6, knit 1 row. Tension dial at 4·· , knit 4 rows. Turn up a

hem. Carr at right. RC 000. Tension dial at 5. Inspection button off. Set carr for plain lace. Working in col sequence as given in notes, knit 64 rows. Mark st 42 each side of centre 0 with waste yarn. Set carr for stockinet. Using waste yarn knit 8 rows and release from machine.

BACK

Push 62 (66, 70, 74, 77) Ns at left and right of centre 0 to B pos. 124 (132, 140, 148, 154) Ns altog. With carr at right and purl side of one peplum facing pick up sts from below waste yarn and place onto Ns in B pos with the 84 sts between marked points onto the centre 84 Ns and gathering remaining sts each side evenly. Inspection button on. Set card to row 1 (29, 25, 21, 17). Point cams 60 (64, 64, 72, 75) at each side of centre 0. Needle 1 cam between Ns 12 and 13 at right of centre 0. Buttons 1 (left) and 2 (right). Take carr across twice without knitting. RC 000. Tension dial at 5. Inspection button off. Set carr for plain lace. Working in col sequence as given in notes (see special note for beginning col sequence), knit 94 rows. Mark both ends with waste yarn *. Knit 94 (98, 102, 106, 110) rows. RC 188 (192, 196, 200, 204). Knit 2 rows col 3 (col 2, col 2, col 2, col 2). Mark st 35 (36, 37, 38, 39) each side of centre 0 with waste yarn. Set carr for stockinet. Using waste yarn knit 8 rows and release from machine.

FRONT

Work as given for back to *. Knit 82 (86, 90, 94, 98) rows. RC 176 (180, 184, 188, 192). Carr at right.
Shape neck
Using nylon cord knit 80 (84, 88, 92, 95) sts at opposite end to carr by hand taking Ns back to A pos. Inspection button on take note of row number showing on pattern panel. Inspection button off. Knit right part as follows:-
Knit 2 rows. * Using nylon cord knit 4 (4, 4, 4, 5) sts at opposite end to carr by hand taking Ns back to A pos in the next row, knit 1 row. Using nylon cord knit 4 sts at opposite end to carr by hand taking Ns back to A pos on the next row, knit 1 row. Using nylon cord knit 3 (4, 4, 4, 4) sts at opposite end to carr by hand taking Ns back to A pos on the next row, knit 1 row. Using nylon cord knit 3 (3, 4, 4, 4) sts at opposite end to carr by hand taking Ns back to A pos on the next row, knit 1 row. Using nylon cord knit 3 (3, 3, 4, 4) sts at opposite end to carr by hand taking Ns back to A pos on the next row, knit 1 row. 27 (30, 33, 36, 38) Ns rem in B pos. Break off yarn *. Using nylon cord knit 27 (30, 33, 36, 38) sts in B pos by hand taking Ns back to A pos. Carr at right. Inspection button on. Set card to number previously noted. Inspection button off. Unravel nylon cord over 44 (48, 52, 56, 59) Ns at opposite end to carr bringing Ns to correct

pos. Keeping col sequence correct knit 1 row. Knit left part as for right part from * to *. Unravel nylon cord bringing all Ns to correct pos. Knit 2 rows col 3 (col 2, col 2, col 2, col 2). Mark st 35 (36, 37, 38, 39) at each side of centre 0 with waste yarn. Set carr for stockinet. Using waste yarn knit 8 rows and release from machine. Remove card.

NECKBAND (2 pieces)

With ribbing attachment and main knitter carr in pos. Set half pitch lever to P and swing indicator to 5. Push 62 (66, 70, 74, 77) Ns at left and right of centre 0 on knitter to B pos. 124 (132, 140, 148, 154) Ns altog. Push corresponding Ns on ribber to B pos. Arrange Ns for knit 1 purl 1 rib. Carr at left. Using col 1 cast on as shown in instruction book. RC 000. Set carr for main knitting. Tension dial at 1, knit 12 rows. Transfer sts from ribber to knitter using Knitmaster rib transfer carriage. Lower ribber. With purl side of back facing pick up sts from below waste yarn and place onto Ns in B pos. Cast off. Rept for front.

SLEEVES (both alike)

With ribbing attachment and main knitter carr in pos. Set half pitch lever to P and swing indicator to 5. Push 42 (42, 42, 45, 45) Ns at left and right of centre 0 on knitter to B pos. 84 (84, 84, 90, 90) Ns altog. Push corresponding Ns on ribber to B pos. Arrange Ns for knit 1 purl 1 rib. Carr at left. Using col 1 cast on as shown in instruction book. RC 000. Set carr for main knitting. Tension dials at 1, knit 15 rows. Carr at right. Transfer sts from ribber to knitter using rib transfer carriage. Lower ribber. Change to lace carriage. Inspection button on. Insert special card into machine and set to row 29. Pattern width indicator 27. Point cams 2 sts in from edge of knitting. Needle 1 cam between Ns 12 and 13 at right of centre 0. Buttons 1 (left) and 2 (right). Take carr across twice without knitting. RC 000. Tension dial at 5. Inspection button off. Set carr for plain lace. Working in col sequence as given in notes, knit 1 (1, 3, 3, 1) rows. Keep point cams 2 sts in from edge of knitting.
1st, 3rd and 4th sizes only
* Inc 1 st (see notes) both ends next and ev foll 3rd row 3 times in all, knit 3 (1, 1) rows *. Rept the last 10 (8, 8) rows from * to * 9 (11, 11) more times.
1st size only
Inc 1 st both ends next and foll 3rd row. Inc 1 st both ends next row.
3rd and 4th sizes only
Inc 1 st both ends next and ev foll 3rd row 3 times in all.
2nd size only
Inc 1 st (see notes) both ends next and ev foll 3rd row 36 times in all.
5th size only
* Inc 1 st (see notes) both ends next and

foll 3rd row, knit 1 row *. Rept the last 5 rows from * to * 20 more times.

All sizes
150 (156, 162, 168, 174) sts. Knit 8 (7, 8, 8, 8) rows without shaping. RC 114. Carr at right.

Shape top
Cast off 12 sts beg next 2 rows, 9 sts beg next 4 rows, 6 (5, 5, 4, 4) sts beg next 2 (4, 8, 4, 8) rows and 7 (6, 6, 5, 5) sts beg next 6 (2, 2, 8, 6) rows.

2nd, 3rd, 4th & 5th sizes only
Cast off (7, 7, 6, 6) sts beg next (4, 2, 2, 2) rows. RC 128 (130, 132, 134, 136). Mark centre with waste yarn. Cast off rem 36 (36, 36, 40, 40) sts.

BELT

Tension dial at 0. Make a cord over 4 Ns as shown for circular cord knitting. Knit 600 rows col 2 and 600 rows col 3.

TO MAKE UP

Pin out to size and steam carefully with a warm iron over a damp cloth. Join shoulder seams by overlapping front neckband over back neckband to marked points and secure with 3 buttons on each shoulder. Set in sleeves. Join side and sleeve seams. Using 3 strands of yarn fold in half and thread through holes made by pattern as shown, using cols 2 and 3 in turn. Make 2 loops each side for belt. Give final light steam.

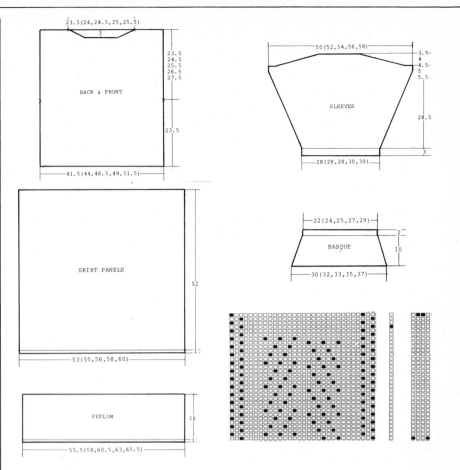

Diagram of finished measurements in centimetres.

HINTS & TIPS

EASY WHEN YOU KNOW HOW

My first threading of an overlocker involved several hours, a flashlight and the assistance of my mum. However, after watching the expert it soon became apparent that however long it takes you the first time you only need ever have the same performance once, for all future threadings simply break the yarn, tie the new ends to the old ones and pull them through . . . if only we had thought of that.

A WEIGHTY PROBLEM

On single bed knitting the small claw weights can often solve some of those annoying little problems. For instance, when you have cast off say ten stitches at the armhole edge and you are ready to knit across the row, the cast off edge tends to curl and get caught in the brush assembly, but by attaching the small claw weight you can keep the edge back in place and no problems. The same applies when you are shaping a neck by using the holding position. The small claw weight attached to the neck edge will ensure that the edge stitches knit correctly and will also prevent the needles in the holding position from moving back into the knitting position without your permission.

LACE WORK

Here's another tip on lace knitting. If stitches are not transferring properly on lace work, and you have checked that the needles are OK, have a look at the sinker posts. If one of these is out of alignment this is sufficient to cause dropped stitches on transfer. If it's happening right across the row make sure that the prongs on the underside of the lace carriage haven't been displaced. Are you using the special wax ring on top of the tension arm? I've found that the yarn gets caught underneath it and drags, which again causes dropped stitches. So if your yarn is pre-waxed you may be better off without the wax ring.

SPRAY WAX

I have been asked to mention the spray wax which is available at most knitting shops these days. Apparently a friend has met several knitters on her travels who do not know about the spray. Well, it is certainly worth knowing about. I would not be without it. For the benefit of those who have not used it, the spray is a silicone wax which is sprayed from the can on to your cone of yarn and it helps to smooth down any bumps, lumps, hairs and other little troubles as the yarn knits through your machine.

If the yarn is in a ball, just spray the outside of the ball and a quick squirt top and bottom will last the ball through. For cones spray the outside well and it will penetrate for quite some distance, but once you have reached the part of the cone where the spray has failed to penetrate you will feel that the row is harder to knit across and you can dive under your knitting table and give a quick spray. It is quite expensive but one can goes a very long way. I found that a white jumper showed the spray, but it did wash out with no trouble. Especially helpful on Shetlands and yarns that break easily, and on mohair. I use it when I knit chunky yarns, even on the chunky machine.

PUNCH LACE

Punch lace is a stitch that is sadly neglected, due mainly I think to the fact that, knitted as the instruction books suggest, with a clear thread, it is not very exciting, but knitted with a fine cotton or shiny thread as the lace thread it becomes quite a different tale.

Lady's jumper and skirt

This garment was designed and knitted on a Knitmaster 260 or 360 machine with the lace carriage. It can be knitted on any machine with a lace carriage and a card from the basic lace pack could be substituted.

MEASUREMENTS

Jumper: to fit 81-106 cms/32-34 ins bust; length from top of shoulder 65 (66, 67, 68, 69 69) cms; sleeve seam 49.5 cms.
Skirt: to fit 86-112 cms/34-44 inch hip; completed length including waistband 64.5 cms (32 ins).

MATERIALS

Argyll Starlite.
Jumper: 1 (1, 1, 1, 2, 2) 340 grm cones in col. 1; 5 buttons.
Skirt: 1 340 grm cone in col. 1; elastic to fit waist.

TENSION

29 sts and 38 rows to 10 cms (4 ins) measured over stockinet. 27 sts and 38 rows to 10 cms (4 ins) measured over lace. Tension dial at approx 6.

NOTES:
Figures in brackets refer to the larger sizes respectively. Dec-ings on skirt should be worked fully fashioned 3 sts. in.

JUMPER

BACK

Push 66 (70, 73, 76, 79, 82) Ns. at left and 65 (70, 73, 76, 79, 82) Ns at right of centre 0 to B pos. [131 (140, 146, 152, 158, 164) Ns. altog.]. Arrange Ns. for 2 x 1. Using waste yarn, cast on and knit several rows ending with carr. at right. Insert card and lock on row 1. Row Counter 000. Tension Dial at 4. Using col. 1, knit 18 rows. Tension Dial at 6, knit 1 row. Tension Dial at 4, knit 18 rows. Turn up a hem. Carr. at left.
1st Size only
Inc. 1 st. at right edge.
6th Size only
Inc. 1 st. at both ends.

All Sizes
132 (140, 146, 152, 158, 166) sts. Row Counter 000. Tension Dial at 6. Set edge pins into pos. Release card and set carr. for plain lace. Knit 25 rows. Dec. 1 st. both ends of next and ev. foll. 22nd row 5 times in all. 122 (130, 136, 142, 148, 156) sts. rem. Knit 21 rows. Row Counter 135. Carr. at right**.

Shape Armholes
Cast off 2 sts. beg. of next 2 rows. Dec. 1 st. both ends of next and ev. foll. alt. row 3 (5, 5, 5, 5, 7) times in all, knit 3 rows. Dec. 1 st. both ends of next and ev. foll. 4th row (5, 4, 4, 5, 5, 4) times in all. 102 (108, 114, 118, 124, 130) sts. rem. Knit 53 (57, 61, 61, 65, 65) rows. Row counter 215 (219, 223, 227, 231, 231). Carr. at right.

Shape Shoulders
Cast off 6 (7, 7, 8, 8, 9) sts. beg. of next 4 rows.

Shape Back Neck
Using a length of col. 1, cast off centre 38 sts. Using nylon cord, knit 20 (21, 24, 24, 27, 28) sts. at left by hand taking Ns. back to A pos. Take note of row number showing on patt. panel.

Knit Right Part as folls.:-
Cast off 6 (6, 7, 7, 8, 9) sts. beg. of next row, 2 sts. beg. of next row and 6 (6, 7, 7, 8, 8) sts. beg. of next row. Dec. 1 st. beg. of next row. Cast off rem. 5 (6, 7, 7, 8, 8) sts.. Carr. at right. Set card at number previously noted and lock. Take carr. across twice without knitting. Unravel nylon cord bringing Ns. back to B pos. Release card. Knit 1 row. Carr. at left. Knit left part as for right part from * to *.

FRONT

Work as given for Back to **.

Divide for Front Opening
Using nylon cord, knit 39 (43, 46, 49, 52, 56) sts. at left by hand taking Ns. back to A pos. Take note of row number showing on patt. panel.

Knit Right Part as folls.:-

Shape Armhole
Cast off 2 sts. beg. of next row, knit 1 row. Dec. 1 st. beg. of next and ev. foll. alt. row 3 (5, 5, 5, 5, 7) times in all, knit 3 rows. Dec. 1 st. beg. of next and ev. foll. 4th row 5 (4, 4, 5, 5, 4) times in all. 73 (76, 79, 81, 84, 87) sts. rem. Knit 29 (33, 37, 37, 41, 41) rows. Row Counter 191 (195, 199, 203, 207, 207). Carr. at right.

Shape Neck
Using a length of col. 1 and counting from left edge, cast off sts. 14 to 31 inclusive (18 sts. altog.). Using nylon cord, knit 13 sts. at left by hand taking Ns. back to A pos. Take another note of row number showing on patt. panel.

Knit Right Part as folls.:-
Knit 1 row. Cast off 3 sts. beg. of next and foll. alt. row, knit 1 row. Cast off 2 sts. beg. of next and ev. foll. alt. row 3 times in all, knit 1 row. Dec. 1 st. beg. of next row. 29 (32, 35, 37, 40, 43) sts. rem. Knit 12 rows.

Row Counter 215 (219, 223, 227, 231, 231). Carr. at right.

Shape Shoulder
Cast off 6 (7, 7, 8, 8, 9) sts. beg. of next and foll. alt. row, knit 1 row. Cast off 6 (6, 7, 7, 8, 9) sts. beg. of next row, knit 1 row. Cast off 6 (6, 7, 7, 8, 8) sts. beg. of next row, knit 1 row. Cast off rem. 5 (6, 7, 7, 8, 8) sts. Carr. at right. Set card at number noted the second time and lock. Take carr. across twice without knitting. Unravel nylon cord from 13 Ns. at right bringing Ns. back to B pos. Release card. Knit 2 rows. Cast off 3 sts. beg. of next and foll. alt. row, knit 1 row. Cast off 2 sts. beg. of next and ev. foll. alt. row 3 times in all, knit 1 row. Fasten off rem. st. Carr. at right. Set card at number noted the first time and lock. Take carr. across twice without knitting. Unravel nylon cord bringing Ns. to B pos. Release card. Reset Row Counter at 135. Knit 1 row. Carr. at left.

Shape Armhole
Cast off 2 sts. beg. of next row, knit 1 row. Dec. 1 st. beg. of next and ev. foll. alt. row 3 (5, 5, 5, 5, 7) times in all, knit 3 rows. Dec. 1 st. beg. of next and ev. foll. 4th row 5 (4, 4, 5, 5, 4) times in all. 29 (32, 35, 37, 40, 43) sts. rem. Knit 40 (44, 48, 48, 52, 52) rows. Place a marker at right edge of last row knitted. Knit 13 rows. Row Counter 216 (220, 224, 228, 232, 232). Carr. at left.

Shape Shoulder
Cast off 6 (7, 7, 8, 8, 9) sts. beg. of next and

foll. alt. row, knit 1 row. Cast off 6 (6, 7, 7, 8, 9) sts. beg. of next row, knit 1 row. Cast off 6 (6, 7, 7, 8, 8) sts. beg. of next row, knit 1 row. Cast off rem. 5 (6, 7, 7, 8, 8) sts.

SLEEVES (both alike)

Lock card on row 1. Push 40 (40, 40, 43, 43, 43) Ns. at left and right of centre 0 to B pos. [80 (80, 80, 86, 86, 86) Ns. altog.]. Using waste yarn, cast on and knit several rows ending with carr. at left. Row Counter 000. Tension Dial at 6. Set edge pins into pos. Release card and set carr. for plain lace. Knit 11 rows. *Inc. 1 st. both ends of next and foll. 8th (7th, 6th, 6th, 6th, 6th) row, knit 8 (7, 6, 6, 5, 5) rows*. Rept. the last 17 (15, 13, 13, 12, 12) rows from * to * 8 (9, 10, 10, 11, 11) more times.

3rd, 4th, 5th and 6th Sizes only
Inc. 1 st. both ends of next row.

All Sizes
116 (120, 126, 132, 136, 136) sts. Knit 5 (8, 14, 14, 13, 13) rows. Row Counter 169. Carr. at right.

Shape Top
Cast off 9 (10, 10, 11, 11, 11) sts. beg. of next 2 rows, 5 (6, 6, 7, 7, 7) sts. beg. of next 2 rows, 3 sts. beg. of next 2 (2, 4, 4, 4, 4) rows, 2 sts. beg. of next 6 (6, 6, 6, 8, 8) rows, 5 (5, 5, 6, 6, 6) sts. beg. of next 2 rows and 8 sts. beg. of next 2 rows. Cast off rem. 44 sts.

CUFF

Push 59 (59, 59, 65, 65, 65) Ns. to B pos. Arrange Ns. for 2 x 1. [40 (40, 40, 44, 44, 44) Ns. rem. in B pos.]. With purl side facing, pick up sts. from below waste yarn and place onto Ns. in B pos. gathering evenly. Row Counter 000. Tension Dial at 4. Using col. 1, knit 18 rows. Tension Dial at 6, knit 1 row. Tension Dial at 4, knit 18 rows. Turn up a hem. Tension Dial at 10, knit 1 row. Cast off using linker or latchet tool. With plain side facing pin out each piece to size and steam carefully with a warm iron over a damp cloth. Brush each piece before removing pins. Join left shoulder.

NECKBAND (2 pieces)

Push 83 Ns. to B pos. With plain side facing, pick up 83 sts. evenly along back neck and left front opening to marker. Tension Dial at 6. Using col. 1, knit 6 rows. Tension Dial at 8, knit 1 row. Tension Dial at 6, knit 7 rows. Using waste yarn, knit several rows and release from machine. Push 70 Ns. to B pos. With plain side facing, pick up 70 sts. evenly around front neck. Tension Dial at 6. Using col. 1, knit 1 row. Inc. 1 st. at right edge on next 5 rows. Tension Dial at 8, knit 1 row. Tension Dial at 6. Dec. 1 st. at right edge on next 5 rows. Knit 2 rows.

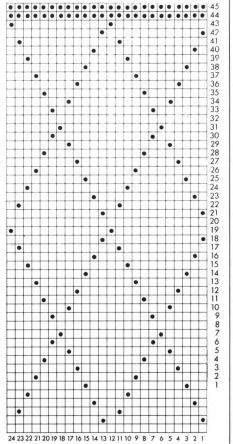

Using waste yarn, knit several rows and release from machine. Join right shoulder and neckband seam. Fold neckband in half onto outside, pin into position and backstitch through open loops of last row knitted in col. 1. Unravel waste yarn.

FRONT OPENING BAND

Push 60 Ns. to B pos. With plain side facing, pick up 60 sts. evenly along right front opening, including neckband. Inc. 1 st. at right edge. Tension Dial at 6. Using col. 1, inc. 1 st. at left edge on next 3 rows. Tension Dial at 8, knit 1 row. Tension Dial at 6, dec. 1 st. at left edge on next 3 rows. Knit 1 row. Using waste yarn, knit several rows and release from machine.

TO COMPLETE MAKE UP

Join side and sleeve seams. Set in sleeves. Work 1 row of double crochet along remainder of left front opening. Fold front opening band in half onto outside, pin into position and backstitch through open loops of last row knitted in col. 1. Unravel waste yarn. Using col. 1 make 5 button loops evenly spaced along edge of front band and neaten lower edge. Sew on buttons to correspond with button loops. Give final light steam and brush.

SKIRT

PANELS (4 alike)

Push 47 (49, 51, 52, 54, 56) Ns. at left and right of centre 0 to B pos. [94 (98, 102, 104, 108, 112) Ns. altog.]. Using waste yarn, cast on and knit several rows ending with carr. at right. Insert card and lock on row 1. Row Counter 000. Tension Dial at 6. Using col. 1, knit 4 rows. Tension Dial at 8, knit 1 row. Tension Dial at 6, knit 4 rows. Turn up a hem. Carr. at left. Row Counter 000. Set edge pins into pos. Release card and set carr. for plain lace. Knit 48 rows. Set machine for single motif lace over centre 24 Ns. as given in Operation Manual pages 59 and 60. Knit 2 rows. Dec. 1 st. (see notes) at both ends of next and ev. foll. 8th row 23 times in all. 48 (52, 56, 58, 62, 66) sts. rem. Knit 4 rows. Row Counter 231. Carr. at right.

Using waste yarn, knit several rows and release from machine.

WAISTBAND (2 pieces)

Pin out each panel to size, steam and brush as given for Jumper. Push 48 (52, 56, 58, 62, 66) Ns. at left and right of centre 0 to B pos. [96 (104, 112, 116, 124, 132) Ns. altog.]. With plain side facing, pick up sts. below waste yarn from two panels and place onto Ns. in B pos. Tension Dial at 6. Using col. 1, knit 7 rows. Tension Dial at 8, knit 1 row. Tension Dial at 6, knit 8 rows. Using waste yarn, knit several rows and release from machine.

TO MAKE UP

Join panels and waistband seams. Fold band in half onto outside, pin into position and backstitch through open loops of last row knitted in col. 1 leaving a small opening for elastic. Insert elastic and close opening. Unravel waste yarn. Give final light steam and brush.

HINTS & TIPS

THE GARTER BAR

This item of equipment seems to hold an air of mystery for some knitters. Doris Coutts, from Sandown, Isle of Wight, has some ideas of her own about it. She says: "The garter bar is one of my favourite accessories; not only for its normal uses, but did you know that it can be turned into a really large stitch-holder? All you need is one of the file binders that you can get from stationers (such as those you use for putting on to the ribber bed to protect the needles), some do-it-yourself shops sell this by length, so you could get it cut to the exact length. When you've got your stitches on the garter bar, pop on the file binder strip. If it is a little loose either put rubber bands round to hold it on the comb, or wind round the loose ends of yarn. Just a word to be careful when you take it off, do it gently otherwise if it is snug it might take off all the stitches as well! It can also be used with the 45 stitch transfer tool.

"Another way I use either the garter bar or the needle stopper is as a very firm straight-edged ruler. Whenever you have a lot of needles to return from H/P to C or B position, or when you're finishing your work and want all the needles at rest, you'll find this ideal for the job, dealing with up to 100 needles at one go."

BELLINKY TIPS

Anyone who uses a Bellinky will tell you what a useful piece of equipment it is and sensibly supplied with it when it is spanking new is a needle threader, but once you have broken or lost this little gadget the next best thing is a small piece of soap kept to hand. Wet the end of the yarn and press it on to the soap and you will be able to thread up without any bother.

Other useful bits on the Bellinky are the little rubber pieces for holding the stitches down on the comb. The only snag is that there aren't really enough and, like the threader, they can be lost . . . The solution is to cut a few one inch pieces of thin electric wire and pull the wire out of the middle and the cases make excellent holders of stitches.

BULGING RIBS

This is not a slimming article but a tip for a neat transfer from ribbing to single bed knitting. When you knit the last row of rib before the transfer from ribber to main bed, knit the last row at a higher tension than the rib — it makes transferring the stitches easier and prevents the rib from bulging at this point when the garment is finished.

RANDOM STREAKS AND BLOTCHES

Sounds awful doesn't it but random yarns, when they decide to be a nuisance really can produce some terrible shapes and patches on your beautifully knitted wooly, especially on the smaller sizes. There are several ways of tackling this problem. Splitting the cone is one way. Wind the yarn into balls and juggle them around, or knit from two cones, changing them frequently, but both these methods take extra time. Industrial randoms can be dealt with successfully by twisting the ends together before you thread the yarn through the yarn break. Thread them with the ends twisted and they will stay that way and produce a nice even random effect.

One of our patterns is a lovely baby duffle coat knitted in a random yarn and our designer wrote to tell us that she had been experimenting with random yarns and has come to the conclusion that a tuck stitch is the answer to breaking up the pattern of the random and is even better if it can be 'let down' in tone by the use of rows of white in between.

KNITTING IN BEADS

What could be more dramatic yet simple to do on a plain sweater than knitting in beads? How about a scatter of sequins on one shoulder of a chenille jacket, or a string of pearls around the neck and sleeves of a soft mohair sweater?

PASSAP OWNERS

Next time you do a circular cast on do 4 rows circular instead of 2 or 3 . . . it's smart.

Party dress

For Knitmaster SK 500 Electronic and standard punchcard machines.

SIZES

To fit 81-106 cms., 32-42 ins. bust.

MATERIALS

2 (2, 2, 3, 3, 3) 200 grm. cones Silverknit Dakota in col. 1. 3 (3, 4, 4, 4, 4) spools Silversmith in col. 2. Dakota shade used is 2824.

To obtain these yarns at a special inclusive price of £11.95 (£11.95, £13.95, £15.75, £15.75, £15.75), write to Sil-

verknit, The Old Mill, Epperstone By-pass, Woodborough, Nottingham NG14 6DH, enclosing a cheque or postal order, payable to Silverknit, quoting Knitting Machine Digest in your order. To ensure fast delivery, mark your envelope in the top left hand corner 'Knitting Machine Digest pattern'.

TENSION

32 sts and 46 rows to 10 cms (4 ins) measured over stockinet platting. Tension dial at approx 4. 32 sts and 47 rows to 10 cms (4 ins) measured over punch lace. Tension dial at approx 3.

SKIRT PANELS (3 pieces)

1st piece
*Push 76 (80, 84, 88, 92, 96) Ns. at left and right of centre 0 to B pos. 152 (160, 168, 176, 184, 192) Ns. altogether. Using waste yarn cast on and knit several rows ending with carr. at right.

Electronic machines
Inspection button on. Insert special card into machine and set to first row. Pattern width indicator 18. Point cams at edge of knitting. Needle 1 cam centre of machine. Buttons 1 (left) and 2 (left).

Punchcard machines
Insert special card into machine and lock on row 1.

All machines
Row counter 000. Tension dial at 3. Set carr. for stockinet platting. With col. 1 in feeder 1 and col. 2 behind feeder 1, knit 4 rows. Tension dial at 5, knit 1 row. Tension dial at 3, knit 4 rows. Turn up a hem, knit 1 row. Carr. at right.

Electronic machines
Inspection button off.

Punchcard machines
Release card.

All machines
Row counter 000. Tension dial at 3. Set carr. for punch lace. With col. 1 in feeder 1 and col. 2 in feeder 2, knit 47 rows. Remove card. Tension dial at 4. Set carr. for stockinet platting. With col. 1 in feeder 1 and col. 2 behind feeder 1, knit 184 rows. Row counter 231*. Using waste yarn mark centre. Using waste yarn knit 10 rows and release from machine.

2nd piece
Work as given for 1st piece from * to *. Counting from the left edge mark st. 38 (40, 42, 44, 46, 48) with waste yarn. Using waste yarn knit 10 rows and release from machine.

3rd piece
Work as given for 1st piece from * to *. Counting from the right edge mark st. 38 (40, 42, 44, 46, 48) with waste yarn. Using waste yarn knit 10 rows and release from machine.

FRONT BODICE

Push 76 (80, 84, 88, 92, 96) Ns. at left and right of centre 0 to B pos. 152 (160, 168, 176, 184, 192) Ns. altogether. Using waste yarn mark Ns. 50 (53, 56, 59, 62, 65) at both sides of centre 0. With carr. at right and purl side of 1st skirt panel facing pick up sts. below waste yarn and place onto the centre 100 (106, 112, 118, 124, 130)

Ns. including marked Ns., gathering evenly and placing marked point on skirt panel at centre 0. Do not unravel waste yarn. With purl side of 2nd skirt panel facing, pick up 38 (40, 42, 44, 46, 48) sts. below waste yarn at left including marked st. and place onto Ns. at right of 1st skirt panel and gather evenly. Do not unravel waste yarn. With purl side of 3rd skirt panel facing pick up 38 (40, 42, 44, 46, 48) sts. below waste yarn at right including marked st. and place onto Ns. at left of 1st skirt panel and gather evenly. Do not unravel waste yarn. *Row counter 000. Tension dial at 4. Set carr. for stockinet platting. With col. 1 in feeder 1 and col. 2 behind feeder 1, knit 146 rows. Carr. at right.

Shape armholes

Cast off 6 sts. beg. next 2 rows and 2 sts. beg next 6 (6, 6, 6, 8, 8) rows. Dec. 1 st. both ends next and ev. foll. alt. row 3 (3, 4, 4, 5, 6) times in all, knit 2 (2, 2, 2, 3, 3,) rows. Dec 1 st. both ends next and ev. foll. 3rd (3rd, 3rd, 3rd, 4th, 4th) row 3 (4, 4, 5, 3, 3) times in all. 116 (122, 128, 134, 140, 146) sts. Knit 2 (3, 3, 2, 3, 3) rows without shaping. Row counter 170 (174, 176, 178, 180, 182). Using waste yarn mark sts. 24 and 36 (26 and 38, 27 and 39, 29 and 41, 30 and 42, 32 and 44) at both sides of centre 0. Using waste yarn mark centre. Using waste yarn knit 10 rows and release from machine*.

BACK BODICE

Join centre back skirt seam. Push 76 (80, 84, 88, 92, 96) Ns. at left and right of centre 0 to B pos. 152 (160, 168, 176, 184, 192) Ns. altogether. With carriage at right and purl side facing pick up rem. 228 (240, 252, 264, 276, 288) sts. below waste yarn on 2nd and 3rd skirt panels and place into Ns. gathering evenly. Do not unravel waste yarn. Work as given for front bodice from * to *.

BACK YOKE

Carr. at right, push 52 (55, 58, 61, 64, 67) Ns. at left and right of centre 0 to B pos. 104 (110, 116, 122, 128, 134) Ns. altogether.

Electronic machines

Inspection button on. Insert special card into machine and set to first row. Pattern width indicator 18. Point cams at edge of knitting. Needle 1 cam centre of machine. Buttons 1 (left) and 2 (left).

Punchcard machines

Insert special card into machine and lock on row 1.

All machines

Take carr. across twice without knitting. Carr. at right. *Using waste yarn mark Ns. 24 and 30 (26 and 32, 27 and 33, 29 and 35, 30 and 36, 32 and 38) at both sides of centre 0. Mark centre 0 with waste yarn*. With purl side of back bodice facing pick up sts. below waste yarn and place onto Ns., matching markers and gathering the 11 sts. between markers on bodice onto

the 5 Ns. between markers on yoke.

Electronic machines

Inspection button off.

Punchcard machines

Release card.

All machines

Row counter 000. Tension dial at 3. Set carr. for punch lace. With col. 1 in feeder 1 and col. 2 in feeder 2, knit 45 (47, 49, 51, 53, 55) rows. Mark both edges with waste yarn, knit 18 rows. Row counter 63 (65, 67, 69, 71, 73). Carr. at left.

Shape shoulders

Set carr. for D pos. shaping. Always taking yarn round first inside N. in D pos. Push 5 (6, 6, 7, 7, 8) Ns. at opposite end to carr. to D pos. on next 4 rows. Carr. at left.

Shape back neck

Using length of col. 1, cast off centre 38 sts. Push rem. 23 (24, 27, 28, 31, 32) Ns. at right to D pos.

Electronic machines

Inspection button on.

All machines

Take note of row number showing on pattern panel.

Electronic machines

Inspection button off.

All machines

Knit left part as follows:-

Knit 1 row. Dec. 1 st. at beg. and push 5 (6, 6, 7, 7, 8) Ns. at opposite end to carr. to D pos. on next row. Knit 1 row. **Dec. 1 st. at beg. and push 5 (5, 6, 6, 7, 7) Ns. at opposite end to carr. to D pos. on next row, knit 1 row**. Rept. the last 2 rows from ** to ** once more. 5 (5, 6, 6, 7, 7) Ns. rem. in B pos. Carr. at right. Using a transfer tool push Ns. at left from D pos. back to B pos. Cast off using a linker or latchet tool. Carr. at left.

Electronic machines

Inspection button on. Set card to number previously noted.

Punchcard machines

Take card to number previously noted and lock.

All machines

Using a transfer tool push 23 (24, 27, 28, 31, 32) inside Ns. at right back to B pos. Take carr. to right without knitting.

Electronic machines

Inspection button off.

Punchcard machines

Release card.

All machines

Knit right part as for left part but read left for right and vice versa.

FRONT YOKE

Carr. at right. Push 52 (55, 58, 61, 64, 67) Ns. at left and right of centre 0 to B pos. 104 (110, 116, 122, 128, 134) Ns. altogether. Work as given for back yoke from * to *. With purl side of front bodice facing pick up sts. below waste yarn and place onto Ns., matching markers and gathering the 11 sts. between markers on bodice onto the 5 Ns. between markers on yoke. Using nylon cord knit 52 (55, 58, 61,

64, 67) Ns. at left by hand, taking Ns. back to A pos.

Knit right part as follows:-

Electronic machines

Inspection button on, set card to first row. Point cams at edge of knitting. Needle 1 cam centre of machine. Buttons 1 (left) and 2 (left).

Punchcard machines

Lock card on row 1.

All machines

Take carr. across twice without knitting. Carr at right.

Electronic machines

Inspection button off.

Punchcard machines

Release card.

All machines

*Row counter 000. Tension dial at 3. Set carr. for punch lace. With col. 1 in feeder 1 and col. 2 in feeder 2, knit 35 (37, 39, 41, 43, 45) rows without shaping. Carr. at left.

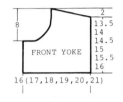

FRONT YOKE

16 (17, 18, 19, 20, 21)

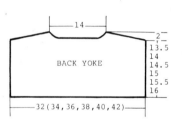

14

BACK YOKE

32 (34, 36, 38, 40, 42)

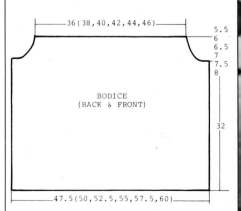

BODICE (BACK & FRONT)

36 (38, 40, 42, 44, 46)

47.5 (50, 52.5, 55, 57.5, 60)

Diagram of finished measurements in centimetres.

72

Shape neck
Cast off 6 sts. beg. next row, knit 1 row. Cast off 3 sts. beg. next and foll. alt. row, knit 1 row. Cast off 2 sts. beg. next and foll. alt. row, knit 1 row. Mark right edge with waste yarn. Dec. 1 st. at left edge on next and ev. foll. alt. row, 3 times in all, knit 2 rows. Dec. 1 st. at left edge on next and ev. foll. 3rd row 3 times in all. 30 (33, 36, 39, 42, 45) sts. Knit 4 rows without shaping. Row counter 63 (65, 67, 69, 71, 73). Carr. at left.

Shape shoulder
Set carr. for D pos. shaping. Always taking yarn round first inside N. in D pos., push 5 (6, 6, 7, 7, 8) Ns. at opposite end to carr. to D pos. on next and ev. foll. alt. row 3 times in all, knit 1 row. Push 5 (5, 6, 6, 7, 7) Ns. at opposite end to carr. to D pos. on next and foll. alt. row, knit 1 row. 5 (5, 6, 6, 7, 7) Ns. rem. in B pos. Carr. at left. Using a transfer tool push Ns. in D pos. back to B pos. Cast off using a linker or latchet tool*. Carr. at left, unravel nylon cord bringing Ns. to correct pos.

Electronic machines
Inspection button on. Set card to first row. Point cams at edge of knitting.

Punchcard machines
Lock card on row 1.

All machines
Take carr. across twice without knitting.

Electronic machines
Inspection button off.

Punchcard machines
Release card.

All machines
Carr. at left. Work as given for right part from * to * but read right for left and vice versa.

SLEEVES (both alike)

Push 54 (58, 61, 64, 67, 71) Ns. at left and right of centre 0 to B pos. 108 (116, 122, 128, 134, 142) Ns. altogether. Using waste yarn cast on and knit several rows ending with carr. at right.

Electronic machines
Inspection button on. Set card to first row. Point cams at edge of machine. Needle 1 cam centre of machine. 1 (left) and 2 (left).

Punchcard machines
Lock card on row 1.

All machines
Row counter 000. Tension dial at 3. Set Carr. for stockinet platting with col. 1 in feeder 1 and col. 2 behind feeder 1, knit 4 rows. Tension dial at 5, knit 1 row. Tension dial at 3, knit 4 rows. Turn up a hem, knit 1 row. Carr. at right.

Electronic machines
Inspection button off.

Punchcard machines
Release card.

All machines
Row counter 000. Tension dial at 3. Set carr. for punch lace. With col. 1 in feeder 1 and col. 2 in feeder 2, knit 24 rows. Remove card. Tension dial at 4. Set carr. for stockinet platting. With col. 1 in feeder 1 and col. 2 behind feeder 1, knit 1 row.

Transfer the 2nd (3rd, 3rd, 3rd, 3rd, 2nd) and ev. foll. 3rd st. onto its adjacent N., leaving empty Ns. in B pos., knit 211 rows. Row counter 236. Carr. at right.

Shape top
Cast off 6 sts. beg. next 2 rows.

2nd, 3rd, 4th, 5th and 6th sizes only
Cast off 4 sts. beg. next (4, 4, 4, 4, 6) rows.

All sizes
Cast off 3 sts. beg. next 6 (2, 2, 2, 2, 2) rows and 2 sts. beg. next 2 (2, 2, 2, 4, 4) rows. Dec. 1 st. both ends next and ev. foll. alt. row 3 (3, 4, 4, 3, 2) times in all, knit 5 (5, 5, 3, 3, 3) rows. Dec. 1 st. both ends next and ev. foll. 6th row 9 (9, 9, 10, 10, 11) times in all, knit 3 (5, 5, 3, 5, 1) rows. Mark both edges with waste yarn. Knit 4 (0, 0, 2, 0, 0) rows.

2nd and 3rd sizes only
Dec. 1 st. both ends next row, knit 3 rows.

All sizes
Dec. 1 st. both ends next and ev. foll. alt. row 3 (2, 2, 2, 2, 2) times in all, knit 1 row. Cast off 2 sts. beg. next 2 (4, 2, 4, 6, 6) rows, 3 sts. beg. next 4 rows and 4 sts. beg next 2 (2, 4, 4, 4, 4) rows. Row counter 326 (328, 330, 332, 334, 336). Cast off rem. 20 (20, 20, 22, 22, 22) sts.

COLLAR

Push 16 Ns. at left and right of centre 0 to B pos. 32 Ns. altogether.

Electronic machines
Inspection button on. Insert special card into machine and set to first row. Pattern width indicator 18. Point cams at edge of knitting. Needle 1 cam centre of machine. Buttons 1 (left) and 2 (left).

Punchcard machines
Insert special card into machine and lock on row 1.

All machines
Take carr. across twice without knitting. Carr. at right. Using col. 1, cast on by hand. Row counter 000. Tension dial at 3.

Electronic machines
Inspection button off.

Punchcard machines
Release card.

All machines
Set carr. for punch lace. With col. 1 in feeder 1 and col. 2 in feeder 2, knit 2 rows. Cast on 8 sts. beg. next 2 rows, 3 sts. beg. next 4 rows and 2 sts. beg. next 4 rows. Inc. 1 st. both ends next and ev. foll. alt. row 5 times in all. 78 sts. Knit 3 rows. Row counter 24. Carr. at right. Using a length of col. 1, cast off centre 34 sts. Using nylon cord, knit 22 sts. at left by hand taking Ns. back to A pos.

Electronic machines
Inspection button on.

All machines
Take note of row number showing on pattern panel.

Electronic machines
Inspection button off.

All machines
Knit right part as follows:-
Inc. 1 st. beg. next row, cast off 3 sts. beg.

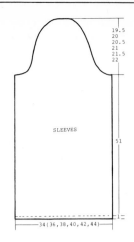

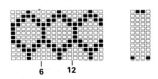

Diagram of finished measurements in centimetres.

PUNCHCARD MACHINES

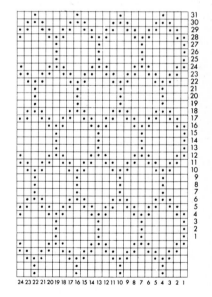

ELECTRONIC MACHINES

next row. Inc. 1 st. beg. next row, cast off 2 sts. beg. next row. *Inc. 1 st. at right edge next row, dec. 1 st. at left edge next row*. Rept. the last 2 rows from * to * twice more. Knit 1 row. Dec. 1 st. at left edge next row, inc. 1 st. at right edge next row. Dec. 1 st. at left edge next and ev. foll. alt. row 3 times in all. Inc. 1 st. at right edge next row, knit 2 rows. Dec. 1 st. at left edge next row. 16 sts. Knit 17 rows without shaping. Row counter 63. Dec. 1 st. at right edge and inc. 1 st. at left edge next row, knit 1 row. Inc. 1 st. at left edge next row, knit 2 rows. Dec. 1 st. at right edge and inc. 1 st. at left edge next row, knit 2 rows. Inc. 1 st. at left edge next row, knit 1 row. Cast on 2 sts. at left edge next row, knit 1 row. Dec. 1 st. at right edge and inc. 1 st. at left edge next row, knit 1 row. *Cast on 2 sts. at left edge and dec. 1 st. at right edge next row, knit 1 row*. Rept. the last 2 rows from * to * once more. Knit 1 row. Dec. 1 st. both ends next row, knit 1 row. Cast off 2 sts. beg. next 4 rows and 3 sts. beg. next 2 rows. Row counter 90. Cast off rem. 6 sts. Carr. at right.

Electronic machines
Inspection button on. Set card to number previously noted.
Punchcard machines
Take card to number previously noted and lock.
All machines
Take carr. to left. Unravel nylon cord bringing Ns. to correct pos.
Electronic machines
Inspection button off.
Punchcard machines
Release card.
All machines
Knit left part as for right part but read left for right and vice versa.

CORDS (knit 4)

Working in stockinet platting make a cord over 4 Ns. as given in instruction book for circular cord knitting. Make 2 cords approx. 25 cms. long and 2 cords approx. 40 cms. long.

TO MAKE UP

Pin out to size and press carefully with a cool iron over a damp cloth. Join skirt seams. Unravel waste yarn. Set in sleeves, matching markers and gathering sts. evenly between markers. Join side and sleeve seams. Slip st. collar into pos. Using col. 1, work 1 row of double crochet along front opening and around edge of collar. Sew cords 25 cms. long into pos. for ties. Thread rem. 2 cords through holes on sleeves. Give final light press.

HINTS & TIPS

POM POMS

A recent visit to the home of my friend Rose had me gazing in awe at little snowmen, brownies, soldiers and other little people, all beautifully made. I could not help noticing that Rose's pom poms were much better than anything we ever managed, so we asked . . . Out came a box containing a child's kit for making pom pom animals. It is called Pom Pom Pets and is made by Spear's. It contains small plastic frames, one small, one medium and an oval, an easy instruction book and some bits of wool, felt for eyes etc., but it is the pom pom frames that are worth every penny, not only for the time they save but the pom poms are lovely and they always turn out the right size with no ragged edges and of course the frames can be used again and again.
The small kits cost £1.60, but we could only find the new, larger kits at £2.40, but I still think I have bought a bargain.

COLOUR CHANGER ON THE KNITMASTER ELECTRONIC MACHINE

Knitting conventions are a great place for picking up and passing on hints and tips and we always learn lots of useful things and the demonstrators from the knitting machine manufacturers are especially helpful. One such lady is Dorothy Silk from Knitmaster. Dorothy was chatting to us about colour changers and was concerned that anyone buying a colour changer to fit on the Knitmaster electronic machine should be aware that they need to fit a little 'T' bar on to the original yarn break so that the aerial tension unit fits on to the 'T' shape.
There is a great deal of interest in colour changers now, possibly because we are able to buy lovely yarns to knit our Jacquard fabrics.

MORE TENSION

Those of us who teach machine knitting do not always practice what we preach and this week I committed one of the oldest sins . . . measured the tension swatch before I had let it settle and, true to form, I had trouble. It settled into shape several hours later and measured a completely different tension . . .
GOLDEN RULE — ALWAYS allow your tension swatch to settle back into shape before you measure it. We are an impatient lot really. I wonder how many unfinished garments there are hidden in drawers and cupboards because they did not look much when they came off the machine after being knitted. It is surprising how different a piece of knitting looks when the ends are sewn in and the pieces are pressed, so never give up until you have finished the whole thing. You might get a very pleasant surprise.

HANDS AND BAGS

Mrs Joyce Warren from Bedford has been enjoying herself at the knitting conventions and passes on a very useful tip for convention goers . . . never take a handbag, always take a shoulder bag — it leaves your hands free to get at the yarn. It made us smile but we do see the sense in it.
Mrs Warren has a couple of other useful ideas. The first one concerns your Christmas present list. Top on the list of labour saving devices this year should go a food processor . . . saves time in the kitchen which of course means more time in the knitting area.

Finally, back to the actual knitting. Mrs Warren says that to finish off a ribbed neckband she removes the knitting from the machine with a knitting needle and casts the stitches off by hand for a neat stretchy neck.
I approve of any hand knitting techniques that help with machine knitting. It is often an old hand knitting technique that saves the day on the tricky bits, so don't ignore the hand knitting patterns, especially some of the older ones in old books.

EATING YOUR WORDS . . .

Ann passed on a cooking tip . . . use a punchcard or the copy paper pattern placed over the Sunday sponge cake and sift the icing sugar over it. We had a big snowflake last weekend . . . now what can we do with the trifle . . ?

SHOULDER TROUBLE?

Have you ever knitted a garment only to find that the width at the shoulders is just a bit too much, especially on the dropped shoulder type of garment? It leaves you looking like the Incredible Hulk and the garment is not too smart. Take heart and a leaf from Mrs Everett's book and do some smocking on the shoulders to pull them in. I saw Mrs Everett at Bournemouth and she was wearing a lovely chenille jacket. She dyed the yarn herself with Dylon, which to us sounded a nice, safe way to dye yarns, and it was very effective.

REVERSE CABLES

Ribber owners . . . if you want a cable on the reverse side of your knitting, knit the cables on the ribber.

Dress and poncho

Haze (B), 1 cone Mulberry Haze (C).
Poncho
1 cone Aran Cream (A), 1 cone Pink Haze (B), 1 cone Mulberry Haze (C).
NOTE:
If both garments are to be knitted you will need 1 cone Aran Cream (A), 2 cones Pink Haze (B), 1 cone Mulberry Haze (C).

TENSION

15 sts and 22 rows to 5 cms (2 ins). Approx tension dial 9·. Rib tension approx tension dial 7.

NOTES:
Unless otherwise stated all welts can be knitted using a ribbing attachment as on 1 x 1 rib, T7/7 and knit half the amount of rows.

PATTERN CARDS

Using a blank punchcard make squares 6 sts by 10 rows.
Make triangles 2 rows 9 sts, 2 rows 7 sts, 2 rows 5 sts, 2 rows 3 sts, 2 rows 1 st.

BACK

With waste yarn cast on 146 (154, 162) sts as 2 x 1 mock rib. Knit a few rows. Carriage at right RC 000, using col B, rib tension, knit 19 rows, T10 one row, ribbing tension 19 rows. Make a hem filling in all empty Ns, knit the row. RC 000 main tension col B knit 10 rows. * Change to col C, knit 6 rows. Col B knit 10 rows, cols B and A pattern 10 rows of squares, col B knit 10 rows, col C 6 rows. Change to col B. ** Continue in B to row 330. *** Col C knit 6 rows, col B knit 10 rows, cols B and A pattern 10 rows triangles, col B knit 10 rows, col C knit 6 rows. **** Continue in col B to row 380. Cast off.

FRONT

Knit as the back to row 300.
Shape neck
Continue the same patterning as on the back whilst shaping as follows:
Put sts on left hand side of carriage on hold. At the end of the next and every foll alt row dec one st 10 times. At end of next and every foll 4th row dec one st 15 times. Continue straight to row 380. Cast off 48 (52, 56) sts. Take left handside off hold and knit as for right hand side reversing all shapings.

SIZES

Dress to fit 86 (91, 97) cms, 34 (36, 38) ins bust. 51 cms, 20 ins sleeve seam. 91 cms, 36 ins length.

MATERIALS

Lister Lee Thermoknit 4 ply.
Dress
1 cone Aran Cream (A), 2 cones Pink

SLEEVES (both alike)

With waste yarn cast on 68 (71, 74) sts as 2 x 1 mock rib, knit a few rows. Carriage at right RC 000 change to col B. Rib tension knit 39 rows, T10 knit one row, rib tension knit 39 rows. Make a hem filling in all empty Ns, and knit the row. RC 000, at each end of next and every foll 4th row inc one st to 114 (118, 122) sts, whilst patterning as follows. Knit 10 rows B, pattern as the back from *** to ****. Continue in col B to row 130. Pattern as the back from * to **. Cast off in col C.

NECKBANDS

Back neck

With wrong side of work facing and beg at right side pick up 50 sts from centre of the back, place on machine as 2 x 1 mock rib. Carriage at right RC 000 rib tension col B knit 15 rows, T10 knit one row, rib tension: knit 16 rows. Cast off.

Sides of neck

With wrong side of work facing and beg at right pick up 71 sts down side of neck and place on machine as 2 x 1 mock rib. Carriage at right RC 000 rib tension col B knit 2 rows. At point of neck of next and every foll alt row dec one st for 13 more rows, T10 knit one row, rib tension at point of neck of next and every foll alt row inc one st for 16 rows. Cast off. Repeat for other side of neck.

TO MAKE UP

Sew shoulder seams together. Sew down neckbands. Place centre of top of sleeves to shoulder seams and sew in place. Sew side and sleeve seams.

PONCHO

TO KNIT

With waste yarn cast on 200 sts as 2 x 1 mock rib. Knit a few rows. Carriage at right RC 000 col C main tension knit 19 rows, T10 knit one row, main tension knit 19 rows, make a hem filling in all empty Ns. Knit the row. RC 000 main tension col C knit 20 rows. * Change to col B, knit 6 rows, col C knit 10 rows, col C and A knit 10 rows squares, col C knit 10 rows, col B knit 6 rows, col C knit 30 rows, col A knit 6 rows, col C knit 10 rows, col C and B knit 10 rows triangles, col C knit 10 rows, col A knit 6 rows. ** Col C knit 30 rows. Repeat patterning from * to **. Knit in col C to row 288.
Divide for neck by putting 55 sts on left hand side on hold. Knit one row. At beg of next row cast off 90 sts, knit the row. Knit 8 more rows put right hand side on hold. Return left hand side to WP and knit 10 rows. Cast on centre 90 sts, return right hand side to WP, knit 10 complete rows.

Continue by reversing patterning of first side of poncho, knitting from ** to * twice. Col C knit 20 rows. Place sts as 2 x 1 mock rib. Main tension col C knit 19 rows, T10 knit one row, main tension knit 20 rows, cast off.

NECKBANDS (two alike)

With wrong side of work facing and beg at right side pick up 90 sts across neck edge and place on machine as 2 x 1 mock rib. Carriage at right RC 000, rib tension, col B, at beg of next 2 rows inc 3 sts. Knit straight to row 140, cast off.

ARMBANDS (two alike)

With wrong side of work facing and beg at right, pick up 160 sts from centre of poncho and place on machine as 2 x 1 mock rib. Carr at right RC 000 col B rib tension knit 15 rows, T10 knit one row, rib tension knit 16 rows, cast off.

TO MAKE UP

Sew neckband together and sew 3 increased sts at beg of neckbands to 10 rows on shoulders. Sew down neckband. Sew down armbands and ribbing at bottom. Sew side seams. Fringe around bottom and armholes.

HINTS & TIPS

INTARSIA

Another popular technique at the moment is the intarsia knitting and the results can be quite spectacular. Ann Groves from Hull sent a useful idea for intarsia patterns. She suggests that I use tapestry and cross stitch designs squared off as needed, as there are some lovely designs and pictures . . . I had a look through some books in our local library and agree and would add that many of the designs could be transferred to punchcards also.

LET'S TWIST AGAIN

Mrs Simmons rang to give me this handy tip for twisting fine yarns to make a random effect. First of all drill a small hole in your knitting table (please take care, I can hold no responsibility for this part of the proceedings), stand your three cones of yarn underneath the hole, which should be in the centre back of the table. Thread the three yarns through your double eye transfer tool and twist them round several times and then thread them through the hole and then carry on and thread the yarn as normal. The yarns will remain twisted and an even random effect will be obtained without any

blotches of one of the colours, as so often happens.

A WORD OF WARNING

I was commissioned last week to knit a cricket sweater for a friend and because I chose double knit yarn I decided to use the spray wax. My tension swatch turned out with cream streaks on it. Further investigation revealed the spray as the source of the trouble. However, it washed out with no bother and I would not be without my spray wax, but if you are knitting with white wool watch out, especially if you are knitting for someone else and you do not want to wash the garment before you part with it.

JACQUARD KNITTING

For those of you who have tried Jacquard knitting and have been disappointed with the results, either because the fabric felt hard or because of that awful 'grinning' through one or other of the colours . . . cheer up and try again. I found that I can knit Jacquard on a much looser tension than you would think. I have just experimented with some of this type of knitting on various machines. My yarn was

a very soft 3 ply and the tensions varied between 6 and 7 and the results were very pleasing. The fabric was soft and, contrary to what I would have expected, the opening up of the stitches prevented the 'grinning' rather than aggravated it. The entire secret of success in all double bed knitting, especially Jacquard, is correct yarn, weights and tension. There are of course other considerations, but if you have these three things right you are half way there.

EASY COUNTING

If you are coping with more than one shaping at a time and you are knitting from a written pattern it is easiest to keep track of your movements if you use your row counter as a check. For example, if you are decreasing at the armhole edge on alternate rows and the neck 'V' shaping is every 7th row, write on a piece of card the row numbers on which the 'V' shapings fall, 7, 14, 21 etc., and then a quick glance at your row counter will tell you whether or not you are due for a decrease. This is very simple, but it works and is much more reliable than ticking off as you go and then wondering did I or didn't I.

Winter warmth from Lister Lee

Knitted in Lister Lee 4 ply Thermoknit

SIZES

Jumper to fit bust 86 (91, 97) cms, 34 (36, 38) ins.
Length 51 (51, 51) cms, 20 (20, 20) ins.
Sleeve seam 31 (31, 31) cms, 12 (12, 12) ins.
Skirt to fit hip 91(97, 102) cms, 36 (38, 40) ins.
Length 71 (71, 71) cms, 28 (28, 28) ins.

MATERIALS

Lister Lee 4 Ply Thermoknit. 1 cone shade A, B, C and D.
Skirt: 1 cone shade A, B, C and D.
Jumper: 1 cone shade A, B, C and D.
Shawl: 1 cone shade A, B, C and D.
Complete outfit: 2 cones shade A, 1 cone shade B, C and D.

TENSION

4 ply Thermoknit qualities. 15 sts and 22 rows to 5 cms (2) ins. Approx tension dial 7.

Always check your tension before commencing.

NOTES:
Unless otherwise stated all welts can be knitted using a ribbing attachment. Cast on as 1x1 rib, T5/5 and knit half the amount of rows. To work larger sizes figures in parenthesis(). When only one set of figures is given this applies to all sizes.

JUMPER

BACK

With waste yarn cast on 104 (112, 120) sts as 2x1 mock rib. K a few rows. Carr at right RC 000 shade A RT k 39 rows, T10 k one row, RT k 39 rows. Make a hem filling in all empty Ns and k the row. RC 000 MT shade A, at each end of next and every foll 4th row inc one st 18 times 140 (148, 156) sts. K to row 90. At each end of next and every foll 3rd row (2nd row 12 times, then every 3rd row, 2nd row 24 times, then every 3rd row) dec one st until 80 sts rem. K to row 180, cast off.

FRONT

K as back to row 150.
Shape neck
Whilst continuing sleeve shaping, shape neck as follows. Put all sts from left of centre on hold. K one row, cast off 12 sts k the row. At neck edge of next and every foll row dec one st, until one st rem. Break yarn and secure. Repeat for left side of neck, reversing all shapings.

NECKBAND

With wrong side of work facing and beg at right hand side pick up 80 sts across back of neck and 92 sts across front of neck. Place on machine as 2x1 mock rib. Carr at right RC 000. Shade A, RT k 15 rows, T10 k 1 row, RT k 16 rows. Cast off.

SLEEVES (2 alike)

With waste yarn cast on 71 (77, 83) sts as 2x1 mock rib. Knit a few rows, carr at right. RC 000 shade B RT k 4 rows, shade A k 45 rows T 10 1 row, RT shade B 6 rows, C k 2 rows, B k 6 rows, D k 2 rows, B k 6 rows, A k 2 rows, repeat last 24 rows once more. A k one row. Make a hem filling in all empty Ns. Knit the row. RC 000 shade A. MT at each end of next and every foll 4th row inc. one st 15 times 101 (107, 113) sts. Knit to row 70. At each end of next and every foll row dec one st 10 (16, 22) times. At each end of next and every foll alt row dec one st until one st remains. Break yarn and secure st.

TO MAKE UP

Sew down neck to double thickness. Place arms in armholes and sew seams together. Sew side and sleeve seams.

SKIRT

TO KNIT (2 pieces alike)

Using shade A MT and all Ns, cast on 200 sts k 29 rows. T 10 1 row. MT RC 000 shade B, k 6 rows, D k 2 rows, B k 6 rows, C k 2 rows, B k 6 rows, A k 2 rows, B k 6 rows, C k 6 rows, D k 2 rows, C k 6 rows, B k 2 rows, C k 6 rows, A k 2 rows, C k 6 rows.***
K shade A 46 rows (RC 106), D k 4 rows, C k 4 rows, A k 46 rows, (RC 160). B k 4 rows, C k 4 rows, A k 46 rows (RC 214). D k 4 rows, B k 4 rows, A k 18 rows (RC 240). Cast off.

BACK WAISTBAND

With right side of work facing arrange one skirt piece evenly along 100 (110, 120) sts using all Ns.* RC 000 MT shade A k 6 rows.

At each end of next and every foll 6th row dec one st 8 times. K to row 59 T 10 k 1 row. Pattern as skirt bottom from ** to ***, whilst shaping as follows. K 6 rows, at each end of next and every foll 6th row inc one st 8 times. K to row 120. Cast off.

FRONT WAISTBAND

With right side of work facing arrange skirt evenly along 100 (110, 120) sts using all Ns. At right hand side of work cast on a further 16 sts. K as back waistband from *.

GUSSETT

Shade A MT RC 000. cast on 3 sts. K 2 rows. At each end of next and every foll 4th row inc one st 14 times. K to row 60. Cast off.

TO MAKE UP

With right sides together sew right skirt and waistband seams together. Fold waistband in half, with right sides together sew both ends of waistband. Turn waistband right way out and sew cast off edge of waistband to top of skirt. Place gussett at top of left skirt seam and sew in place. Sew remainder of skirt seam. Turn bottom 30 rows of skirt as hem. Make 4 button loops evenly along edge of waistband. Arrange buttons on waistband to match loops.

SHAWL

TO KNIT

Right side (2 pieces alike)
Using all Ns shade C RC 000 MT, cast on 200 sts, k 2 rows. At the beg of next and every foll alt row dec one st whilst patterning as follows. C k 4 rows, A k 2 rows, C k 6 rows, D k 2 rows, C k 6 rows, B k 2 rows, repeat first 16 rows once more.
A k 6 rows, D k 2 rows, A k 6 rows, B k 2 rows, A k 6 rows, C k 2 rows. Repeat rows 40 to 56 once more.
D k 6 rows, B k 2 rows, D k 6 rows, C k 2 rows, D k 6 rows, A k 2 rows, repeat rows 80 to 96 once more.
B k 6 rows, C k 2 rows, B k 6 rows, A k 2 rows, B k 6 rows, D k 2 rows, repeat rows 120 to 136 once more.
Repeat these 160 rows once more, then first 78 rows once more. One st remains. Break yarn and secure.

Left side (2 pieces alike)
Using all Ns, shade C RC 000, MT cast on 200 sts. Knit 2 rows. At end of next and every foll alt row dec one st whilst patterning as right side of shawl.

TO MAKE UP

With right sides together, sew one right side of shawl to left side twice. With right sides together sew diagonals of shawl. With wrong sides together sew cast on edges together.

HINTS & TIPS

ROLLING BACK

At Littlehampton knitting club we were discussing the use of curtain weights for keeping hems in place and it brought one or two amusing tales I can tell you but, joking apart, one member suggested using curtain weights in a stocking stitch band for edge to edge jackets to prevent that awful rolling back . . . well sufficient to say I tried it and it works.
Another way to prevent that rolling is to knit the band in with the fronts. Just add sufficient extra stitches to each front (this is for a round neck edge to edge jacket), leave one needle in the non working position for the fold edge and have about three or four stitches for folding in. When the garment is finished you can fold the edge in and stitch petersham ribbon to it to make a facing. The effect is professional and neat. This method can also be used for a button band.

THREADING THE BELLINKY

A useful tip passed to me last week by my friend Thelma was for threading the Bellinky. Take the finest of the two wool needles that you get in those packets of two and thread up your yarn

into it. It is fine enough to thread through all the holes etc. for the Bellinky and then can be used with the needle threader to get the yarn through the eye of the needle. A useful time saver this one.

THE HOLDING POSITION

All machines have a needle position for holding stitches, either for a neck shaping or perhaps a dart, heel or toe of a sock etc. If you want those stitches to stay held then you need to set your carriage to hold them. However, this needle position is very useful in many circumstances, for instance if you have just picked up a hem or a neck edge and you have two stitches, sometimes more, on one needle then the next row is going to be hard work for both you and the machine. By putting the needles into this holding position you are doing half the work for the machine and making the row easier to knit because the stitches are already behind the latches. Leave the carriage set to knit, NOT to hold, and the row will knit easily.
On a fully fashioned decrease, such as on a raglan sleeve shaping, the edge of the raglan is sometimes tight. When you have made the decrease leave the

needles out at the holding position with the carriages set to knit and this will help the raglan edge to stay looser. This principle applies to ribbers as well as single bed machines, especially if you have just transferred stitches for a special needle arrangement. Quite often the next row will be stiff and this will solve the problem. If the yarn you are using is a very soft yarn such as Shetland, then this method may well save your yarn from breaking.
You can if necessary take it a step further and if you think that the yarn is very soft and may well break away, or if the yarn is very thick and you think that the carriage might not make it across, knit that one row by hand, taking the yarn across the needle hooks one at a time with the needles out to the holding position first, ready to receive the yarn. It does not take long and is much better than jamming the carriage or bending the needles.
This position is also useful when you are knitting a single bed Fair Isle pattern that has long floats. If you bring the edge needle nearest the carriage out to the holding position every row, it will knit the end stitch in the second colour and thus prevent ragged or tight edges. It slows you down a little, but not much.

Unisex yoke sweater

An easy to follow pattern for the ever popular yoked sweater.

To suit most makes and models of punch-card machines.

SIZES

To fit 91 (96, 101, 106) cms, 36 (38, 40, 42) ins bust or chest.

MATERIALS

Pure Shetland wool 2/8's. Approx 320 (340, 370, 400) grms main colour, shade A, 30 grms shade B. Oddments of shades C, D, E, F.

TENSION

27 sts and 38 rows to 10 cm (4 ins) measured over stocking stitch. Tension dial at approx 8. 30 sts and 37 rows to 10 cm (4 ins) measured over Fair Isle. Tension dial at approx 9.

NOTES:
A garter bar may be used instead of WY when reducing sts on the yoke. Oiled Shetland wool should be knitted at 1 full tension larger than is normal for stocking stitch, and Fair Isle 2 tensions larger. Use a 2 x 1 rib, it gives a good tight welt with plenty of stretch when using Shetland wools.

BACK

Cast on 138 (144, 152, 158) sts in a 2 x 1 rib. Rib T3. Knit 32 rows. Transfer sts to main bed. RC 000 T8. Knit 128 (128, 136, 136) rows. Carr at right.
Shape raglan armholes
RC 000. Cast off 6 sts at beg of next 2 rows. Dec Ff 1 st at each end of next and every foll alt row 14 (15, 16, 17) times altog, 98 (102, 108, 112) sts, 30 (32, 34, 36) rows. Mark the centre 2 sts with a contrast yarn. Using WY knit 8 rows. Release from machine.

FRONT

Follow instructions for back until the armhole is reached.
Shape raglan armholes
RC 000. Carr at right. Push 69 (72, 76, 79) Ns on the left of centre 0 to holding pos. Push 9 (9, 10, 10) Ns to the right of centre 0 to holding pos. Cast off 6 sts at armhole edge. Always wrapping the first inside needle in holding pos, knit 2 rows. Push 6 Ns to holding pos at opposite end to carr, dec Ff 1 st at armhole edge. Knit 2 rows. Rept the instructions for the last 2 rows. Push 3 Ns to holding pos at opposite end to carr. Dec Ff 1

st at armhole edge. Knit 2 rows. Rept from ★ 2 more times. ★★ Push 2 Ns to holding pos at opposite end to carr. Dec Ff 1 st at armhole edge. Knit 2 rows. Rept from ★★ 9 (10, 11, 12) times altog 30 (32, 34, 36) rows. RC 000. Carr at left. Leave the Ns on the right of centre 0 in holding pos. Push the Ns to the left of centre 0 into WP, using a transfer tool. Rept from ★★★ to ★★★ reversing shapings. Knit 1 row across all the sts. Mark the centre 2 sts with a contrast yarn. Using WY knit 8 rows. Release from machine.

SLEEVES

Cast on 62 (64, 66, 68) sts in a 2 x 1 rib. Rib T3. Knit 32 rows. Transfer sts to main bed. RC 000 T8. Inc 1 st at each end of every 8th row 20 (21, 22, 23) times. Knit to row 174 (180, 188, 196), 102 (106, 110, 114) sts. Carr at right.
Shape raglan top
RC 000. Cast off 6 sts at beg of next 2 rows. Dec Ff 1 st at each end of next and every foll alt row 14 (15, 16, 17) times altog 62 (64, 66, 68) sts. Mark the centre 2 sts with a piece of contrast yarn. Using WY knit 8 rows. Release from machine.

YOKE (back and front alike)

Push 158 (164, 172, 178) Ns into WP. Starting with the back, and with the purl side facing, replace the sts held on WY onto the centre 98 (102, 108, 112) Ns, putting the marked sts on either side of centre 0. At the left replace sts held on WY at the top of the right sleeve, starting with the marked stitch in the centre, putting it onto the edge needle and placing the last stitch at the raglan edge on top of the first raglan edge needle of the back. Rept at the right side with the left sleeve. Inc 1 st at each end 160 (166, 174, 180) sts. RC 000 T9. Insert card and knit in Fair Isle, using col A in feeder 1 and col C in feeder 2. Knit 10 rows. With col B in feeder 1 and col C in feeder 2. Knit 10 rows. Lock card. Using WY knit 8 rows. Release from machine. Push 128 (133, 140, 144) Ns into WP. Starting at the left, replace sts onto the needles putting 2 sts onto the 2nd (2nd, 4th, 2nd) needle and every foll 4th needle 32 (33, 34, 36) times altog. Unlock card. With col B in feeder 1 and col D in feeder 2 knit 13 rows. Lock card. Using WY knit 8 rows. Release from machine. Push 103 (107, 112, 116) Ns into WP. Starting at the left, replace sts onto the needles putting 2 sts onto the 4th (4th, 2nd, 4th) needle and every foll 4th needle 25 (26, 28, 28) times altog. Unlock card. With col B in feeder 1 and col E in feeder 2. Knit 17 rows. Lock card. Using WY knit 8 rows. Release from machine. Push 83 (86, 90, 93) Ns into WP. Starting at the left, replace sts onto the needles putting 2 sts onto the 4th (3rd, 3rd, 3rd) needle and every foll 4th needle 20 (21, 22, 23) times altog. Unlock card. With col B in feeder 1 and col F in feeder 2 knit 11 rows. Lock card. Using WY knit 8 rows. Release from machine. Push 67

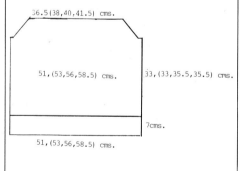
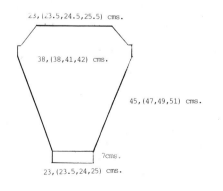

Diagram of finished measurement in centimetres.

(69, 72, 75) Ns into WP. Starting at the left, replace sts onto the needles putting 2 sts onto the 4th (2nd, 2nd, 4th) needle and every foll 4th needle 16 (17, 18, 18) times altog. Unlock card. With col B in feeder 1 and col C in feeder 2. Knit 6 rows. Remove card. Using WY knit 8 rows. Release from machine. Replace sts from front onto machine and knit to match back.

NECKBAND (2 Pieces)

Push 67 (69, 72, 75) Ns into WP. With purl side of back facing, replace sts held on WY onto needles in WP. T 8 using col A, knit 1 row. Transfer sts to ribber for a 2 x 1 rib. T3, Knit 14 rows. T6, knit 1 row. T3, knit 14 rows. Using WY knit 8 rows. Release from machine. Replace sts from front onto machine and knit to match the back.

TO MAKE UP

Join yoke and neckband seams. Fold neckband to inside. Stitch down. Join side and sleeve seams.

HINTS

Wash garment in fairly hot water using good quality washing up liquid. This is to release the oil from the wool. The garment will then be beautifully soft and fluffy. Remember to wash the tension square using the same treatment. Press the garment with a damp cloth and a hat iron.

HINTS & TIPS

STILL ON BOUCLE

I did some stripes on boucle and was disappointed, the very nature of the yarn hid the stripes and they did not look effective. I tried again (I always do) and this time the boucle was the main yarn and I did the stripes in a 4 ply acrylic. Result, much more effective and looked even better using the wrong side of the knitting as the right side, which is usually the case with boucles. Interest was added to the stripes because the stripe is not just one line but is more obvious because the background colour breaks up the first and last rows on the stripes.

NEAT EDGES TO YOUR WEAVING

When you are weaving bring the second needle from the edge out to the holding position at the side nearest the carriage on every row. This will give a neat edge to the weaving and give you a knit stitch to sew up on. When you set off across the row always take up any slack on the weaving yarn with your spare hand and pull it upwards away from the carriage as you start to weave the row. This will also help to give a neat edge and stop any tangles at the beginning of the row.

Opposite: **Fine knit jacket, skirt and vest** (see pattern on page 45)

Sweater with Fair Isle circular yoke

For **KNITMASTER 260/360 and SK560 machines with ribbing attachment. For stockists write to KNITMASTER Ltd., 30-40 Elcho Street, London SW11.**

SIZE

To fit 96-112 cms, 38-44 ins chest.

MATERIALS

Wendy Shetland double knit. 12 (13, 14, 15) 50 grm balls col 1 (hebrides); 2 50 grm balls col 2 (islay); 2 50 grm balls col 3 (pasture); 1 50 grm ball col 4 (tartan blue).

TENSION

26 sts and 35 rows to 10 cms (4 ins) measured over stockinet. 29 sts and 32 rows to 10 cms (4 ins) measured over Fair Isle. Tension dial at approx 9. 42 rows to 10 cms (4 ins) measured over 1 x 1 rib. Tension dial at approx 4.

Colour sequence
*   With col 1 in feeder 1 and col 4 in feeder 2, knit 3 rows.
    With col 1 in feeder 1 and col 3 in feeder 2, knit 6 rows.
    With col 1 in feeder 1 and col 2 in feeder 2, knit 4 rows.

With col 3 in feeder 1 and col 2 in feeder 2, knit 4 rows.
    With col 1 in feeder 1 and col 3 in feeder 2, knit 5 rows*.
** With col 1 in feeder 1 and col 2 in feeder 2, knit 9 rows.
    With col 2 in feeder 1 and col 3 in feeder 2, knit 2 rows.
    With col 3 in feeder 1 and col 4 in feeder 2, knit 2 rows.
    With col 2 in feeder 1 and col 3 in feeder 2, knit 2 rows.
    With col 1 in feeder 1 and col 2 in feeder 2, knit 9 rows**.
***With col 1 in feeder 1 and col 3 in feeder 2, knit 5 rows.
    With col 3 in feeder 1 and col 2 in feeder 2, knit 5 rows.
    With col 1 in feeder 1 and col 2 in feeder 2, knit 11 rows***.

BACK

With ribbing attachment in pos set half pitch lever to P and swing indicator to 5. Push 65 (68, 71, 74) Ns at left and right of centre 0 on knitter to B pos. 130 (136, 142, 148) Ns altog. Push corresponding Ns on ribber to B pos.
Needle arrangement
· 1· 1· 1· 1
1· 1· 1· 1·
With carr at left and using col 1, cast on as shown in instruction book for knit 1 purl 1 rib. Set carr for main knitting. RC 000. Tension dial at 4, knit 33 rows. Carr at right. Push empty Ns on knitter to B pos. Transfer sts from ribber to knitter using Knitmaster Rib Transfer Carriage. Lower ribber.
260/360 machines
Insert special card into machine and lock on row 1. Take carr across twice without knitting.
SK560 machines
Inspection button on. Insert special card into machine and set to first row. Pattern width indicator 24. Point cams edge of knitting. Needle 1 cam 12 at right of centre 0. Buttons 1 (left) and 2 (left). Take carr across twice without knitting.

All machines
RC 000. Tension dial at 9. Set carr for Fair Isle.
260/360 machines
Release card.
SK560 machines
Inspection button off.
*All machines***
Knit 22 rows of pattern as given in notes

Opposite: **Jogging suit** (see pattern on page 50)

from ★ to ★. Remove card. Set carr for stockinet. Continue in col 1, knit 10 rows. Inc 1 st both ends next and ev foll 15th (15th, 15th, 12th) row 5 (5, 5, 6) times in all. 140 (146, 152, 160) sts. Knit 35 rows without shaping. RC 128. Carr at right★★★.

Shape raglan armholes
Cast off 6 sts beg next 2 rows.
1st, 2nd and 3rd sizes only
Dec 1 st both ends next and ev foll alt row 4 times in all.
All sizes
★Dec 1 st both ends next and foll alt row★. Rept the last 3 rows from ★ to ★ 4 (4, 4, 6) more times.
4th size only
Dec 1 st both ends next row.
All sizes
100 (106, 112, 118) sts. RC 152. Carr at right. Push 50 (53, 56, 59) Ns at left to D pos. Set carr for D pos shaping.
Knit right part as follows:-
Always taking yarn round first inside N in D pos, push 18 Ns at opposite end to carr to D pos and dec 1 (1, 1, 0) st beg next row, dec 0 (0, 0, 1) st end next row. Push 7 (8, 9, 9) Ns at opposite end to carr to D pos and dec 1 st beg next row, dec 1 (1, 1, 0) st end next row. Push 7 (8, 8, 9) Ns at opposite end to carr to D pos and dec 0 (0, 0, 1) st beg next row, dec 1 st end next row. Push 7 (7, 8, 9) Ns at opposite end to carr to D pos and dec 0 (1, 1, 1) st beg next row, dec 0 (0, 0, 1) st end next row. Push rem 7 (7, 8, 8) Ns in B pos to D pos. Break off yarn. Take carr to left. Using a transfer tool bring 50 (53, 56, 59) Ns at left from D pos to B pos. Knit left part as for right part. Push all Ns in D pos to C pos. Mark centre with waste yarn. Using waste yarn knit 8 rows and release from machine.

FRONT

Follow instructions for back to ★★★. Mark centre with waste yarn. Push 70 (73, 76, 80) Ns at left to D pos. Set carr for D pos shaping.
Knit right part as follows:-
Always taking yarn round first inside N in D pos, push 10 Ns at opposite end to carr to D pos and cast off 6 sts beg next row, knit 1 row. Push 6 Ns at opposite end to carr to D pos and dec 1 st beg next row, knit 1 row. Push 6 Ns at opposite end to carr to D pos and dec 1 st beg next row, dec 0 (0, 0, 1) st end next row. Push 6 Ns at opposite end to carr to D pos and dec 1 (1, 1, 0) st beg next row, dec 0 (0, 0, 1) st end next row. Push 5 Ns at opposite end to carr to D pos and dec 1 st beg next row, dec 1 (1, 1, 0) st end next row. Push 4 (5, 5, 5) Ns at opposite end to carr to D pos and dec 0 (0, 0, 1) st beg next row, dec 1 st end next row. Push 3 (4, 4, 5) Ns at opposite end to carr to D pos and dec 1 (1, 1, 0) st beg next row, dec 0 (0, 0, 1) st end next row. Push 2 (3, 4, 5) Ns at opposite end to carr to D pos and dec 1 st beg next row, dec 1 (1, 1, 0) st end next row. Push 2 (2, 3, 4) Ns at

opposite end to carr to D pos and dec 0 (0, 0, 1) st beg next row, dec 1 st end next row. Push 2 (2, 3, 3) Ns at opposite end to carr to D pos and dec 1 (1, 1, 0) st beg next row, dec 0 (0, 0, 1) st end next row. Push 2 Ns at opposite end to carr to D pos and dec 1 st beg next row, dec 1 (1, 1, 0) st end next row. Push 1 N at opposite end to carr to D pos and dec 0 (0, 0, 1) st beg next row, dec 1 st end next row. Push rem N to D pos. Break off yarn. Take carr to left. Using a transfer tool bring 70 (73, 76, 80) Ns at left from D pos to B pos. Knit left part as for right part. Push all Ns in D pos to C pos. Using waste yarn knit 8 rows and release from machine.

LEFT SLEEVE

With ribbing attachment in pos set half pitch lever to P and swing indicator to 5. Push 28 (28, 31, 31) Ns at left and right of centre 0 on knitter to B pos. 56 (56, 62, 62) Ns altog. Push corresponding Ns on ribber to B pos.
Needle arrangement
·1·1·1·1
1·1·1·1·
With carr at left and using col 1 cast on as shown in instruction book for knit 1 purl 1 rib. Set carr for main knitting. RC 000. Tension dials at 4, knit 25 rows. Carr at right. Push empty Ns on knitter to B pos. Transfer sts from ribber to knitter using Rib Transfer Carriage. Lower ribber. Foll instructions for back from ★★ to ★★. Working in pattern as given in notes from ★ to ★ knit 1 (8, 6, 1) rows. Inc 1 st both ends next and ev foll 5th (4th, 4th, 4th) row 5 (4, 4, 6) times in all, knit 0 (1, 3, 0) rows. RC 22 (end of pattern). Remove card. Set carr for stockinet. Continue in col 1, knit 4 (2, 0, 3) rows. Inc 1 st both ends next and ev foll 5th (4th, 4th, 4th) row 26 (30, 31, 32) times in all. 118 (124, 132, 138) sts. Knit 12 (23, 21, 14) rows without shaping. RC 164★★★. ★★★★(knit 1 row extra for right sleeve only). Carr at right.
Shape raglan top
Cast off 6 sts beg next 2 rows. Dec 1 st both ends next and ev foll alt row 6 times in all, knit 1 row. Push 47 (50, 54, 57) Ns at left to D pos. Set carr for D pos shaping.
Knit right part as follows:-
Always taking yarn round first inside N in D pos, push 13 Ns at opposite end to carr to D pos and dec 1 st beg next row, knit 1 row. Push 9 (9, 9, 10) Ns at opposite end to carr to D pos and dec 1 st beg next row, knit 1 row. Push 8 (8, 9, 9) Ns at opposite end to carr to D pos and dec 1 st beg next row, knit 1 row. Push 6 (7, 8, 9) Ns at opposite end to carr to D pos and dec 1 st beg next row, knit 1 row. Push 5 (7, 8, 9) Ns at opposite end to carr to D pos and dec 0 (0, 1, 1) st end next row. Carr at right. Push rem N in B pos to D pos. Break off yarn. Take carr to left. Using a transfer tool bring 47 (50, 54, 57) Ns at left from D pos to B pos.

Knit left part as follows:-
Push 8 Ns at opposite end to carr to D pos and dec 1 st beg next row, knit 1 row. Push 6 Ns at opposite end to carr to D pos and dec 1 st beg next row. Knit 1 row. Rept the last 2 rows once more. Push 5 (5, 5, 6) Ns at opposite end to carr to D pos and dec 1 st beg next row, knit 1 row. Push 4 (4, 5, 6) Ns at opposite end to carr to D pos and dec 1 st beg next row, knit 1 row. Push 3 (3, 4, 5) Ns at opposite end to carr to D pos and dec 1 st beg next row, knit 1 row. Push 2 (3, 4, 4) Ns at opposite end to carr to D pos and dec 1 st beg next row, knit 1 row. Push 2 (3, 3, 3) Ns at opposite end to carr to D pos and dec 1 st beg next row, knit 1 row. Push 1 (2, 2, 3) Ns at opposite end to carr to D pos and dec 1 st beg next row, dec 0 (0, 1, 0) st end next row. Carr at left. Push rem N in B pos to D pos. Break off yarn. Push all Ns in D pos to C pos. Mark centre with waste yarn. Using waste yarn knit 8 rows and release from machine.

RIGHT SLEEVE

Foll instructions for left sleeve to ★★★. Now foll instructions from ★★★★ to end but reverse the shapings by noting alterations in number of rows worked and reading left for right and vice versa.

FRONT YOKE

First section
Join front raglan seams. ★Carr at right. Push 48 (48, 56, 56) Ns at left and 56 (64, 64, 64) Ns at right of centre 0 to B pos. With purl side of front facing pick up 49 (52, 55, 58) sts on left half of front and place onto Ns as folls:-
1st size only
Place the sts onto the 56 Ns at right of centre 0, placing the first 2 sts at left tog onto the first N at right of centre 0 and increasing required amount of sts evenly.
2nd size only
Place the sts onto the Ns at right of centre 0 placing the first 2 sts at left tog onto the 4th N at right of centre 0 and increasing required amount of sts evenly.
3rd and 4th sizes only
Place the first 2 sts at left tog onto the 4th N at left of centre 0 and increase required amount of sts evenly.

All sizes
Pick up 42 (45, 48, 51) sts to marked point on sleeve at left and place onto the empty Ns in B pos at left, placing the first 2 sts tog onto the first inside empty N and increasing required amount of sts evenly. Inc 1 st at each end.
260/360 machines
Insert special card into machine and lock on row 1. Take carr across twice without knitting. Release card.
SK560 machines
Inspection button on. Insert special card into machine and set to first row. Pattern width indicator 24. Needle 1 cam 12 at right of centre 0. Point cams edge of

knitting. Buttons 1 (left and 2 (left). Take carr across twice without knitting. Inspection button off.
All machines
Set carr for Fair Isle. RC 000. Tension dial at 9. Knit 22 rows of pattern as given in notes from * to *.
260/360 machines
Lock card.
SK560 machines
Inspection button on.
All machines
Set carr for stockinet. Knit 1 row col 1. Using waste yarn knit 8 rows and release from machine*. For other half of front and sleeve work as given from * to * but read right for left and vice versa throughout. Do not reverse pos of buttons and needle 1 cam on electronic machine. Keep carr at right to start.
Second section
Join centre front seam of first section. Push 85 Ns at left and right of centre 0 to B pos. With purl side of first section facing pick up sts from below waste yarn and place onto Ns in B pos gathering evenly. Using col 1, knit 1 row stockinet.
260/360 machines
Release card.
SK560 machines
Inspection button off.
All machines
Set carr for Fair Isle. Knit 24 rows of pattern as given in notes from ** to **.
260/360 machines
Lock card.
SK560 machines
Inspection button on.
All machines
Set carr for stockinet. Knit 1 row col 1. Using waste yarn knit 8 rows and release from machine.
Third section
Push 65 Ns at left and right of centre 0 to B pos. With purl side of second section facing pick up sts from below waste yarn and place onto Ns in B pos gathering evenly. Using col 1, knit 1 row stockinet.
260/360 machines
Release card.
SK560 machines
Inspection button off.
All machines
Set carr for Fair Isle. Knit 11 rows of pattern as given in notes from *** to ***.
260/360 machines
Lock card.
SK560 machines
Inspection button on.
All machines
With col 1 in feeder 1 and col 2 in feeder 2, knit 1 (4, 8, 11) rows. Set carr for stockinet. Using waste yarn knit 8 rows and release from machine.

BACK YOKE

First section
Join back raglan seams. *Carr at right. Push 40 (48, 48, 48) Ns at left and 48 (56, 64, 64) Ns at right of centre 0 to B pos.

With purl side of back facing pick up 46 (48, 51, 53) sts on left half of back and place onto Ns as follows:-
1st and 2nd sizes only
Place the sts onto the 48 (56) Ns at right of centre 0, placing the first 2 sts at left tog onto the first N at right of centre 0 and increasing required amount of sts evenly.
3rd and 4th sizes only
Place the first 2 sts at left tog onto the 4th N at right of centre 0 and increase required amount of sts evenly.
All sizes
Pick up 38 (41, 44, 48) sts rem on sleeve at left and place into the empty Ns in B pos at left, placing the first 2 sts tog onto the first inside empty N and increasing required amount of sts evenly. Inc 1 st at each end.
260/360 machines
Lock card on row 1. Take carr across twice without knitting. Release card.
SK560 machines
Inspection button on. Set card to first row. Needle 1 cam 12 at right of centre 0. Point cams edge of knitting. Take carr across twice without knitting. Inspection button off.
All machines
Set carr for Fair Isle. RC 000. Tension dial at 9. Knit 22 rows of pattern as given in notes from * to *.
260/360 machines
Lock card.
SK560 machines
Inspection button on.
All machines
Set carr for stockinet. Knit 1 row col 1. Using waste yarn knit 8 rows and release from machine*. For other half of back and sleeve work as given from * to * but read right for left and vice versa throughout. Do not reverse pos of buttons and needle 1 cam on electronic machine. Keep carr at right to start.
Second section
Join centre back seam of first section. Push 61 Ns at left and 85 Ns at right of centre 0 to B pos. With purl side of first section facing pick up sts from below waste yarn and place onto Ns in B pos placing the centre seam on the 12th N at right of centre 0 and gathering evenly. Using col 1, knit 1 row stockinet.
260/360 machines
Release card.
SK560 machines
Inspection button off.
All machines
Set carr for Fair Isle. Knit 24 rows of pattern as given in notes from ** to **.
260/360 machines
Lock card.
SK560 machines
Inspection button on.
All machines
Set carr for stockinet. Using col 1, knit 1 row. Using waste yarn knit 8 rows and release from machine.
Third section
Push 49 Ns at left and right of centre 0 to B pos. With purl side of second section

facing pick up sts from below waste yarn and place onto Ns in B pos gathering evenly. Using col 1, knit 1 row stockinet.
260/360 machines
Release card.
SK560 machines
Inspection button off.
All machines
Set carr for Fair Isle. Knit 11 rows of pattern as given in notes from *** to ***.
260/360 machines
Lock card.
SK560 machines
Inspection button on.
All machines
With col 1 in feeder 1 and col 2 in feeder 2, knit 1 (4, 8, 11) rows. Set carr for stockinet. Using waste yarn knit 8 rows and release from machine. Remove card.

PUNCHCARD CHART

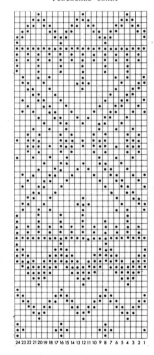

ELECTRONIC CHART

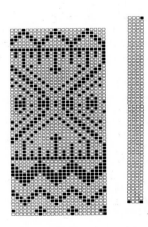

NECKBAND (2 pieces)

Push 99 Ns to B pos. With plain side of front yoke facing pick up sts from below waste yarn and place onto Ns in B pos gathering evenly. *Tension dial at 4. Using col 1, knit 1 row. Transfer sts to ribber for 1 x 1 rib. Knit 20 rows. Transfer sts from ribber to knitter using Rib Transfer Carriage. Knit 2 rows. Using waste yarn knit 8 rows and release from machine*. Push 63 Ns to B pos. With plain side of back yoke facing pick up sts from below waste yarn and place onto Ns in B pos gathering evenly. Foll instructions from * to *.

TO MAKE UP

Pin out and steam carefully with a warm iron over a damp cloth. Join neckband and yoke seams. Join side and sleeve seams. Fold neckband in half onto the outside. Pin into pos and backstitch through the open loops of last row knitted in col 1. Unravel waste yarn. Give final light steam.

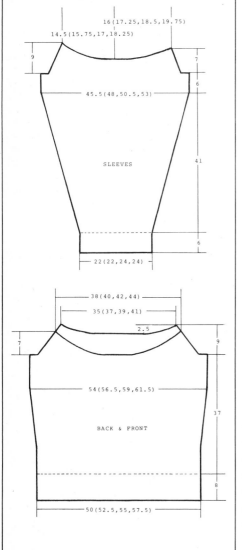

Diagram of finished measurements in centimetres.

SHEEP

There are lots of sweaters about at the moment with various types of sheep sauntering across them but this one is one of the best we have seen. The punchcard was sent to us by Brenda Saxon from Wollengers. Brenda and I have chatted over the 'phone about all sorts of things from leg warmers to the secrets of circular skirts (which started the article for the next issue rolling). Below is the punchcard for you to copy and the colour sequences are as follows:-

Rows on the card 1–20 grass green and white.

On row 20 lock the card and knit 10 rows green only.

21–32 green and brown.

33–36 green and darker green.

37–60 sky blue and darker green.

Many thanks Brenda – any more?

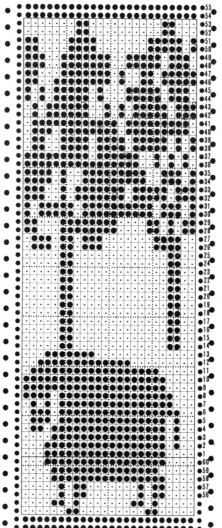

HINTS & TIPS

TOP TIP

I find this a very useful little chart, though we must stress that because of the great variation in types of yarn it can only be described as approximate. The table gives a guide as to the approximate yarn required for a long sleeve, round neck sweater.

Size	3 ply	4 ply	DK
71cm (28in)	200g	250g	350g
76cm (30in)	225g	300g	400g
81cm (32in)	300g	375g	450g
86cm (34in)	350g	425g	500g
91cm (36in)	400g	450g	525g
96cm (38in)	450g	500g	575g
101cm (40in)	525g	550g	600g

1kg equals 2lb 3oz. 230g equals 8oz.

KNITMASTER PUNCH LACE EDGES

I like the punch lace and feel that it is often neglected. One of the grumbles seems to be that knitters have trouble with tatty edges. Mrs Sharon Johnson wrote to me with a tip for just this problem.

She says do not follow the instruction book (do we ever?). Set both front levers to I (to set the machine to hold). At the carriage side bring the end needle out to D position. Knit 1 row. * At the carriage side bring the end needle out to D position, and at the opposite end to the carriage push the end needle back to C position (upper working position). Knit 1 row. * Repeat from * to * for each row.

This ensures that both the yarns wrap around the end needles on each side of every alternate row, regardless of the punchcard.

A CLOSED EDGE CAST ON FOR KNITMSTER 260 AND 360 LACE

If you are using your lace carriage you cannot use the normal hand cast on and pull the needles out to the HP for those first few tricky rows. Try this instead. Cast on from left to right using the latch tool to crochet cast on. Leave the needles out at HP and then knit the stitches back by hand. Thread up (carriage on left) and knit the first row or two slowly and you will have a very neat cast on edge.

HANG THAT WOOL

Mrs Rogers from Newcastle passed on a super tip for storing yarn (do we need storage space . . .).

Take a wire coat hanger and straighten it out, leaving the hook on. Thread your cones of yarn on to it and turn up the end sufficiently to hold the bottom cone. Hang the coat hanger in a wardrobe and start looking for somewhere else for your clothes.

Quilted jerkin

SIZES

Instructions are for garment fitting man, size 96-107 cms/38-42 ins chest. Adding or subtracting 2 rows in each tuck will result in about 9 cms (3½ ins) difference in size. Length can be varied easily.

MATERIALS

2 cones main, 1 cone contrast of Knitting Concepts Sophie.
Approx 1m 20cm terylene wadding.
Open ended 60 cm zip.

TENSION

8 sts and 12 rows to 2.5 cm (1 inch) using yarn double, and tension 4 on Knitmaster. This is the tension obtained when work is simply measured in usual way; however, the wadding alters the size considerably and if you are calculating changes in length, then allow only 7 sts to the inch.

TO KNIT

Start by cutting the wadding into 5 cm (2 ins) strips, each long enough to go between needles 90 each side of centre.
Garment is knitted sideway and picked up into tucks as the lining is knitted with the wadding inserted as this is done.
With main, cast on by hand 147 sts between needles 84 at left and 63 at right. Knit 4 rows (this will form facing for zip). RC 000. Work in stripes of 2 rows contrast, 22 rows main for the whole of outside of jacket. When starting second contrast stripe (RC 24) increase 1 st at neck alternate rows 11 times (right hand side of work) and then cast on 10 sts. Work straight until end of 6th stripe repeat (RC 144). At right cast off 70 sts (or leave on waste yarn) for armhole, work across and back, casting on 70 sts for back of armhole. Work straight to end of 18th stripe pattern (RC 432). Work armhole as before. Work straight to end of 22nd

stripe pattern (RC 528). Shape neck by casting off 10 sts at beginning of next row, then decrease at neck edge alternate rows 11 times. Work straight to end of 24th stripe pattern (RC 576). Work 2 rows contrast, 4 rows main and cast off.

LINING

Worked in contrast throughout. Cast on 147 sts as before. Work 4 rows for zip facing. RC 000. Hold outside piece of garment with neck edge at right, and pick up sts from centre of first contrast stripe and hang on to needles. Work 24 rows. Lay stripe of wadding between layers of knitting and pick up sts from next contrast stripe. The wadding stays in place quite well against the fluffy yarn so this is not difficult. It sticks out beyond the work at each end, and this is trimmed away later. Continue in this way, inserting wadding and picking up sts every 24 rows, and shaping neck and armholes to match piece already knitted. Pick up armhole sts from outside of garment before casting them off together with lining, and instead of casting on sts to replace them, use the sts from armhole edge of outside of garment. End with 4 rows for zip facing and cast off.

TO MAKE UP

Pin wadding in place at each end of tucks and trim edges. Join shoulders by mattress stitching on outside and again on inside of garment, catching in the wadding as you sew so that it stays in place.
Collar
Use main yarn 4 fold, pick up about 120 sts round neck, picking up through wadding as well as knitting. Work 50 rows tension 7, increasing each end every 4 rows. Work 50 rows more decreasing each end every 4 rows. Cast off and sew edge down to cover seam. Neaten ends of collar.
Welts
Pick up about 134 sts from front edge to centre back. Using 4 ends of main yarn work 3 rows tension 7, transfer sts for 2 x 1 mock rib and work 60 rows T5··. Return empty needles to WP and work 3 rows tension 7. Cast off and sew down to cover seam, again catching in wadding as you sew. Work other half of welt to match. Join centre back seam neatly. Insert zip between facings.

Gent's chunky knit sweater with cable

SIZE

Finished measurements 96 (101, 106, 112) cms, 38 (40, 42, 44) ins chest.

MATERIALS

Aran on cone from Wollengers, 50% wool 50% acrylic. Each cone is 800 grms. Our size 101 cms (38 ins) took 400 grms (see Yarn Break, issue 9).

TENSION

4 sts and 6¾ rows to 2.5 cm (1 in). Tension dial approx (5). 2 x 1 rib T(3).

NOTE:
Cables worked as follows:-
3 sts each side of 0 and needles 17, 18, 19, 20, 21 and 22 to right and left of centre. Leave one empty needle each side of the six cable needles. Knit 6 rows. Bring empty needles in WP. Knit 2 rows. Drop sts off the empty needles (this gives extra yarn for the cabling). Work the cable 3 needles around from right to left, then 3 from left to right, leave them out to the HP and continue.
Two side cables – cable 8 times altogether.
Centre cable finish as near to 'V' shaping as possible.

BACK (plain – no cabling)

Cast on by hand 78 (82, 86, 90) sts. T(3) knit 30 rows. Work 2 x 1 rib by dropping down 2nd and every foll 3rd stitch and latching up. RC 000. Main tension (5) knit 88 (90, 94, 96) rows.
Shape raglan armholes
RC 000. Cast off 2 sts at beg of next 2 rows (all sizes). Ff dec 1 st at each end of ev 4th row 6 (7, 6, 7) times altog and then each end of ev alt row 18 (18, 21, 21) times altog. Run remaining sts off on waste yarn.

FRONT

Cast on by hand 78 (82, 86, 90) sts. T(3) knit 30 rows. Work rib as for back. RC 000. Main tension (5) knit 2 rows and then start cable as notes. Keeping cables correct knit to row 88 (90, 94, 96).

See colour plate on back cover

AT THE SAME TIME

Shape the 'V' neck

Keeping the raglan decreases on row 8 (8, 10, 10) after the beg of the armhole shaping. Ff dec 1 st at the neck edge every 4th row 12 (13, 13, 14) times altog. Continue with raglan decreases until 2 sts remain. Cast off.

Shape raglan armholes

RC 000. Cast off 2 sts at beg of next 2 rows (all sizes). Ff dec 1 st at each end of ev 4th row 6 (7, 6, 7) times altog and then each end of ev alt row 18 (18, 21, 21) times altog.

NECKBANDS (knitted in 3 pieces)

(See note at end). Join two front raglan seams.

Two front neckbands knitted the same

Cast on by hand 45 (45, 48, 48) sts. Knit 11 rows T(3). Work 2 x 1 rib by dropping 2nd and 3rd and ev foll 2nd and 3rd sts and latching up to make rib. (You are latching up 2 instead of 1 as on the other ribs because you are putting the rib onto the right side of the garment.) With wrong side of knitting facing you pick up down one front 'V' edge and top of one sleeve. Knit one row T(10). Cast off with latch tool. Knit 2nd front band the same.

Back neckband

Cast on by hand 26 (28, 28, 30) sts. Knit as for front bands.

SLEEVES (two alike)

Cast on by hand 40 (40, 42, 42) sts. T(3) knit 20 rows. Work rib as for back and front. Main tension (5). RC 000. Commence cable on row 3 over centre 6 needles. Inc 1 st at each end of every 9th (8th, 8th, 7th) row 11 (12, 12, 14) times altog. 62 (64, 66, 70) sts. Knit to row 108 (108, 108, 108).

Start raglan shaping

RC 000. Cast off 2 sts at beg of next 2 rows. Ff dec 1 st at each end of every 4th row 6 (7, 6, 7) times altog then dec 1 st each end of ev alt row 18 (18, 21, 21) times altog. Run remaining sts off on waste yarn.

TO MAKE UP

No pressing required. Join the other two raglan seams. Join side and sleeve seams. Neaten neck at centre by overlapping the end and stitching down neatly.

NOTES ON NECKBAND:

When you attach the neck edge to the knitted band leave 2 sts at the 'V' end of the band free without attaching the garment to them. Cast these two sts off when you join the band to the garment and sew them down when you neaten the 'V' at the finish.

HINTS & TIPS

IT'S WORTH A CHECK

A note from Doris Coutts, Isle of Wight, had me checking my ribber clamps. Doris says that she found that the main clamps holding the ribber bed had worked forwards on the table (she thinks it may have taken 2½ years) and they were nearly off the table. One member of Doris's club had had both beds fall off the table and the same thing had happened there, so obviously it is well worth a check from time to time. I do tend to check the small additional clamps but not so much the large ribber clamps. Everybody check.

DROPPED STITCHES

As if I ever have any . . . well if I do they are a nuisance anyway, but on a ribber garment they are even worse and usually it is easier to hold the dropped stitch somehow until the garment is finished and then repair the error after the garment is removed from the machine. A safety pin is the common tool for this operation, but stitches have a habit of getting fast in the pin and then you are in for more trouble. A better tool for the job is an ordinary hair clip. It slides into the stitch and will hold it until you are finished and then it slides off just as easily.

MAKE IT COME TO LIFE

Joan has just knitted a child's jumper with a row of horses round the bottom edge. The horses came to life because she knitted them in white boucle. I remember doing the same with a swan motif and it made all the difference. Ballerinas with a bit of sparkle, frogs with tweedy skins, chicks with fluffy bodies, they all go to make that little extra something that lifts the garment from the routine.

FISHERMAN'S RIB — TROUBLE SHOOTING

Doris Coutts has also written to me with some helpful hints on Fisherman's rib. Doris says: 'Although this is one of the easiest of patterns for the newcomer to the ribber, I know quite a few difficulties can be experienced. Sometimes these can be corrected by switching to a higher tension and, of course, the height of the ribber bed needs to be checked carefully. Even with some of the newer ribbers, whose height is supposed to be constant, I find it advisable to loosen the holder screws, lift the ribber bed up towards the main bed and re-tighten the screws. I do this from time to time, as when you consider that the whole weight of the ribber is dependent on these fittings, it is not surprising if readjustment is needed. If you are having trouble with one or two special needles not forming the loops properly, and a visual check of the needles reveals nothing wrong, you can work a test piece and use this to check on the needles at fault. Using a fine yarn (2 x 2/30s) at T(4) or (5) cast on in full needle rib over as many stitches as you want to check, say 150 each bed, or the whole bed if you wish. Work in the half fisherman's rib setting first on one bed, then on the other — say about 50 rows of each — to give you a good sample. Then take a long piece of contrast yarn and knit off the stitches marked 10, 20 and 30 on both sides of the main bed, letting the yarn run between the beds from needle to needle. Either note the position of the corresponding 10, 20 needle on the ribber bed, usually to the right of the main bed, or you could use a different contrast yarn to mark these needles after a further few rows. Then strip the work off the machine and see where there are faults occurring in the knitting. The marked stitches make it easy to work out which needles are at fault; you can then examine these for bent latches, also for a bent shaft if the butt has been knocked or forced out of alignment. Even though this is hardly discernible on the needle bed, it's enough to cause an error.'

SINGLE MOTIFS

Try a butterfly punchcard single motif in random yarn or a giraffe in shades of brown, and if you do not have random yarn mix several different colours of industrial acrylic — it is just as effective.

A PASSAP TIP

When increasing on the single bed, leave the edge springs on the knitting until you have knitted across the new needles, THEN move the springs out . . . it saves the stitches from dropping.

PIN IT THIS WAY

A tip from our sewing expert, Rose. When you are pinning pieces together, e.g. setting in the sleeve head, place the pins crossways and NOT lengthways. This holds the pieces together much better and is easier to handle as you sew. I've tried it, she is right.

Man's cable T-shirt

A Singer Design
Suitable For All Machines

SIZE

To fit size 96 (101, 106) cms, 38 (40, 42) ins. Garment chest size 98-108 cms (39-43 ins). Length from shoulder 65 (66, 66) cms (26 ins) approx. Sleeve seam 11 (12, 12) cms (4¾ ins) approx.

MATERIALS

Aryll 2 ply.
Main colour 265 (275, 285) grms.
Small quantity contrast colour.

TENSION

34 stitches and 50 rows to 10 cms (4 ins) measured over stocking stitch. Suggested tension 4. Check tension first to ensure accuracy.

Cable pattern (front only)

— 111 111 —
1 2 3 4 5 6 7 8 drop stitches 1 and 8.
Cable 6 as follows:
Twist stitches 2, 3, 4 behind stitches 5, 6, 7.
Knit 6 rows.
Drop stitches 1 and 8. Cable 6.
Knit 6 rows.
Drop stitches 1 and 8. Cable 6.
Knit 18 rows.
30 rows form pattern. Work stitches 1 and 8 into purl stitches after knitting, using latch tool.

BACK

Using main colour cast on 167 (175, 183) stitches in rib. Main tension minus 3, rib 50 rows. Transfer to stocking stitch. Increase to 168 (176, 184) stitches*. RC 0. MT. Work in stocking st. Knit to RC 164.
Shape raglan
RC 0. Cast off 7 (8, 9) stitches beginning of next 2 rows. When RC 4 decrease 2 sts each end, this and following 4th rows to 46 (48, 50) stitches remain. Knit to RC 112 (116, 120). Remove stitches on to waste yarn.

FRONT

Work as for back to *. RC 0. MT. Knit 6 rows.
Set position of cables — drop stitches 4, 21 and 28 each side of centre. Work cables over 6 stitches between dropped stitches, as set in cable pattern. Note*: In order to avoid the rib stitches from dropping small loops of waste yarn at the top of the rib section should be used. When RC 164 shape raglan.
RC 0. Shape as for back. When RC 45 (46, 47) (before decreasing over dropped stitch, purl up using latch tool).
Shape neck
Work on 55 (58, 61) stitches nearest carriage, remaining stitches in holding position, decrease 1 stitch at neck edge every 3rd row, and continue raglan shaping to RC 108 (112, 116).
Decrease 2 stitches, knit 2 rows. Remove on to waste yarn. Join main yarn to remaining stitches and shape other side to match.

SLEEVES

Using contrast colour cast on 105 (109, 113) stitches for rib. Using main colour, main tension minus 3, rib 24 rows. Transfer to stocking stitch increase 1 stitch to 106 (110, 114) stitches RC 0. Increase 1 stitch each end 8th rows to 114 (118, 122) stitches. Knit to RC 36 (40, 40).
Shape raglan
RC 0. Cast off 7 (8, 9) stitches beginning of next 2 rows. Decrease 2 stitches each end RC 4 and following 4th rows to 48 (54, 60) stitches remain. RC 52 (48, 44).
Decrese 1 stitch each end 4th rows to 20 (22, 24) stitches remain. Knit to RC 112 (116, 120). Remove on to waste yarn.

NECKBAND (left)

Salect 63 (67, 71) needles on main machine. Set for double rib (close rib) using contrast colour. Cast on. Re-set for 1x1 rib. Using main colour and main tension minus 3, rib 19 rows. Transfer front bed (ribber) stitches to main machine. Remove on to waste yarn.

NECKBAND (right)

Select 109 (115,122) needles on main machine. Work as for left band, remove on to waste yarn.

TO MAKE UP

Join side, shoulder and sleeve seams. Insert sleeves. Join neckband seam at left shoulder, back stitch and form mitre at centre front.

Cheer up a classic for the gents

TENSION

7 sts and 10 rows to 2.5 cm (1 inch). Main T(7). 2x2 rib T(4).

BACK

Knitted plain.
Cast on 134 (140, 148) sts in 2x2 rib.
Ribbers and double bed machines
K 28 rows 2x2 rib.
Single bed machines
K 56 rows 2x2 mock rib and turn up hem.
Transfer all sts to main bed.
RC 000 MT(7). K 140 (140, 150) rows.
Shape armholes
RC 000.
Cast off 5 sts at beg of next 2 rows.
Cast off 4 sts at beg of next 2 rows.
Cast off 3 sts at beg of next 2 rows.
Cast off 2 sts at beg of next 2 rows.
Dec 1 st at each end of the next and ev foll alt row 3 (3, 5) times altogether.
Continue knitting to row 78 (82, 86).
Shape shoulders
Cast off 7 (9, 8) sts at beg of next 2 rows.
Cast off 7 (7, 8) sts at beg of next 2 rows.
Cast off 7 (7, 8) sts at beg of next 2 rows.
Cast off 7 (7, 7) sts at beg of next 2 rows.
Cast off.

FRONT

Knit as for back until
Shape armholes
RC 000. Starting with the first stitch to the left of centre 0 transfer that stitch and ev foll 6th stitch to its adjacent needle. Leave the empty needle in the NWP. Work to the right and left to the edges of the knitting.

NOTE:
As you decrease bring the empty needles into the WP and use them.
Cast off 5 sts at beg of next 2 rows.
Cast off 4 sts at beg of next 2 rows.
Cast off 3 sts at beg of next 2 rows.
Cast off 2 sts at beg of next 2 rows.
Dec 1 st at each end of the next and ev foll alt row 3 (3, 5) times altogether.
Continue knitting to row 48 (52, 56).
Shape neck
Hold 20 sts in the centre and all sts to the left of these sts.
Work on the right hand set of needles only.
Dec 1 st at the neck edge on every row 12 (13, 14) times continue straight to row 78 (82, 86).
Shape shoulders
Cast off 7 (9, 8) sts at beg of next row. K 1 row.

SIZES

Finished measurements 96 (101, 106) cms, 38 (40, 42) ins chest.

MATERIALS

Argyll Sportsday. 1 340 grm cone 50% wool 50% acrylic.

Cast off 7 (7, 8) sts at beg of next row. K 1 row.
Cast of 7 (7, 8) sts at beg of next row. K 1 row.
Cast off the remaining sts.
Leave centre 20 sts in H/P.
Return left hand set of needles to WP and knit left side to match right side reversing the shaping. Cast off.

SLEEVES (both alike)

Cast on 64 (66, 68) sts for 2x2 rib. Knit rib as for back and front.
RC 000. Main T(7). Transfer sts as for front (make sure that you leave the empty needles in the NWP).

NOTE:
As you increase and decrease count the empty needles as working needles.
Inc 1 st at each end of every 7th row 19 (20, 20) times altogether. 102 (106, 108) sts. Knit to row 160 (160, 170).

Shape sleeve cap
Cast off 6 (6, 5) sts at beg of next 2 rows.
Dec 1 st at each end of the next and ev foll alt row 19 (21, 22) times altog.
Cast off 3 (4, 3) sts at the beginning of the next 8 (6, 6) rows.
Cast off the remaining sts.

NECKBAND

Ribbing attachments and double bed machines.
Cast on for 2x1 rib.
Rib T(4). Knit 24 rows rib.
Transfer all sts to main bed.
MT (7). Knit 3 rows and run off on WY.
Single bed machines
Join one shoulder seam.
With right side of knitting facing you pick up sts evenly round neck edge. K 1 row. MT.
Transfer sts for mock 2x1 rib.
Rib T(4) knit 48 rows.
Bring all needles to WP.

MT. K 3 rows.
Run off on WY.

TO MAKE UP

Ribbing attachments and double bed machines
Block and press according to yarn instructions.
Join shoulder seams.
Pin neckband onto right side of garment and backstitch through the open loops of the last row knitted in main yarn. Remove WY.
Turn edge of band to inside neck and catch loosely down.
Single bed machines
Join second shoulder seam.
Turn neckband down onto right side of knitting pin into place and backstitch through open loops of last row knitted in MY. Remove WY.
Join side and sleeve seams.
Give final press.

HINTS & TIPS

DO IT YOURSELF STITCH HOLDER

Mrs Roland from Ramsgate sent us a very useful stitch holder which she had made from a wire coat hanger and bent into the shape of a safety pin thus:

Mrs Rowland says that she uses it instead of the nylon cord or putting needles into the holding position and thus avoids a fluffy line on her knitting at the neck shaping. The holder is light enough to hang on the work without dragging the knitting while you shape one half.

360 HOLES

Phyllis sent us a tip for a quick row of holes (useful for threading a cord etc.). On the Knitmaster 360, using the lace carriage, take lace card 4 from the basic pack, lock it on row 1 and knit 1 row with the lace carriage and then continue in plain knitting. This will give you a row with a hole every 8th stitch. Other machines can of course do the same sort of thing.

REHANGING STITCHES ON TO THE MACHINE

If you have a long edge to pick up on to the machine, say perhaps for a button band, or you may be picking up and knitting a hem on to the bottom of a garment, here is how to make an easy job of it.
Bring out the required number of needles to the working position, take your carriage across them empty to straighten them up and then pick up your stitches as follows. Put one or two sts. on at each end, then a couple in the middle. Now pick up a couple in the middle of each side and continue, picking up in the middle of each space until all the sts. are on. You will see at a glance that you are picking up evenly and it seems to take much less time than if you start at one end and struggle along the row from end to end . . . usually finishing with some short or some to spare if you are like me.

PILE KNITTING — WHICH IS THE PILE THREAD!

Pile knitting on the Knitmaster ribbing attachments makes a super fabric and is really quite easy to do.
The pile thread is a finer thread used to lock the loops formed so that they do not come undone. The actual loops are formed by the main yarn which is threaded into the main feeder. The pile thread, the finer yarn, is threaded into the pile feeder marked with a 'P' on your ribber arm.
We find the pile feeder easiest to thread if you part the two carriages, thread up into the pile feeder and then push the yarn to the right of the carriages and down between the two beds. Anchor the yarn either to a clamp or tie it round one of your ribber weights and put it well under the ribber on the floor and this will ensure that the thread clears the sinkers on the first row of knitting and engages properly on that first row.
The 'P' carriage is really just a safety measure to ensure that the ribber needles knit correctly on each row. This is the procedure:
Carriage on the left, cam lever set to 'S' for slip, right hand side lever is back and left hand side lever is forward so that the needles on the main bed will pick up a loop on the row from left to right and slip across without knitting as you go from right to left.
All stitches are on the ribber, half pitch and corresponding needles in the WP on the main bed.
Take the 'P' carriage from left to right across the ribber and this will bring the ribber up to 'C' position. Knit across. Both yarns will have knitted on the ribber needles and the main yarn will have gathered a loop on the main bed only.
Carriage is now on the right, take the 'P' carriage across the ribber needles again from left to right and knit across with the carriage. Top bed slips and both yarns knit on the ribber. This locks the loops.
Now take the 'P' carriage across the main bed needles from right to left and back again and this will strip the loops off the main bed.
Start again from the beginning and just keep repeating this sequence, it is quite easy once you get into it. The small piece of metal called the 'P' presser which can be attached to the 'P' carriage is not really essential and we found it easiest to work without it. If you should slip with the 'P' carriage and you need to straighten out your line of needles before you knit across, simply push them all out to HP.
Working with the pattern cards is just the same procedure, but remember to preset your pattern card from right to left before you start to pattern.

YARN FOR THE BABY LOCK

Using a Baby Lock machine for sewing up your knitwear? Try substituting one of the cotton threads with a 2/30s industrial acrylic.

Man's shirt-style sweater

For All Punchcard Machines
A 2 ply Design From Argyll Wools

These instructions are written for punchcard machines. We used a Jones + Brother KH840.

SIZES

To fit 96 (101, 106) cm, 38 (40, 42) ins chest. Length to shoulder 65 (66, 67) cm (26 ins) approx. Sleeve seam 13 cm (5¼ ins).

MATERIALS

Argyll 2 ply cones (50% acrylic/50% nylon). 1 (1:1) x 250g cone in Aran white 338.

3 buttons.
For best results you should use the specified yarn. If you have any difficulty in obtaining this yarn, please write to Argyll Wools Ltd., P.O. Box 15, Priestley Mills, Pudsey, West Yorkshire LS28 9LT.

TENSION

25 stitches and 92 rows to 10 cm (4 ins) measured over double length tuck stitch (tension dial approximately 3).
Tension must be matched exactly before starting the garment.

NOTE:
Purl side of tuck stitch is used as right side.
Punchcard pattern
Punch the following card, if required, before starting to knit.

BACK

Push 128 (134, 143) Ns to WP. Push every 3rd N back to NWP. Using MT and WY, cast on and k a few rows ending with carriage at left. Set RC at 000. Using MT-2 and MY, k 55 rows. Push Ns from NWP to WP and make a hem by placing loops of first row worked in main yarn evenly along the row. Unravel WY when work is completed.
Inc 1 (1, 0) st. 129 (135, 143) sts.
Insert punchcard and lock on first row. Set carriage for patt. Set RC at 000. Using MT, k 1 row. Release card and continue in double length pattern. Continue in tuck st★.
K 341 rows. RC shows 342.
Shape armholes
Cast off 4 sts at beg of next 2 rows. Dec 1 st (3 sts in) at each end of every 4th row until 103 (107, 107) sts rem, then on every foll 6th row until 95 (99, 103) sts rem. K 150 (156, 160) rows. RC shows 554 (564, 572).
Shape shoulders
Cast off 4 sts at beg of next 12 rows and 2 (3, 4) sts at beg of foll 2 rows. Cast off rem 43 (45, 47) sts.

FRONT

Work as for back to ★.
K 323 rows. 18 rows less have been worked to armhole than on back.
Front opening
Note pattern row on card. Using a length of yarn, cast off centre 7 sts. Push 61 (64, 68) Ns at left to H/P and continue on rem sts for first side. K 18 rows. Front matches back to armhole.
Shape armhole
Cast off 4 sts at beg of next row, k 1 row. Dec 1 st (3 sts in) at armhole edge on every 4th row until 48 (50, 50) sts rem, then on every foll 6th row until 44 (46, 48) sts rem. K 81 (87, 91) rows. 69 rows less have been worked to shoulder than on back.
Shape neck
Cast off 3 (4, 5) sts at beg of next row. Dec 1 st (3 sts in) at neck edge on every 3rd row until 26 (27, 28) sts rem. K 23 rows. Front matches back to shoulder.
Shape shoulder
Cast off 4 sts at beg of next and foll 5 alt rows, k 1 row. Cast off rem 2 (3, 4) sts.

With carriage at left, push Ns from H/P to WP by hand. Lock card on number previously noted. Set carriage for pattern and take to right without knitting. Release card and set for double length pattern. Continue in tuck st. K 1 row. Finish to correspond with first side reversing shapings.

SLEEVES

Push 89 (92, 95) Ns to WP. Push every 3rd N back to NWP. Using MT and WY, cast on and k a few rows ending with carriage at left. Set RC at 000. Using MT-2 and main yarn, k 33 rows. Push Ns from NWP to WP and make a hem by placing loops of first row worked in main yarn evenly along the row. Unravel WY when work is completed.
Inc 0 (1, 2) sts. 89 (93, 97) sts.
Insert punchcard and lock on first row. Set carriage for pattern. Set RC at 000. Using MT, k 1 row. Release card and set for double length pattern. Continue in tuck st. K 91 rows. RC shows 92.
Shape top
Cast off 4 sts at beg of next 2 rows. Dec 1 st (3 sts in) at each end of every 6th row until 37 (39, 43) sts rem, then on every foll 4th row until 25 sts rem. Cast off.

BUTTONHOLE BAND

Push 61 (65, 69) Ns to WP. With purl side facing, pick up 61 (65, 69) sts evenly along left edge of front opening and place on to Ns.

Inc 1 st at left edge. 62 (66, 70) sts.
Set RC at 000. Using MT and MY, k 8 rows. Counting from right edge, make buttonholes over 7th, 8th, 9th, 10th; 30th, 31st, 32nd, 33rd; 53rd, 54th, 55th, 56th (7th, 8th, 9th, 10th; 32nd, 33rd, 34th, 35th; 57th, 58th, 59th, 60th; 7th, 8th, 9th, 10th; 34th, 35th, 36th, 37th; 61st, 62nd, 63rd, 64th) sts. K 17 rows. Make buttonholes over same sts as before. K 8 rows. Using WY, k a few rows and release from machine.

BUTTON BAND

Work as for buttonhole band omitting buttonholes and reading right for left.

COLLAR

Using main yarn, cast on 170 (177, 184) sts by hand. Set RC at 000. Using MT, k 99 rows. Using WY, k a few rows and release from machine.

TO MAKE UP

Block each piece by pinning out round edges, cover with a wet cloth and leave until dry. Join shoulder, side and sleeve seams. Set in sleeves. Fold front bands in half to right side and pin in position. Unravelling WY as required, backstitch through open loops of last row worked in main yarn. Lap buttonhole band over button band and sew lower edge into position. Sew cast on edge of collar

into position, fold in half to right side and pin in position. Backstitch as for bands. Neaten open ends of collar. Finish buttonholes. Sew on buttons.

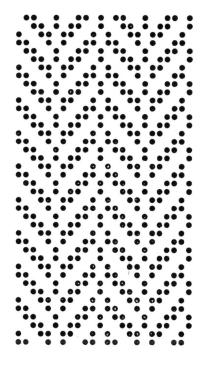

HINTS & TIPS

EASY GRAFTING

A lovely lady called Linda from Cheadle showed this to me and I was supposed to be teaching her how to graft. Linda says she learnt it at her class, but I had not seen it done this way before.
To graft two edges together, run the stitches off on waste yarn as usual, have the two right sides facing each other and the waste yarn tucked down between the two. Graft the stitches together, working from the wrong side of the knitting, take the first stitch and put the needle through it, across to the opposite stitch, then to the next stitch on the same side and then across to the first stitch on the same side and then across to the one you have just left and continue in this way. Pull the stitches together carefully, putting the same tension on as in the knitted stitch so that all stitches are the same size and the join will be invisible.

CASTING ON PROBLEMS

Many a potential garment must have been abandoned because the knitter could not cast on, due either to a tricky stitch type or a difficult yarn, or a combination of both. The secret is to cast on first of all with waste yarn and

get a good few rows of knitting in an easy yarn firmly established on the machine, then change to the tricky yarn or the difficult stitch and you will probably find that your troubles have disappeared. This also applies where weights are essential to the knitting. Lace knitting is a good example, and this method is also very ueful to start off a woven garment.
Even if you have to knit the rib and attach it later, it is no trouble and much better than having knitted a rib, transferred all the stitches to the main bed, started the pattern and whoops! You know the feeling!

TIP FROM EASTBOURNE

Joan asks do I often lose or break my nylon cords (as if I would)? But should that mishap occur a super substitute is a length of lurex thread. Not the fine industrial but the 3-4 ply thickness that you can buy on small cones. It is strong and does not break, it does not tangle easily and it shows up well on the knitting. I tried it (just for practice) and it works.

LACE COLLARS

One of the advantages of visiting the

many conventions and knitting shows around the country is that you are almost sure to gather together at least a couple of useful hints and tips just from watching the other visitors.
At the Battle and Hastings gathering I saw a lady in a lovely lace collar attached to a round neck sweater. The last time I tried this the collar was too tight to get the neck over the wearer's head. The collar I am describing now was split at the back as well as at the front, and so this problem did not arise. My thanks to the lady who was wearing it.

A USEFUL BUTTONHOLE

This is a quick and easy buttonhole for the single bed. It is big enough for a lady's cardigan button and is quite neat. Do remember that on single bed button bands you will always need to work two holes to allow for turning the band over. To work the buttonhole — transfer one stitch to the right and one to the left, leaving two empty needles in the working position. Put one needle to the holding position and leave one in the working position. Set your machine to hold stitches. Knit two rows. Set the machine back to normal knitting and continue.

Mother and daughter snowman sweaters

SIZES

To fit 61 (66, 71, 76, 81, 86, 91, 96) cms, 24 (26, 28, 30, 32, 34, 36, 38) ins chest. 35.5 (41, 43, 44.5, 44.5, 46, 47.5, 49) cms, 14 (16, 17, 17, 17½, 18, 18½, 19) ins sleeve seam (adjustable).

MATERIALS

Lister Lee Thermoknit 4 ply. 1 cone of each col will make 2 sweaters, using different main cols e.g.
Daughter – main: red; contrast 1: white; contrast 2: navy
Mother – main: navy; contrast 1: white; contrast 2: red.

TENSION

15 sts and 21 rows to 5 cms (2 ins) measured over stocking stitch at MT (approx T6) and the same tension over Fair Isle pattern at FT (approx T7).

NOTE:
All welts may be knitted using a ribbing attachment. Use T5/5 and knit half the rows stated with Ns arranged for 2 x 2 true rib.

BACK

Insert card and lock on row 1. With waste yarn cast on 96 (104, 112, 120, 128, 136, 144, 152) sts as 2 x 1 mock rib. K a few rows, carriage on right.
Change to main RT. RC 000. K to RC 20. T10, k 1 row. RT k 20 rows. Make a hem and k the row, setting Ns for Fair Isle.
Fair Isle T RC 000. Release card and set machine for Fair Isle.
* With main col in main feeder and contrast 1 in contrast feeder k 24 rows.
With main col in main feeder and contrast 2 in contrast feeder k 4 rows.
With main col in main feeder and contrast 1 in contrast feeder k 2 rows. *
Repeat these 30 rows * to * to RC 102 (102, 120, 120, 146, 146, 170, 170).
Shape armholes
Continue col sequence, cast off 10 sts at beg next 2 rows. 76 (84, 92, 100, 108, 116, 124, 132) sts.
K to RC 150 (150, 180, 180, 210, 210, 240, 240) (ending last row of 30 row sequence).
**
MT RC 000. Change to main col and stocking stitch.
K 24 (26, 26, 28, 28, 30, 30, 30) rows, carriage on right.
Shape shoulders
Cast off 5 (6, 7, 8, 8, 9, 10, 11) sts at beg next 4 rows.
Cast off 5 (6, 7, 8, 9, 10, 10, 11) sts at beg next 2 rows.
Cast off 4 (5, 6, 7, 9, 10, 11, 11) sts at beg foll 2 rows.
38 (38, 38, 38, 40, 40, 42, 44) sts rem.
Change to waste yarn, k a few rows and remove from machine.

FRONT

K as back to **.
Shape neck: first side
Carriage on right, MT RC 000. Change to main col and stocking stitch. All Ns left of 14th (14th, 14th, 14th, 15th, 15th, 16th, 17th) right into H/P. K on rem sts, dec 1 st at neck edge on every row 6 times. 19 (23, 27, 31, 34, 38, 41, 44) sts rem.
K to RC 30.
Shape shoulder
Carriage on right. Cast off 5 (6, 7, 8, 8, 9, 10, 11) sts at beg next and alt row. K 1 row.
Cast off 5 (6, 7, 8, 9, 10, 10, 11) sts at beg next row. K 1 row.
Cast off rem 4 (5, 6, 7, 9, 10, 11, 11) sts.
Second side
K 26 (26, 26, 26, 28, 28, 30, 32) sts at centre front onto waste yarn and complete to match first side reversing shaping.

SLEEVES

Insert card and lock on row 1. With waste yarn cast on 54 (54, 56, 56, 60, 60, 60, 60) sts as 2 x 1 mock rib. K a few rows, carriage on right.
RT RC 000. Change to main col. K 30 rows. T10, k 1 row. RT k 30 rows. Make a hem and k the row, setting Ns for Fair Isle.
Release card and set machine for Fair Isle. Fair Isle T RC 000. K row sequence as for back from * to *, AT THE SAME TIME inc 1 st at each end 1st and every foll 4th (4th, 4th, 4th, 4th, 4th, 5th, 5th) row, 24 (24, 29, 29, 34, 34, 28, 28) times in all, AT THE SAME TIME changing to MT, stocking stitch and main col at RC 120 (120, 150, 150, 150, 150, 150, 150). 102 (102, 114, 114, 128, 128, 136, 136) sts.
K to RC 126 (148, 158, 164, 164, 168, 174, 180).
Inserting marking threads at each end next row, k a further 10 rows. Cast off loosely.

NECKBAND

Join one shoulder seam.
With waste yarn cast on 100 (104, 104, 108, 112, 116, 120, 124) sts as 2 x 1 mock rib. K a few rows, carriage on right.
RT RC 000. Change to main col. K 10 rows. T10 k 1 row. RT k 10 rows. Make a hem and k the row.
With wrong side of work facing, pick up 38 (38, 38, 38, 40, 40, 42, 44) sts from back of neck, 18 (20, 20, 22, 22, 24, 24, 24) sts from each side of front neck shaping and 26 (26, 26, 26, 28, 28, 30, 32) sts from front neck.
100 (104, 104, 108, 112, 116, 120, 124) sts. T10 k 2 rows and cast off loosely.

TO MAKE UP

Join top edges of sleeves to armhole edges with rows above marking threads joining cast off sts of armhole shapings. Join rem shoulder seam. Join side and sleeve seams. Do not press.

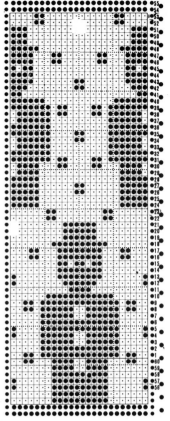

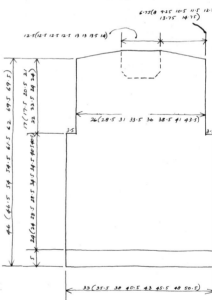

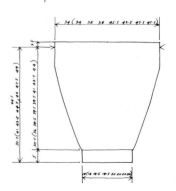

Diagram of finished measurements in centimetres.

94

Chunky knit sweaters

These two lovely knits were supplied by Corona and were designed and knitted on the Corona Jumbo knit. They can be knitted on any chunky knit machine.

CHILD'S ROUND NECK SWEATER

MEASUREMENTS

To fit size 67 (72, 77) cms, 26 (28, 30) ins chest. Body length 42 (45, 48) cms, 16½ (18, 19) ins. Sleeve length 36 (38, 40) cms, 14 (15, 16) ins.

MATERIALS

All sizes one 50 grm. ball each colour of cols. 1-4 Sirdar Sea Pearl and 2 balls 50 grms. Sirdar Country Style DK. Used double for ribs, single on garment stripes.

TENSION

14 sts and 24 rows to 10 cms (4 ins). Tension dial approx (6). Rib tension (1).

BACK

Cast on with waste yarn 48 (52, 56) sts. Knit a few rows ending with the carriage at the left. Knit 1 row with the nylon cord. Carriage on right R.C. 000. Main tension (6) knit in stripes as follows:
11 rows col. 1. 2 rows col. 5. 11 rows col. 2. 2 rows col. 5. 11 rows col. 3. 2 rows col. 5. 11 rows col. 4. 2 rows col. 5. 11 rows col. 1. 2 rows col. 5. 11 rows col. 2. 2 rows col. 5. 11 rows col. 3. 2 rows col. 5 and 5 (11, 17) rows col. 4 until row counter reads 96 (102, 108).
AT THE SAME TIME
Shape armholes
On row 57 (61, 65) carriage on left cast off 4 sts. at the same end as the carriage and knit to the right, cast off 4 sts. on the right side knit to row 92 (98, 104).
Shape shoulders
Carriage on left cast off 4 (4, 5) sts. at the right and knit across to the left.
Knit the left part first
Set carriage to hold. Put into H/P 22 (24, 25) needles on the right leaving 14 (16, 18) needles in WP. on the left. Cast off 4 (4, 5) sts. on the left. Knit to the right. R.C. 94 (100, 106). Cast off 3 sts. at the right (neck

edge) and knit 1 row. Cast off 3 (4, 5) sts. at the left and dec. 1 st. at the right, knit 1 row cast off 3 (4, 4) sts. at the right and break the yarn.
Knit the right part
Turn R.C. to 93 (99, 105). Return to the WP. 10 (12, 13) Ns. at the right leaving 12 needles still in hold at the left. Carriage on left allow the loose end of garment yarn approx. 4 ins. to hang below the feeder and knit across to the right. With the loose end cast off 3 sts. at the left side (neck edge) and at the same row cast off 3 (4, 5) sts. at the right. Knit 1 row to the left. Dec. 1 st. at neck edge and knit 1 row cast off 3 (4, 4) sts. Run remaining sts. off on waste yarn.

FRONT

Cast on 48 (52, 56) sts. and work as for back until R.C. 77 (83, 89) with carriage on left side. 40 (44, 48) sts. remain.
Shape shoulder and neck at same time
Bring 6 sts. in the centre and all sts. to the right of centre 6 sts. in the H/P leaving 17 (19, 21) needles at the right in the WP. Run these stitches off on waste yarn. Bring the 6 centre sts. back to the WP. and run these off on waste yarn.
Knit the left half as follows
Carriage on left knit 1 row to the right R.C. 78 (84, 90). Dec. 1 st. 4 times at right side (neck edge) of next 4 rows. R.C. reads 82 (88, 94) and 13 (15, 17) needles remain. Knit 1 row. Dec. 1 st. at right edge, knit 3 rows. R.C. 86 (92, 98). Dec. 1 st. at right edge, knit 4 rows. R.C. 90 (96, 102). Dec. 1 st. at right edge and knit 3 rows R.C. 93 (99, 105) carriage at left and 10 (12, 14) needles remain. Cast off 4 (4, 5) sts. at left and knit 2 rows. Cast off 3 (4, 5) sts. at left and knit 1 row. Cast off. Turn row counter back to 77 (83, 89) and work right half with carriage at left as follows:- follow instructions for left half of front but reverse the shapings until row 90 (96, 102) then dec. 1 st. at left (neck edge) and knit 2 rows. R.C. 92 (98, 104) and 10 (12, 14) needles remain with carriage on right. Cast off 4 (4, 5) sts. at right and knit 2 rows. Cast off 3 (4, 5) sts. at right and knit 2 rows. Cast off.

RIBS FOR FRONT AND BACK (alike)

Using colour 5 double, tension (1), purl side facing pick up sts. from waste yarn knit 13 rows, drop alternate sts. down and latch up as for rib. Knit 1 row T.(10). Cast off.

NECKBAND

Join one shoulder seam. With right side of knitting facing pick up sts. evenly round neck shaping. Have the carriage on right and knit the first row from left to right BY HAND. Knit 24 rows T.(1) drop down alternate sts. and latch up for rib. Main T. Knit 3 rows run off on waste yarn. Join second shoulder seam.

SLEEVES (two alike)

With purl side facing pick up 42 (44, 46) sts. along armhole edge. R.C. 000. Carriage on right knit the first row from left to right by hand.

NOTE:

For colour changes, proceed as follows:- knit 0 (4, 7) rows col. 2. 0 (2, 2) rows col. 5. 12 (11, 11) rows col. 1. 2 rows col. 5. 11 rows col. 4. 2 rows col. 5. 11 rows col. 3. 2 rows col. 5. 11 rows col. 2. 2 rows col. 5. 11 rows col. 1. 2 rows col. 5. and 7 rows col. 4. R.C. 74 (78, 82).

AT THE SAME TIME

For the shaping:- dec. 1 st. on each side every 13th row 5 times until 32 (34, 36) needles remain and R.C. reads 65 (65, 65). Then knit straight 9 (13, 17) rows. R.C. 74 (78, 82). Dec. 1 st. on each side and with col. 5 double knit 13 rows T.(1). Drop down alt. sts. and latch up for the rib. Knit 1 row T.(10). Cast off.

TO MAKE UP

Sew down neckband by back stitching through the open loops of the last row knitted in the main yarn. The neckband is turned over to the right side of the garment for sewing down. Join neckband seam. Join side and sleeve seams.

LADIES 'V' NECK SWEATER

MEASUREMENTS

To fit bust 33½ (35½, 37½) ins., 85 (90, 95) cms. Body length 24½ (25, 26) ins., 62 (64, 66) cms. Sleeve length 21 (21¼, 21½) ins., 53 (54, 55) cms.

MATERIALS

First and second sizes, 2 balls each of colours 1-4 50 grm. balls Sirdar Sea Pearl. Third size, 3 balls each of colours 1-4 Sirdar Sea Pearl. All sizes, 2 balls Sirdar 50 grms. Country Style DK.

TENSION

14 sts. 24 rows to 10 cms. Tension dial approx. (6).

BACK

Cast on with waste yarn 62 (66, 70) sts. Knit a few rows. Finish with carriage on left. Knit 1 row with nylon cord. Carriage on right R.C. 000. Main T.(6) Garment yarn col. 1 knit 15 rows. Change to Col. 5 and knit 2 rows. Col. 2 knit 15 rows. Continue to knit 2 rows col. 5. 15 rows col. 3. 2 rows col. 5. 15 rows col. 4. 2 rows col. 5. 15 rows col. 1. and 1 (2, 2) rows col. 5 until row counter 84 (85, 85). For bigger two sizes knit further (3, 7) rows col. 2 until R.C. reads (88, 92).

Shape armholes

With carriage on right cast off 5 (5, 5) sts. at the same end as carriage with col. 5 (2, 2). Knit 1 row with col. 5 (2, 2) across to left. R.C. 85 (89, 93) cast off 5 (5, 5) sts. on left side. Knit 15 (11, 7) rows with col. 2 until R.C. 100 (100, 100). Continue to knit 2 rows col. 5. 15 rows col. 3. 2 rows col. 5 and 12 (16, 20) rows col. 4 until R.C. 131 (135, 139) with carriage on left.

Shape shoulders

With col. 4 cast off 4 sts. at the beg. of the next 2 rows and then 3 (4, 4) sts. at the beg. of the next 2 rows. 38 (40, 44) sts. remain R.C. 135 (139, 143) with carriage on left.

AT THE SAME TIME

Shape shoulder and neck

Knit left part first

Put into H/P 25 (26, 28) Ns. on the right, leaving in the WP. 13 (14, 16) Ns. on the left. With carriage on left cast off 3 (4, 4) sts. on the left and knit 1 row. Cast off 2 sts. at the right (neck edge). Knit 1 row. Cast off 3 (3, 4) sts. at left side at the same time dec. 1 st. at right side, knit 1 row. R.C. 138 (142, 146) and 4 (4, 5) sts. remain. Dec. 1 st. at right side and knit 1 row. R.C. 139 (143, 147) cast off 3 (3, 4) sts. Break yarn.

Knit right part

Turn R.C. back to 135 (139, 143) and with carriage on left push back 13 (14, 16) Ns. on right opposite the carriage leaving in H/P 12 Ns. on the left side. Begin to knit from the left. Allow the loose end of the garment yarn to hang about 4 ins. below the feeder and knit across 13 (14, 16) Ns. to the right. With the loose end of yarn cast off 2 sts. at the left side (neck edge). At the same row cast off 3 (4, 4) sts. at right. Knit 1 row. Dec. 1 st. at neck edge and knit 1 row to right. Cast off 3 (3, 4) sts. at the right and at the same time dec. 1 st. on the left. Knit 1 row across to left. R.C. 139 (143, 147). Cast off.

FRONT

Cast on 62 (66, 70) sts. and work as back until R.C. 84 (88, 92) carriage on right.

Shape armholes and front neck

Cast off 5 sts. on the right side. Knit to the left with col. 5 (2, 2) R.C. 85 (89, 93). Cast off 5 sts. on the left side. 52 (56, 60) Ns. remain. Divide in the centre for neck and knit left half first. Bring into H/P 22 (28, 30) Ns. on the left side. With waste yarn run off the other 26 (28, 30) Ns. on the right. Reset R.C. to 85 carriage on left.
NOTE: for 54 rows until R.C. reads 139 (143, 147) you should change colour as follows. Knit 15 (11, 7) rows col. 2 until R.C. 100. 2 rows col. 5. 15 rows col. 3 R.C. 117. 2 rows col. 5 and 20 (24, 28) rows col. 4 until R.C. 139 (143, 147). Knit 5 rows across 26 (28, 30) Ns. R.C. 90 (94, 98) carriage on right. Dec. 1 st. at right (neck edge) knit 5 rows over 25 (27, 29) needles until R.C. 95 (99, 103). Dec. 1 st at right and knit 5 rows. R.C. 100 (104, 108). Dec. 1 st. at right and knit 5 rows. Dec. 1 st. at right and knit 5 rows. Dec. 1 st. at right and knit 5 rows. Dec. 1 st. at the right and knit 5 rows. Dec 1 st. at the right and knit 5

rows. Dec. 1 st. at right and knit 1 row. R.C. 131 (135, 139) carriage on left.

Shape shoulder and neck

Left half

Cast off 4 sts. at left side knit 2 rows. Cast off 3 (3, 4) sts. at left knit 2 rows. Cast off 3 (3, 4) sts. at left and at the same time dec. 1 st. at right. Knit 2 rows. Cast off 3 (3, 4) sts. at left knit 2 rows across. Cast off remaining sts.

Right half

Replace sts. from waste yarn onto machine. R.C. reset to 84 (89, 93). Begin with carriage on left. Work same as left half but shape neck on left side by dec. 1 st. at left (neck edge) every 5th row, until 17 (19, 21) sts. remain. Carriage on right. Proceed as follows.

Knit 2 rows cast off 4 sts. at right knit 2 rows. Cast off 3 (3, 4) sts. at right. Knit 1 row. Dec. 1 st. at left, knit 1 row. Cast off 3 (3, 4) knit 2 rows. Cast off 3 (3, 4) sts. at right knit 1 row. Cast off remaining sts.

RIBS FOR BACK AND FRONT

Using col. 5 double and T.(1) pick up with purl side facing, the stitches from the bottom of the garment piece (back and front both alike). Knit 17 rows. Drop down alternate sts. and latch up for rib. Knit 1 row T.(10). Cast off.

NECKBAND (knitted in two pieces)

Join one shoulder seam. With purl side facing you pick up sts. evenly along one neck edge, and back neck. Carriage on right knit the first row from left to right by hand, with col. 5 double. T.(1) knit 13 rows, drop down alternate sts. and latch up for rib. Knit 1 row T.(10) cast off. Knit second side of neck edge to match. Join second shoulder seam.

SLEEVES (two alike)

With purl side facing you pick up 54 sts. from armhole edge. Carriage on right. Knit the first row from left to right by hand. R.C. 000.

NOTE for col. changes proceed as follows:-

10 (12, 14) rows col. 2. 2 rows col. 5. 15 rows col. 1. 2 rows col. 5. 15 rows col. 4. 2 rows col. 5. 15 rows col. 3. 2 rows col. 5. 15 rows col. 2. 2 rows col. 5. 15 rows col. 1. 2 rows col. 5 and 15 rows col. 4. R.C. 112 (114, 116).

AT THE SAME TIME

Dec. 1 st. on each side every 12th row 7 times until 40 sts. remain. Then knit 28 (30, 32) rows. Dec. 2 sts. at the right side and 1 st. at the left side with col. 5. T.(1) knit 17 rows, drop down alternate sts. and latch up for rib. Knit 1 row T.(10) cast off.

TO MAKE UP

Sew neckband seam. Mitre centre neck by sewing on the inside. Join side and sleeve seams.

Opposite: **Lady's two piece evening outfit** (see pattern on page 54)

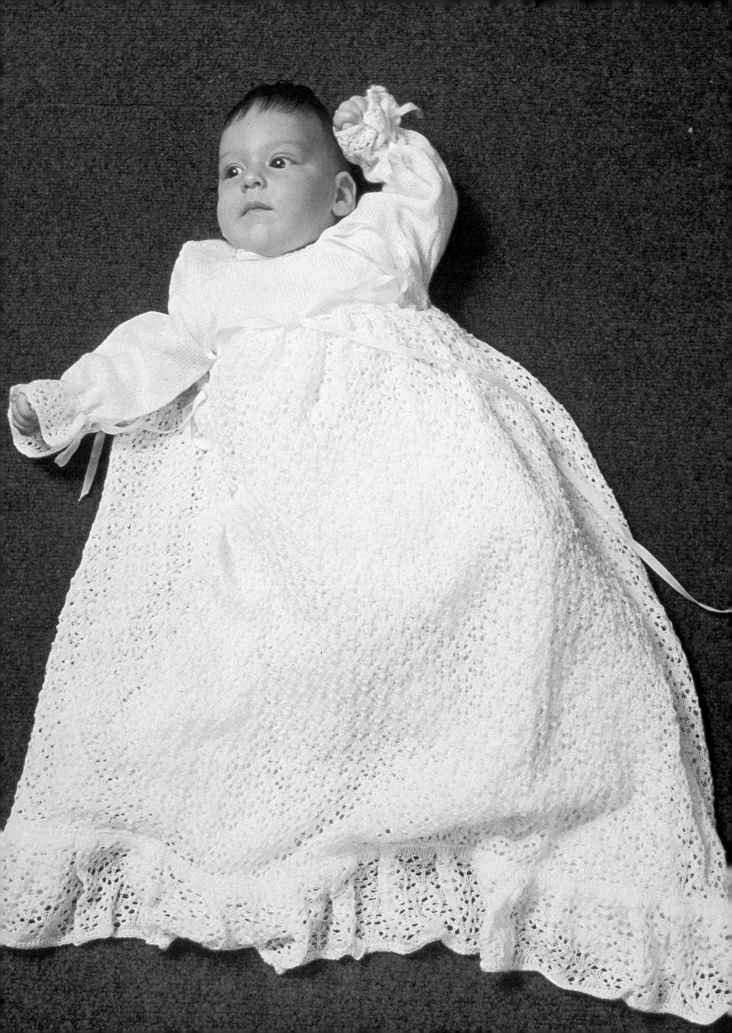

Round neck sweater with saddle shoulder

MEASUREMENTS

61 (71, 76, 91, 101) cms, 24 (28, 36, 38, 40) ins. chest.

TENSION

7 sts 10 rows to 2.5 cm (1 in) over st st. Approx 7 (7..) on tension dial.

MATERIALS

Any 4 ply. Approx. quantities – 140, 180, 280, 310, 340 grs.

The pattern as given was knitted on a Knitmaster with Ribbing Att., but any double bed m/c would be suitable. However, the sweater can just as easily be knitted in st. st. on a single bed machine, using mock-rib. All dec. should be worked on the 3rd st. in. **Please read pattern notes before starting to knit.**

BACK

Set the machine for K1 P1 rib, MT-4. Cast on 92 (106) 134 (140) 148 sts. and knit 24 rows. Transfer sts. to main bed. MT. RC.000. Work in st. st. without shaping 76 (90) 130 (130) 140 rows.

ARMHOLE

RC.000. Cast off at the beg. of the next 2 rows 6 (5) 8 (7) 8 sts. then dec. 1st at each end of every 4th row 9 (11) 14 (15) 16 times alto. work without shaping until RC. reads 42 (50) 64 (68) 70. Now dec. 1st at each end of every row 17 (21) 26 (28) 29 times. Cast off rem. 28 (32) 38 (40) 44 sts.

FRONT

Set the machine for K1 P1 rib, MT-4. Cast on 92 (106) 134 (140) 148 sts. and knit 24 rows. Arrange needles for pattern (see note no.1) MT on main bed MT-1 on front bed. RC.000 Following racking pattern knit 76 (90) 130 (130) 140 rows.

ARMHOLE

RC.000. Cast off 6 (5) 8 (7) 8 sts. at the beg. of the next two rows then dec. 1st. at each end of every 4th row until RC. reads 34 (38) 50 (54) 56

NECK

(See note no.3.) Cast off at centre 20 (20) 24 (26) 30 sts. Put sts. at L into HP. Continue to dec. 1st at the shoulder edge until a total of 9 (11) 14 (15) 16 sts. have been dec. **At the same time** dec. 1st at the neck edge of the next and every alt. row 4 (6) 7 (7) 7 times alto. K1 row. RC. reads 42 (50) 64 (68) 70. Cast off rem. 17 (21) 26 (28) 29 sts.

SLEEVES

Both alike. Knit in contrast col. if preferred. Set M/C for K1 P1 rib – MT-4. Cast on 46 (54) 64 (66) 68 sts. and knit 24 rows. Transfer sts. to main bed. MT. RC.000 Continue in st. st. Inc. 1st at each end of the next and every following 8 (8) 7 (7) 7th row 11 (12) 19 (20) 21 times alto. Knit without further shaping until RC. reads 90 (110) 160 (160) 160. (68 (78) 102 (106) 110 sts.)

ARMHOLE

RC.000. Cast off at the beg. of the next 2 rows 6 (5) 8 (7) 8 sts. then dec. 1st at each end of every alt. row 20 (24) 31 (33) 34 times alto. RC. reads 42 (50) 64 (68) 70. Knit without shaping 24 (30) 38 (40) 42 rows. Cast of rem. 16 (20) 24 (26) 26 sts.

NECKBAND

Set machine for K1 P1 rib, MT-4. Cast on 80 (96) 116 (124) 132 sts. and knit 30 (40) 50 (50) 50 rows. Transfer to main bed. Change to MT and knit 1 row. Break off yarn, and rejoin with waste yarn, (preferably in contrast col.) knit approx 5 rows and remove from machine.

SEWING UP

Join shoulder seams by backstitching as near to edge as possible matching shaping on bend of shoulder.*
* Then join underarm seams and side seams.
Neckband: Join seam, then pin into position round neck on the outside of work and backstitch through the one row of st. st. ** remove waste wool. Turn in cast-on edge of neck band and slip st. to inside.
** This operation is easier if the waste wool is lightly pressed before pinning on to neck.

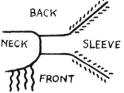

ABBREVIATIONS

MT	main tens.	RC.	row counter
sts.	stitches	st.st.	stocking
beg.	beginning		stitch
CB	Cam box	HP	Holding pos.
dec.	decrease	alt.	alternate
rem.	remaining	alto.	altogether
WP	working pos.	RH.	Right hand
LH.	Left hand	cont.	continue.

Opposite: **Christening gown** (see pattern on page 118)

PATTERN NOTES

With H/P lever still on the P (pitch) posn. set needles for pattern as follows:

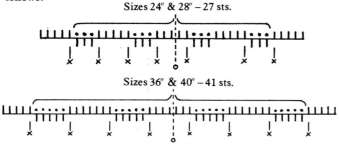

Sizes 24″ & 28″ – 27 sts.

Sizes 36″ & 40″ – 41 sts.

(All ndls. either side of panel should be on the main bed.) Bring ndls. marked x into WP, pick up a loop from below an adjacent st. and hang it on the empty ndl. Now turn your H/P lever to H (half pitch). Your setting will now look like this.

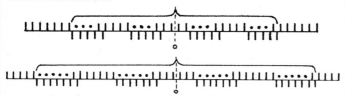

Work pattern as follows:
Knit 2 rows then rack 1 posn. to the L.
Knit 2 rows then rack 1 posn. to the R.
Repeat.

Weights must be retained throughout while knitting FRONT
Ribber should be in closest position possible.
Add side weights if necessary.
Knit steadily – end sts. may not knit properly if movement is too fast.
If the weights reach the floor – possible when knitting larger sizes – roll up comb and rehang weights.

NECK SHAPING

After the centre sts. have been cast off, transfer the sts. on front bed to the left of centre onto needles on main bed (make note of racking pos.) before putting these needles into HP. This will enable you to rack while working the RH side of neck. When this has been completed, return these sts. to front bed, check racking posn. and complete LH side to match.

The numbers given for casting off and decreasing at neck refer to spaces covered on main bed. The extra sts. (those marked x in diag.) must be 'lost' by transferring to adjacent needles as shaping proceeds.

Alternative pattern panels for single bed m/cs.

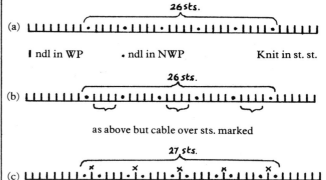

(a)

26 sts.

❙ ndl in WP   • ndl in NWP   Knit in st. st.

(b)

26 sts.

as above but cable over sts. marked

(c)

27 sts.

❙ ndl in WP   • ndl in NWP put ndl marked x into HP
knit 3 rows.
put ndl marked x into Ret pos. knit 1 row.
repeat

If knitting the garment for a boy or man use a plain rib setting or (a) or (b) above.

HINTS & TIPS

FAIR ISLE KNITTING WITHOUT A PUNCHCARD

In our article entitled Safety Knits there is a pattern for a scarf with writing on it. The card is designed for the electronic machines, but any machine capable of Fair Isle could knit the lettering by using hand selection. On the Knitmaster punchcard machines the yarn is threaded in as for normal Fair Isle, the carriage is set for Fair Isle with the side levers forwards (towards you). All the needles that you want to knit in the second colour are brought to the holding position on each row and the front or Russell levers are on 11 so that they knit back each time. The needles you have brought out into the holding position will knit in the second colour. So you see you can select anything you wish without the restrictions of the punchcard.
For Jones & Brother punchard machines thread up for Fair Isle in the usual way and press the MC button. Bring the needles you want to knit in the second colour out to the holding position and have the holding lever on N so that they knit back each time.
For the Toyota 901 set the colour button and thread up as for normal Fair

Isle and select the needles as already described.
As for your letters, design them first of all on graph or squared paper then they will be easy to follow and REMEMBER to have the letters and the words back to front so that they come out the right way when they are knitted. An easy way to check the pattern before you start to knit is to hold it up to the mirror and see if you can read it.
Below the first line of your lettering, number the stitches from the centre 0 out to the left and right, and again number up the side for the rows and then you can keep track as you knit.

WHICH KNITTING MACHINE?

It must be the most popular question from new knitters to the very experienced. New knitters ask which machine shall I buy, and the knitters who have several wonder which one to buy next, or ask: 'If you could only have one, which one would you have?' To anyone who is contemplating buying a knitting machine and feels really at sea, then write to us, enclose a stamped, addressed envelope and we will do our best to help. If you already

have a knitting machine then, providing that it is not damaged or faulty in any way, you have got the best machine because it is yours. It will do everything that the makers say it will do . . . and more. *THIS IS THE TIP.* If you are struggling with your knitting make your mind up here and now that you are going to master it, not change it. The lady sitting next to you at knitting club is not knitting better things than you because she has a better machine, she is getting on faster for some other reason which has nothing to do with the machine. there is plenty of help available for machine knitters. If you can't get it in person you can get it by post. If you can't find it try us, we will do our best to find it for you. The chances are that all you need is a little encouragement, so stop thinking 'which machine' and start thinking 'which pattern'.

WEAVING . . . OR IS IT?

Weaving is great, but it does slow you down considerably. For a change try a Fair Isle pattern used inside out, it looks remarkably like weaving and is much quicker.

Mother and daughter sweaters

Jean Nissan

SIZES

To fit bust 71 (76, 81, 86, 91, 96, 101) cms, 28 (30, 32, 34, 36, 38, 40) ins.

MATERIALS

Argyll Starlite, 1 cone each in main and contrast. (Note: The sweaters illustrated were both made from the original two cones, by reversing the colours. This can probably be done for sizes up to 36″).

TENSION

29 sts 39 rows = 10 cm (4 ins) in stocking stitch, approx T(7).
29 sts 32 rows = 10 cm (4 ins) in Fair Isle, approx T(8).

NOTES

1. When casting off for armholes and shoulder shaping, rather than break off one colour or have a clumsy edge, try casting off at side AWAY from carriage using an odd length of one colour yarn. This method is useful for all fairisle and woven garments.
2. Stripes in bands look nice but the loose edge sts. caused by the ends of wool can look messy in the seams, and personally I get very flustered if I have to cope with lots and lots of ends all over the place. Try these methods. If using ribber, work one row in the new colour, then thread the loose end into a needle, hold it over the first few sts between the needle beds and drop the needle down; the next row you knit will enclose the end. If working in stocking stitch, push the first few needles forward and lay the end of the new wool over and under alternate needles; set the machine to knit them back, they will be woven in and not show on the right side.

BACK

Cast on 109(115,121,129,137,143,151) sts for 1 x 1 rib, having the extra stitch to LEFT of centre. Work T (4), 8 rs. M, 2 rs. C, 4 rs. M, 2 rs. C, 8 rs. M.
Before finishing rib insert card and lock at row 33(23,11,11,11,11,11). Transfer sts to main bed.
If no ribber available work 2 x 1 mock rib, tension (5), first working 24 rows main, then 1 loose row, then stripes as above. Turn up hem.
Release card. Change to fairisle, T (8), RC 000. Work straight to RC 82(92, 104,104,104,104,104).

ARMHOLE

Using odd end of yarn, cast off at side away from carriage on alternate rows at each side, 6 sts once, 3 sts once, then dec 1 st each side alternate rows until there are 79(85,93,101,105,109,115) sts. Work straight to RC 132(144,158,162,166, 170,174).

SHOULDER

Cast off using spare end of wool at side away from carriage. At each side alternate rows cast off 6 sts 3 times (7 sts 3 times) (6 sts twice, 5 sts twice) (6 sts 4 times) (6 sts twice, 7 sts twice) (6 sts twice, 7 sts twice) (7 sts 4 times). Leave remaining 43 (43,49,53,53,57,57) sts on waste yarn.

FRONT

Work as back to RC 80(90,102,102, 102,102,102). Note row showing on card. Take centre st off on to waste wool. Using nylon cord knit sts at side of neck away from carriage by hand pulling needles back to A position. Knit 2 rows. At armhole side shape to match back. **At the same time** dec 1 st at neck edge alternate rows until there are 18(21,22, 24,26,,26,28) sts. Work straight until same length as back to armhole. Work shoulder as back. Reset card and RC and work second side of neck to match.

NECKBAND

Join shoulders. Cast on 159(169,185, 193,195,197,199) sts. T (5). Dec 1 st each side alt rows and work in stripes 3M, 2C, 2M, 2C, 3M for first 2 sizes and 4M, 2C, 2M, 2C, 4M for remaining sizes. Work 1 row tension (8). T (5), work same number of rows as before increasing 1 st each side alt rows. Turn up hem and knit across. Allowing for back neck sts attach neckband as follows. Starting with centre front st on waste yarn pick up front neck sts and hang on to same needles as neckband with right side of front facing machine. Cast off these sts. Now hang on back neck sts and cast off, and then hang sts down other side of front neck, ending into same st, from waste yarn.

SLEEVES

With wrong side facing, pick up sts round armhole. Pick up 85(89,95,99,103, 109,115) sts. Using main colour and stocking st. T (7), work 1 row. On next 2 rows at side away from carriage push 34(34,38,38,40,42,44) needles to HP. Return sts to WP as follows: *First 2 sizes:* 3 sts end of next 6 rows, 2 sts end of next 6 rows, 1 st until there are 7 sts each side in HP, then 3 sts next 2 rs, 4 sts next 2 rs. *All other sizes:* 3 sts end of next 6 rs, 2 sts end of next 4 rs, 1 st end of each row until there are 9 sts each side in HP then 3 sts next 2 rs, 6 sts next 2 rs.

RC 000. Insert card and lock at row 11, all sizes. Work 2 rows. Change to Fairisle T (8), release card and work 22 rows, finish sleeve in st. st. T (7). **At the same time** decrease 1 st each side every 6 rows, all sizes. Work to RC 112(116,144,144, 144,148,148). Transfer sts for rib and work as back welt.

MAKING UP

Join sleeve and side seams. Join centre front of neck band. Brush with teazle brush, using long even strokes of brush.

NOTE

Punchcard is No.409 on page 133 of Jones Punchcard Pattern Vol. III.

ABBREVIATIONS

M	Main Colour
C	Contrast
T	Tension
RC 000	Row counter 0

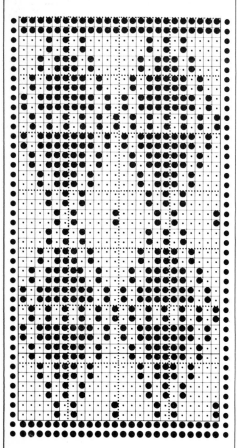

HINTS & TIPS

THE RISE AND FALL

Most standard 'V' neck shapings start at the same time as the beginning of the armhole shaping. The work is divided, half the stitches are put into the holding position and the shaping starts at the neck edge. At the same time we are often shaping the armhole as well.

Shaping always causes a tightening of the stitches, especially fully fashioned shaping, and this can cause the 'V' to drag upwards and becomes even worse when we attach the band.

ATTACHING THE BAND

This is where care is needed. DO NOT dig down too deeply into the 'V' in an attempt to take the band to the very point. You will cause the drag that I mentioned.

IF YOU ARE KNITTING THE BAND FIRST and then attaching the neck edge to the band, proceed as follows: Decide how many stitches you need for the band by holding the neck edge to the machine and then cast on that number of stitches for your band, PLUS 2 or 3 extra at the 'V' end. Knit the band in your usual way and then when you come to attach the garment neck edge to the band, attach it all except the 2 or 3 extra stitches at the 'V' end. Just cast these off as you cast the join of the band and the edge off. When you are completing the garment these are just sewn down at the 'V' and prevent any pulling of the 'V'.

SIMILARLY

If you are knitting the band on to the neck edge, when you pick up the stitches cast on an extra two or three at the 'V' end (by winding them on) and then treat them as I have said in the previous instruction.

CABLING

If you are knitting cables and there is a central cable which is to finish at the 'V', always finish it about six rows before the start of the 'V' neck shaping, or again it will pull the 'V' out of shape.

ANOTHER BAND

If you want a ribbed band but do not want it to pull too tightly, knit as follows:

Let's say we are doing a 2 x 2 rib. Set your carriages so that you are doing two rows knit and then two rows circular. This leaves a bar across the knitting between the ribs and opens the rib up a little. Wool, or a wool mixture or any yarn that can be damp pressed, gives the best results on this type of band. Press the band lightly when you have finished and the rib will not pull in too much.

LET'S TAKE NUMBER ONE

As I mentioned earlier, decreasing does tend to tighten the stitch, and so care must be taken on this part of the shaping. The method we use mostly is the holding position, e.g. if you have a neckband which is to be 22 rows in all (this is a stocking stitch band), you will decrease at the neck edge on alternate rows for 11 decreases and then increase on alternate rows 11 times. To do the decreases simply put the needle into the holding position, so . . . with carriage at the right (for the first band 'V' is at the left) set your carriage to hold and knit to the left, bring the first needle at the left out to the holding position, knit to the right . . . continue in this way for 11 decreases. To increase put the needles back into the knitting position one at a time on alternate rows.

You will find that you need to hang your small claw weight at the 'V' point or hold the knitting down at this point with your hand to ensure that the stitches knit off properly.

NOW FOR METHOD NUMBER TWO

I like this method when I am using a ribbed band. It is quick and easy and very neat, and a discreet examination of most 'V' necks in the shops will tell you that this method is used a great deal in the industrial production of knitwear.

Knit the band straight, it can either be knitted separately or on to the neck edge but make sure once again that you have those extra stitches at the 'V' end. Turn the garment inside out and sew a straight line across the ends of the band at the point of the 'V' and then sew down the two little flaps on the inside of the garment. Check as you sew that you are keeping it straight. A 1 x rib band knitted lengthways and sewn on to the neck shaping looks very smart handled in this way and it is possible to get an excellent fit to the band. Always knit more than you need and then unravel the surplus as you reach the end.

Mother and daughter top

Designed and knitted on Knitmaster 260 & 360 machines with Lace Carriage.

MEASUREMENTS

To fit 76-101 cms/30-40 inch chest/bust; length 56 (66, 67, 68, 69, 70) cms; sleeve seam to wrist 35 (42.5, 42.5, 42.5, 42.5, 42.5) cms.

MATERIALS

1 (1, 1, 2, 2, 2) cones Silverknit Jupiter in col. 1. Yarn available from Silverknit, Dept. K, the Old Mill, Epperstone-By-Pass, Woodborough, Notts. Card 396 from series 63.

TENSION

29 sts and 41 rows to 10 cms (4 ins) measured over lace pattern. Tension dial at approx 3.

NOTE:

Figures in brackets refer to the larger sizes respectively.

BACK

Push 150 (158, 164, 172, 178, 186) Ns. to B pos. ★ Tension Dial at 3. Using waste yarn, cast on and knit 8 rows. Carr. at right. Insert card L-6 and lock on row 6. R.C. 000. Using col. 1, knit 5 rows. Set carr. for plain lace and place edge pins into pos. Knit 1 row. Set carr. for stockinet. Remove card. Knit 5 rows. Turn up a hem. Carr. at left. Insert card 396 and lock on row 1. R.C. 000. Knit 1 row. Release card. Set carr. for plain lace ★. Knit 16 rows. Mark both edges with waste yarn for threading cord. (Also mark centre on Front). Dec. 1 st. at both ends of next and ev. foll. 9th (12th, 12th, 12th, 12th, 12th) row 15 times in all. 120 (128, 134, 142, 148, 156) sts. ★★. Knit 9 (3, 3, 3, 3, 3) rows. R.C. 153 (189, 189, 189, 189, 189). Carr. at right.

Shape armholes

Cast off 7 sts. at beg. of next 2 rows and 2 sts. at beg. of next 6 rows. Dec. 1 st. at both ends of next and ev. foll. alt. row (3 (4, 4, 5, 5, 6) times in all, knit 3 rows. Dec. 1 st. at both ends of next and ev. foll. 4th row 3 times in all. 82 (88, 94, 100, 106, 112) sts. Knit 20 (20, 22, 22, 24, 24) rows. Mark both edges with waste yarn. Knit 5 (7, 9, 11, 13, 15) rows. Inc. 1 st. at both ends of next and ev. foll. 6th row 3 times in all. 88 (94, 100, 106, 112, 118) sts. Knit 1 row. Carr. at right.

Shape shoulders

★★★ Using nylon cord, knit 4 (5, 5, 6, 7, 7) sts. at opposite end to carr. by hand taking Ns. down into A pos., knit 1 row. Using nylon cord knit 1 st. at same side as carr. by hand taking N. down into A pos. ★★★. Rept. from ★★★ to ★★★ once more. (78 (82, 88, 92, 96, 102) Ns. in B pos.).

Shape neck

Note row number showing on patt. panel. Using a length of col. 1, cast off 34 sts. in centre. Using nylon cord, knit 22 (24, 27, 29, 31, 34) sts. at left hand by hand taking Ns. down into A pos.

Knit Right Part as folls.:-

Knit 1 row. ★★★★ Using nylon cord, knit 4 (5, 5, 6, 6, 7) sts. at opposite end to carr. by hand taking Ns. down into A pos. Dec. 1 st. at beg. of next row. Using nylon cord, knit 1 st. at same side as carr. by hand taking N. down into A pos. Knit 1 row. Using nylon cord, knit 4 (4, 5, 6, 6, 7) sts. at opposite end to carr. by hand taking Ns. down into A pos. Dec. 1 st. at beg. of next row. Using nylon cord, knit 1 st. at same side as carr. by hand taking N. down into A pos. Knit 1 row. Using nylon cord, knit 4 (4, 5, 5, 6, 7) sts. at opposite end to carr. by hand taking Ns. down into A pos. Dec. 1 st. at beg. of next row. Using nylon cord, knit 1 st. at same side as carr. by hand taking N. down into A pos., knit 1 row. 4 (5, 6, 6, 7, 7) Ns. in B pos. Set carr. for stockinet. Unravel nylon cord over Ns. at right bringing Ns. back to B pos. Knit 1 row. Cast off ★★★★. With carr. at left, lock card on number previously noted. Take carr. to right. Unravel nylon cord over 22 (24, 27, 29, 31, 34) Ns. at right bringing Ns. back to B pos. Release card. Set carr. for plain lace. Knit left part as for right part from ★★★★ to ★★★★ reading left for right.

FRONT

Foll. instructions for Back to ★★. Knit 7 (1, 1, 1, 1, 1) rows. Carr. at right.

Front opening

Note row number showing on patt. panel. Using nylon cord, knit 60 (64, 67, 71, 74, 78) sts. at left by hand taking Ns. down into A pos. Knit Right Part as folls.:-
Knit 2 rows. Carr. at right.

Shape armhole

Cast off 7 sts. at beg. of next row, knit 1 row. Cast off 2 sts. at beg. of next and ev. foll. alt. row 3 times in all, knit 1 row. Dec. 1 st. at beg. of next and ev. foll. alt. row 3 (4, 4, 5, 5, 6) times in all, knit 3 rows. Dec. 1 st. at beg. of next and ev. foll. 4th row 3 times in all. 41 (44, 47, 50, 53, 56) sts. Knit

14 (16, 20, 22, 24, 24) rows.
4th, 5th & 6th Sizes Only
Mark right edge with waste yarn. Knit (0, 2, 4) rows.
All Sizes
Shape neck
Cast off 10 sts. at beg. of next row, knit 1 row.
3rd Size Only
Mark right edge with waste yarn.
All Sizes
Cast off 2 sts. at beg. of next row, knit 1 row.
2nd Size Only
Mark right edge with waste yarn.
All Sizes
Cast off 2 sts. at beg. of next row, knit 1 row.
1st Size Only
Mark right edge with waste yarn.
All Sizes
Cast off 2 sts. at beg. of next row, knit 1 row. Dec. 1 st. at beg. of next and foll. alt. row. Inc. 1 st. at beg. of next row. Dec. 1 st. at beg. of next and foll. 4th row. Inc. 1 st. at beg. of next and foll. 6th row. 24 (27, 30, 33, 36, 39) sts. Knit 2 rows. Carr. at left.

Shape shoulder
Using nylon cord, knit 4 (5, 5, 6, 7, 7) sts. at opposite end to carr. by hand taking Ns. down into A pos., knit 1 row. Using nylon cord, knit 1 st. at same side as carr. by hand taking N. down into A pos. Knit 1 row. Using nylon cord, knit 4 (5, 5, 6, 6, 7) sts. at opposite end to carr. by hand taking Ns. down into A pos., knit 1 row. Using nylon cord knit 1 st. at same side as carr. by hand taking N. down into A pos. Knit 1 row. Using nylon cord, knit 4 (4, 5, 6, 6, 7) sts. at opposite end to carr. by hand taking Ns. down into A pos. Knit 1 row. Using nylon cord, knit 1 st. at same side as carr. by hand taking N. down into A pos., knit 1 row. Using nylon cord, knit 4 (4, 5, 5, 6, 7) sts. at opposite end to carr. by hand taking

Ns. down into A pos., knit 1 row. Using nylon cord, knit 1 st. at same side as carr. by hand taking N. down into A pos. Knit 1 row. (4 (5, 6, 6, 7, 7) Ns., in B pos.). Set carr. for stockinet. Unravel nylon cord over Ns. at right bringing Ns. back to B pos. Knit 1 row. Cast off. With carr. at left, lock card on number previously noted. Take carr. to right. Unravel nylon cord bringing Ns. back to B pos. Release card. Set carr. for plain lace. Knit 1 row. Knit left part as for right part reading left for right and vice versa.

SLEEVES

Push 82 (88, 88, 94, 94, 100) Ns. to B pos. Foll. instructions for Back from ★ to ★. Knit 8 rows. Mark both edges with waste yarn for threading cord. Inc. 1 st. at both ends of next and ev. foll. 28th (34th, 21st, 21st, 17th, 17th) row 6 (6, 9, 9, 11, 11) times in all. 94 (100, 106, 112, 116, 122) sts. Knit 3 (3, 5, 5, 3, 3) rows. R.C. 153 (183, 183, 183, 183, 183). Carr. at right.
Shape top
Cast off 4 (5, 6, 6, 6, 7) sts. at beg. of next 2 rows and 2 sts. at beg. of next 2 rows. Dec. 1 st. at both ends of next and ev. foll. alt. row 2 (2, 3, 4, 5, 6) times in all, knit 3 rows. Dec. 1 st. at both ends of next and foll. 4th row, knit 7 (6, 6, 5, 5, 4) rows. Dec. 1 st. at both ends of next and ev. foll. 9th (9th, 8th, 7th, 6th, 6th) row 3 times in all, knit 7 (6, 6, 5, 5, 4) rows. Dec. 1 st. at both ends of next and ev. foll. alt. row 3 (4, 4, 5, 5, 5) times in all knit 1 row, mark both edges with waste yarn. Dec. 1 st. at both ends of next and ev. foll. alt. row 2 (3, 4, 5, 6, 7) times in all. Cast off 2 sts. at beg. of next 4 rows, 3 sts. at beg. of next 4 rows and 4 sts. at beg. of next 2 rows. Mark centre with waster yarn. Cast off rem. 30 sts.

NECKBAND (2 pieces)

Join shoulder seams.
First piece
Carr. at left. Push 88 Ns. to B pos. With plain side facing, pick up 88 sts. around one front edge and back neck edge and place onto Ns. ★ Tension Dial at 3. Using main carr. and col. 1, knit 1 row. Change to lace carr. Insert card L-6 and lock on row 3. Knit 4 rows. Set carr. for plain lace and place edge pins into pos. Knit 1 row. Set carr. for stockinet and remove card. Knit 6 rows. Using waste yarn, knit 8 rows and release from machine ★.
Second piece
Push 38 Ns. to B pos. With plain side facing, pick up 38 sts. around one front neck edge and place onto Ns. Foll. instructions for First Piece from ★ to ★.

CORDS

Using main carr. and col. 1, make a cord over 4 Ns. as shown in instructions book for circular cord knitting. Make 1 cord 140 (145, 150, 155, 160, 165) cms long for lower edge, 2 cords 40 cms long for wrists and 2 cords 25 cms long for ties. Fasten off.

TO MAKE UP

Pin out each piece to size and press carefully with a warm iron over a damp cloth. Join side and sleeve seams. Set in sleeves, matching markers and gathering tops. join shoulder seam in neckband. Fold neckband in half to right side and pin into pos. and backstitch through open loops of last row knitted in col. 1. Unravel waste yarn. Insert cords in lower edge and sleeves on marked rows. Using col. 1 work 1 row of crab stitch along front opening. Sew ties to neck edge.

HINTS & TIPS

METHOD NUMBER 3

This is quick and easy and suitable especially for children's sweaters where the 'V' gets a lot of pulling on and off. Once again, make sure that you have those extra stitches at the end so that the 'V' is well covered. The ends of the band are overlapped and sewn down one over the other. Sew on the right side of the garment by sewing neatly over the bar of each stitch.

MITRING THE 'V'

You have three main alternatives when it comes to shaping the mitre at the 'V'.
1. You can decrease and then increase to shape a mitre.

2. You can sew the end to look like a mitre.
3. You can overlap the ends without any mitre.

RIBS. SINGLE BED

To steam a single bed mock rib into shape before sewing up — most knitters are quite well behaved and remember to do this (if you don't, please give it a try it is worth it) — the rib is pulled tight by means of the steamer bar or any flat bar (a ruler will do) and the pressing cloth is put over the top. Have the cloth slightly damp and then let the heat of the iron penetrate but DO NOT PRESS ON. This will set the rib and help it to keep its shape BUT when it comes to round necks you must NOT

pull the rib into a straight line, you will ruin it . . . thread your nylon cord or a piece of yarn through the neckband and gently pull it into a circle and then hold it in this position and steam as for the cuffs etc.

AVOID THE OIL

When you are holding stitches at the left for a neck shaping the yarn tends to fluff up and sometimes you get an oil mark where the brushes are continually passing over the same place. To avoid this mark hang a tension swatch over the sinkers to cover the piece of knitting that is on hold. Alternatively, you can use an old punchcard in the same way. Masking tape or a piece of fine material will also do the trick.

Smart shirt in six sizes

This jazzy shirt was designed for the kids but we liked it so much we decided to write it in larger sizes for us all.

The pattern is a two colour tuck stitch and can be produced on a punchcard, a semi automatic machine, electronic or on manual selection, so we can all have one . . . or two.

For colour changes see notes after pattern instructions.

SIZES

Finshed measurements 76 (81, 87, 92, 97, 102) cms, 30 (32, 34, 36, 38, 40) ins bust.

MATERIALS

2 150 grm. balls Studley 4 ply Acrylic main col., 1 (1, 2, 2, 2, 2) 150 grm. balls 2nd col.

TENSION

15 rows and 6¾ sts per 2.5 cm (1 in) measured over tuck stitch. Tension dial approx (8).

1 x 1 rib S/S 3/3. The 'knit' side is used as the right side throughout.

COLOUR CHANGERS:

Owners of colour changers can use them to knit this pattern. We used a Knitmaster 2 colour changer and knitted with the ribber arm and the ribber up in position. Because the colour changers had to be on the left each time, we started knitting the pattern from the left so that we were changing every 4th row as we should. When we divided for the front neck opening we worked on the left hand set of needles first and then the right which made it easier to use the colour changer. When we cast off at the armhole edge we cast off at the right with the yarn we were using and on the same row we cast off at the left with the yarn in the col. changer. We kept the ribber comb and weights on throughout.

BACK

With main col. cast on 102 (108, 114, 122, 128, 136) sts. for 1 x 1 rib.

Ribbers and double bed machines knit 24 rows rib S/S 3/3. Transfer sts. to main bed. Single bed machines knit 48 rows 1 x 1 mock rib and turn up the hem.
R.C. 000. Start pattern, knit 4 rows main col. 4 rows 2nd col. throughout.
Knit 136 (150, 180, 180, 196, 196) rows straight.★
Shape armholes
R.C. 000. Cast off 13 (13, 14, 15, 16, 17) sts. at beginning of next 2 rows.
Knit straight to row 102 (106, 112, 124, 132, 138).
Stop pattern, knit 2 rows stocking stitch and run off on waste yarn.

FRONT

Knit as for back until ★.
Shape armhole
Put all sts. to left of centre 0 into H/P. (Make a note of the number of pattern row on card).
Work on right hand set of needles only.
Cast off 13 (13, 14, 15, 16, 17) sts. at beg. of next row. Knit straight to row 56 (54, 60, 72, 72, 78).
Shape neck
Cast off 10 sts. at neck edge on next row.
Dec. 1 st. at neck edge on next and ev. foll. alt. row 6 (9, 9, 10, 11, 12) times altog.
Knit straight to row 102 (106, 112, 124, 132, 138).
Stop pattern. Knit 2 rows stocking stitch and run off on waste yarn.
Return the left hand Ns. to WP. Reset card and work left half to match right, reversing all shapings.
Join both shoulder seams
Join shoulder seams either by grafting or by replacing the seams right sides together onto the machine, knit 1 row T.(10) and cast off.

SLEEVES (two alike)

With purl side of knitting facing you pick up 92 (94, 102, 112, 118, 124) sts. from armhole edge. Knit 1 row stocking stitch and then start pattern.
Dec. 1 st. each end of every 8th (10th, 8th, 8th, 8th, 8th) row 21 (20, 22, 26, 28, 30) times altog. Knit straight to row 196 (225, 225, 240, 254, 270).
Ribbers and double bed machines
Transfer stitch to 1 x 1 rib.
Main col. S/S 3/3. Knit 24 rows rib. Knit 1 row T.(10) still in rib.
Transfer all sts. to main bed and cast off.

Single bed machines

Transfer sts. to 1 x 1 mock rib. Knit 48 rows T.(3).
Pick up alt. sts. from first row and put on to empty Ns. K.1 row T.(10). Cast off.

COLLAR

Collar is knitted in main col. in three pieces: the back neck piece and two front pieces.

Two front pieces

With purl side facing you pick up 30 (32, 34, 36, 38, 40) sts. round one side of front neck shaping. T.(8) inc. 1 st. at front neck edge ev. alt. row (inc. at end opposite carr. for a neat increase) 10 times altog. K.1 row T.(10).
T.(8) dec. 1 st. at front neck edge ev. alt. row 10 times altog. Pick up alt. sts. from first row knitted. Knit 1 row (.(10). Cast off.
Knit a second piece the same for the other side.

Back neck piece

Knit as for two fronts but omit the shapings.
Join the collar seams with mattress stitch.

Front opening edge

Knitted in one piece.
With purl side facing pick up the edge of the opening in one piece.
T.(8) knit 8 rows. Pick up alt. sts. from first row knitted on to alt. Ns. K.1 row T.(10). Cast off.

TO MAKE UP

Neaten edges of border and collar.
Join side and sleeve seams. Sew button and loop for fastening and two buttons on collar for decoration.
No pressing is needed.

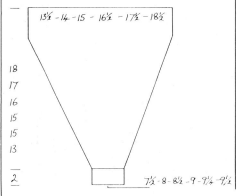

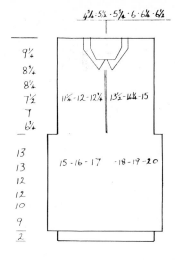

Diagram of finished measurements in inches.

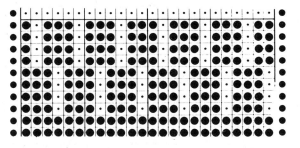

HINTS & TIPS

A PICOT RAGLAN

If you have used the picot trim on a garment, you might like to carry it out also on to the raglan slant.
1. Make single decrease stitch by moving 7th stitch on to 8th stitch and moving all the stitches in take up the empty needle.
2. Make picot transfer on the 4th or 5th stitch from the edge. Move in either direction. Just do the same way each time. Leave the empty needle in work of B position.
3. Repeat step 2 every 2 rows.
4. Repeat step 1 on decrease rows as needed.
Variations. Instead of making picot transfer in only one direction, try transferring to the left one time then transferring next time to the right. Alternate these decreases.
For a very pretty accent, lace contrast colours through the holes made by the picot transfers.

BUTTON BANDS

I have a feeling that we have mentioned this before, but it keeps cropping up. Have you seen a cardigan spoilt because the button and buttonhole bands pull upwards away from the bottom of the garment, spoiling the line?

This mostly occurs when the button band is picked up and knitted sideways on to the garment, or if the band is knitted and then the edge of the garment is hung on to the band. In either case the solution is simple, increase one or two stitches at the bottom end of the band and then when you finish the edge off you will not take away the bottom of the band from the bottom of the garment. You will have enough length for the band to be neatened at the edge and still lie in line with the bottom of the garment.
If the band is knitted first and the garment edge attached to the band, then you can cast on an extra two or three sts. right from the outset and this will do the job just the same. The same technique should be applied to 'V' neckbands to prevent them from dragging at the 'V'.

MY FAVOURITE

So often, little hints and tips that always seem to work are what the men would probably call definitely female and NOT logical, but the lovely thing about them is that they always seem to work and this one from Gwen Lovelock, Kent, is no exception. If you cast on the same number of stitches for the neckband as you cast on for the welt it fits perfectly — try it.

SUPERBA/SINGER ELECTRONIC MACHINES

If you have the transfer carriage and not the garter carriage and you want to transfer all the stitches from one bed to the other, transfer alternate stitches manually and then transfer the rest with the transfer carriage — cuts the work in half.

STILL WITH THE FRENCH ELECTRONIC MACHINES — DRAWING YOUR OWN DESIGNS

If you have a large design to draw, either on the geometric or the decorative sheets, mark the outline with the Letraset and then fill the rest in with a pen. This will give you a good, bold outline but speed up the process for the rest of the drawing.

TIGHT RAGLANS

If you suffer from tight raglans try this tip (another of Joan's little gems that she reminded me of). When you do the raglan decrease do the decrease at the carriage end only. So, if the pattern reads decrease one stitch at each end of every alternate row then you decrease at the beginning (i.e. carriage end) of every row. Hang your little claw weights at the edges and keep moving them up.

Specials for school

It won't be long before we have to think about the children's school uniform again, so here are two versions of school woollies each with a variation to make them extra special.

SIZES

61 (66, 71, 76, 81), 24 (26, 28, 30, 32) ins chest finished measurement.

MATERIALS

1 cone Argyll Superwarm. 340 grm. cone 4 ply. Small amount of contrast for 'V' neck sweater. As a guide size 32 took 200 grms.

TENSION

30 sts. and 42 rows to 10 cms. (4 ins.). Tension dial approx. T.(6..). Main tension. 1 x 1 rib approx. T.(4..).

NOTES:

Raglan shapings on the cardigans are done by using the 7 prong multi-transfer tool set as follows 1...111 Key: 1 = prong in action. . = prong out of action. This makes a fully fashioned decrease as follows. Working from the outside edges stitch 3 is transferred to needle 4 and stitch 2 to needle 3, stitch 1 to needle 2 (this is the usual fully fashioned transfer decrease). At the same time stitch 7 is transferred to needle 8 and the empty needle is left in the WP. This creates the hole which produces an attractive decrease.

If you do not have a multi tool you can still do this decrease with your 3 by 1 transfer tool but you will need to do it in two movements instead of just one.

'V' NECK CARDIGAN

BACK

Cast on 90 (98, 106, 112, 120) sts. 1 x 1 rib. RT. approx. (4..). Ribbers knit 24 rows and transfer all sts. to main bed. Main tension. Single bed machines knit 48 rows and turn up the hem. Main tension. R.C. 000. Knit 66 (72, 76, 80, 102) rows.

Shape armholes

R.C. 000. Cast off 2 sts. at beg. of next 2 rows. Ff. (see notes) Dec. 1 st. at each end of the next and every foll. alt. row 27 (30, 33, 35, 38) times altog. R.C. 56 (62, 68, 72, 78). Cast off rem. 32 (34, 36, 38, 40) sts.

FRONT (right)

Cast on 45 (49, 53, 56, 60) sts. for 1 x 1 rib and knit as for back until shape armhole. R.C. 000. Cast off 2 sts. at the beg. of the next row. Knit 1 row. Ff. (see notes) dec. 1 st. at the beg. of the next and every foll. alt. row 27 (30, 33, 35, 38) times altog. R.C. 56 (62, 68, 72, 78).

AT THE SAME TIME SHAPE THE 'V' NECK

Use the triple transfer tool to give a Ff. dec. Dec. 1 st. at the neck edge every 3rd row 16 (17, 18, 19, 20) times altog. and then continue with the raglan shaping only until all sts. are decreased.

FRONT (left)

Knit as for right front but reverse shapings.

See colour plate on back cover

SLEEVES (two alike)

Cast on 46 (48, 52, 56, 60) sts. for 1 x 1 rib. Knit cuffs as for back and front ribs. R.C. 000. Main tension. Inc. 1 st. at each end of every 6th (6th, 6th, 7th, 8th) row 11 (13, 15, 15, 16) times altog. 68 (74, 82, 86, 92) sts. Knit straight to row 70 (90, 102, 112, 134).

Shape armholes
R.C. 000. Cast off 2 sts. at beg. of next 2 rows. Ff. dec. (see no s) 1 st. each end of alt. rows 27 (30, 33, 35, 38) times altog. R.C. 56 (62, 68, 72, 78). Cast off rem. sts.

BUTTON BAND

Ribbers. Cast on 18 sts. for 1 x 1 rib. Rib tension knit 6 rows and make a buttonhole over the centre 2 needles. Knit 24 rows rib and repeat buttonhole. Make 4 buttonholes altog. Knit band until it is long enough to fit round cardigan when band is slightly stretched.

Single bed machines. Cast on 20 sts. Rib tension knit 6 rows and then make the first buttonhole over needles 5 and 6 counting from each edge (2 holes each time because the band is folded double). Knit 24 rows, repeat buttonhole, make 4 buttonholes altog. Knit band until long enough to fit round the cardigan with band slightly stretched.

TO MAKE UP

Give light press with a warm iron and dry cloth. Join raglan seams, join side and sleeve seams and sew on button band stretching slightly as you sew. Sew on buttons (remember to sew a spare button inside the cardigan for emergencies).

'V' NECK JUMPER

BACK

Ribbers and double bed machines
Cast on 90 (98, 106, 112, 120) sts. Cast on for 2 x 2 rib. The sequence after the cast on rows is 3 rows knit, main col. 2 rows circular contrast col. and then 4 rows knit, main col. 2 rows circular contrast col. until row 27. Transfer all sts. to main bed. Set needles as follows: work from centre 0, first to the right and then to the left and transfer the 6th and every foll. 6th stitch to its opposite needle on the ribber. Ribber is at 'P'. Leave the empty needle in the N.W.P. Ribber set to Fisherman's Rib (1 row knit, 1 row tuck). Top carriage set for stockinet.

Single bed machines
Cast on 90 (98, 106, 112, 120) sts. for mock 2 x 1 rib. Rib tension knit 24 rows main colour then knit 2 rows contrast col. 4 rows main col. for 24 rows and turn up hem.

Transfer stitches for pattern as follows. Working from centre 0 first to the right and then to the left transfer the 6th and every foll. 6th stitch to its adjacent needle,

leaving the empty needles in non working position. R.C. 000 knit 66 (72, 76, 80, 102) rows.

Shape armholes
R.C. 000. Cast off 2 sts. at beg. of next 2 rows. Ff. dec. 1 st. at each end of the next and every foll. alt. row 27 (30, 33, 35, 38) times altog. R.C. 56 (62, 68, 72, 78). Run stitches off on waste yarn. 32 (34, 36, 38, 40) sts.

FRONT

Knit as for back until armhole shaping. R.C. 000. Put all stitches to the left of centre 0 to the H/P. Work on right side only. Cast off 2 sts. at beg of next row, knit 1 row. Ff. dec. 1 st. at beg. of the next and every foll. alt. row 27 (30, 33, 35, 38) times altog. R.C. 56 (62, 68, 72, 78).
AT THE SAME TIME SHAPE THE 'V' NECK
Fully fashioned shapings using the triple transfer tool. Dec. 1 st. at the neck edge every 3rd row 16 (17, 18, 19, 20) times altog. and then continue with raglan shapings only until all sts. decreased. Return left hand needles to WP. and shape to match the right reversing the shapings.

SLEEVES (two alike)

Ribbers and double bed machines
Cast on for 2 x 2 rib (single bed machines 2 x 1 mock rib) 46 (48, 52, 56, 60) sts. Knit as for back and front ribs. Transfer sts. for pattern R.C. 000 MT. Inc. 1 st. at each end of every 6th (6th, 6th, 7th, 8th) row 11 (13, 15, 15, 16) times altog. 68 (74, 82, 86, 92) sts. Knit straight to row 70 (90, 102, 112, 134).

Shape armholes
R.C. 000. Cast off 2 sts. at beg. of next 2 rows. Ff. dec. 1 st. each end of alt. rows 27 (30, 33, 35, 38) times. altog. R.C. 56 (62, 68, 72, 78). Cast off rem. sts.

NECKBAND

Join three raglan seams leaving the back left hand seam open. Band is knitted in 2 parts.
Ribbing attachments and double bed machines
To estimate the number of stitches required, hold the knitting up to the machine and bring out the corresponding needles. First band is along one front neck edge, top of one sleeve and back neck. (Neck and sleeve edges will have stitches on waste yarn so will need no calculating.) Cast on for 2 x 2 rib. Rib tension and using the same pattern sequence as for the ribs and cuffs knit 13 rows. Transfer all sts. to main bed. With wrong side of knitting facing you pick up the neck edge, top of sleeve and back and place onto band. Knit 1 row T.(10). Cast off. Repeat for other half of neck and the other sleeve top.
Single bed machines
Main tension minus (1). Work in two pieces. Join three raglan seams leaving the left back seam open. With wrong side of knitting facing you pick up sts. evenly from front neck edge, top of sleeve and back. Knit 2 rows contrast, 14 rows main
AT THE SAME TIME TO MITRE THE 'V' put one needle into the H/P at the neck edge every row 8 times and then put one needle at the neck edge back to the W.P. every row 8 times. NOTE. When you put the needle out to the H/P remember to wrap the yarn round the needle to prevent a hole. Pick up the first row of the band onto alt. needles. Knit 1 row at T.(10) and cast off.

TO MAKE UP

Give light press with a warm iron and dry cloth. Join fourth raglan seam. Join side and sleeve seams.
Double bed neckband, either mitre the centre by sewing or overlap the ends and sew down neatly. Single bed bands, neaten the inside of the mitre. Give final light press.

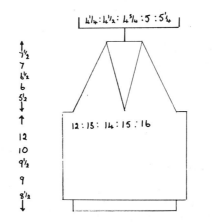

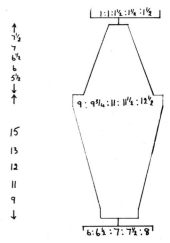

Diagram of finished measurements in inches

Christmas 'quackers'

JUMPER HAT & MITTS SET with Fair Isle ducks and flowers. It's enough to drive you quackers.

SIZES

To fit 61 cms (24 ins) chest.
Jumper: Finished measurements 63 cms (25 ins).
Length 38 cms (15 ins).
Sleeve seam 32 cms (12⅜ ins).
Hat: Round head 53 cms (21 ins).

Mitts: Length 18 cms (7 ins). Round hand about thumb 16.5 cms (6½ ins).

MATERIALS

Acrylic 4 ply. Main colour Black.
The whole set – 250 grms black and approx 20 grms of each of the following 6 colours:—
Red, green, orange, white, blue, yellow.
Jumper only 190 grms black col as above.

TENSION

30 sts and 40 rows to 10 cms (4 ins) measured over stocking st. Try T7 Fair Isle MT plus 2 dots. Rib 4/4.

NOTES:
Punch the card as illustrated. Keep black in main feeder always. Change colours in Fair Isle feeder as follows:—4 rows green, 5 rows red, 4 rows black only. 6 rows orange, 5 rows white, 13 rows blue, 11 rows yellow, 7 rows red.

JUMPER

BACK

Push into WP 98 needles.
Machines with ribbers.
Set for k2 p2 rib. K 24 rows.
Machines without ribbers.
Set for mock k2 p2 rib. K 40 rows and seal hem.
All machines.
K6 rows stocking st. Set for Fair Isle and work completely through the punch card once changing cols as given in patt notes. After the duck is completed, continue in stocking st to RC 70.
Shape armhole
Cast off 4 sts beg next 2 rows.
RC 000. Dec 1 st at beg every row until 26 remain (RC 64). See helpful hints 6. K a few rows WY. Remove from machine.

FRONT

Work as for back until 40th row of rag-shaping (50 sts remain). Push centre 16 to hold. Push to H/P all needles remaining on LHS. Work on RHS needles, dec as before at armhole edge. At neck edge dec 1 at beg of next 10 alt rows. RC 60. Fasten off remaining st. Reset RC to 40.
Work all sts on LHS of centre 16 to correspond.
Using WY k a few rows over centre 16. Remove from machine.

SLEEVES

Left sleeve
Push 54 needles to WP. Arrange to match the body rib. K 30 rows (ribbers) or 44 and seal hem (single beds). All machines RC 000. Working in stocking st only inc 1 st both ends every 7th row until there are 80 sts. K to RC 100 (add extra length here if required). Cast off 4 sts beg next 2 rows. RC 000. Dec raglan as before until 12 sts remain. RC 60. COR.

Right sleeve

*Push 4 sts to H/P at opposite end to carriage. K the row, and place yarn under needle stem to avoid a hole (or do an automatic type 'e' wrap). K back to RHS. Repeat once more the last 2 rows. RC 64. Set machine to k back to WP. K 1 row only. 12 sts remain. Using WY k a few rows and remove from machine. *

Left sleeve. K 1 row. COL. Repeat from * to *.

NECKBAND

Replace front onto machine purl side towards you as follows:— Centre 16 onto 16 needles. Pick up 18 sts at either side of neck curve. (52 sts) replace 12 sts of r sleeve onto RHS of front. Bring to WP 11 empty needles. Replace 11 sts and the 12th st onto the top of the end neck front st.
Replace the sts of l sleeve to correspond on LHS (74 sts).
Replace the 26 sts of the back onto 24 empty needles, by dec 1 in the centre and overlapping the end st on top of the last sleeve st 98 sts. K 1 row stocking st at MT. Arrange for rib as before. Single beds k 26 row dec and increase tension see your instruction book.
Ribbers
K 25 rows k2 p2 rib.
All machines.
Using double eyed transfer tool take all sts onto a long length of black.

TO MAKE UP

Join 4 raglan seams, including edge of neck rib. Put both hands into neck opening. Stretch neck rib as large as possible. Leave in the black yarn through sts. Turn neckband towards inside and catch down slackly. Join side sleeve seams.

HAT

TO KNIT

Push 170 sts to WP, arranging rib to match jumper rib.
Single beds.
K 60 rows. Seal hem.
Ribbers
K 30 rows.
All machines
RC 000. K 6 rows stocking st set for Fair Isle duck beg Fair Isle on 14th row of punchcard. 6 rows orange contrast starts off the colours. Complete duck and knit in stocking st to RC 56. Insert punchcard upside down. K the flower with 5 rows red, 4 rows green Fair Isle. K in stocking st to RC 70. Transfer every alt st to next needle. Checking empty needles are left in NWP. T3 k 4 rows. Again transfer alt sts (every 4th needle now in work). T2 k 1 row. Thread sts on a length of black as for jumper neck.

TO MAKE UP

Turn patt to inside. Join seam. Pull thread to gather the sts at top secure. Make a black pom pom and sew in position. Turn the edge ribs to inside by folding only (not sewing.) It will encase the first few rows of Fair Isle floats.

MITTS

TO KNIT

Push 54 needles to B. Arrange to match jumper rib.
Ribbers
K 18 rows k2 p2 rib.
Single beds
K 36 rows and seal hem.
All machines
RC 000. K 4 rows stocking st set for Fair Isle and k the 9 rows of card only. (Flower). Continue in stocking st to RC 17 (left mitt) or RC 18 (right mitt). Using a contrast odd length of yarn k manually the 9 sts at opp end to carriage. Check needles are in WP. K in stocking st to RC 48 COR. Push all 24 sts at left of "0" to H/P. Work on the RHS 24 sts. Dec 1 st at both ends of next 6 rows. K a few rows WY and remove from machine. Work the remaining 24 sts on LHS of "0" to correspond.
Thumb
Push 18 needles to WP. Unravel coloured yarn. First pick up the 9 sts that are above the Fair Isle. Pick up 9 sts from the rem opening. Check no loops left to "run". Cross the 2 centre sts (as for a cable) to prevent a hole forming. K 20 rows stocking st. Transfer every st to alt needles, Empty needles in NWP. T2 k 1 row. Place sts on a thread.

TO MAKE UP

Gather thumb sts and sew small thumb seam. Graft top sts tog or join by replacing on machine right sides to inside and cast off all tog. Close side seam and small seam at other side of top.

HELPFUL HINTS

1. A black background means less washing! Navy is a good choice for the same reason but does not show up the many contrasts quite so colourfully.

2. A white background works lovely and shows off all the colours well – but its always in the washer! But if you do choose white, knit the 6 underbody rows of the duck in black or navy!

3. The duck is ideal for single motif knitting. It is also a good chance to use up tiny amounts of left over colours. He shows up well in plain white on a red background.

4. This design is not suitable for a single bed colour changer, there are uneven numbers of colour rows. It helps to speed up the work when changing colours by hand, to cut the colour just completed about 6 in above the cambox. Thread up the next contrast, knot it to the used one, pull the knot through, and hold firmly down right under the machine for a couple of rows. Let go.

5. If your machine will not knit Fair Isle, it is still possible to achieve a colourful effect by knitting a variety of bright stripes across the yoke for the whole of the raglan shaping. Check they will match when sewn up, do not do more than 6 rows of each colour at a time, and the black neckband will provide a good finishing touch. Stripe the hat to match.

6. If you do fully fashioned rag decreasings or use a multiple T tool, it helps to knit the 1 extra row which always comes at the top of the left sleeve (and possibly disturbs the shaping dec just where it will show) across straight after the armhole cast off. Reset to 000 and work with COL. This helps on all raglan garments.

7. Try to find a make of yarn with a good range of bright colours. If you have one or more balls of a different make check they are compatible for washing as well as for yarn content. Sirdar, Phildar and Patons all make a large colour range in 4 ply.

M. Loraine

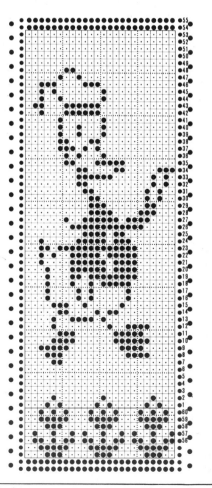

Teenage jumper — nice 'n' easy

To suit most makes and models of double bed machines with 5 mm needle gauge.

SIZES

To fit chest size 91-97 cms (36-38 ins). finished back length 60 cms (23½ ins). Sleeve seam 41 cms (16 ins).

MATERIALS

Lister Lee Tropicana: 16 x 25g balls.

TENSION·

18 sts and 23 rows to 10 cms (4 ins) measured over stocking st (approx T10).

NOTE

Garment is knitted on alternate needles.

BACK

*Cast on 90 sts for 1 + 1 rib. RT. RC 000. Knit 21 rows. Transfer all sts onto main bed.
Knit a few rows in waste yarn. Remove from machine.
Bring 180 Ns into WP on main bed. Move alt no. into NWP.
Place rib onto Ns in WP on main bed. MT. RC 000.
Knit 71 rows straight. **Note: Adjust length here.
Dec 5 sts at beg of next 2 rows.
Dec 2 sts at beg next 4 rows.
Cast off rem sts.

FRONT

Knit as back from * to **.
Dec 5 sts at beg next 2 rows.

RC: 73.
***Divide for neck; Place all Ns from 0 to the opposite side to the carriage into H/P. Work on Ns from 0 to the same side as the carriage only.
Dec 2 sts at armhole edge at beg next row.
Dec 1 st at neck edge on next and every foll alt row 17 times in all.
Knit 3 rows.
Dec 1 st at neck edge at beg of next row.
Knit 3 rows.
Dec 17 sts at armhole edge at beg next row.
Knit 1 row. Cast off rem sts.
Knit other side the same from *** reversing all shapings.

SLEEVES

Knit 2 the same.
Cast on 46 sts in 1 + 1 rib. RC 000. RT.
Knit 21 rows. Transfer all sts onto main bed.
Knit a few rows in WY. Remove from machine.
Bring 92 needles into WP on main bed. Move alt Ns into NWP. Place rib onto Ns in WP on main bed. RC 000 MT. Knit 5 rows straight.
Inc 1 st at beg of next 2 rows. Knit 6 rows.
Repeat from * to * once more.
Inc 1 st at beg of next 2 rows. Knit 4 rows.
Repeat from ** to ** 7 more times.
Inc 1 st at beg of next 2 rows.
Note: Adjust Length Here.
Dec 4 sts at beg of next 2 rows.
Dec 2 sts at beg of next and foll row 10 times altogether.
Dec 1 st at beg of next and every following row 20 times.
Dec 3 sts at beg of next 2 rows.
Cast off rem sts.

NECK BAND

Cast on 110 sts in 1 + 1 rib.
RC 000 RT. Knit 8 rows.
Knit a few rows in waste yarn and remove from machine.

TO MAKE UP

Pin out pieces to size and press according to ball band. (Excluding ribs). Sew up shoulder and side seams using a back stitch. Sew sleeve seams. Set in sleeves. Place neckband around neck edge, sew onto right side around neck edge with a back stitch unravelling waste yarn. Mitre V at centre front.

A sweater for beginners

15) Main tension, knit 114 (114, 138) rows to the armhole. RC 000.
16) Cast off loosely 10 (10, 10) sts at the beg of the next 2 rows.
17) Insert punchcard no.1 and lock on row 1.
18) *Knit master machines* knit 4 (6, 8) rows. *Other machines* knit 3 (5, 7) rows. Set the machine to bring the needles to patterning position. K 1 row.
19) *All* machines. Release the card and set for Fair Isle.
20) With main yarn in feeder 1 and 1st contrast in feeder 2 knit 10 rows.
21) Break off 1st contrast.
22) K 2 rows main yarn only.
23) With main yarn in feeder 1 and 2nd contrast in feeder 2 knit 28 rows.
24) Break off 2nd contrast.
25) K 2 rows main yarn only.
26) With main yarn in feeder 1 and 1st contrast in feeder 2 knit 10 rows.
27) Break off 1st contrast.
28) Lock *or* remove the card from the machine.
29) Return the machine to stocking st setting. RC 58 (60, 62).
30) K 21 (21, 23) rows. RC 79 (81, 85). Carr at left.

Shape the shoulders with the automatic wrap as follows:
31)) Set the machine to hold pos.
32) Bring 5 (6, 7) needles at the opposite side to the carriage to hold pos.
33) Knit across to the right.
34) Bring the 1st needle nearest the carriage to hold pos 6 (7, 8) sts in hold pos at the right.
35) Bring 5 (6, 7) needles at the opposite side of the carriage to hold pos.
36) Knit across to the left.
37) Bring the 1st needle nearest the carriage to hold pos 6 (7, 8) sts in hold pos at the left.
38) Repeat steps 32-37 two more times.
39) Bring 6 (7, 7) needles at the opposite side to the carriage to hold pos at the right.
40) Knit across to the right.
41) Bring the 1st st nearest the carriage to hold pos.
42) Bring 6 (7, 7) needles at the opposite side to the carriage to hold pos at the left.
43) Knit across to the left.
44) Bring the 1st needle nearest the carriage to hold pos.
45) K 1 row. Carriage at the right.
46) Break off the main yarn.
47) With waste yarn, k 8 rows on the 36 sts remaining in WP.
48) Break off the waste yarn.

SIZES

To fit 71 (76,81) cms, 28 (30, 32) ins bust. Sleeve length 43 (44.5, 44.5) cms, 17 (17½, 17½ ins).

MATERIALS

Agryll Starlite.
1 cone of white – main colour Nimbus.
Oddments of pale pink 1st contrast Aries.
Oddments of lavender 2nd contrast Jupiter.

TENSION

28 sts and 40 rows to 10 cms (4 ins). Main tension (approx T7).

BACK

1) Bring to WP 106 (114, 120) needles.
2) Position the needles for 2 x 1 rib.
3) Cast on with waste yarn.
4) Knit about 8 rows ending with the carriage at the right. RC 000.
5) Break off the waste yarn.
6) Thread the main yarn in feeder 1.
7) T4 knit 22 rows.
8) T7 knit 1 row.
9) T4 knit 22 rows. Carr at the left.
10) Bring the empty needles to WP.
11) Pick up the sts for the hem.
12) Bring all the needles to hold pos.
13) Set the machine to knit the sts back to B pos.
14) T10 knit 1 row. RC 000.

49) With both feeders empty take the carriage across the knitting twice. The sts on waste yarn will fall off the needles.
50) Put the empty 36 needles back to A pos.
51) Take the 25 (29, 32) needles nearest the carriage back until the sts are just behind the open needle latches.
52) With the main yarn k 1 row. Break off main yarn.
53) With waste yarn k 8 rows.
54) With both feeders empty remove the sts as before and return the needles to A pos.
55) Repeat from 51 once on the remaining sts.

FRONT

1) Work as the back from steps 1-29.
2) K 2 (2, 2) rows. Carriage at the right.

Shape the neck as follows:

31) Set the machine to hold.
32) Bring 10 needles at the right of 0 and all the needles at the left to hold pos.
33) Work only on the sts on the right.
34) Bring 1 st at the neck edge to hold pos every row for the next 8 rows.
35) K 13 (13, 15) rows on the remaining sts. Carriage at the left.
36) Bring 5 (6, 7) needles at the opposite side of the carriage to hold pos.
37) Knit 1 row.
38) Bring the 1st needle nearest the carriage to hold pos 6 (7, 8) sts in hold pos.
39) K 1 row. Repeat steps 36-39 two more times.
40) Bring 6 (7, 7) needles at the opposite side of the carriage to hold pos.
41) Knit 1 row.
42) Bring the 1st needle nearest the carriage to hold pos.
43) Knit 1 row. Carriage at the left.
44) Take the needles back until the sts are just behind the latches.
45) Knit 1 row. Break off main yarn.
46) With waste yarn k 8 rows.
47) Release the sts in waste yarn from the machine. Carriage at the right.
48) Take the needles 11-43 (47, 50) at the left back until the sts are just behind the open latches.
49) Knit 1 row.
50) Bring the 1st st nearest the neck edge to hold pos, every row for 8 rows.
51) Knit 7 (7, 9) rows. Carriage at the right.
52) Bring 5 (6, 7) needles at the opposite side to the carriage to hold pos.
53) K 1 row to the left.
54) Bring the 1st needle nearest the carriage to hold pos 6 (7, 8) sts in hold pos.
55) K 1 row. Repeat steps 52-55 two times more.
56) Bring 6 (7, 7) needles at the opposite side of the carriage to hold pos.
57) K 1 row.
58) Bring the 1st needle nearest the carriage to hold pos.
59) K 1 row. Repeat steps 44-47 once.
60) Bring 12 (12, 14) needles at each side of the sts still in hold pos to B pos.

61) Hook the straight side of the neck sts onto the empty needles.
62) Bring the needles to hold pos.
63) Set the machine to knit the sts back.
64) With main yarn k 1 row.
65) Break off main yarn.
66) With waste yarn k 8 rows.
67) Release from the machine.

SLEEVES (2)

1) Carriage at the right RC 000.
2) With main yarn, cast on by hand *or* with the weaving method 122 (122, 126) sts.
3) Knit 74 (76, 80) rows in stocking st.
4) Break off the main yarn.
5) With the 2nd contrast yarn k 2 rows.
6) Break off the contrast yarn.
7) Insert punchcard 2 and lock on row 1.
8) Thread up with main yarn.
9) *Knitmaster Machines*. Knit 6 rows. *Other machines*. Knit 5 rows. Set the machine to bring the needles to patterning position. K 1 row.
10) *All Machines*. Unlock the card. Set the machine for Fair Isle.
11) Thread feeder 2 with the 1st contrast yarn.
12) K 7 rows Fair Isle.
13) Place markers at each end.
14) K 6 rows Fair Isle.
15) Break off the contrast yarn.
16) Return the machine to stocking st setting.
17) Lock the card *or* remove from the machine.
18) Knit 6 rows stocking st.
19) Break off the main yarn.
20) With the 2nd contrast yarn knit 2 rows.
21) Break off the contrast yarn.
22) With the main yarn knit 73 (75, 79) rows.
23) Cast off loosely.
24) Form a pleat at each end by folding the knitting over the hearts, the stripes meeting at the markers.
25) Bring 52 (52, 56) neeedles to B pos. Carriage at the left.
26) Hook the bottom edge of the sleeve onto the needles gathering the sleeve by putting 2 sts on needles where necessary.
27) Bring all the needles to hold pos.
28) Set the machine to knit the sts back.

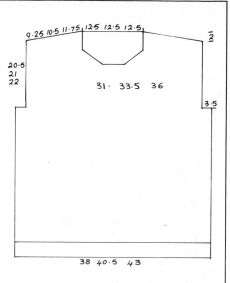

Diagram of finished measurements

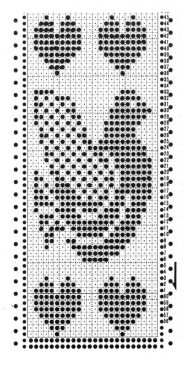

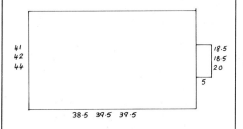

Diagram of finished measurements in centimetres.

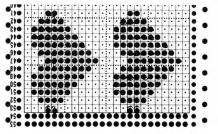

29) T10 Knit 1 row. Carriage at the right. RC 000.
30) Transfer every third st onto the next needle and return the empty needle to A pos.
31) T4. K 22 (22, 22) rows.
32) T7. K 1 row.
33) T4. K 22 (22, 22) rows. Carriage at the left.
34) Bring the empty needles back to B pos.
35) Turn up the hem by picking up the first row of the cuff.
36) Bring all the needles to hold pos.
37) T10. K 1 row.
38) Cast off loosely.

JOINING THE SHOULDER SEAM

1) Bring to B pos 25 (29, 32) needles.
2) With the knit side of the back facing you, hook the shoulder sts on the right onto the needles.
3) Bring the needles forward.
4) Push the sts back until they are just behind the open latches.

5) With the purl side of the front facing you hook the shoulder sts on the right onto the needles.
6) Holding the knitting with one hand and using the straight edge of the 1 x 1 selector, take the needles back to B pos. The sts behind the latches will go over the sts in the latches leaving only one set of sts on the needles.
7) Cast off loosely.

NECKBAND

1) Bring to B pos 100 (100, 104) needles. Carr at the left.
2) Hook the sts from the waste yarn onto the needles, purl side facing you adding 2 sts at shoulder seam on each side.
3) Bring all the needles to hold pos.
4) Set the machine to knit the sts back.
5) T7. K 1 row.
6) Transfer every 3rd st onto the next needle to give the 2 x 1 rib setting.

7) Put the empty needles back to A pos. RC 000.
8) T4. K 22 rows.
9) T7. K 1 row.
10) T4. K 22 rows. RC 45.
11) Bring the needles in A pos back to B pos.
12) Hook the 1st row of the neckband back onto the needles to form a hem.
13) Bring all the needles to hold pos.
14) T10. K 1 row.
15) Cast off loosely.

TO MAKE UP

1) Join the remaining shoulder sts as before.
2) Mattress st or back stitch the neckband.
3) Join 5 cms each end of the sleeve to make a pleat.
4) Place the marker on the sleeve against the shoulder seam and backstitch the sleeve into the armhole.
5) Join side and sleeve seams.

HINTS & TIPS

BUTTONHOLES ON 2 x 2 RIBS

How to get a neat buttonhole on a 2 x 2 rib.
Key 1 = Needle working.
    = Needle not working.
DIAGRAM ONE
        b d
111..11..11..111
    11..11..11
        a c
DIAGRAM TWO
  11..11..11..11
     11..11..11

For the buttonhole, transfer the stitch from needle a to needle b and the stitch from needle c to needle d. Leave the needles a and c in the working position and knit two rows.
The yarn will make a loop over needles a and c, pick the loop up and place it on to needle a or c, it doesn't matter which one. Continue knitting.
DIAGRAM TWO shows the standard needle setting, but DIAGRAM ONE, with the extra needles on the top bed at each end, gives a firmer edge and makes the band easier to sew on.

Some extras from Pam Turbett to help you with your cut and sew. Some necessary items of equipment for successful cut and sew work.

Having written these instructions, it has occurred to me that some readers may not know exactly what I mean by 'a *wooden pounder'*. It is simply a block of hard, untreated wood; a one foot length of bannister rail from a builder's wood merchant does the job

admirably. The idea is that when you want to achieve a really flat, sharp-edged look (as on a pocket edge or on a hem), you press with a damp cloth, remove the iron, whip off the damp cloth and bring the wood block down with a hefty thump (warn the neighbours first!) and hold it there for a few seconds. The weight of the block plus the absorption of the steam by the untreated wood gives you a beautiful sharp edge on your fabric.
Buy a really good *steam iron* — one, preferably, which will take tap water, will give an extra shot of steam, will also spray moisture and which has plenty of steam holes and a good smooth sole plate. This is *such* a valuable aid! Keep it on your ironing board, switched on, while you sew; then you can press as you go — the professional way.
Pins: Buy the fairly long kind made of fine steel with coloured glass or plastic heads. These are essential for knitted fabrics and have the added bonus that they are less easily lost.
Scissors: Large, not too heavy, and very sharp for cutting fabric. As previously mentioned, hide them away from predators! Also have a small pair for thread snipping.
A stitch-unpicker: A tiny, sharp blade in a plastic case for undoing those things which we ought not to have done — we all need this!
Tape measure: An analogical fibreglass tape measure — your old linen one may have stretched. Try to get one which has a brass end and is exactly 1.5cm wide — it makes a very useful guide for judging your seam allowance.

HEM . . . HEM . . . HEM . . .

The problem of hems keeps cropping up, if you will excuse the pun, and this time one of my friends wanted to lengthen a circular skirt.
If only a little extra length was needed then crochet would probably be the answer, providing that the yarn was suitable for crochet. Crochet could be plain, using crab stitch or a fancy edging, depending of course on the type of skirt. A knitted or bought trimming could be sewn on and once again the choice would be dependent on the fabric of the skirt.
However, my favourite method for hems, and one which would suit almost any type of skirt, is to pick up the bottom of the skirt and knit the hem downwards. This usually needs to be done in several sections, depending on how full the skirt is. Have the wrong side of the knitting facing you and pick the edge up neatly on to the machine and then knit the hem twice as deep as you need it. Pick up the first row again and knit one row at tension (10) and cast off.
This type of edging makes the skirt hang well and there are many variations you can use to add interest to the hem. A small Fair Isle pattern looks well, so does a stripe or the introduction of a contrast colour which perhaps you have used elsewhere on the outfit. A row of holes with the contrast yarn or ribbon threaded through is another possibility. The ideas are endless, so if you have a skirt that is too short don't send it to the jumble sale, lengthen it and give it a new lease of life.

Child's duffle coat

For Knitmaster 120 machines with SR120 ribbing attachment. For stockists write to Knitmaster Ltd., 30-40 Elcho Street, London, S.W.11.

SIZES

To fit 61-81 cms, 24-32 ins chest.

MATERIALS

Lister Lee Thermo-knit double knitting. 14 (14, 15, 15, 16) 50 grm balls in col 1.
6 toggles.

TENSION

21 sts and 28 rows to 10 cms (4 ins) measured over double rib. Tension dials at approximately 1.

NOTES:

Inc, dec and casting off are given for knitter only, sts on ribber should be inc, dec or cast off automatically when they occur.
Always transfer towards the centre of the pattern.
*Knit 2 rows with the following needle arrangement

Knit 2 rows with the following needle arrangement

Knit 2 rows with the following needle arrangement

Rept from * to * throughout. When transferring end sts, pick up the *loop* from the adjacent st and place onto the N.

BACK

With ribbing attachment in pos, set half pitch lever to H and indicator scale to 5. Push 39(42, 44, 47, 50) Ns at left and right of centre 0 on knitter to B pos. 78 (84, 88, 94, 100) Ns altog. Push corresponding Ns on ribber to B pos. Carr at right. Using col 1 cast on as shown in instruction book for double rib using ribber as right side throughout. Set carr for main knitting. Row Counter 000. Tension Dials at 1.
Knit 88 (106, 124, 140, 156) rows. Carr at right.
Shape armholes
Cast off 4 sts at beg of the next 2 rows.
1st, 2nd, 3rd and 4th sizes only
Dec 1 st at both ends of the next and ev foll 4th row 3 (6, 2, 3) times in all, knit 4 rows.
All sizes
Dec 1 st at both ends of the next and ev foll 5th row 5 (3, 7, 7, 10) times in all. 54 (58, 62, 66, 72) sts. Row Counter 124 (144, 166, 186, 204). Carr at right.
Shape shoulders
Set carr for partial knitting. Always taking yarn round the first inside N in E pos, push 5 (5, 6, 6, 7) Ns at opposite end to carr to E pos on the next 6 (8, 4, 8, 4) rows and 4 (5, 5, 5, 6)

Ns on the next 4 (2, 6, 2, 6) rows. 8 Ns rem in B pos. Break off yarn. Mark centre with waste yarn. Using a transfer tool bring Ns in E pos back to B pos. Cast off.

LEFT FRONT

Push 39 (42, 44, 47, 50) Ns at right and 6 Ns at left of centre 0 on knitter to B pos. 45 (48, 50, 53, 56) Ns altog. Push corresponding Ns on ribber to B pos. *Carr at right. Using col 1 cast on in double rib. Tension Dials at 1. Set carr for main knitting, knit 1 row. Carr at left. Working the pattern over Ns 13 to 26 inclusive at right of centre 0 (with the centre 2 Ns in the arrangement on Ns 19 and 20) transfer sts for the following arrangements:—

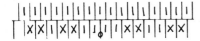

Knit 1 row. Carr at right*. Row Counter 000. Working in pattern as given in notes throughout knit 28 (34, 40, 46, 52) rows. Counting from the centre 0 mark the 13th st and the 36th (38th, 40th, 44th, 46th) st with waste yarn for pocket pos. Take a note of the needle arrangement.
Knit 30 (34, 36, 40, 42) rows. Mark the same sts as before. Knit 30 (38, 48, 54, 62) rows. Row Counter 88 (106, 124, 140, 156). Carr at right.
Shape armhole
Cast off 4 sts at beg of the next row, knit 1 row.
1st, 2nd, 3rd & 4th sizes only.
Dec 1 st at right edge on the next and ev foll 4th row 3 (6, 2, 3) times in all, knit 4 rows.
All sizes
Dec 1 st at right edge on the next and ev foll 5th row 4 (2, 6, 6, 9) times in all. 34 (36, 38, 40, 43) sts. Knit 2 rows. Row Counter 121 (141, 163, 183, 201). Carr at left.
Shape neck
Cast off 12 sts at beg of the next row, knit 1 row. Cast off 3 sts at beg and dec 1 st at right edge on the next row, knit 1 row. Row Counter 125 (145, 167, 187, 205). Carr at left.
Shape shoulder
Set carr for partial knitting. Always taking yarn round the first inside N in E pos, push 4 (4, 4, 5, 5, 6) Ns at opposite end to carr to E pos and cast off 2 sts at beg of the next row, knit 1 row. Rept the last 2 rows once more. Push 3 (4, 4, 5, 6) Ns at opposite end to carr to E pos on the next row, knit 1 row. 3 (4, 4, 5, 5) Ns rem in B pos. Using a transfer tool bring Ns in E pos back to B pos. Cast off.

RIGHT FRONT

Work as given for left front but reverse the shapings by reading left for right and vice versa throughout.

LEFT POCKET

Push Ns 13 to 36 (38, 40, 44, 46) inclusive at right of centre 0 to B pos. 24 (26, 28, 32, 34) Ns. Push corresponding Ns on ribber to B pos. Carr at right. Using col 1 cast on in double rib using ribber as right side. Set carr for main knitting. Tension dials at 1. Transfer sts for needle arrangement previously noted over the first 14 Ns at left. Working in correct sequence knit 24 (28, 30, 34, 36) rows. Half pitch lever to P, transfer sts for 1x1 rib. Knit 10 rows. Transfer sts from ribber to knitter, knit 1 row. Using waste yarn knit 8 rows and release from machine.

RIGHT POCKET

Work as given for left pocket but read left for right and vice versa throughout.

RIGHT SLEEVE

Push 21 (21, 21, 23, 23) Ns at left and right of centre 0 on knitter to B pos. 42 (42, 42, 46, 46) Ns altog. Push corresponding Ns on ribber to B pos. Carr at right. Using col 1 cast on in double rib. Tension dials at 1. Set carr for main knitting, knit 1 row. Carr at left. Working the pattern over the centre 14 Ns (with the centre 2 Ns in the arrangement on the centre 2 Ns) transfer sts for the following arrangement:—

Knit 1 row. Carr at right. Row counter 000. Working in pattern as given in notes throughout knit 7 (11, 0, 11, 1) rows. Inc 1 st at both ends of the next and ev foll 3rd (3rd, 4th, 4th, 5th) row 17 (19, 21, 21, 23) times in all. 76 (80, 84, 88, 92) sts. Row counter 56 (66, 81, 92, 112). Knit 8 (8, 7, 8, 8) rows without shaping. Carr at right.
Shape top
Cast off 4 sts at beg of the next 2 rows. *Cast off 3 sts at beg of the next 2 rows and 2 sts at beg of the next 2 rows*. Rept the last 4 rows from * to * 3 (4, 4, 4, 4) more times.
1st, 3rd, 4th & 5th sizes only.
Cast off 3 (2, 2, 2) sts at beg of the next 2 (2, 4, 6) rows.
All sizes
22 sts. Row counter 84 (96, 112, 116, 148). Knit 18 (20, 24, 28, 30) rows. Carr at right. Cast off 11 sts at beg of the next row, knit 1 row. Dec 1 st at right edge on the next and ev foll 3rd row 5 times in all, knit 3 rows. 6 sts

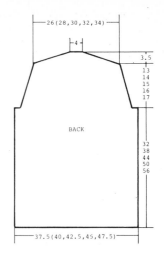

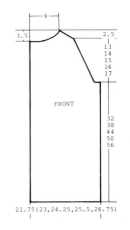

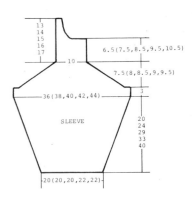

Diagram of finished measurements in centimetres

114

rem. Tuck knob up. Side levers on ribber up. Using waste yarn knit 8 rows on knitter only and release from machine. Side levers on ribber back to knitting pos. Knit 8 rows waste yarn and release from machine.

LEFT SLEEVE

Work as given for right sleeve but reverse the shapings by reading right for left and vice versa throughout.

HOOD (2 pieces altog)

Push 36 Ns at right of centre 0 on knitter to B pos. Push corresponding Ns on ribber to B pos. Carr at right. Using col 1 cast on in double rib. Set carr for main knitting. Row counter 000. Tension dials at 1. Knit 1 row. Inc 1 st at right edge on the next and ev foll alt row 4 (4, 6, 6, 6) times in all. 40 (40, 42, 42, 42) sts. Knit 55 (57, 57, 57, 63) rows without shaping (knit 1 row extra for second piece). Carr at left. Set carr for partial knitting. Always taking yarn round the first inside N in E pos, push 13 Ns at opposite end to carr to E pos on the next row, knit 1 row. Push 3 Ns at opposite end to carr to E pos on the next row, knit 1 row.

1st & 2nd sizes only.
Push 2 Ns at opposite end to carr to E pos on the next and ev foll alt row 10 times in all, knit 1 row.

3rd, 4th & 5th sizes only.
Push 2 Ns at opposite end to carr to E pos on the next row, knit 1 row. Push 3 Ns at opposite end to carr to E pos on the next row, knit 1 row. Rept the last 4 rows from * to * once more. Push 2 Ns at opposite end to carr to E pos on the next and ev foll alt row 6 times in all, knit 1 row.

All sizes
4 Ns rem in B pos. Using a transfer tool bring Ns in E pos back to B pos. Cast off. Knit another piece in the same way but reverse the shapings by noting alteration in the number of rows worked and then reading right for left.

TO MAKE UP

Join sides of sleeve extensions to the shoulder edges of back and fronts. Set in sleeves. Join side and sleeve seams. Fold top of pockets in half onto the right side. Pin into pos and backstitch through the open loops of the last row knitted in col 1, unravel waste yarn. Sew pockets into pos using markers as a guide. Join the 2 pieces of hood tog at cast on edge. Join back seam. Sew curved edge of hood into pos around neck edge.
Using a latch tool make 3 chain stitch cords 24 cms long and 3 chain stitch cords 7 cms long. Make fastenings with long cords and decorative trims with short cords as shown in photograph. Sew on in 3 evenly spaced places, positioning 1 level with pocket top.

HINTS & TIPS

EASY DECREASES

When you are decreasing a large number of stitches over one row, if, for example, you have to lose 30 sts., the work is run off on waste yarn and you then bring to the working position the number of needles on to which you are going to rehang the knitting. Before you start to rehang the knitting bring forward each needle that should have two stitches put on it. It may be every fourth needle so many times and then every sixth needle and so on, but if you prepare the way as described it saves counting the stitches as you go along and makes life easier. Every time you reach a needle that is brought forward you know that you have to put two stitches on it.

DO IT YOURSELF WAISTCOATS

Waistcoats are useful garments for many reasons. Apart from being a handy addition to any wardrobe they make an easy project to knit when you are trying a new yarn or a new stitch because you have no holding stitches for neck shapings and the whole garment does not take very much yarn.
To adapt a drawn block for one of the charting devices from a set in sleeve to a sleeveless waistcoat is easy. All you need to do is take off the amount required for the armbands. If you then want an armband one inch wide, you need to draw a line on the block one inch in from the edge round the armhole shaping. This would be half an inch on the half scale charting devices. See the diagram below. The dotted line is the line to draw.
For a button up waistcoat use the round neck shaping and for a 'V' neck, draw in your own line starting at the same point as the beginning of the armhole shaping and finishing at the shoulder. See the diagram.
The armbands on a waistcoat could be ribbed if you want them to fit snugly or stocking stitch is smart for a not so tight fitting and for summer and evening waistcoats you might consider crochet or bought lace or braids — think about these little finishing touches, they make all the difference.

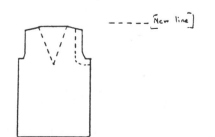

WELL BEHAVED WAISTBANDS

Have you got a knitted skirt, or any skirt for that matter, where the waistband curls over and causes you annoyance? It need not be. Ann Taylor from Littlehampton brought me some Peta Stretch (Dewhurst), which is uncurlable elastic specially for waistbands etc. — perfect for the job. For your nearest stockist you can write to English Sewing Ltd., 56 Oxford Street, Manchester M60 1HJ.

GRAFTING

Here are some clear instructions for grafting.
Lay the two pieces to be joined, edge to edge with the right sides facing.
Put the needle from the back to the front through the first stitch on the right hand side of the lower piece.
Put the needle into the first look on the upper piece from back to front . . . pull the thread through.
Put the needle into the front of the first stitch on the right of the lower piece and through the back to the front of the next stitch on its left. Repeat with the first two stitches on the upper section and continue in this way until all the loops are joined. Close the loops, taking care not to pull too tightly.

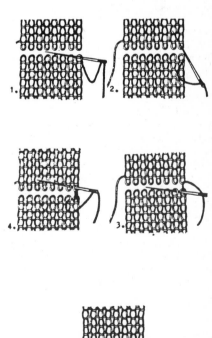

Baby's dress

SIZES

Birth – 6 months. To fit chest 41–46 cms (16–18 ins).
Dress length: 30 cms (11¾ ins). Sleeve length: 12 cms (4¾ ins).

MATERIALS

8 25 grm balls Lister Lee Target Baby Love 4 ply acrylic/wool, colour 57.
Crochet hook. 4 small buttons. 5 m Offray Tone-on Tone Jacquard floral ribbon pattern 5451, colour 7 Ivory. 1.5 m Offray 14 double faced satin ribbon Ivory.

TENSION

30 sts and 42 rows to 10 cms (4 ins) measured over stocking stitch. MT approx T5.

NOTE:
To suit most makes and models of machine.
Purl side is right side.

BACK

RC 000. MT. Closed edge cast on 104 sts. Working in stocking stitch knit 4 rows*. Using a transfer tool, place loops of braid edging over needle hooks. (Note: braid will frill slightly). Leave 2.5 cms (1 in) spare on each end of braid for seam allowance. Knit across braid. Knit a further 8 rows**. Repeat twice more from * to **. Knit to RC 80. Knit several rows in waste yarn. Release from machine.
Yoke
Bring 64 needles to WP. Unravel waste yarn and replace skirt, purl side facing.

Dec 40 sts evenly along the row ***.
RC 000. Work in stocking stitch. Trans every third st onto adjacent needles, leaving empty needles in WP. Knit 2 rows.
Divide for back opening
Push 32 sts at left to H/P. Work on rem 32 sts. Knit 2 rows.
Shape armhole
Cast off 6 sts at beg of next row. Knit straight to RC 42.
Shape shoulder
Cast off 7 sts at beg of next and foll alt row. Knit 1 row. Cast off. Work left side to match, reversing shaping.

FRONT

Knit as back to ***. RC 000. MT. Work in stocking stitch. Knit 4 rows.
Shape armhole
Cast off 6 sts at beg of next 2 rows. Knit straight to RC 32.
Shape neck
Push 33 sts at left to H/P. Work on rem 19 sts. Knit 1 row. Dec 1 st at neck edge on next and foll rows 5 times altogether. Knit straight to RC 42.
Shape shoulder
Cast off 7 sts at beg of next row. Knit 1 row. Cast off. Cast off next 14 sts in H/P. Knit on rem 19 sts, to match right side, reversing shapings.

SLEEVES

RC 000. MT. Closed edge cast on 42 sts. Working in stocking stitch, knit 4 rows. Place loops of braid over needle hooks as for dress skirt front and back. Knit 6 rows straight. Inc 1 st each end of next and every foll sixth row 6 times altogether. 54 sts. Knit straight to RC 56. Cast off. Knit second sleeve.

TO MAKE UP

Join shoulder seams. Set in sleeves. Join side and sleeve seams, sewing through ribbon strips by hand or on a sewing machine.
Trim raw edges of ribbon to 1 cm (½ in) and finish out edge with a zig-zag stitch to prevent fraying. With crochet hook work 1 row of DC along back opening and 1 row of cord edging, making 4 loops on one side. Work 1 row of DC round neck, then 1 row of loop or shell pattern. Sew on buttons. Thread narrow ribbon through holes at waist and tie in front.

First size matinee coat and bonnet

This first size baby outfit is for ribbing attachments and double bed machines only. Apart from being a delightful little set it also shows you just how easy double bed patterns can really be. If there are no new babies around at the moment then knit it anyway just to show yourself how easy it is.

For double bed machines and machines with ribbing attachments.

SIZE

First size only. Could be easily adjusted.

MATERIALS

2 strands of 2/30 Acrylic. A baby 3 ply could be substituted.

TENSION

Approx. T.(4) main bed and (6) ribber. 26 sts. and 100 rows to 4 ins. This pattern is suitable for all double bed machines and ribbing attachments.

PATTERN

Main bed on slip. Knit 6 rows on ribber only. Knitmaster machines run 'P' carriage across to make sure that all sts. knit off. (Other machines, if sts. do not knit off easily, push all needles on front bed up to the H/P). Knit 2 rows full needle rib.

COAT

BACK

Cast on 90 sts. Full needle rib. Knit 2 circular rows.
Main tension knit 4 rows double rib. Knit in pattern until work is 6 inches, 26 rows, 15 tucks. Transfer all sts. to main bed. Run off on waste yarn.

BOTH FRONTS

Cast on 46 sts. as for back and work as for back.

SLEEVES

Use an extra strand if 2/30 yarn is used. Cast on 48 sts. 1 x 1 rib and knit 12 rows. Change to 2 strands and pattern and work 108 rows as for back.

YOKE

Push up 118 needles on back bed to WP. With wrong side of knitting facing you replace sts. onto machine, front, sleeve, back, sleeve, front, decreasing evenly across the row.
T.(3) knit 36 rows straight. Run off on waste yarn. Replace the work, 2 sts. on every needle. 59 sts. Knit 6 rows. T.(2) 1 row T.(6) 6 rows T.(2). Pick up from first row and latch off.

FRONT BANDS

With wrong side of work facing you.
Left
Pick up 60 sts. down front of work. T.(3) knit 10 rows, 1 row T.(6) 10 rows T.(3). Pick up first row and latch off.
Right
Knit as for left but make three single stitch button holes over the yoke part.

TO MAKE UP

Join yoke down for 1½ inches. Then join side and sleeve seams.

BONNET

Cast on full needle rib 76 sts. Knit 28 rows tubular for the hem. Work in pattern for 64 rows (8 pin tucks).
Cast off 24 sts. at beg. of next 2 rows. Knit 80 rows on remaining sts. Transfer sts. to main bed and run off on waste yarn.
Pick up 24 sts. from side edge then replace sts. from waste yarn, 2 sts. on each needle and 24 sts. from the other side edge. 60 sts. Transfer sts. to 1 x 1 rib and knit 14 rows. Cast off.
Turn back the rib rows and catch down and this makes neckband for ribbon. Join side seams.

Christening gown

Made on a Jones + Brother 830 machine. Card number 414 from small design pack.

SIZES

To fit up to a 8–9 month old baby.

MATERIALS

9 ozs Bright Courtelle 2/28 in white, used double throughout.
4 yds white ribbon ¼ inch wide.
½ yd white silky material to line the skirt.
A very fine crochet hook.

TENSION

Approximately 3 for stocking stitch and 3 for lace.

SKIRT (3 panels)

Work in two strands throughout.
Main panel
RC 000 T3. Cast on 'e' wrap over alternate needles the width of the bed. Knit 1 row, bring needles in A position to B position, 200 needles. Knit 6 rows (it helps to bring needles to D position each row and then knit back). Now insert long cast-on comb. Knit 1 row at tension 7. Knit 7 rows at tension 3. RC 15.
RC 000. Insert lace card and knit in lace pattern till RC registers 250 (you may need claw weights on the cast-on comb). Remove card and knit 4 rows stocking stitch. RC 254. Take off on waste yarn.
Back panels (knit two)
RC 000. T3. Bring 50 alternate needles to B position and cast on 'e' wrap. Knit 1 row, bring needles in A position to B position (100 needles). Knit 6 rows (insert cast-on comb). Knit 1 row at T7. Knit 7 rows at T3. RC 15.
RC 000. Insert lace card and knit in lace pattern till RC registers 250. Remove card and knit 4 rows in stocking stitch. RC 354. Take off on waste yarn.

BODICE

Continue knitting in two strands.
Bring 100 needles to WP and take *main* panel with wrong side facing you, replace 2 sts onto each needle.
RC 000. Knit 2 rows in stocking stitch. RC 002, transfer every 4th stitch to 5th needle and leave empty needle in WP. Knit 6 rows stocking stitch. RC 008.
RC 000. Decrease 1 st at each edge 8 times. RC 016. Knit to row 50 carriage at the right.
Put all needles left of centre 0 to H/P plus 12 sts at right of centre. Decrease 1 st at neck edge every 2 rows 6 times. Knit to row 24 and take off on waste yarn.
Shape the other side to match and take off onto waste yarn.

BACK

T3. Use two strands throughout.
Bring to WP 45 needles left of centre 0 and five needles right of centre 0. Replace one back panel, wrong side facing you, 2 stitches to each needle.
Bring to WP 45 needles right of centre 0 (total of 50 needles on right) and replace the other back panel in the same manner, over lapping in the centre with the other panel. This leaves the back open from the centre down and allows the skirt to be draped for photographs, and minimises disaster from nappies!
RC 000. Knit 2 rows in stocking stitch. Transfer every 4th stitch to 5th needle and leave empty needles in WP. Knit 6 rows in stocking stitch.
RC 000. Decrease 1 stitch on each edge 8 times. RC 016. Knit to row 36, place half the stitches in H/P and * knit 30 rows on the other half. Place half of these stitches onto waste, and knit 8 rows on the remainder. Take off onto waste yarn.
Repeat from * to match the other side.
Graft together both shoulder seams.

SLEEVES

T3. Use two strands throughout.
With wrong side of garment facing you, pick up round the armhole side of garment approximately 90 stitches.
RC 000. Knit 1 row and break yarn. Keeping the centre 30 stitches on WP, place the others on both sides into H/P. Bring to WP 2 needles on the side opposite to carriage on each row till all needles are in WP.
RC 000. Knit in stocking stitch to row 14. Decrease 1 st each side every 7 rows 8 times. Transfer every 4th st to 5th needle and leave empty needles in WP. Knit 3 rows. RC 66.
Insert lace card and work in lace till RC registers 84. Knit 2 rows stocking stitch and cast off round sinker pegs.
Knit other sleeve in same way.

Turn up the hem round the bottom of the skirt and slip stitch loosely in place. This hem is hidden by the frill, but is necessary to give weight to the garment.
At this point, pin out each skirt piece, wrong side up, onto a flat area and pull out to equal size, cover with a damp cloth and press with hot iron, killing the yarn to get a draping effect. Press edge lace on sleeves in the same way. *Do not* touch the upper part of the sleeves or bodice. Sew up the seams, and place garment in a clean plastic bag.

FRILL (3 pieces)

Cast on 'e' wrap with two strands over 200 needles, bring to D position and knit back for 4 rows, and insert cast-on comb.
Insert lace card and work in lace until RC registers 44 (row 32 on card). Knit 4 rows in stocking stitch and cast off round sinker pegs.
Make two more pieces the same.

TO MAKE UP

Pin out onto flat surface, wrong side up, cover with a damp cloth and press with hot iron.
Join the pieces into one long strip and pin carefully onto hem of the skirt, pleating in the frill to fit round – the cast off edge fitting onto the hem. This leaves small holes from the cast off. Back stitch the frill in situ through these holes.
Crochet 2 rows of double crochet round the bottom of the frill and the edge of the sleeves. 1 row of double crochet round the neck, removing waste yarn as you go. Work 2nd row of crochet round the neck as follows – 1 treble, 3 chain, 1 treble, making a place for the ribbon to thread through the crochet. Thread the ribbon round the neck to tie at the back. Pull the centre front of the ribbon out, and make into a bow at the front. Thread ribbon through the sleeves and through the eyelets at the top of skirt, leaving long streamers of ribbon down the front when tied.
Make a hem top and bottom of the silky material and insert elastic into the top, and stitch two tapes either side, and two tapes inside the lace skirt. This keeps the lining in place and is easy to remove.
By altering the ribbons, pulling in or letting out, this garment should fit babies in a variety of sizes.

See colour plate opposite page 97

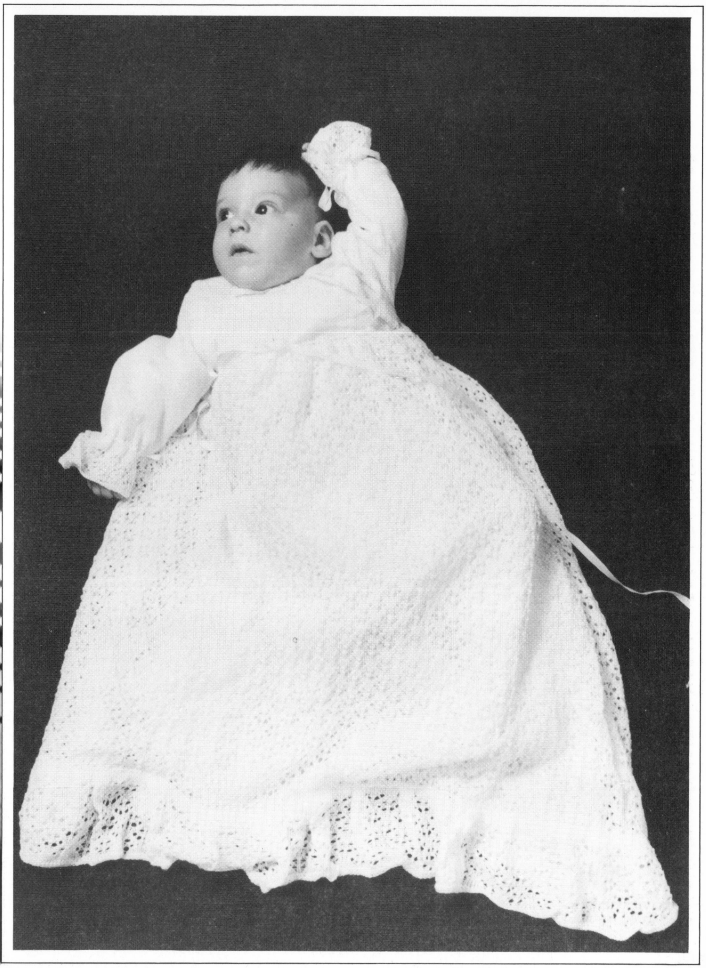

Baby sized set

SIZES

To fit age 9-18 months.
Poncho: Length 38.5 cm (15 ins) counting the fringe but *not* the neck rib.
Mitts: Length 14.5 cm (5¾ ins), width 7.5 cm (3 ins).
Hat: At first, depth 15 cm (6 ins), around head 22 cm (17 ins). When turned, depth 19 cm (7½ ins). The rib band is 9 cm (3½ ins).

MATERIALS

Sirdar Wash 'n' Wear double knit crepe (40 grm size balls).
The whole set: 10 balls white, 2 balls pink.
Poncho only: 8 balls white, 2 balls pink.
4 small buttons.
3.00 size crochet hook.

TENSION

Stocking stitch: 28 sts and 34 rows to 10 cms (4 ins) (try T9.).
Fair Isle: Main tension, plus two dots.

Ribs: Approx 3 whole numbers lower than MT (try T 6.).
Fringe: All at T 6.

NOTES:
Flower border: Knitmaster set M1001, pattern M 12.
Elephant border: 'Memomatic Book', pattern 16 on page 5.
Weight garment edges as if it was a raglan. If the sts jump off after 'e', wrap cast on, use weaving brushes for the first few rows. They will not be needed as soon as the knitting grows long enough to hang in a claw weight.

PONCHO

PANELS (four alike)

Onto the basic shape work the Fair Isle.
Basic shape
Using white 'e' wrap method cast on 122 sts (61 each side of '0'). Leave an end of approx 24 ins as this is enough to sew the side seam.

RC 000. Carriage on right.
Dec 1 st both ends of every 4th row to RC 36. 106 sts.
Dec 1 st both ends of every alternate row. RC 110. 30 sts.
Using waste wool k 6 rows and release.
AT THE SAME TIME commence flower border on RC 9, work 9 rows Fair Isle. RC 17, carriage on left. Do not break pink yarn. Remove from feeder and leave at the side. K 8 rows stocking stitch. Carriage on left, RC 25.
Commence elephant border on RC 26 and k 20 rows Fair Isle. RC 45, carriage on left. Cut pink yarn.

NECKBAND

Push 113 needles to WP. Carriage on right.
Replace each panel as follows, starting with the end needle on the right.
PANEL 1 – Dec 2 sts in the centre. 29 needles full.
PANEL 2 – 1st st on top of the last st of panel one, so begin on the 29th needle. Dec 1 st in centre. 57 needles full.
PANEL 3 – 1st st on top of the last st of panel two, dec 1 st in centre. 85 needles now full.
PANEL 4 – 1st st on top of last st of panel three. Dec 1 st in centre. All 113 needles now full.
Knit 1 row in stocking stitch towards the left on MT.

Machines with ribber
RC 000. Set for k 1 p 1 rib. Knit 36 rows. Carriage on left. Knit one row towards the right on highest tension possible. Transfer all sts to main bed and loop off using latch tool.
Machines without ribbers
RC 000. Choice of 2 methods.
a. Set for rib of your choice (over 113 needles) from your instruction book and work 70 rows. Seal hem and cast off at same time.
b. On two whole tensions lower k 35 rows in stocking stitch and make into rib by crocheting up every alternate st with a latch tool. If you do this – say every 10 rows – it is easier. Having crocheted rib stitches 'up to date' and knitted the last row on a larger tension, loop off with latch tool. This method takes longer, but is well worth the effort – the finish is much nicer.

FRINGE

On each side of '0' push into WP needles 20, 21, 22, 23, 24. Cast on with waste wool. K 6 rows. There should be a long bar of wool reaching from needle No. 20 across '0' to the other needle No. 20 and a knitted solid edge at both sides. Hold the loops down slightly as you knit.

RC 000. Using white, knit 630 rows. Marking the edge sts of rows 160, 320, 480 with waste wool helps to position the fringe onto the 3 centre garment seams. K 6 rows waste wool and release.

MITTS (both alike)

Machines with ribbers

Cast on 41 sts in k 1 p 1 rib. K 10 rows. Transfer to main bed by putting each rib st on top of the sts already there (not onto empty needles). Push all needles to WP. This will automatically make holes for a tie when the 1st row of stocking stitch is knitted.

Machines without ribbers

Arrange the rib setting of your choice (to match poncho neck) over 41 needles. Cast on using waste wool. K 6 rows. Using white k 20 rows. Seal hem. Make a row of holes for tie by placing every alt st onto the next needle, leaving the empty ones in WP (or crochet up after RC 10 and transfer as above).

All machines

Dec 1st. 40 sts (20 each side of '0').

RC 000. MT, k 6 rows stocking stitch. Work the 9 Fair Isle rows of the flower border. Cut pink wool. Work in stocking stitch to RC 34. Carriage on right.

RC 000. Set cam box for H/P. Push the 20 needles on left to H/P. Working on the 20 needles on the right hand side, dec 1 st beg of next 4 rows, 12 sts remain. Remove on waste wool. Work the 20 sts on left hand side to match. Join the top either by grafting or replacing onto 12 machine needles (right sides tog) 12 sts, then the other 12 on top of the first set. Cast off tog.

Crochet tie

Using white yarn double work 96 chain.

HAT

Machines with ribbers

Cast on 121 sts as for mitts. K 30 rows. Transfer to main bed ready for stocking stitch.

Machines without ribbers

Cast on 121 sts to match the rib used for the mitts and poncho neck. K to RC 30 (if crocheting up the sts with a latch tool) or RC 60 if sealing the hem.

All machines

RC 000. MT, k 10 rows stocking stitch. Work the Fair Isle elephant border over the next 20 rows. Continue in stocking stitch to RC 54. Transfer every alternate st to the next needle on the right. Put empty needles into 'A' so they will not knit. Set tension much smaller (try T 3). K 6 rows. Leaving a long end of yarn, break off and thread onto a double eyed transfer tool or sewing needle. Take the sts straight from the machine onto thread. Make a large white pom pom.

TO MAKE UP

Poncho

Join the 3 centre seams. The overlapped stitch at the neck rib provides a tiny seam allowance. Join the centre front seam to within 3½ ins (9 cm) of neck ribs. Crochet round edge of neck rib and opening, making 4 small buttonholes, 3 on the stocking stitch and the other about one third of the way up neck rib. Sew on buttons. (It is easiest to start at one collar point and finish at the other.)

Commencing at the centre back, pin on edge of the fringe to the poncho edge, by placing the 5 sts right (stocking stitch) side up in line with each panel. (The thread markers help here, one for each 3 centre seams.) Sew using tiny back stitch. Turn up the other edge of the fringe to the inside and catch down. The poncho edge should now be sandwiched between the loops, the five smooth stitches on each surface weighting the panels down. Graft together the 5 sts on the outside, then the 5 inside. Do NOT cut the loops – they tend to twist tog with wear, looking like crochet bunches. Turn down top of neck rib to form collar.

Mitts

Sew up the side seam and tiny top shaping seam. Thread tie through holes, finishing each end with a tiny knot.

Hat

Draw up sts at crown and secure. Right side is inside. Join stocking stitch as far as the rib. Turn work other way out. Join rib rows. Sew pom pom to crown.

Press all parts according to ball bands.

HELPFUL HINTS

1. Push the hat ribs to the inside. The rib will not show, is doubly warm and clings to the head. As baby grows, make the hat larger by laying the rib flat then turning up the cast on edge on the right side below the elephants' feet. The hat now has a brim, is larger inside because the rib is not taking up room, and will last a growing baby for longer.

2. It is easy to ring the changes by substituting your own favourite Fair Isle borders. Pick a smaller one which will fit on the mitts and a larger one to go on the hat. Place the smaller one under the larger on the poncho.

3. If your machine will not do Fair Isle, there are many pretty baby colours with which to stripe the poncho. Try peach, lemon, blue, pink and apple green, one after the other on white. As with the Fair Isle borders, if you start the next band of colour on the same row number of the panels, the seams will match.

4. One ball of white will make one panel (and a bit over to use up in the pom pom). Begin a new ball for each panel and there will be no white ends to sew in.

HINTS & TIPS

CUT AND SEW GARMENTS

Many knitters avoid using any cut and sew methods, but the time comes to us all when it is a case of taking the scissors to the mistake or knitting the whole thing all over again. Usually the tragedy is at the neck shaping, the neck being too small. To cut a decent shape of the right size for the wearer, make a template, using a well fitting garment as a guide. Make it out of card or thick brown paper and you have a permanent pattern for the next time. Cut and sew necklines can be great time savers and often they are the easy solution to that tricky yarn or complicated pattern when holding stitches would be a nightmare, or in some cases of double bed patterns quite impossible.

Cut and sew should not be regarded as second best or the last resort. A well shaped and finished cut and sew neckline can give a garment a professional finish that cannot always be achieved by other more conventional methods.

NECK SHAPING ON CHILDREN'S GARMENTS

Still on the subject of cut and sew necklines, we need to take extra care with our measurements on a child's neckline. The head of a child is out of proportion to the rest of its body. When it comes to fitting a neck shape it needs to go over without any screams and yet sit closely once it is on. Allow a 7.5cm (3in) cut as with an adult sweater, because there will not be as much width and so that extra depth is needed to compensate.

There are alternatives if the neck is too tight. Buttons in the back left raglan will suffice but they do tend to look rather like an afterthought than a planned part of the design. Leaving one shoulder open and fastening it with a neat row of buttons on a set in sleeve jumper looks OK and you could do the same on both shoulders. An extra piece knitted on to allow for the overlap will make them sit properly and fasten tidily.

WINDING THE YARN

If you are winding your yarn with the electric winder, thread the yarn through the aerial tension unit on your machine and then to the winder. This will give the yarn an even tension as it winds and you will not need to hold it at all. Leave the yarn on the plastic cone and knit from the outside.

Toddler size three-piece outfit

Just the thing for a little girl's visit to playgroup, and easily altered to fit an older child.

SIZES

Finished measurements:
Dress length 41 cm (16 ins) (see Helpful Hints 1).

Skirt length 23 cm (9 ins).
Top: back length 32 cm (12½ ins); sleeve seam 6 cm (2½ ins).
Pants: top to front crotch 20 cm (8 ins); hips 40 cm (20 ins).

MATERIALS

Phildar Option 4 ply 50 grm balls.
The whole set: 3 balls red, 3 balls white.

Skirt: 2 balls red, 1 ball white.
Top: 2 balls white and a few yards red.
Pants: 1 ball red and a few yards white.

TENSION

15 sts and 21 rows to 5 cm (2 ins) measured over stocking stitch. Try T6··, ribs T3.

NOTES:
Fair Isle border is Knitmaster No.127 from set 30/31.

SKIRT

BACK AND FRONT (both alike)

Push 147 needles to WP. Return every alternate needle to A. Using WY cast on, knit several rows ending with carr on right. Change to red yarn. Work hem as follows:-

K 1 row to left hand side. Push ALL needles including those in A to H/P. Set machine to knit back to WP. K 1 row carr on right. RC 000. MT minus a dot. K 10 rows MT + a whole number higher, work 1 row. MT k to RC 22. Seal hem by picking up long loops only, onto alternate needles. Push all needles to H/P and k 2 rows. Carr on right. Remove WY from hem. Dec 1 st. 146 sts (73 each side of '0'). Hem is completed.
RC 000. Work 6 rows stocking stitch. MT + two dots commence Fair Isle border on RC 7, ending on RC 46. Decrease T by 2 dots back to MT. Continue stocking stitch to RC 66. Using WY or hand knitting needle, remove from machine. No need to break red yarn.
Waist rib
Push 81 needles to WP. Replace as follows:-
2 sts onto first needle, 1 st onto next needle, 8 times.
2 sts onto each of the next 33 needles.
2 sts onto first needle, 1 st onto next needle, 8 times.
Work 1 row stocking stitch on MT.
Machines with ribbers
Change to k 1 p 1 rib. Using a tension approx 3 whole numbers smaller than MT, rib 10 rows. Work another row on largest tension possible on both dials. Transfer all sts to main bed and using a latch tool, chain off.
Machines without ribbers
Using a smaller tension as above, k 10 rows and 1 more row on largest tension possible. Drop every alternate st and crochet up. Cast off as above.

STRAPS (knit 2 alike)

Machines with ribbers

Set for k 1 p 1 rib. Cast on 11 sts, (6 on main bed 5 on ribber). Push 1 extra needle to 'B' each side of the end st on main bed. This gives a neat edge because it curls under, also giving a right and wrong side to the work. 8 sts now on main bed, 5 on ribber. Using rib tension work approx 220 rows. Leave a long length of red. Remove on WY.

Machines without ribbers

Cast on 13 sts e wrap method. Work 220 rows on a small tension as used for waitband, latching alternate sts up approx every 10 rows. Note the first latch up st will be 3rd from the end. OR Cast on 22 sts. K in stocking stitch, sew seam and turn to right side out.

PANTIES

TO KNIT

Machines with ribbers

Using red cast on 81 sts k 1 p 1 rib. Make holes on row 3 by transferring every alt main bed st to nearest ribber needle. Continue to RC 10.

Machines without ribbers

Cast on 81 sts e wrap method. Using ribber tension work 3 rows. Crochet up with latch tool. Transfer every 3 rd needle to next needle. Work to RC 10. Crochet up sts.

All machines

Set for stocking stitch at MT.
Push 6 sts to H/P beg of next 8 rows.
Push all sts at left hand side in hold to the position on your machine model that will knit back to WP. K 1 row to left. Set machine to k back remaining sts in H/P. Work 1 row carr on right.
RC 000. Inc 1 st at both ends of rows 10, 20, 30 (87 sts). Continue to RC 38.
RC 000. Cast off 2 sts beg every row until 19 sts remain. RC 34. K 10 rows (RC 44). Cast on 2 sts beg every row until there are 59 sts (RC 64).
Cast on 8 sts beg next 2 rows, cast on 6 sts beg next 2 rows (87 sts).
RC 000. K 38 rows, dec 1 st at both ends on RC 8, 18, 28.

Machines with ribbers

Change to k1 p 1 rib, work 6 rows, make holes as before. Work to RC 10. Work 1 row on largest tension possible. Transfer all sts to main bed and chain off.

Machines without ribbers

Using rib tension complete to match the back rib, making holes at RC 6.

LEG RIBS (two alike)

Machines with ribbers

Cast on 95 sts k 1 p 1 rib. Work 10 rows red, rows 11 and 12 white. Continue in red to RC 16. Transfer to main bed. Work 1 row stocking stitch at MT. Remove with WY.

Machines without ribbers

Having the *right* side of garment facing you, pick up 95 sts round leg edge. Stocking stitch in rib tension work 10 rows red, rows 11 and 12 white. Red to RC16, crochet up alt sts using latch tool. Work 1 row stocking stitch MT. Remove with WY.

TOP

BACK

Using white cast on 85 sts and work 20 rows rib.

Machines without ribbers

Latch up alt sts.

All machines

Set for stocking stitch MT. RC 000. K to RC 60. Cast off 2 sts beg next 2 rows.
RC 000. Raglan. Dec 1 st beg every row. Work to RC 22. Divide for back opening by transferring centre st to needle on right hand side. Using nylon cord k 32 sts on left hand side to A. Dec at armhole edge only, work to RC 54. Cast off. Finish other side to match.

FRONT

Work as back to raglan.
RC 000. Shaping raglan as before, work 32 rows. Divide for neck. Using spare length of white, cast on centre 19 sts. Using nylon cord k 15 sts on left hand side back to A. Dec on armhole edge as before. At the neck edge dec 1 st on next 6 alt rows. Dec only at armhole edge until 2 sts remain. Fasten off. Work the left hand side of neck to match.

SHORT SLEEVES

Using white cast on 59 sts in k 1 p 1 rib. Work 10 rows, using red for rows 4 and 5 as a trim.

Machines without ribbers

Latch up as before.

All machines

RC 000. Inc 1 st both ends. Change to stocking stitch and MT. K 2 rows. Inc 1 st both ends every alt row until there are 65 sts. K to RC 12. Cast on 2 sts beg next 2 rows.
RC 000. Work raglan as on back to RC 54. Cast off.

NECKBAND

Machines with ribbers

Using white cast on 89 sts k 1 p 1 rib. Work to RC 13. Using red (as a trim) work rows 14 and 15. Using white continue to RC 19. Transfer to main bed. Work 1 row stocking stitch MT. Remove on WY.

Machines without ribbers

Cast on 89 sts e wrap method. Work as above for 19 rows. Crochet up every alt st. Work 1 row on MT. Remove on WY.

TO MAKE UP

Skirt

Join side seams using mattress st. In red, work herringbone st over end of elastic on inside of waist rib, using k rib sts as a guide. Thread elastic through as you go along. Join elastic ends. Sew on buttons 4 ins (10 cm) from cast on edge of each strap (see Helpful Hints 2). Remove WY and sewing through open loops and join straps to skirt waistband on inside top row of stocking stitch. Catch together on last row of rib top for strength Make 2 button loops on skirt front on top edge of ribs.

Panties

Sew ribber made leg bands round each leg by back stitching through open loops. Join side seams. Catch down lightly to inside, hiding raw edge. Sew main machine made bands down on right side, backstitching through open loops and removing WY. Thread elastic through waist rib and join ends.

Top

Join side and sleeve seams. Sew 4 raglan seams. Pin neckband to right side of garment and join by backstitching through open loops and removing WY. Turn to inside and catch down hiding raw edge. Crochet round back opening, making 4 buttonholes. Sew on buttons.

HELPFUL HINTS

1. Any children's border of Fair Isle would be suitable, provided the floats on the back are short. Try one of the new 6 designs from Knitting Machine Digest Punchcard Library. An arrangement of stripes is also attractive.

2. By leaving spare strap length below the buttons, they can be moved down, so lengthening the skirt as the child grows.

3. Use fully fashioned dec where possible. It always adds a little style to the finished garment.

4. Children of this age seem to spend so much energy moving about, they tend to grow taller and stay the same width! The set will fit an older child by adding straight rows above the Fair Isle border, 2 ins or so. (Add 50 rows to each strap.) Remember the panties too will fit so add the same number of rows before the back leg shaping and again after the front leg shaping. The jumper already has an extra 2 ins allowed on the body length.

5. Ring the changes with other good contrasting colours. A navy skirt and pale pink top for instance. Or add two colours in the Fair Isle border and trim the top with both colours in the neck and sleeve ribs (one above the other).

6. Knit the pants in blue, jumper top in white (only k to RC 50 before armhole) and there's a set for a little boy.

For your little treasure

A circular shawl in tuck lace for christening day
by Muriel Loraine.

SIZES

Approx 64 in diameter including fringe.

MATERIALS

2'30s acrylic 400 grms including fringe. 360 grms without fringe. A fine to medium crochet hook.

TENSION

4⅔ 16 sts 60 rows = 10 cm (4 ins). See Helpful Hints (1).

NOTES:

Use the illustrated punchcard as a guide to making your own card. 3 sts and 6 rows = 1 pattern repeat. Needles in "A" not knitting are not counted, and are represented on the punchcard by vertical lines. Only actual working needles are counted throughout this design. See Helpful Hints (2). *The yarn is knitted two fold throughout.*

before starting – decide which way the seam is to be joined. The most satisfactory finish is to graft, as was done on the original. If you cannot graft, cast on "e" wrap method do not use WY. Cast off *very* slackly.

SHAWL

Needle setting – Bring to WP needle number 97 at left. Push every alt needle to WP across width of machine until there are 95 needles. The last one on the right should be needle number 92. The needle on the left of the central "0" on the needle bed should be a working needle in "B". The one on the right of central "0" should be non-knitting, left in "A". This is important as the correct formation of the stitch pattern depends on these needles. 95 actual needles are in "B" that is 31 group of 3 pattern sts counting from the left, and 2 more on the right which form the shell edge.

Using WY cast on. K several rows ending with COL. Join in white. K 1 row to right. Release card. Set for tuck stitch. Use LEFT weaving brush throughout — (not both). Hang a claw weight at right edge only. Move it up 2 or 3 times during each section and always at the start of a new one.

*000. Set for H/P.

1. Push 3 needles at left to H/P. K to left.
2. Take yarn under end needle to prevent a hole forming. (Automatic e wrap is not possible on this stitch set up). K to right.
3. K to left.
4. Take yarn under the same end needle as in row 2. K to right.

5. K to left. *Do not wrap needle on this row*.
6. K to right.

These 6 rows form the pattern. During rows 1 to 4 every 3rd working needle will hold tuck loops. Rows 5-6 knit stocking stitch. Knitting all held loops up to date. As the work progresses it becomes obvious that of each little group of 3 forming the pattern repeats, the 2 left sts are continually knitting stocking stitch. Only the right one is a tuck stitch. Continue until only 2 sts at RHS of needle bed are still knitting all other needles are in H/P.

RC 180. K rows 1 to 4 again. Set machine to k all needles from H/P to WP. K rows 5 and 6 across the width of machine. RC 186. This completes one section.★

Work from ★ to ★ 16 more times. 17 sections completed BUT the final section ends after row 5. COL. Join in WY. K row 6, then several rows (not less than 10). Remove from machine.

TO MAKE UP

Either graft the sts and remove WY or sew the seam. Run a gathering thread neatly round the inner edge twice for strength, draw up tightly to close the hole. Fasten off.

THE FRINGE

Cut lengths of yarn approx 10 ins long by wrapping round a piece of cardboard 5 ins wide and snipping one edge. Take 6 single strands of yarn at a time, fold in half, insert crochet hook through each edge shell, pull the loop through, then the ends through the loop and tighten. Repeat through every edge shell right round. Spread out the shawl on a flat area and with a clothes brush (bristle type) brush the fringe out away from the centre, in the direction it should hang. Trim round to neaten.

HELPFUL HINTS

1. The tension dial number of 4⅔ to give the sts and rows to 10 cms is not absolutely vital. If you have it tighter the worst that will happen is the shawl be a little smaller – larger and the shawl will be bigger. The important thing is to make a fabric that will drape and fold softly. It should never be stiff and tight. It is a good idea to try out a sample first – just a small one, no need to work H/P shapings, knit straight. Repeat at different dial numbers until the feel of the work is satisfactory. Use that dial number.
2. As in (1) above, try out a sample to see how easily the pattern forms, and that your needle setting is correct before casting on the whole width of the machine. It's no trouble to pull out a small test bit if wrong but once you have got into swing across the whole machine width – well it's a different story.

3. Do you want a simpler shawl more quickly made? If so only complete 15 sections (not 17). It will be full enough to still form a circle. Leave off the fringe – if you have moved up the claw weights the edge should be perfect and will curl in on itself to form little shells that are quite pretty enough to leave as a finished edge.
4. Do you want to make the shawl that bit "extra special"? Sew on tiny little white bows of narrow ribbon – one bow on each panel centre 2 ins in from the fringe. *OR* thread VERY narrow ribbon right round the shawl 2 ins in from fringe through the lacy ladders. I found white ribbon hardly shows, so does not justify the extra expense. Pink/blue or lemon would be ideal. Buy it only after completing the shawl so you can measure how much is needed. Pick nylon taffeta and not satin ribbon.
5. If your patience wears a bit thin when fringing, (mine does . . .) fringe 2 sections at a time only. Do the shopping, have a break etc, then fringe another 2 sections. It may take longer, but it's better than trying to complete the lot in one mammoth sitting!
6. A crochet fringe or edging would be another way to put a pretty finish to the shawl. Why not make a little crochet circle to match – 2 ins across no more – sew it into the centre hole instead of gathering it together.
7. Once you get into the swing of the pattern, there really is no need to keep your row counter working. Remove it from the machine or set the trip on the cambox out of action. Jot down the number of panels you have made instead. You will have knitted a grand total of 3,162 rows by the finish of the shawl.

HINTS & TIPS

CASTING ON EXTRA STITCHES

Casting on lots of extra stitches presents a problem, especially if you need to weight the knitting straight away. Pulling all the needles out to the holding position for a few rows until it gets going is one method. Another way is to put the nylon cord over the extra stitches again until it gets started, and this will work OK. If you know that you are going to have to cast on say 60 extra stitches at some stage, then a good idea is to knit a piece of knitting 60 sts. wide and run it off on waste yarn before you start the garment and then you can rehang it on to the machine at the appropriate point and you will have no problems. This technique is especially useful if you need to weight the knitting at once and again if you are starting straight into pattern on the extra stitches.

A KNIT LEADER TIP

The Knit Leader is a full scale charting device and uses large plastic sheets for the pattern blocks. One of the disadvantages of these sheets is that it is rather expensive to have many in use at once. If you draw your blocks on to art paper you can put it behind the knit leader sheet, attach it with masking tape and run it through the knit leader as normal. This saves buying extra sheets and saves wiping and redrawing blocks.

V NECK

When you divide for the neck, transfer the two centre stitches, one to the right and one to the left. This makes the divide clearly defined and makes it easier when you are attaching the band to work from the exact centre.

For the star of the show on christening day

This garment was made on a Brother machine.

SIZES

Cape shoulder to hem 43.5 cm (17 ins). Width round hem 132 cm (52 ins) around face edge 33 cm (13 ins). Bootee foot length 9 cm (3½ ins).

MATERIALS

1 cone Roselan DK white, 1 cone 2'30s white (available from The Dalesknit Centre, Kirkgate, Settle, N. Yorks.). 135 cm (1½ yds) white ribbon 4 cm (1½ ins) wide for cape. 90 cm (1 yd) white ribbon narrow for boots. 9 motifs of white rosebud trim (optional). Ordinary white sewing cotton. 63 cm (24 ins) wide shirring elastic. 180 cm (2 yds) white swansdown trim.

TENSION

25 sts and 42 rows to 10 cm (4 ins) sq measured over patt.
24 sts and 32 rows to 10 cm (4 ins) sq measured over stocking st on DK.
T10 for DK yarn. T6 for 2'30s yarn.
Although it is always best to have correct tension here is a pattern where tension is not absolutely vital! Too large and the cape will simply be longer. The correct tension is one which shows clearly the strip in the fabric to give a soft texture which is comfortable for baby to wear. A stiff fabric means the tension is too tight.

NOTE

The purl side of the knitting is the right side when finished. The 2'30s is used double always. A single bed colour changer makes quick work of yarn changes. Thread DK into feeder 2 and 2'30s used double in feeder 1, the texture is just stocking st.

CAPE

TO KNIT

The skirt is knitted sideways. Using WY cast on 85 sts. 75 left of 0 and 10 right.
Knit a few rows ending on left. Change to 2'30s yarn T6 k3 rows. COR. Cast on another 27 needles at RHS 'e' wrap method (for neck opening). 112 needles now working. K1 row to left. T10 using DK knit 2 rows.
RC 000.
Step 1
Push 8 needles at RHS to H/P.
Set carriage for H/P.
T6. Using 2'30s k6 rows, always taking yarn under needle no. 30 to prevent a hole forming. (It is not possible to use automatic wrap on this pattern. It would spoil the line of shoulder gathers).
Step 2
Set carriage to k back all sts in H/P to WP.
T10 Using DK K2 rows.
At right edge transfer stitch no. 33 onto needle 34 leaving empty needle in WP. (This makes a vertical ladder of holes for neck ribbon).

Important

The work will knit on the curve. LHS is hem edge where yarns are changed. Use a claw weight and move it up *often* **or the bar of yarn will be tight as it is carried up the side, and spoil the finished hem.**

RHS is neck edge, with 8 sts always knitted in DK only. Use a claw weight here too. As the knitting grows it will be necessary to move up the left claw weight far more often than the right claw weight. Repeat steps 1 and 2 to RC 504. (62 ribbon holes should have been made on neck edge at RHS). Do not make anymore ribbon holes. Continue in patt to RC 512. COL. Using 2'30s yarn k1 row to right across all needles. C off 27 sts (slacking for neck opening) at beg of next row. Using WY k a few rows over remaining 85 sts and release.

HOOD

Cast on 85 sts using DK for k1 p1 rib. Both beds T8. Rib 16 rows. (If you do not have a ribber drop alternate sts and latch up into true rib). Transfer sts for stocking st. T10 k1 row to left.
Starting with 2'30s T6 repeat steps 1 and 2 noting the knitting will be straight. (Do not push any needles in H/P or make lace ladder on RHS). Work 59 rows. The 7th DK ridge has been completed. Carriage should now be at RHS T6 2'30s knitting 4th row of step 1. Cast off 26 sts at beg of next 2 rows. Centre 33 remain. Keeping patt correct, k to RC 110. Cast off slackly.

TO MAKE UP

Thread sewing needle with 2'30s double. Graft the 85 sts that are held on WY at centre front. The neck opening stitches leave — the fabric "curl" neatens them automatically. Join 2 head seams on hood. Turn face rib to inside and catch lightly down on 2nd ridge of DK leave side face edges free. Pin the hood centre back to the cape centre back right sides facing.
Pin the face edges of hood to cape front edges leaving 5cm (2in) free of cape top at each side to fit under chin. Sew bonnet to hood leaving inner turned under rib edges free to reduce bulk. 6 or 7 actual rows of rib should be all that show around the finished face edge. Thread wide ribbon through neck holes. Tie in a bow, trim ends. Using white sewing cotton, sew swansdown length of 33cm (13in) on to first DK ridge of hood. The 6 rib bands should still show giving a snug fit, and because the swansdown is not at the actual edge, it should not touch the face.
Turn 1in of cape hem to inside and catch down with 2'30s yarn one st into each DK ridge. Measure 132cm (52in) of swansdown and sew round lower edge using white sewing cotton. (See Helpful Hints 5.) Place six rosebud trims (6.5cm (2½in) above hem) evenly around garment. Approx every 11th ridge. Sew on with sewing cotton. Place a 7th rosebud trim near top of hood back.

BOOTIES

TO KNIT (two alike)

Foot Part
Use DK T10 "e" wrap Cast on 14 sts. k 18 rows carriage set for H/P from now on. COR hang claw weight.
Shape toe
*Push N nearest carriage to H/P. K1 row to left.
Push N nearest carriage to H/P. K1 row to right.
Repeat last 2 rows until 6 centre sts only are knitting. Rehang claw weight.
Push 1 N to UWP (where it will knit and return to WP) at beg of next 8 rows.
Rehang claw weight. * RC 34 k16 rows straight RC 50.
Shape heel
Work as toe from * to * RC 66 cast off.
Top Part
Using 2'30 cast on 25 sts. Knitting straight fabric repeat steps 1 and 2 of cape patt until RC 96 (12th DK ridge completed). K1 row in 2'30s. Cast off.

TO MAKE UP

Remember purl side is right side. Join one side seam of foot part. The cast off and cast on sts now make a straight edge. Join one side of top part to this straight edge purl sides facing as follows:
Oversew one DK ridge edge into first st of foot part leave all 6 2'30s rows free.
Oversew next DK ridge in next alt foot stitch to end. The top part will be slightly gathered on to foot part and there should be small gaps showing where the 6 2'30s rows were left free. These make holes through which the ribbon is later threaded. Join the remaining side seam from two to ankle and up top part. Turn top edge to inside and catch down on top of other sts holding edge to foot part. (Do not close ribbon holes.) Cut shirring elastic in half. Thread the 31cm (12in) into a sewing needle. Use it double and past along the top edge on the inside. It will not drop down to ankle if caught through a DK ridge st all the way round. Knot ends and using latch tool pull them on to inside of fabric fold where they will not show. Cut narrow ribbon in half, thread through ankle holes and tie. Sew a white rosebud trim near top edge on centre front. Cut a 1½in length of swansdown for each foot. Fold in half and sew on top of toe section.

HELPFUL HINTS

1. Knit slowly. It is a good idea to make the bootees' top parts first as they are straight and knitters get into a rhythm quite soon once they "get the hang of it".

2. Should you need to pull out a row or two and "get lost" on the big numer rows on the RC, after the 2nd row of DK on T10 the RC number is always divisible by eight.

3. As the work grows on the body of the cape it becomes easier to see at a glance which needle to transfer for the lace ladder and which to push to H/P. This speeds up knitting — no need to count 8 end sts any more.

4. Try using 2'30s of a different colour — lemon, pink or blue — still with white DK it makes an interesting texture and changes the look completely of the finished garment. But white is still the main part. If you work this the other way around — white 2'30s and used a coloured DK then the colour will become the main part. A different effect altogether.

5. Before cutting swansdown for lower edge tie a red marker thread around it 132cm (52in) from end. Tie a blue marker thread 65cm (26in) from the end you will start to sew. Catch a red marker thread through centre front of cape hem, and a blue through centre back. Pin on matching the marker threads. This way you will not run out of edging and it will be sewn on evenly all the way round.
Please note the following about swansdown:
If you decide to remove it before washing, only catch down with sewing cotton firmly in LARGE sts. This makes it easier to remove quickly.
Swansdown looks beautiful and puts a luxury finish to all it touches. However, this cape and bootees set was designed with a christening in mind and will be worn when baby is under the watchful eyes of adults at all times. It is not intended as a garment for baby to be put down to sleep in, or left alone at any time when wearing either the cape or bootees.

6. Everyday version — to save pennies substitute a fringe or braid which can be bought, machine knitted or crocheted in place of swansdown. Or turn up the hem with an embroidery trim all the way round. Place also round face and on bootee tops. Knit fewer rows in the body section of cape. It will not be as full. Subtract groups of 16 rows so there will be an even number of ribbon holes left round the neck or the ribbon will not begin and end on the outside to tie.

7. The cape without the hood looks quite nice.
Why not knit the hood and attach it to a length of 75cm (30in) narrow knitted strip, gathering slightly to make a bonnet? Together with the bootees it would make a nice present for any baby.

Tiny cardis with matching bootees

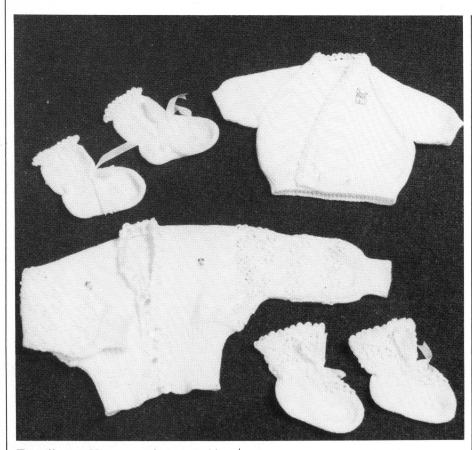

For all new Mums wanting something special to bring baby home from hospital; these little cardi's are made to fit size – birth to 2 months.

Muriel Loraine

SIDEWAYS KNITTED CARDI

SIZES

To fit chest 41 cm (16 in), length 21.5 cm (8½ in), sleeve seam 16.5 cm (6½ in).

MATERIALS

20 grm balls Keynote acrylic 4 ply.
Girl's Cardi: 4 balls. 68 cm (¾ yd) narrow ribbon, 4 tiny buttons, 2 bought motifs or embroidery thread (optional), 2.5 crochet hook.
Boy's Cardi: 5 balls, 4 tiny buttons.

TENSION

31 sts and 44 rows to 10 cm (4 ins) measured over stocking stitch. Try T6. K1 p1 rib approx 3 whole numbers smaller.

NOTES:
Card 414 Jones Vol.6 (small designs) if using a machine with separate lace carriage:-
Increasing – move lace carr BEFORE the inc.
Decreasing – move lace carr AFTER the dec.

GIRLS VERSION (As illustrated)

BODY (knitted in one piece – starting with right sleeve, ending with left

Using waste yarn cast on 57 sts, having odd st on right. k a few rows. Join in main yarn. K 6 rows stocking stitch.
RC 000. Begin wrist lace border. K 12 rows lace, 8 stocking stitch. RC 20. Begin middle lace border. K 12 rows lace, 8 stocking stitch. RC 40.
Begin shoulder lace border. K 4 rows lace, then cast on 'e' wrap method 12 sts at beg of rows 45 and 46. 81 sts (see Helpful Hints No.3).
Work in lace to RC 64. This completes the third lace border. K 40 rows stocking stitch. RC 104. Using nylon cord k back to

A all sts left of '0'.
Working on rem 41 sts at right hand side of '0' k 24 rows stocking stitch. Using waste yarn k a few rows and remove from machine.
At left bring 40 Ns held on nylon cord to WP. K 1 row to left hand side. Set machine for H/P.
Shaping the front edge – at right hand side push 14 needles to H/P. K 2 rows (taking yarn under end needle so a hole will not form). Again push another 14 needles to hold. K 2 rows. 12 sts remain.
Important. Note their position, it should be needles 40 to 29 left of '0'. Set machine to k sts back to WP. K 1 row to right on largest tension possible and cast off using a latch tool.
This completes slope of the right front edge – the work is no longer on machine.
To commence slope of left front edge place carriage on right. Using main yarn cast on 12 sts ('e' wrap method) over needles 29 to 40 left of '0', which are the same Ns whose position was previously noted. K 2 rows.
Cast on 14 sts over needles 15 to 28 left of '0'. K 2 rows.
Cast on 14 sts over needles 1 to 14 left of '0'. K 1 row. Carriage on left.
All needles 1 to 40 now hold sts. This completes the left front slope.
Replace (purl side facing you) 41 sts from waste yarn on 41 Ns at right. K 1 row to right. 81 sts. RC 000. K 40 rows stocking stitch.
Begin shoulder lace border. K 24 rows lace, casting off 12 sts at beg of rows 59 and 60 (see Helpful Hints 3). RC 64. 57 sts remain.
* K 8 rows stocking stitch. K 12 rows lace border. * = RC 84. Rep from * to * once. RC 104. K 6 rows stocking stitch. Using waste yarn k a few rows and remove from machine.

CUFFS (both alike)

Cast on 45 sts for k 1 p 1 rib. Work to RC 17. Transfer all sts to main bed. Using the straight edge of needle pusher or a ruler, ease the needle butts slightly forward in a straight line until each st is just behind the latch. Replace the 57 sleeve cuff sts (held on waste yarn) into needle locks in front of OPEN latches, purl side facing you. Unravel the waste yarn as you go. Dec 12 sts across the sleeve width by replacing 2 sts onto the same Ns 6 times as evenly as possible (use '0' as a guide. 3

dec each side). Hold work down and with needle pusher or ruler, push all needle butts back to WP all at once. The rib sts will have 'knitted over' the garment sts and each needle will now hold only a single st. Cast off slackly.

Join sleeve and tiny 12 st side seams next.

BODY RIB

Cast on in k 1 p 1 rib 123 sts and rib to RC 36. Transfer all sts to main bed. Push needle butts forward slightly as for cuff. Around lower edge of cardi pick up 123 sts and place in hooks. Pick up the front edges first – one at each end of machine approx 34 sts each front. The back section is replaced last. Pick up sts to go onto Ns in centre area and if necessary 'double up' onto some Ns to dec the stocking stitch back to correct width of rib. If work is tight, move each needle butt individually to k over the picked up st because of width of work it is not advisable to move all Ns back at once as on sleeve cuffs.

CROCHET FRONT BAND (made in 3 rows)

1st row to form a firm edging
1 DC into each edge row of rib, also each individual cast off (or cast on) front edge sts including back of neck row edges, until rib is reached again. Work as start of row to end.
2nd row to form spaces in which to slot ribbon
4 chain to turn. * 3 chain, 1 treble into 3rd stitch of previous row * to end.
3rd row to form picot edge trim
1 chain to turn. * 2 DC into space where ribbon will go, 4 chain (to form picot), 2 DC into same space *. Repeat from * to * in each space to end. Fasten off.

TO MAKE UP

Neaten any ends by darning into seams. Thread ribbon in and out of large spaces round crochet edge. Pull slightly until front band stays flat. Secure ends by turning ribbon over garment edge and back on itself. Cut off any surplus and catch down with sewing cotton.

Using convenient picots as button loops; sew on buttons to correspond, 3 spaced out over rib, 4th where the V begins. Sew on motif or embroider fronts as illustrated (if liked).

BOOTEES

SIZES

Foot length 9 cm (3½ in) approx.

MATERIALS

1 ball 4 ply, 1 yd narrow ribbon, 2 motifs or embroidery thread if liked.

RIGHT FOOT (girls version as illustrated)

* Using waste yarn cast on 43 sts having odd st on right. K 8 rows. This is simply to provide fabric in which to hang claw weights as it is not always easy to knit a first row of transfer lace right after the cast on row.
Join in main yarn. Push all 43 Ns to H/P. Cast on 'e' wrap method with main yarn. K 2 rows stocking stitch.
RC 000. Work 18 rows lace. K 2 rows stocking stitch. Make a row of holes by transferring every alt st to next needle. All empty Ns in WP. K 2 rows. *
Push 22 Ns at right hand side to H/P. Remove main yarn and hook it round machine bed out of the way. K several rows waste yarn on 21 sts at left hand side of '0', release from machine. Using multi-transfer tool or hard k needle, move all sts 3 needles to left. Dec 1 st at right hand side. 21 sts.
RC 000. ** K 4 rows stocking stitch, 18 rows lace (either select Ns to make a small motif of 4 lace flowers or work lace right across the sts).
RC 22. Complete bootie in stocking stitch.
Shape toe
Set machine for H/P. Push 1 N at edge of work on same side as carriage to H/P and k across. Do this another 9 times. 11 Ns still knitting, 5 either side in H/P. Return 1 N at same side as carriage to WP on the next 10 rows, starting with the H/P N that is next to the 11 Ns still knitting. RC 42. Knit 22 rows straight for under the foot.
Shape heel
Repeat the 20 rows of toe shaping. RC 84. Using waste yarn k a few rows. Remove from machine.
Graft these sts to the other set of 21 already on waste yarn. Remove the waste yarn from cast on edge. **

LEFT FOOT

Work as for right foot from * to *. Break main yarn. Push 22 sts at left hand side to H/P. Using waste yarn k a few rows over 21 remaining Ns. Release. Return left hand Ns back to WP. Move all sts 2 needles to right. Dec 1 st at left hand side. 21 sts remain. Work as for right foot from ** to **. See Helpful Hints 2.

TO MAKE UP

Join side seam which will be on the inner side of leg when finished. Close other tiny foot seam.
Crochet edging
1st round as row 1 on coat front band. Join with slip st to end the round.
2nd round. * 1 DC, 4 chain, 1 DC all into first st of previous round, 1 DC into next st of previous round * to end. Fasten off. Thread ribbon through holes at ankles. Tie in a bow.

SIDEWAYS KNITTED CARDI – BOYS VERSION (not illustrated)

TO KNIT

Omit lace patterns and work throughout in stocking stitch. Work body and sleeve ribs as girls pattern. All row counter numbers will be the same. Omit ribbon/crochet front band.
Front band
Cast on in k 1 p 1 rib 9 sts. Work until required length – approx RC 200, making 4 small button holes evenly spaced where needed. Sew on the band to garment edge. Sew 4 buttons on to correspond with button holes. See helpful Hints 6.

BOOTEES (not illustrated)

Work as for girl, omitting lace, working in stocking stitch. Make a row of holes for ribbon at ankle as for girls pattern. See helpful Hints 4. Crochet round top edge.

SHORT SLEEVE CARDI IN CROSS-OVER STYLE

SIZES

To fit chest 46 cm (18 in), length 21 cm (8¼ in), sleeve seam 4.5 cm (1¾ in).

MATERIALS

4 balls Keynote acrylic 4 ply (20 grm balls) for coat.
2 buttons, 1.75 size crochet hook, bought motif or embroidery thread.

TENSION

30 sts and 40 rows to 10 cm (4 in). Try T6··. Ribs 2 or 3 whole numbers tighter.

BOYS VERSION (as illustrated)

BACK

Cast on 71 sts in k 1 p 1 rib. K 12 rows. Inc 1 st.
RC 000. Work in stocking stitch to RC 28. Cast off 2 sts beg next 2 rows. RC 000.
Raglan shaping (see Helpful Hints 1)
Use a multi-transfer tool with 4 prongs in action. Take 4 sts from arm hole edge onto tool, move inwards towards centre needle. Push empty Ns to A. The 4th N from edge now holds 2 sts. Using a one-eyed tool take the 5th st from edge and place on top of the 2 sts already on the 4th needle, which will now be holding 3 sts. Check the empty 5th needle is in WP so it will pick up and knit, making a decorative hole. Do the same at the other arm hole edge to correspond. K 2 rows. Continue to RC 42. (26 sts). Set machine for H/P.
Shape back neck over 4 rows
Push to H/P at left hand side 15 sts. * Still dec as before at arm hole edge, k 1 row, place yarn under end needle in H/P to

prevent a hole forming and k back. *
Repeat from * to *. Push rem 6 sts to H/P.
Break yarn. Place carriage on left of work.
Replace 11 sts at edge into WP. Complete
to match right hand side. 22 sts remain. K
1 row to bring all sts from H/P to WP. Cast
off.

RIGHT FRONT

Cast on in k 1 p 1 rib 45 sts. Work 12 rows.
Change to stocking stitch and working
with carriage on right, dec 1 st on next and
every 4th row at front edge until finishing
off at shoulder. This shapes the front
edge. At the same time – k 28 rows, cast off
2 sts on next row, k 1 row.
RC 000. Dec at arm hole edge as on back
until no sts remain.

NOTE:
At RC 38 6 sts remain (19 holes made by
decreasing). It is now no longer possible
to make a hole by moving the 5th st from
the edge, so transfer the edge 4 and knit.
At RC 40 there are 5 sts. Put both edge sts
onto next N in K 1 row. 3 sts. Dec as
before. A stitch remains. Fasten off.

LEFT FRONT

Cast on as for right front and rib 5 rows.
Make a buttonhole over 3rd st from the
right. (This is the 2nd needle working on
main bed). Make a second buttonhole on
the 17th st from the right. (This is the 9th
st working on main bed). K to RC 12.
Change to stocking stitch. K 1 row to left
hand side. From now on work with
carriage on left. Complete as for right
front, reversing shapings.

RIGHT SLEEVE

*Cast on 43 sts in k 1 p 1 rib and work 6
rows. Continue in stocking stitch. Inc 1 st
at beg of next 10 rows. K 2 rows. 53 sts. *
Cast off 2 at beg of next 2 rows.
RC 000. Dec as on back to RC 38 (11 sts).
It is no longer possible to make holes for
lace, so transfer the centre st to one side to
make the last decorative hole. K 2 rows.
As next dec is arranged centre needle
should hold 3 sts. K 2 rows. RC 42 (7 sts).
Dec 1 st at right hand side. Set machine
for H/P. Push 3 sts at left to H/P. K 2 rows.
Dec 1 st at right hand side. Set to knit back
to WP. K 1 row. 5 sts left. Cast off.

LEFT SLEEVE ONLY

Work from * to *. K 1 row to left.
RC 000. Work as for right sleeve to end
noting you will be working from the left
hand side. (holes of dec will then match).
Therefore read carriage on left for carriage on right, and vice versa.

FRONT BAND

Cast on 5 sts in k 1 p 1 rib.

. . .
.
. . . .

Push 1 needle at left edge to WP.

. . . .
.
. . . .

Now inc 2 sts on main bed by 'e' wrap
method. Cast on at right edge of work.
Needle setting is now

. . . . x .
.
. . . .

RC 000. Rib 4 rows. Transfer st marked
'x' onto right edge needle. Leave needle in
WP to make a hole.
Repeat these 4 rows to RC 250 or length
required. See Helpful Hints 2.

TO MAKE UP

Join sleeve and side seams. Sew in
sleeves. Sew on front band, edge without
holes to garment edge.
Work only one crochet now
* 1DC into hole, 4 chain, 1 DC into same
hole * to end. Fasten off.
Sew on 2 buttons on waist rib. Sew on
motif or embroidery if liked.

GIRLS VERSION (not illustrated)

TO KNIT

Work back, both fronts and front bands as
before, but make buttonholes on the right
front, counting needles from left hand
side. After the sleeve ribs, knit both
sleeves completely in any all-over lace
(small repeat) design of your choice. It is
not necessary to do the lace hole dec on
the 5th st of body parts.

BOOTEES

SIZES

Foot length 10 cm (4 in).

MATERIAL

1 ball and left over yarn from coat for the
crochet edge row. 90 cm (1 yd) narrow
ribbon.

BOYS VERSION (as illustrated)

Cast on in k 1 p 1 rib 43 sts and work 6
rows. Change to stocking stitch and work
to RC 18. Complete as for previous bootee
pattern starting with the row of holes for
ankle ribbon.
Crochet trim now – as crochet row of front
band, but working into each cast on. Knit
rib st on right side instead of each hole in
band edge.

GIRLS VERSION (not illustrated)

After the six rows rib, work 18 rows in lace
pattern to match the sleeves. Complete in
stocking stitch as for boys version.

Copies of Passap model book 34 have duly
arrived in the Dalesknit Centre and as
usual have been snapped up by Passap and
non Passap owners alike. The issue is not
only a feast of colour but a treasury of
fashion and knitting ideas as well. I've
had a lot of queries about yarn and tension
since this column last appeared. One
common query is "Where can we get
yarns similar to those used in garments in
the Passap model book?" Most of the
Passap garments we admire so much are
knitted in branded European yarns samples of which are offered for matching
purposes.

We all knit the special garment in the
special yarn but on the whole British
machine knitters have not been accus-
tomed to paying a lot for yarn but we must
realise the disadvantages as well as the
advantages of the situation. Branded
yarns have been tested in all kinds of ways
and have been chosen by the designer as
'just right' for the planned outfit. A
substitute yarn may produce a garment
different from the model garment in the
photograph. Most of us are prepared for
that and can adjust.

HINTS & TIPS

CHILDREN'S KNITTING

Children grow faster than we can knit.
Next time you knit a sweater for a
growing child try knitting it from the
top downwards. The length on both
back and front and on the sleeves can
then be easily added to if need be.
A sideways knitted sleeve can also be
an economy. Knit the sleeve sideways,
make it nice and wide, and then gather
it on to a tight cuff. No shaping on the
sleeve is required, simply knit it
straight. When the arms grow the
extra width will let the sleeves grow
with them. The cuff can be doubled
over at first and then pulled down to
give a few more inches. The whole cuff
could be easily removed and a new one
knitted.

A PRESSING PROBLEM

I have recently been asked advice on
what kind of surface to press garments
on. Well, there are several options. If
you can afford a press then it is a wel-
come luxury, but if you are planning to
make your own pressing surface then
you have to go back to the good old
days. Remember seeing the ironing
being done on the kitchen table, with
the table covered by several thick-
nesses of blanket and then a piece of
old sheeting? Well this is ideal, and if
you make the sheet on the top either
striped or checked then you have some
straight lines for easy pinning out of
your garment pieces.

Child's chinoise

A design from the Ryder range

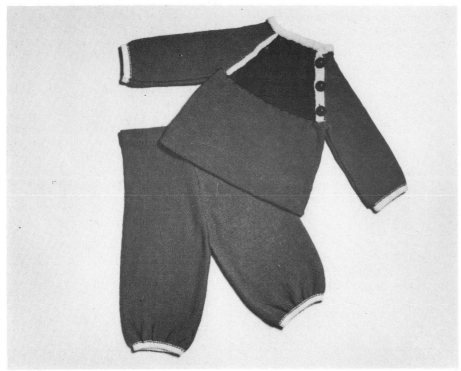

This little top and pants is a useful addition to any baby's wardrobe and can look pale and dreamy in pastel shades or bright and busy in the stronger colours. You could substitute mock rib for the ribber parts of this garment though the effect will not be quite so successful.

SIZES

41 (46, 50) cms, 16 (18, 20) ins.

MATERIALS

1 cone Argyll Ferntex in main colour; small quantities of two contrasting colours; 3 buttons; press stud fastener; length of 2 cms (¾ ins) elastic for waist.

TENSION

28 sts. and 40 rows to 10 cms. (4 ins.).

TOP

BACK AND FRONT (alike)

(Reverse side of work is right side of fabric throughout).
With main col. cast on by hand 79 (84, 89) sts.
Working in MT. k. 66 (78, 88) rows.
Shape raglan
Cast off 10 sts. at beg. of next 2 rows.
Place rem. 59 (64, 69) sts. into 3 x 2 rib

setting as shown below.

Break off main col. yarn.
Join in first contrast yarn and work in rib at main tension minus 1. Work 2 rows then dec. 1 st. each end of every alt. row until 23 (24, 25) sts. rem. Work 2 rows. Chain cast off.

SLEEVES

With main col. cast on by hand 60 (68, 74) sts.
K. straight to 68 (80, 94) rows. (Adjust length here if required).
Shape raglan
Cast off 4 (5, 5) sts. at beg. of next 2 rows. Dec. 1 st. each end of every alt. row until 16 (18, 20) sts. rem. Chain cast off.

SLEEVE BANDS

With reverse side facing pick up 3 sts. on 2 needles across cast on edge 40 (45, 47) sts. K. 1 row in MT.; 4 rows MT. minus 1; 1 row MT.; 3 rows MT. minus 1; 1 row T.10. Chain cast off.

TO MAKE UP

With reverse side of sleeve facing pick up 36 (38, 40) sts. along raglan. Using 2nd contrast yarn k. 1 row MT.; 4 rows MT.

minus 1; then, with wrong side of back facing, pick up 36 (38, 40) sts. from bodice raglan and k. tog. with sts. already on needles at T.10. Chain cast off.
Work a further back raglan and sleeve seam to match and also the right front seam.

LEFT FRONT RAGLAN OPENING

Button band
Pick up 36 (38, 40) sts. on left sleeve front raglan and work as sleeve band.
Buttonhole band
(This band is not reverse fabric to facilitate making buttonholes).
With wrong side facing pick up 36 (38, 40) sts. along front bodice raglan. Work as button band but make three closed buttonholes equally spaced along the band.

NECKBAND

With right side of work facing, pick up 2 sts. from buttonhole band; 21 (22, 23) sts. across front neck; 2 sts. from raglan band; 14 (16, 18) sts. across right sleeve top; 2 sts. from raglan band; 21 (22, 23) sts. across back neck; 2 sts. from raglan band; 14 (16, 18) sts. across left sleeve top and 2 sts. from button band. 78 (84, 90) sts. Work as sleeve band.
Join side and sleeve seams. Turn sleeve bands and neckband to wrong side and slip st. into place.
Attach buttons to correspond with buttonholes and sew press stud at neckband.

TROUSERS (make 2 pieces)

With main col. cast on by hand 102 (110, 116) sts. In MT. k. 70 (86, 100) rows. Adjust length here if required.
Dec. 1 st. each end of next and every 4th row until there are 70 (78, 84) sts. K. to 76 (80, 84) rows. Take off on waste yarn.

TO MAKE UP

Waistband
Join centre front seam. With reverse side facing, pick up 3 sts. on 2 needles across top of trousers. 94 (104, 112) sts. Work 1 row in MT.; 8 rows MT. minus 1; 1 row MT.; 9 rows MT. minus 1; 1 row T.10. Chain cast off.
Leg hems (alike)
Pick up 2 sts. on each needle 51 (55, 58) sts. Work as for sleeve bands. Join leg seams and back seam. Fold waistband to wrong side and slip st. in position. Thread elastic through band and secure.

Lacy baby set — angel top and pants

After the baby has outgrown our first size outfit this little ensemble will take him/her through the next few weeks. It is not too difficult to knit and is easy to wear accommodating both baby and nappy. The punchcard used is from a Jones/Brother pack as mentioned but Jones/Brother have kindly allowed us to print the card for those of you who do not have it. Readers with other makes of machine can easily substitute another lace card — see Anne's notes.

MEASUREMENTS

To fit chest 45cm (18 ins) top. Length 30½ cms. (12 ins.) pants. Completed side seam 15½ cm (6 ins.), around crotch 45 cm (18 ins.).

MATERIALS

Hayfield Babykin 3 ply. 8 balls. (Top alone takes 5½ balls). 4 small buttons. ½

metre narrow elastic. 1 pair plain white plastic baby pants for lining.
3 metres approx. pink and green 3 ply for embroidery. (3 metres of each col.).

TENSION

33 sts. and 48 rows to 10 cms (4 ins.) over stocking stitch. Approx. T.(4). Ribs (1..)/(1..)

NOTES:
Card 449 from Jones/Brother Vol.12 was used BUT knit 6 rows plain at steps 36 and 72 on the card. 44 actual knitted rows equal 1 pattern. You may substitute any lace card you choose.

TOP

BODY (knit 2, back and front alike)

Using waste yarn cast on 119 sts. with the uneven stitch on the right, knit 6 rows. R.C.000. Using main yarn make a picot edge by knitting 6 rows, transfer every alt. st. to the next needle, leaving empty needles in the WP. and using a whole number higher tension, knit 1 row to the left. Main tension knit 6 more rows. Turn up the hem. Carriage on the right. Knit 2 rows stocking stitch. R.C.000. Working in lace pattern knit 82 rows. Place marker thread at both edge sts. Knit 12 rows stocking stitch. Run off on waste yarn.

SLEEVES (knit two)

Using waste yarn cast on 59 sts. with the uneven stitch on the right. Knit 6 rows. R.C.000. Using main yarn knit 6 rows stocking stitch, then commence the lace pattern and work to R.C.66. Place marker threads at both edge sts. Knit 12 rows stocking stitch. Run off on waste yarn.

CUFFS

Cast on 39 sts. in 1 x 1 rib. Knit 24 rows, using a higher tension for the last row. Transfer sts. to the main bed. Replace onto these needles the wrist edge of the sleeve, decreasing evenly across the row. Knit 1 row on a high tension and cast off.

YOKE (knitted in 3 steps)

Step 1
199 needles to WP. Starting at the right, replace one sleeve onto 39 needles:- first stitch onto first needle, 2 sts. onto next needle to last 2 sts. Put onto the 39th needle.

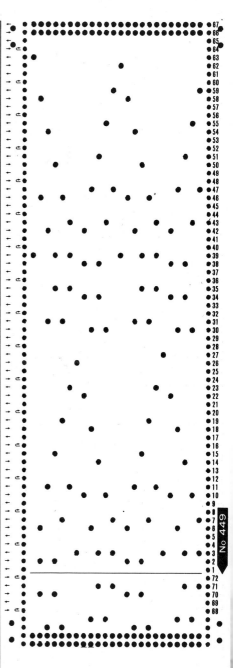

No 449

Onto the next 60 needles replace the front:- 2 sts. onto every needle to the last stitch, place on needle No.60. Replace the next sleeve onto the next 39 needles as before and the back onto the next 60 needles as before.
Knit 16 rows in stocking stitch. Run off on waste yarn.
Step 2
100 needles to WP. Starting at the right replace 2 sts. to each needle and the last

stitch singly. Knit 2 rows stocking stitch. Working in lace knit to step 36 on the card marking. Knit 4 rows stocking stitch. (R.C.22). Run off on waste yarn.

Step 3

67 needles to WP. Starting at the right replace 1 st. onto the first needle, 2 sts. onto the next needle to the last stitch. Place on 67th needle. Knit 1 row stocking stitch. Transfer sts. to 1 x 1 rib and knit 19 rows rib. Using a double eye tool place all sts. on a thread and remove from machine.

TO MAKE UP

Using mattress stitch join tiny yoke seams (4) above markers. Join side then sleeve seams. Turn cuff to inside and catch down where it meets the stocking stitch. Turn neck rib to inside and, leaving the thread holding the sts. in position, catch down loosely onto first row of rib, stitch for stitch.
Crochet round neck opening, making 4 buttonholes on sleeve edge of raglan. Sew on 4 buttons.
If you wish, embroider flowers on front yoke on the plain 16 rows stocking stitch of step 1.
Press lightly.

HELPFUL HINT

It is easier to handle the garment to embroider, if embroidery is done after joining the tiny raglan seams and before completing the rest of the sewing up.

PANTS

BACK

Using waste yarn cast on 83 sts. with the uneven stitch on the right. Knit 6 rows. Hem. Using main yarn k. 16 rows and turn up hem.
Back dart shaping
Put 3 needles to the H/P at opposite end to the carriage on the next 12 rows. (Don't forget to put yarn under needle as usual to prevent a hole). Push needles in H/P at left to UWP. Knit to the left, push needles at the right to UWP. knit to the right. All needles in WP.
Commence lace pattern and knit to row 54.
R.C.000. Cast off 2 sts. at beg. of next 18 rows, then dec. 1 st. at beg. of every row to R.C.40. 25 sts. remain. Run off on waste yarn.

FRONT

Work the hem as for the back, omit the dart shaping and knit in pattern to row 54.
R.C.000. Cast off 5 sts. at beg. of next 2 rows. Cast off 2 sts. at beg of next 24 rows. Knit 18 more rows straight. Do not start another lace panel after the 4th. Just knit stocking stitch. 25 sts. left. Run off on waste yarn.

LEG BANDS (knit 2)

Cast on 99 sts. in 1 x 1 rib knit 19 rows. Transfer sts. to main bed, k. 1 row only in stocking stitch. Run off on waste yarn.

TO MAKE UP

First graft the 25 sts. between the legs. Sew leg band to garment by back stitching through the open loops. Join side seams (leaving opening for elastic on inner part of hem). Turn leg ribs to inside and catch down. Embroider a row of flowers in the space between the 3rd and 4th lace borders on the back. Thread elastic through waist hem and join.
Press lightly. Pop the bought plastic pants inside to line.

HELPFUL HINTS

1. Press each piece of the garment before removing the waste yarn. It is so much easier to replace the stitches.
2. If you do not embroider the yoke and pants, they look pretty trimmed with rows of bought lace, provided it is already gathered when purchased. Sew on by hand.
3. If you do not have a lace machine, either work a row of diamonds manually above picot edge and step 2 of yoke, or just knit plain and sew on lace as before. White with pink lace or pink with white lace would make a pretty change.
4. If you do not have a ribber, do mock rib, any stitch setting you choose, according to your instruction book.

HINTS & TIPS

A FULLY FASHIONED INCREASE HOW TO DO IT

A fully fashioned increase makes a neat edge, especially where you require a straight edge for neat sewing up, perhaps on trousers or a skirt or wherever the edge will be in evidence. To increase fully fashioned you have to transfer the outside stitch out one needle, leaving an empty needle. This needle then needs to be filled in, otherwise you will have a hole when you knit across. To fill in the hole, pick up the bar of the stitch below and to the left of the empty needle and put it on to the empty needle. See the diagram. You do not have to operate on the very edge stitch, you could move three or more stitches out one space and then fill in and this will give you a fully fashioned increase in the same way as you would do a fully fashioned decrease using the triple transfer tool.

COLOUR CHANGERS

Sometimes I hear nasty rumours about colour changers; that they are difficult to use etc. This is not so, and most people who have had a go with one under the guidance of a demonstrator or tutor will agreed that they are quite easy to operate once you have seen how it is done. The problems start when we want to turn all those lovely little squares and samples into something wearable.
The key word is SIMPLICITY. Take a leaf from the books of the confirmed double bed knitters. Most of their designs are very effective but also very simple. Avoid lots of curves and fancy shapings, stick to straight lines and simple shapes. Take a classic set in sleeve pattern and where the curve comes for the armhole adapt the curve to a straight line so that instead of decreasing say 20 sts. over several rows, cast off 20 sts. all on the one row. If you are using your colour changer, cast off 20 sts. at the right with the yarn in the main feeder and 20 sts. at the left with one of the yarns in the colour changer. This will keep your

weights evenly balanced and the shaping will look much better if it is all on the same pattern row.
The sleeve heads can be straight and set into the sweater, and if you find it easier to decrease than increase then knit the sleeve from the top downwards and put the cuff on afterwards. If you are doing 2 x 1 or 1 x 1 rib first and then going into the Jacquard knitting after the rib, bring all the needles into the working position (don't forget half pitch if you are not already on half pitch), knit two circular rows and then go into your full needle rib. This fills in the gaps nicely and takes you smoothly into full needle rib.

STORING YOUR YARN

We all buy more yarn that we can ever hope to find time to knit up and we store it by the cupboardful. We take care to guard against moth and damp, but many a cone of yarn is ruined by heat. If the cones are in a place that is too warm the oil from the yarn will dry out and the yarn will be unfit for knitting.

Dainty duffle coat and mitts in double knit

SIZES

To fit 51-56 cms (20-22 ins) chest. Length 33 cms (13 ins). Sleeve seam 19 cms (7½ ins). Raglan depth 13 cms (5 ins). Hood round face 42 cms (16½ ins). Mitts width 8 cms (3 ins). Length without rib 10 cms (4 ins).

MATERIALS

8 balls Poppleton, Fragrant Baby DK main col. (white). 6 balls contrast (Rosebud Random).
6 white toggle buttons, small size. 2.5 crochet hook.

TENSION

21 sts and 52 rows to 10 cms (4 ins) measured over pattern. Try T.(9.). Use the same tension for all stocking stitch facings as well as pattern.

NOTES:

4 sts. and 8 rows make a complete pattern sequence and this makes this pattern suitable for all punchcard machines, electronics and semi automatic machines and can also be done by manual selection on the older machines.

The purl side is used as the right side. Work 2 rows contrast, 2 rows main, throughout, STARTING with the contrast.
Rows 1 and 2, 5 and 6, should tuck with the random yarn, rows 3 and 4, 7 and 8 should knit with plain white.

COLOUR CHANGERS:

Single bed colour changers are ideal for this pattern. Simply thread white through feeder 2 and random through feeder 1. Remember after turning work to knit 1 extra row to the left so cam box is at the side for colour changer. Using double bed colour changers see pattern notes for 'SHIRT IN SIX SIZES'.

DUFFLE COAT

BACK

Cast on by hand 83 sts. using white. K.10 rows stocking stitch. Turn work using either a garter bar waste wool or a hand knitting needle. Knit 1 row carriage on right. (Colour changers here is where your extra row is needed).
R.C. 000. Commence pattern and dec. 1 st. at both ends every 10th row 10 times. 63 sts. remain. Work to R.C. 116.
R.C. 000.
Shape raglan
Cast off 4 sts. at beg. of next 2 rows. K.2 rows. Dec. 1 st. at beg. of next and ev. foll. 4th row until 21 sts. remain. R.C. 68. Cast off.

LEFT FRONT

Cast on by hand 47 sts. Using white k.10 rows stocking stitch. Turn work as before.
R.C. 000. Commencing pattern, dec. 1 st. at right edge only, every 10th row until 37 sts. remain. Work to R.C. 116.
R.C. 000.
Shape raglan
Cast off 4 sts. at beg. of next row and knit 3 rows. Dec. 1 st. at beg. of next row and every foll. 4th row (right edge only) to R.C. 60.
AT THE SAME TIME at row 45 (22 sts. in work)
Shape neck
Cast off 10 sts. at left hand side, then 2 on the next alternate row twice altog. Dec. 1 st. at neck edge every time cam box is at neck edge until 3 sts. remain. Put both edge sts. onto centre needle and fasten off.
R.C. 60.

RIGHT FRONT

Work as for left front, dec. on left edge and noting that neck shaping begins on row 44 and not 45.

SLEEVES

*Cast on by hand 37 sts. using white and knit 8 rows stocking stitch. Turn work as before. Commence pattern and knit 20 rows only. Again turn work as before.
Machines with ribbers
Transfer to 1 x 1 rib and work 14 rows T.(6) both beds. Transfer sts. to main bed ready for pattern.
Single bed machines
Set for mock 2 x 1 rib and work 13 rows on a tension two whole numbers lower than the main tension. Bring all needles to WP. k.1 row*. Commence pattern. Inc. 1 st. at both ends of every 16 rows until there are 47 sts. Knit straight to R.C. 84.
Shape raglan
R.C. 000. Cast off 3 sts. at beg. of next 2 rows. Dec. 1 st. at each end of next and every foll. 4th row to R.C. 60.
Left sleeve only
Still dec. at right hand side. Dec. 1 st. at left hand side at beg. of next 8 rows by knitting down to N.W.P. with nylon cord.
Bring back to WP., knit 1 row and cast off (9 sts.) R.C. 68.
Right sleeve
Reverse the above shapings.

FRONT FACINGS
(two alike, knitted sideways)

Using white, cast on by hand 65 sts. Working only in stocking stitch, k.16 rows. Knit a few rows in waste yarn and run off machine.

HOOD

Cast on by hand 95 sts. Work from * to * as for sleeve.
R.C. 000. Commence pattern and knit to R.C. 50. Cast off 32 sts. at beg. of next 2 rows. 31 sts. remain.
R.C. 000. Dec. 1 st. both edges of every 10th row until 21 sts. remain.
Work to R.C. 76 and cast off.

MITTS

Machines with ribbers
Using white cast on 33 sts. for 1 x 1 rib. Work 14 rows and transfer to main bed.
Single bed machines
Using waste yarn cast on 32 sts. (arrange for 2 x 1 rib) knit a few rows and change to

main yarn (white). K.28 rows on a tension two whole numbers smaller than main tension. Turn up a hem. Remove waste yarn and inc. 1 st. at right hand side, 33 sts.

R.C. 000.

Commence pattern. K.50 rows. Set for stocking stitch using a tension three whole numbers smaller than main tension. K.4 rows. Cast off tightly.

CROCHET FASTENINGS

Always use white yarn double. All are simple chain stitch.

Duffle Coat
Crochet 3 lengths each 20 cms (8 ins) long.

Mitts
Make one length of 1 metre (36 ins).

TO MAKE UP

Coat
Join side seams. Turn up facing right along edge, catching lightly through a 'bobble'. Sew a facing to each front edge, purl side of facing to right side of garment. Turn back and catch down lightly to inside, stitch for stitch, unravelling the waste yarn. The stocking stitch side of the facing should show on the coat inside to match the remaining facings.

Join sleeve seams from first row of white rib to armhole. Turn to right side. Join turn back cuff and catch down facing around sleeve edge. Set in the sleeve joining the shorter raglan edge of each sleeve with the coat front and the longer edge with the back.

Hood
Join 2 hood seams. Catch down brim at both face edges. Pin hood to coat matching back panel with back panel of coat and the hood seams with the back raglan seams. Leave 1 in. free at each neck edge and cast off on centre front so they will overlap. Sew on hood.

Sew on 6 buttons as shown and join each chain into a loop round a pair of buttons. Catch chain down at garment edge to make a button loop and also round the other button.

Mitts
Join side and top seam. Join one end of long chain to inner seam at edge of mitt. Thread inner seam at edge of mitt. Thread chain up one coat sleeve across the chest and out down the other sleeve. Join chain to other mitt.

Pressing
Press according to ball bands.

HELPFUL HINTS

1. The stocking stitch 'bubble' side of the fabric is also attractive and a garment with quite a different look and texture will result if made up with this as the right side.

2. No colour changer and in a hurry? Just use one colour only. 13 balls are needed, make up on either side.

3. Try using white as a main colour and a self colour, not a random as here for contrast. The 'bubbles' will then show up more clearly in an alternating pattern.

4. Instead of knitting front facings, turn under ½ in., 2 cm. of front edges and insert a zip. Be sure to sew hood edges right up to centre front edges.

5. Make a bonnet to match the mitts. Knit hood. Knit a long strip of ribbing approx. 1 in. wide, 3 cms. and 1¼ metres long. Sew hood to this, gathering side edges very slightly.

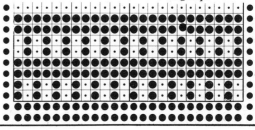

HINTS & TIPS

ON THE MOVE

We all have to move our machines around from time to time, even if it is only to dust the skirting board behind it . . .

The machine plus ribber and all the bits and pieces on the table take some shifting, especially if the machine table is on a thick carpet.

My friend Joan Godfrey runs the Eastbourne knitting club and they have sent me this useful tip for an easy shift around. Put furniture cups under the legs of your knitting table and it will glide easily along when you want to move it. It does not shift when you are knitting. The cups come in several sizes and the smallest size is sufficient.

TIP FROM BETTY ABBOT

We recently had the great pleasure of meeting Betty Abbot from Christchurch, New Zealand. Many of you will no doubt already have enjoyed knitting some of Betty's lovely designs. While discussing circular skirts, Betty showed me how to wrap the yarn on a dart so that the dart does not show at all. If the pattern says hold 10 sts., carriage is on the right and you are holding 10 sts. on the left, then the usual method is to put 9 sts. out to the holding position, knit to the left and then bring out the 10th needle so that the yarn wraps around it as you knit back. Betty knitted as follows: carriage on the right, 9 needles brought out to the holding position at the left, knit to the left, wrap the yarn round the inside needle in the holding position AND THEN bring the 10th needle out to the holding position and knit back to the right. The yarn is, in effect, now wrapped round two needles and the wrap does not show at all on the right side of the fabric. I have tried it since on shoulder shapings too, and it is super. Many thanks Betty for passing that tip on.

WEIGHT FOR IT . . .

Weighting knitting and reweighting once the knitting has reached the floor has always been a challenge to machine knitters and the problem seems to bring out the inventor in us; however, the most successful solutions are usually the simplest and this idea is no exception. When you need to rehang your weights, wind the knitting round the comb and secure it with a large bulldog clip, either one in the centre or one at each end, and if you need to you can hang a weight on to the clip, slotting the hook into the hole provided.

If the knitwear is fine or lacy it would be worthwhile to have one or two clips lined so that they do not snag the knitting.

It is sometimes a mistake to add weights as your knitting grows, quite often the reverse is required and you need to take some of the weight off, which makes sense when you think about it because the weight of the knitting itself is more.

SHAPING UP

I was asked recently about shaping the bottom of a skirt panel when there is to be a band of pattern at the bottom of the skirt. The simple answer is to shape either before you start the pattern or immediately afterwards. However, another alternative is to wait until the panel is almost finished and do the dart shaping at the top of the skirt. This has exactly the same effect on the bottom of the panel as if you had done the shaping at the beginning.

Toddler size rompers

This pattern can be easily adapted to a two piece outfit.

SIZES

To fit 51 cm (20 in) chest. Finished measurements 53.5 cm (21 in). Length 43 cm (17 in). Sleeve seam 20 cm (8 in).

MATERIALS

3 50 grm balls Phildar 'Option' 4 ply main col (red), 1 ball contrast (white).
4 small fish-eye buttons.
A small size crochet hook.

TENSION

30 sts and 42 rows to 10 cm (4 in) measured over stocking stitch. Approx tension 6··.

Fair Isle – increase tension by one dot. k1, p1 rib3/3.

NOTES:
Punchcard is from set M1002 design 40 Knitmaster.

BACK

Cast on 19 sts by hand. 'e' wrap. K 6 rows. Increase 2 sts at beginning of every row until there are 91 sts. RC 42.
RC 000. K 58 rows to waist line, decreasing 1 st every 10th row 3 times (85 sts).
Back dart shaping
Bring 8 needles to H/P at beg of next 8 rows. Carriage on right. Push needles from H/P to NWP at left hand side. K 1 row. Return needles at right hand side to work position. K 1 row. RC 60 of 'straight knitting' (do not count the 8 rows of shaping).

Make a row of holes by transferring every 3rd st. K 2 rows. RC 62.
RC 000. Set machine for Fair Isle.
IMPORTANT NOTE:
Take main (red) from feeder one, and replace with contrast (white).
Put main in feeder two.
K 34 rows Fair Isle. Cast off 2 st at beg of next 2 rows.
RC 000. Shape raglan. Decrease 1 st at beg of the next 50 rows. K 6 rows on waste yarn and release from machine.

FRONT

Cast on 19 sts by hand. 'e' wrap method. K 12 rows.
Inc 2 sts beg of every row until there are 63 sts.
Inc 8 sts at beg of next 2 rows, and inc 6 sts at beg of next 2 rows. RC 38 (91 sts now working).
RC 000. Work 60 rows to waist, dec side edges as on the back.
Make a row of holes (as given on the back) RC 62.
Set machine for Fair Isle (remember to change yarn as given for the back).
RC 000. Work 34 rows of raglan shaping (as on the back). With nylon cord knit centre 13 sts to A for neck. Also knit to 'A' all sts on left hand side.
TAKE NOTE OF CARD ROW NUMBER.
Working on right hand side sts only, and still decreasing at side edge, decrease 2 sts at neck edge by taking to A with nylon cord on every alternate row to RC 46. 3 sts remain. Place on centre needle and fasten off.
Return all sts on the left hand side of neck to WP. Reset card to previous row number and RC to 34 (leave centre 13 and all sts on right hand side which are knitted with nylon cord in A).
Work to match right hand side.
Return all sts now held by nylon cord to WP, and using waste yarn release after 6 rows.

SLEEVES

Rib tension. Cast on 47 sts for k1, p1 rib. Work 24 rows. Inc 1 st (48 sts).
RC 000. Work in stocking stitch. T6··.
Inc 1 st both ends of every 7th row until there are 64 sts. Continue to RC 60.
Cast on 2 st beg next 2 rows.
RC 000. Shape raglan. K 4 rows straight.
Dec 1 st beg of every row to RC 50. Push 2 needles to left hand side to hold on next

and following alternate row. K 1 row. K 1 row right across all sts (this shapes top of raglan for right sleeve). Work 6 rows on waste yarn. Release.

Work the left sleeve as above until RC 51. Push 2 needles to hold at right hand side on next and following alt row. K 1 row. K 1 row across all sts (this shapes sleeve top for left sleeve). Work 6 rows on waste yarn and release.

NECK BAND

Replace sts from front onto machine. Inc 7 sts each side of neck. Replace sts on right hand side from right sleeve top, overlapping one st. Replace sts from left sleeve on left hand side, overlapping one st. Replace sts from back at left hand side, overlapping one st. There should now be 103 sts. Push all needles to hold position. Set cam box to knit them back and work 1 row on main tension. Transfer for k1, p1 rib, k 21 rows. Transfer all sts back to main machine. Break off yarn approx 1 metre away from last st. Thread this end through double-eyed bodkin tool and take all sts off machine onto end of yarn.

LEG BANDS (two in main colour)

Cast on 99 sts for k1, p1 rib and k to RC 19 (rib tension). Transfer all sts to main bed and k1 row stocking stitch on main tension. K 6 rows on waste yarn and release.

WAIST TIE (in contrast colour)

Cast on by hand 4 sts. T2··. Set machine to slip in one direction and knit 550 rows. Thread the 4 sts onto yarn end using double bodkin tool.

TO MAKE UP

Join side seams, sleeve seams and sew raglan seams and tiny neck rib seam. Put both hands into neck rib and stretch as large as possible. Turn rib to inside and catch down on the top row of stocking stitch. Because this neckband has no cast on or cast off edge, it should stretch easily to slip over the head. If it will not, undo about 3 ins of the raglan seam where the neckband joins, and make tiny button loops and sew on 3 buttons, but this should not be necessary.

Pin the leg bands evenly round each leg, over the 12 straight rows of the front, round the edge but NOT over the 6 straight rows of the back. Back stitch in place through open loops, removing waste yarn. Turn the cast on edge to the inside and sew down.

Lightly catch down the 6 rows straight on the back to the inside. This forms a small facing on which to sew the 2 centre buttons. Sew the other 2 onto the edge of the leg ribs. Crochet across the front, 1 row dc, then 1 row to make 4 buttonholes. Make 2 small pom poms in contrast colour. Thread waist tie through holes and sew a pom pom to each end firmly.

HELPFUL HINTS

1. Red with white looks cosy and warm for a winter baby. Using pale blue as the main with navy contrast would look cool for a summer baby.
2. Substitute any Fair Isle pattern of your choice so long as it is only a small design, and so will not have long floats behind. No more than 8 st repeat.
3. It is so simple to change this pattern into a jumper. Knit the sleeves and neckband as in the main pattern.
   BODY: Main. Cast on 63 sts. K1, p1 rib. Work 18 rows. Transfer to main bed and set for Fair Isle (don't forget to change wool in feeders as before).
   Work 52 rows straight to arm hole. Follow main pattern for back from there, then follow the pattern for front. This will only take 2 balls main and 1 of contrast BUT, don't waste contrast colour, there will only be inches left!
4. The lower half of garment is simple to change into a pair of pants. Work both back and front from main pattern as far as the waist. Change to rib, work 21 rows and cast off. Knit leg bands. Turn waist rib to inside, catch down on first row of stocking stitch and insert narrow elastic. Join seam between legs (no buttons and loops needed).
   By making a jumper and matching pants baby will also have a two piece outfit, and again only 3 balls main, 1 contrast are needed!

HINTS & TIPS

MEASURING FOR A NECKBAND

There are many mathematical calculations offered for the working out of neckbands. This is a rule of thumb, but it usually works. Take the back or front of the garment and wrap the welt round your head and pin it. Take it off and measure by counting the stitches. Cast this amount of stitches on for the neckband and it will fit OK.

Quite often it works out that you need almost the same number of stitches on the neckband as you do on the rib for the back or front.

SEWING A NECKBAND DOWN

If you have attached a separate neckband and you are turning the band in to make a double edge, sew the edge down with shirring elastic instead of yarn and you will have a stretchy edge that will not break when you pull the garment over your head. Sometimes a fine yarn will not produce a decent rib and one way around this problem is to knit the rib twice as long as you require and then double it in and sew it down. As with the neckband you can sew the double rib down with shirring elastic and it will not break with wear.

WEIGHING THE YARN

If you knit a garment from a radar, or knit leader block or indeed anything other than a written pattern, it is a good idea to weigh the finished garment and keep a note of the amount of yarn used, noting also the type of yarn. This information will be useful if you want to use the pattern at some time in the future.

CLEAN MACHINES

Take it from me, many a problem has been solved simply by giving the machine a good clean. Wipe off all the old oil. To really clean it put a drop of methylated spirit on your cloth. Brush out all the hairs and bits of fluff etc. from between the needles and from the underside of the carriage. Put the nozzle of your vacuum cleaner on the needle bed, it will clear lots of dust and fluff.

Check that your brushes are spinning freely. If they are not, unscrew them and see that underneath them is free from wool and fluff.

If the bristles are badly frayed then replace them. Check for and replace any bent needles. Check that none of the sinker pins are bent. If they are then carefully straighten them. If you have any rough patches on the needle bed, smooth them down with emery paper and then wipe over with an oily cloth. Finally, oil lightly with light machine oil on a clean cloth as per the machine instruction book. Do not over oil. Don't forget the bodywork and lid. A wipe over with a cloth soaked in a biological washing powder and then a shine over with furniture polish works wonders.

TRANSPORTING YOUR KNITTING MACHINE

When you pack your machine up to take it away on holiday with you . . . do remember to secure the carriage to the machine with the locking bar, otherwise the carriage will slide around and be damaged. Getting all the tools and bits and pieces back into the case the way they were when you first bought your machine is just about impossible. Rather than struggle, it is better to have a separate carrying case in the form of a tool box or the like and put all the extras into this. Store your pattern cards flat and away from heat.

Snuggle

designed by Denise Musk

RC 96. Mark each end with contrast yarn. Knit straight to RC 152. Mark each end with contrast yarn. Knit to RC 192. COL. Transfer sts to main bed. Place remaining 2 edge frills on to needles with *right sides* facing machine. Knit 1 row T8. Knit 1 row T10. Cast off or link off.

SLEEVES

1st sleeve L/R 50/50
COL with cast off edge of ribbing (right side of main frill facing machine) on left side of centre '0'. Cast on edge of ribbing (wrong side of main frill facing machine) on right side of centre '0' pick up sts between markings in centre of main part of garment. With right side of 1 sleeve frill facing machine pick up sts of frill. Knit 1 row T8. Knit 1 row T10. Cast off or link off.

2nd sleeve
As above but reverse main body.
Cast off edge of ribbing on right. Cast on edge of ribbing on left. Pick up centre sts from frill with right side of frill facing machine.

TO MAKE UP

Place garment as diagram. Fold in half along centre line using contrast yarn markers (RC 96) as guide. Join main frill, side seam and sleeve frill ie A to A, (wrong side and right side of frills joined here is correct) along ribbing to BB then sleeve frill to CC. Repeat at other side.

All machines with lace carriage and ribber. Actual garment knitted on Jones 881. Lace punchcard. Basic Pack 17J.

SIZE

To fit most figures.

MATERIALS

"Shalimar" by Yarn-a-rama, The Cornmill, Church Street, Barrowford, Nelson, Lancs.

TENSION

Knitted on T.5 for lace frills and T.7/7 rib. No need for a tension square.

EDGE FRILLS (knit 4 alike)

Cast on in full needle rib. L/R 73/73 sts. Knit 1 zig-zag row T0/0. Hang comb and weights. RC 000. T1/1 knit 1 row. T3/3. Push to H/P every 3rd needle. Set machine to hold and knit 3 rows. Release hold. Knit 2 rows full needle rib. COR (RC 6). Transfer sts to main bed T5. RC 000. Knit 4 rows plain. Knit mesh lace to RC 44. Knit 2 rows plain RC 46. Transfer ev alt needle. Push empty needles to NWP. Knit 1 row. Strip off with WY.

SLEEVE FRILLS (knit 2 alike)

Work as edge frills but cast on L/R 100/100 sts. *N.B.* Watch out for end needle selection when working on full needle bed.

MAIN PART

Push to WP L/R 73/73 sts on main bed. Replace 2 edge frills with right sides facing machine placing 1 stitch on each needle. Transfer every 3rd stitch to ribber bed and set machine and ribber for 2x1 rib. (98 sts on main bed actually in work). Knit 1 zig-zag row. T1/1. Insert comb and weights. Knit 2 circular rows. T7/7. Knit to RC 40. Mark each end with contrast yarn. Knit straight to

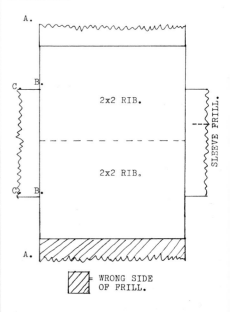

Diagram of finished measurements

Knitted nightdress

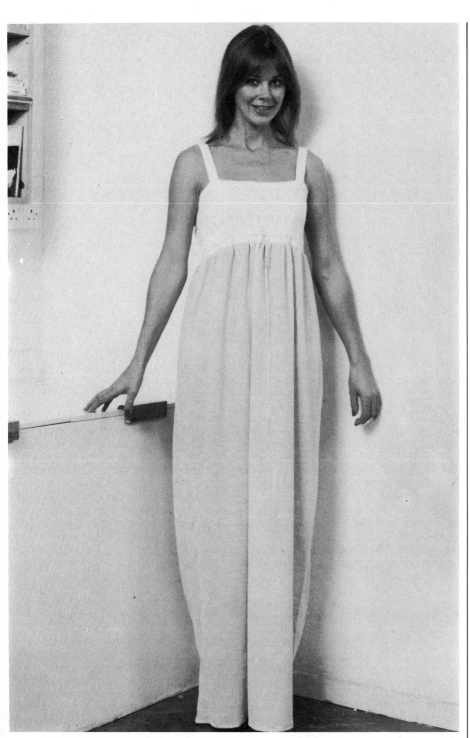

Approx 2.5 metres Singer fabric 'Bianca' 90 cm wide, blue (£2.15 per metre).
2 metres Offray satin ribbon 3 mm wide, colour light-blue.

TENSION

26 sts and 40 rows to 10 cms (4 ins) square measured over stocking stitch (approx tension 7-8). Check tension before starting garment.

TOP (two alike)

RC 000 MT cast on 47 (51, 54, 58) sts.
Knit 8 rows. Transfer every alt st onto adjacent needle, bringing empty Ns back into WP. Knit 8 rows.
Start pattern with con col 1, changing colours as indicated, to RC 35. Continue in main col to RC 48 (56, 60, 64). Knit row 1 of pattern only. Knit 8 rows. Transfer every alt st onto adjacent needle, bringing empty Ns back into WP, knit 8 rows. Turn hem to row 1 of pattern to form picot border. Cast off all sts.

STRAPS (two alike)

Knit a cord 8 sts wide in main col. Knit to required length. Cast off.

TO MAKE UP

Press pieces according to instructions on ball band.
Join two top pieces at side seams.
Place straps and sew into position.
Skirt
Cut fabric for skirt into two pieces 76 cms wide x (required length + 3.5 cms for hems).
Join side seams, trim and finish with a narrow zig-zag stitch. Turn up 1 cm double hem at bottom edge, and finish top edge with a zig-zag stitch.
Run a gathering thread 1 cm from zig-zagged edge and draw up to fit top. With right sides together tack top to skirt and sew using a straight stretch stitch or small zig-zag stitch.
Thread ribbon through holes under bustline and tie with a bow at the centre front.

To suit most makes and models of punchcard machines.

SIZES

To fit bust sizes 81 (86, 91, 96) cms, 32 (34, 36, 38) ins.

MATERIALS

5 (5, 5, 6) 20 grm balls white (main col), 1 20 grm ball blue (con col 1), 1 20 grm ball green (con col 2) of Sirdar Snuggly quick knit baby wool.

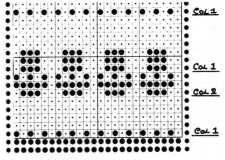

Cassie caterpillar

MATERIAL

Argyll Ferntex 4 ply and small amount of contrast.
Card 1A of Basic Knitmaster set.

TENSION

Any 4 ply tension between 6–7.

BODY

Cast on 20 sts main colour T7. Knit 2 rows. Insert card 1A. Lock on row 1. Inc 1 st both ends of next and every alt row 10 times (40 sts).
* Set machine to slip – card still locked – T9 using contrast colour knit 10 rows.
Set machine to stocking stitch T7 main colour, k 20 rows.
T2 knit 4 rows
T7 knit 20 rows *

Repeat from * to * 5 times more – knit 10 rows.
Shape head
Dec 1 st at each end of every alt row 10 times (20 sts).
Inc 1 st at each end of every alt row 10 times (40 sts)
Knit 30 rows.
* Knit 4 rows T2, knit 42 rows T7 *.
Repeat from * to * 5 times in all. (It is helpful to put the RC to 000 after each section of 46 rows).
Knit 4 rows T2, knit 22 rows T7.
Dec 1 st at each end of next and every alt row 10 times, 20 sts cast off.

SUCKERS (knit 10)

Cast on 7 sts T7. Set machine to knit a circular cord. Knit 50 rows cast off.

TO MAKE UP

Sew up side seams and around head, matching tight sections. Leave the tail end open – stuff and sew up the end. Run a thread through the tight tension rows on the upper body and draw in slightly. Fold back the head and stitch to the first hump. Cut small circles of white felt for the eyes and add beads. Black felt for the eyelashes and a small piece of red felt for the mouth. Embroider a knot for the nose. Roll the strips of circular cord tightly – secure and stitch to underside of body in pairs for the first five segments.
Cut a 10 ins circle of material for Mob cap (draw around a plate). Turn under raw edges and add trimming. Stitch a gathering wool 1½ ins from the edge and draw up to fit the head. Put ribbon around the neck.

Rabbit

MATERIALS

DK yarn – blue, white oddments.

TENSION

Tension 8. Not vital – the bigger the stitch –
the bigger the bunny.

BACK (blue)

Cast on 18 sts. K 2 rows. Inc 1 st each end of
alt rows to 24 sts. K 6 rows. Dec 1 st each end
alt rows 3 times. K 2 rows. Inc 1 st each end
every row to 24 sts. K 6 rows. Dec 1 st each
end every row to 8 sts. Cast off.

FRONT (white)

Cast on 7 sts. K 4 rows. Inc 1 st each end alt
rows to 15 sts. K 8 rows. Dec 1 st both ends
alt rows to 11 sts. K 4 rows. Inc 1 st each end
alt rows to 21 sts. Change colour to same as
back. Knit to row 43. Dec 1 st each end every
row to 8 sts. Cast off.

EARS (2 pieces blue, 2 pieces white)

Cast on 5 sts. Inc 1 st each end alt rows to 11
sts (each end). K 6 rows. Dec 1 st each end to
5 sts. Cast off.

ARM (2, blue)

Cast on 12 sts. K 18 rows. Run thread
through stitches and draw together, sew up
seam, leaving end open for stuffing.

LEG (2 blue)

Cast on 21 sts. K 1 row. Dec 1 st each end
every 3rd row to 11 sts. K 2 rows. Cast off.

FOOT PADS (2 pieces)

With white wool cast on 5 sts. K 2 rows. Inc
each end 1st alt rows to 9 sts. K 2 rows. Dec 1
st each end to 5 sts. Cast off.

NOSE

Knitted same as foot pads.

TO MAKE UP

Seam back and front all round leaving small
opening for stuffing, stuff and sew up. Sew
nose piece on with small amount of stuffing.
Sew seam of foot, sew in foot pad. Stuff and
sew on to bottom at front.
Stuff arms and sew on seam at sides.
Sew blue and white ear piece, lightly stuff
and sew on to top seam. Make carrot with felt
and sew on to ends of arms, joining them
together.
Make eyes with pieces of white felt with black
embroidery at top of felt. Embroider nose
and mouth. Make pom-pom for tail.

TOY OR DRAUGHT EXCLUDER SNAKE

TO KNIT

Using 4 ply yarn Tension 7 cast on 60 sts.
Knit 70 rows in stocking stitch. Change to
Fair Isle pattern of your own choice. T8
knit 220 rows or required length. Change to
1 x 1 rib. Knit 10 rows T5. Knit 10 rows T4.
Knit 20 rows T3. Break yarn and thread
through last row of sts. Draw up and fasten
off. Fold in half right side in. Sew up
leaving a 3in gap in centre. Lay work flat
placing seam in centre. Stitch a curved line
at stocking stitch end to shape snake's
head. Turn to right side through 3in gap.
Stuff, sew up gap and add facial features.

Lady's gloves

SIZES

Small, medium and large.

MATERIALS

Approx 50 grms 4 ply wool.

TENSION

7 sts and 10 rows to 2.5 cm (1 in). Tension dial approx (6).

TO KNIT

Left and right gloves both knitted alike.
Cast on 46 (50, 54) sts in 2 x 1 rib. Rib tension (4). Knit 30 rows.
Single bed machines knit 60 rows mock rib and turn up hem.
Transfer to stocking stitch and main tension.
Knit 12 rows.
*Move 21 (23, 25) needles at each side 1 stitch out (fill in the hole as you would on a fully fashioned increase). Knit 3 rows. *
Repeat from * to * 5 more times. 58 (62, 66) sts.
Now put 21 (23, 25) sts at each side of knitting onto waste yarn. This leaves 16 sts.

THUMB

Carriage at the right. Cast on 4 extra stitches at the right. 20 sts. Knit 20 rows.
To shape the top of the thumb
** Run work off on waste yarn. Replace the knitting 2 sts onto each needle. Knit 2 rows. **
Repeat from ** to **.
Remove from machine and thread end of yarn through last row of knitting.
With the purl side facing you pick up both sets of 21 (23, 25) sts and replace on machine leaving four empty needles in the centre.
Pick up four extra stitches from the base of the thumb and place onto empty needles. 46 (50, 54) sts.

Knit 16 (18, 22) rows.
Run work off on waste yarn.

FIRST FINGER

Pick up 12 (12, 14) sts in centre onto machine, knit 1 row.
Inc 1 st each side of alt rows twice 16 (16, 18) sts. Knit 22 (24, 26) rows.
Shape top as for top of thumb.

SECOND FINGER

Pick up 6 (7, 7) sts from either side of first finger leaving 2 empty needles in centre.
Pick up loops from row below to fill in centre 2 stitches.
Inc 1 st each side of next row 16 (18, 18) sts. Knit 28 (30, 32) rows.
Shape top as for top of thumb.

THIRD FINGER

Pick up 6 (7, 7) sts from either side of second finger leaving 2 empty needles in the centre. Pick up loops from row below to fill in centre 2 sts. Inc 1 st each side of next row 16 (18, 18) sts. Knit 26 (28, 30) rows.
Shape top as for top of thumb.

FOURTH FINGER

Pick up 5 (5, 6) sts at each side of third finger leaving two empty needles in the centre. Pick up loops from the row below to fill in the two centre needles. Increase one stitch at each side of the next row. Knit 24 (26, 28) rows.
Shape top as for top of thumb.

TO MAKE UP

Run in ends, sew up seams. Give light press if necessary.

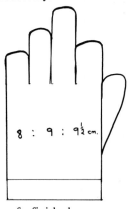

Diagram of finished measurements in inches.

Lace curtains

Knitted on a Knitmaster 360 – lace carriage throughout.

SIZE

To fit a bathroom window 60 cm (24 in) wide by 90 cm (36 in) long.
Finished width of each curtain 50 cm (20 in). Length 97 cm (38 in).

MATERIAL

1 cone of Argyll 2 ply — 100 cm (40 in) of light curtain weights if needed.

TENSION

30 sts and 50 rows of 10 cm (4 in) measured over lace pattern.
Tension 3 Card 396 Pack 63. Knitmaster.

TO KNIT (2 curtains alike)

Cast on with W yarn 150 sts knit 25-30 rows to hang the weights on. Carr at r Main Yarn T3 k 7 rows – transfer the sts for a Picot hem. K 1 row. K 7 rows. Turn the hem and insert the punchcard locked on row 1. K to the R. Release the card – set edge pins into position. K 450 rows moving the weights up as you go. RC 000 k 1 row T3. K 1 row T5 with main yarn and a strand of coloured cotton to mark for

picking up the loops k 36 rows T5. Turn hem and cast off loosely or knit an extra row at T8 and latch off or use the linker.

TO MAKE UP

You must pin the 2 curtains together on a blocking and pressing board measuring as you go. Press with a wet cloth and hot iron so that it drapes well. Leave to dry on the board. Insert the string of weights into the hem. I found I did not need them but you may like the weight. Hang on a pole, wire or sew on curtain tape.
If you need extra width this yarn will also knit well on T6. You could also sew bought fringing or bobbles on the hem, if desired.

Cushion patterns

If Santa brought you a knitting machine or if you are just getting round to mastering your machine and its various functions then you could not do better than to practise with our easy cushion cover patterns.

Joan's patterns for beginners have been amongst the most popular of our patterns and the cushions will be no exception. Each cushion measures 16 ins by 16 ins.

CUSHION IN FAIR ISLE

MATERIALS

Any 4 ply yarn, 2 colours. Amounts vary according to yarn but use up any oddments. Pattern card used was No. 4 from the Knitmaster 360 basic set but any Fair Isle card will do.

TENSION

31 sts and 37 rows to 10 cms (4 ins) at T(6·) measured over Fair Isle.

TO KNIT

Cast on in colour 1 by hand 124 sts. Knit 5 rows stocking stitch.
RC 000. Set machine for Fair Isle, thread in 2nd colour, knit 152 rows in pattern. Set machine for stocking stitch. Knit 5 rows colour 1. Cast off. Knit another piece exactly the same.

TUCK STITCH CUSHION

MATERIALS

We used Y.M.O. Park 4 ply but any 4 ply will do. We used a basic tuck card from the Toyota 901 set but again any tuck stitch card will suffice.

TENSION

23 sts and 72 rows to 10 cms (4 ins) at T(6).

TO KNIT

Cast on by hand 94 sts. Knit 6 rows stocking stitch. Set machine for pattern. RC 000. Knit 276 rows in pattern. Set for stocking stitch and knit 6 rows. Cast off. Knit another piece exactly the same.

WOVEN CUSHION

MATERIALS

Any 4 ply for the background yarn and any double knit for the weaving yarn.

TENSION

45 rows and 23 sts to 10 cms (4 ins) at T(6).

TO KNIT

We used a card from the Jones 840 basic pack but any suitable card for weaving can be used. Keep to a fairly small pattern so that threads will not pull easily if the cushion gets used by the wearers of buckled shoes etc.
Cast on 94 sts by hand and knit 5 rows stocking stitch in the 4 ply.
RC 000. Start weaving and weave 183 rows. Change back to stocking stitch and knit 5 rows. Cast off.
Make another piece exactly the same.

TO MAKE UP CUSHIONS

Mattress stitch three sides and finish the openings by sewing on Velcro or snap fastenings or a zip fastener – we like Velcro best.

Any suitable stuffing can be used. Use up all your reject tension squares and sew them into a washable cover or use a foam stuffing.

If you want to take it a bit further you can try any amount of trimmings and edgings either knitted or bought to jazz up the cushions.

A PASSAP CUSHION COVER

Card used is Passap card 95. This card is a good introduction to 4 colours in a row, without the hassle of shaping. The trim is a one way racking pattern, again good for a beginner to recognise the position of the beds.

SIZE

50 cms by 36 cms (20 ins by 14½ ins).

MATERIALS

Approx 2 ozs of Bright Courtelle in orange, 2 ozs brown, 2 ozs rust, 2 ozs fawn. 9 inch zip.

TO KNIT

Passap Duo 80 Tension (3½). Cast on K/K (full needle rib) 90 sts on each bed.
Lock $\frac{N}{N}$. Knit 8 rows main colour.
Lock on right $\frac{BX}{BX}$ ⟷
Tension dial 4 Card number 95. Thread up the other 3 colours. Fit Deco on 2 and programme pattern. Knit 1016 rows in 4 colour Fair Isle (i.e. 8 rows for every one row of pattern – 127 rows).
Lock $\frac{N}{N}$. Tension dial (4½) thread four colours through one eyelet. Knit 214 and cast off.

TO MAKE UP

Insert zip and sew up sides. Make edging as follows:-
Handle down, orange strippers, orange yarn, 2 strands. Cast on 5 sts each bed then arrange as follows

!!DIAGRAM!!

Make trim long enough to go right round cushion. Cast off and stitch trim in position.

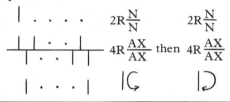

Lacy lampshade

Ann Taylor

SIZE

Lampshade to fit 14 cms (5½ ins) by 17 cms (6¾ ins) base.

MATERIALS

2 strands of blue industrial acrylic 2/30.
2 stands of white industrial acrylic 2/30.
Lampshade base covered with white silk taffeta.
Any small Fair Isle card and some shirring elastic and braid to go round the bottom and top of the shade – approx 1 yard.

TO KNIT

Cast on by hand with blue yarn, 136 sts.
Bring all needles out to the holding position for the first few rows until the knitting gets going.
Knit 5 rows at tension (5). Knit 1 row at tension (10). Knit 6 rows at tension (5). RC 12.
RC 000. Begin Fair Isle pattern.
Knit 10 rows tension (5). Knit 10 rows at tension (4). Knit 10 rows at tension (3).
Knit at tension 2 until RC 70.
Set for stocking stitch, blue yarn only. Knit 3 rows at tension (2).
Knit 1 row at tension (4) and 3 rows at tension (2). Cast off.

TO MAKE UP

Press with a damp cloth and a hot iron.
Turn down hems at both ends and lightly stitch. Insert shirring elastic and draw up at top. Join centre seam then pull down over shade base. Turn hem to inside and catch round with blue yarn. Stitch braid to top and bottom.

Dress a Sindy doll

Most young ladies have a Sindy doll or a doll of similar size and it is quite an expense to keep these little folk well dressed in the latest fashions. Here we have the start to Sindy's spring collection.

SIZES

To fit a doll 28 cms (11 ins) high.

MATERIALS

Oddments of 4 ply yarn, an old watch strap, one press stud and one small bead for a button.

TENSION

8 sts and 9 rows to 2.5 cms (1 in). Tension dial approx (6).

TROUSERS

TO KNIT (in two pieces)

Cast on by hand 20 sts. Knit 8 rows. Inc 1 st at each end of the next and every following 9th row until you have 30 sts. Knit straight to row 46.
Shape top
Dec 1 st at each end of the next row, dec 1 st at the end of the next row. Knit 2 rows. Repeat these 4 rows twice more. Knit 4 rows and cast off. Knit a second piece reversing the shaping.

TO MAKE UP

Join seams, work one row of double crochet round the waist and bottom of the trousers, make loops on waist for belt.

SLEEVELESS TOP

TO KNIT

Cast on 44 sts by hand. Knit 16 rows.
Divide for armholes
Put 32 sts at left into the H/P. 12 sts left in the WP at the right. Cast on 3 sts for the placket. Knit 10 rows on these 15 needles. Cast off. Put 20 needles at the right back into the WP and knit 9 rows. Use a piece of waste yarn and cast off the centre 8 sts and put the 6 sts to the left of the centre into the H/P. Knit 1 row on the remaining 6 sts and cast them off. Put the left hand 6 sts back to the WP. Knit 1 row on these and cast them off. Put the remaining 12 sts back into the WP and knit 10 rows and cast off.

TO MAKE UP

Work 2 rounds of double crochet in the main colour round the hem and one round in a contrast colour round the armholes. Fasten with a press stud. Embroider a little flower on the front.

SKIRT

TO KNIT

Cast on by hand 42 sts. Knit 46 rows. Carriage on the right, cast on 4 sts for placket. Knit 6 rows. Run off on waste yarn. Leaving the 4 extra sts as they are, place 2 sts on each needle across the row. Knit 2 rows, cast off.

TO MAKE UP

Sew seam as far as placket and catch bottom of placket. Finish with a press stud. Do one round of double crochet round the top. Twist a small cord and thread through to draw up skirt as required. Work one row of double crochet round the bottom of the skirt.

JACKET

TO KNIT

Cast on by hand 24 sts. Knit 16 rows. Cast on 7 sts at the beg of the next 4 rows. Continue on these 52 sts for 8 more rows.

Carriage at the right, put 22 sts into the H/P at the opposite end to the carriage. Knit 1 row. Cast off 8 sts, knit 1 row. Inc 1 st each row at the neck edge for the next 3 rows. Knit 3 more rows, carriage at the right. Cast off 7 sts, knit across. Knit 1 row to the right. Cast off 7 sts, continue on these 11 sts for 16 rows. Cast off. Work the other side to match reversing the shapings.

TO MAKE UP

Sew the seams and work one row of double crochet round the bottom, the front edges and the cuffs. Sew on a small bead for a button and make a loop for the fastening.

HAT

TO KNIT

Cast on by hand 47 sts. Knit 18 rows and run off on waste yarn. * Return to the needles by placing 2 sts onto each needle. Knit 2 rows ** and repeat from * to ** once more.

TO MAKE UP

Thread a wool needle and remove the stitches from the machine onto the yarn threaded through the needle. Gather up and fasten off. Sew back seam and allow the hem to roll to form the brim.

RAGLAN SHAPINGS

When a raglan pattern shaping reads decrease one stitch at each end of every alternate row you will get a better result if you decrease one stitch at the beginning of every row, that is at the end nearest the carriage. This makes a neat edge and stops the raglan from pulling so tight. Any fully fashioned shaping tends to pull tight. The small claw weights added to each edge and moved up at regular intervals also helps the situation.

There are many interesting variations to raglan shapings and these really do add to the finish of a garment, especially when it is otherwise plain. A lacy effect raglan looks well on a summer top. This is done by working a row of eyelet holes within the raglan shaping. Two stitches are decreased but an empty needle is left in the working position, say 5 sts in, so actually only one decrease is performed and a hole is made. Decreasing two stitches every fourth row instead of one stitch every alternate row is attractive and has the added bonus of speeding up the knitting. Decreasing 5, 6 or even 7 sts in on a raglan shaping looks very smart. When you are knitting a garment that has raglan shapings don't be discouraged if the pieces look small, you will be surprised at how much bigger they are when all the bits are fitted together.

Sew your raglan seams together with mattress stitch for a really smart finish.

ARMHOLE SHAPING ON STRAIGHT SLEEVES

The 'T' shape sweater is very popular, especially with new knitters. Almost any set in sleeve pattern can be adapted to this method and it is suitable for pattern stitches, double bed knitting and fancy yarns. The idea is that the line of the garment is simple, leaving the stitch pattern or the special yarn to do the job of making the garment look good. If a set in sleeve decreases to take the sleeve shape in say two inches, then you will be adapting the pattern to decrease in one row, but when you do only take the line in for one inch, not the usual amount. The sleeve will sit better in the smaller shape and the edge of the sleeve will not intrude on the front of the garment and pull it out of line. This type of shaping gives an easy line but it is just a little smarter than the drop sleeve, where no shaping is done whatsoever.

Action man

MATERIALS

3 ply yarn. Oddments.

TENSION

7½ sts and 11 rows 2.5 cms (1 in).

TROUSERS

TO KNIT (2 pieces alike)

Cast on 25 sts. K 10 rows 1 x 1 rib. Transfer sts for plain knitting. Row counter 000. Inc 1 st both ends every 6th row to 37 sts. K to row 38. Dec 1 st each end next and every following alt row 5 times. K 2 rows. Cast off.

HOODED JACKET

BACK

Cast on 28 sts. K 10 rows 1 x 1 rib. Transfer for plain knitting. K 22 rows.★ Cast off 6 sts beg next 2 rows. K 16 rows. Cast off.

FRONTS

Cast on 15 sts. Knit as back to ★. Cast off 6 at beg next row. K 16 rows. Cast off. Knit 2nd piece reversing shaping.

SLEEVES

Cast on 24 sts. K 8 rows 1 x 1 rib. K 34 rows plain. Cast off.

HOOD

Cast on 35 sts. Rib 1 x 1 8 rows. K 16 rows plain. Cast off.

SKINNY RIB SWEATER

BACK AND FRONT (both alike)

Cast on 34 sts. K 64 rows 2 x 2 rib. Cast off 10 sts each side ★. Run remaining 14 sts on to waste yarn. Knit 2nd piece to ★. Replace sts of first piece on to machine next to sts remaining on second piece. K 10 rows 1 x 1 rib. Cast off.

SLEEVES

Cast on 24 sts. K 34 rows 1 x 1 rib. Cast off.

TO MAKE UP

Trousers and jacket
Sew seams of trousers and thread shirring elastic through top. Sew up sides and shoulders of jacket and sleeve seams. Join back seam of hood. Turn back ribbing of hood on to right side of plain knitting and join on to neck, leaving ½ cm (¼ in) at each end for fastening at fronts. 1 row double crochet down fronts and sew on snap fasteners.
Skinny rib sweater
Sew up seams leaving 2.5 cms (1 in) open for armhole. Sew pieces of felt or leather over shoulders 2.5 cm (1 in) by 1 cm (½ in).

Lacy summer poncho and bonnet

SIZES

Poncho length (including fringe) 36 cm (14 ins). See Helpful Hints 4.
Bonnet around face 36 cm (14 ins). Depth 13 cm (5 ins).

MATERIALS

1 cone Roselan D.K. 100% acrylic in white, available from The Dalesknit Centre, Settle (send S.A.E. for shadecard). Poncho 225 grms, Bonnet 40 grms. 1 metre white ribbon, 11 motifs of Rosebud trim (optional), 1 crochet hook size 2·5.

TENSION

24 sts and 36 rows to 10 cms (4 ins) over lace. Try T9.

NOTES:
Card 411 Jones Vol. 6 "Small Designs".
8 sts and 12 rows to 1 pattern repeat.
Known as "Falling leaf" pattern.

PONCHO

PANEL A (knit two alike)
(One is left front, one is right back)

Hem
* Push 89 needles to B, having the odd st on right hand side. Return alt Ns to A. Using waste yarn cast on over the alt needles in WP and knit several rows, ending with carriage on right. Using white k 1 row to left hand side.
Push all needles to H/P (including those in A). Set machine to k back to WP and k 1 row to right hand side.
RC 000. K 2 rows. Make a picot edge by transferring every alt st to next needle and leaving empty needles ready to k in WP. K 4 rows. Seal by picking up only the long loops of 1st row white and placing onto alt needles. K 1 row to left hand side.
DOUBLE SEAL by picking up the shorter loops onto alt needles starting with 2nd st from edge. K 1 row to right hand side. Remove waste yarn *. Use weights. Set machine for lace and k 84 rows.

AT THE SAME TIME

Dec both edges as follows:-
Left edge – dec 1 every 4th row 20 times.
Right edge – dec 1 every alt row 42 times. This is easy to remember if you lose count, quickly divide the RC number by 4. If it divides evenly dec at both edges. If 2 left over, dec only at right hand side.
85th row, k in stocking stitch to left hand side.
86th row, Transfer sts as for picot edge. K to right hand side using largest T possible on dial. Cast off slackly.

PANEL B (knit 2 alike)
(One is right front, one is left back)

Knit as panel A reversing all shapings, i.e. dec every alt row at left hand side and every 4th row at right hand side.

CORD

Cast on by hand 3 sts only. MT 3 whole numbers.
Set machine for cord knitting and work to RC 700. Cut yarn, take the 3 sts onto the end with a double eyed T tool. Fasten off.

TO MAKE UP

The shorter seams are the shoulders. The longer seams are centre front and centre back.
Join shoulder and centre back seams. Join centre front seam from bottom to within 10 cms of neck. Leave that open. Using 2·5 crochet hook and starting at top of seam work the 10 cms to neck in double crochet. Work round neck edge into alt. Cast off sts of knitting as follows:
1 double crochet 4 chain, 1 double crochet into a neck edge st. Miss the next st, until the top of the 10 cm open front seam is reached. Work in double crochet only down to start of sewing. Fasten off.
Thread cord through top straight row of holes. Tie each end in a small knot to trim.

FRINGE

Cut yarn into 25.5 cm lengths (10 ins). Insert crochet hook *sideways* along through each point of the picot edge, (do not push hook through from front to back direction). Taking 4 strands at a time, loop, pull through and knot. A good idea is to wind yarn 44 times round a piece of 5 ins card and cut. This is enough for 11 picot points at a time. Trim lightly to neaten when complete.

Arrange 2 rosebud motifs along lower edge of each panel and sew on using white ordinary sewing thread. Or – embroider small flowers onto "leaf" shapes in the pattern.

BONNET

TO KNIT

Push 85 needles to B, having odd needle on right hand side. Work hem from * to * as on poncho. Break off white. K a few rows waste yarn and remove from machine. This is for the picot edge trim next to the face.

Again over the 85 needles, work hem from * to * as on poncho. Do not break white. K 2 rows.

Replace the 85 sts of picot face trim, purl side facing you, over the 85sts already there, and unravelling waste yarn as you go, k 2 more rows carriage on right. This has joined the 2 picot edges together into one piece of knitting.

Set machine for lace, use weights.
RC 000. K 42 rows straight.
Using a spare length of white, remove 26

sts from left hand side. K 1 row. Using another length of white remove 26 sts from right hand side. K 1 row carriage on right. 33 centre needles hold sts.
RC 000. K to RC 36, dec 1 st at both ends every 6th row. 21 sts remain. K a few rows with waste yarn and remove from machine.

TO MAKE UP

Close the 2 small head seams. No need to cast off the sts on length of white. Catch them neatly into the seam.
Neckband
Replace the 21 sts of centre back onto machine with the stocking stitch side of bonnet facing you. Pick up 25 sts at each side to face edge. 71 sts. Do not pick up sts at tiny edge of picot frills – leave them free.
With white, k 8 rows stocking stitch. Using waste yarn k a few rows and release from machine.
Turn the 8 rows of neckband onto the right side of bonnet at neck edge. Sew down back stitching through rows of open loops and remove waste yarn.
The picot edge will curl over towards the back of head. Just catch down the one end st by the face at both ends in that direction. This will form a decorative brim around face.
Thread ribbon through neckband.
Sew 3 rosebus motifs, one in centre and

one at each face edge (or embroider to match poncho on 3 "leaves").

HELPFUL HINTS

1. Knit slowly, making sure the end st is never transferred by machine during a lace sequence.
2. There will be enough yarn left on the cone to make an 18-20 ins baby cardigan or jumper.
3. If you do not crochet, leave the neck as it is. It is quite neat when drawn up with the cord.
4. The set is quite versatile 'size wize'. With bonnet it is suitable for a small baby in arms or pram. When the child outgrows the bonnet, the poncho will fit for quite a while, even to age 24 months. It looks nice then over a toddler's summer dress and makes a pleasant change from a cardigan. Just remove any 'babytype' rosebuds or embroidery.
5. Any lace pattern would be suitable providing it was only an 8 sts repeat as DK tends to make the lace design much larger. A 24 st repeat would therefore be most unsuitable for this garment.
6. A pink (or blue) poncho with white rosebud trim would be pretty, or make a contrasting colour fringe and tie on the poncho – face trim on the bonnet. The yarn is available in several suitable shades for young children.

Baby doll sleeping bag

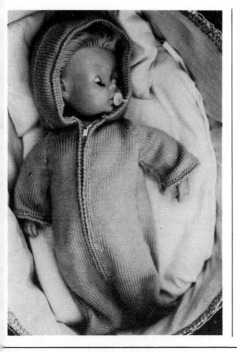

SIZE

To fit 41 cm (16 in) doll.

MATERIALS

Approx 75 grms soft 4 ply 23 cm (9 in) zip.

TENSION

7 sts and 10 rows to 2.5 cm (1 in). T dial approx (7).
Accurate sizing is not vital.
Measure front opening on finished garment before you buy the zip.

BACK

Cast on by hand 56 sts. MT throughout. Knit 102 rows.
Dec Ff 2 sts each end of next and ev foll 4th row 8 times altogether. Knit 3 rows. Cast off.

FRONT

Cast on by hand 56 sts. Knit 34 rows. Put 28 sts at left into H/P. Work on right hand set of

stitches. Knit to row 102. Dec Ff 2 sts at beg of next and ev foll 4th row 8 times altogether. Cast off.
Bring left hand Ns to WP and knit as for right shaping arm decreases on left.

SLEEVES (two alike)

Cast on by hand 44 sts. Knit 20 rows. Dec 2 sts at each end of next and ev foll 4th row 8 times altogether. Cast off.

HOOD

Cast on by hand 24 sts. Knit 62 rows. Cast on 40 sts at beg of next 2 rows. Knit 52 rows. Cast off.

HOOD BAND

Cast on 104 sts by hand. Knit 18 rows. Run off on WY. With wrong side of work facing you hang long edge of hood onto machine. Place band (wrong side facing you) back onto the machine. K 1 row T10. Cast off.

TO MAKE UP

Finish garment by crocheting down each side of front opening with 2 rows of crochet – 1 row crochet and 1 row crab stitch.
Insert zip. Work same crochet round edge of hood band and face edge, also edges of sleeves. Crab stitch is done by crocheting back without turning the work round.

Doll's outfit

**Dress – cape
pants and dungarees**

pink 2 ply for smocking and edgings. 60 cm (24 in) baby ribbon for waist. 3 small buttons. Small length of shirring elastic.

TENSION

9 sts and 12 rows to 1 in measured over stocking stitch. T dial approx (5). Same tension used throughout.
Pattern stitch
We used A 1x1 4 row tuck but any small tuck stitch would be suitable.

FRONT

Cast on by hand 91 sts. K 6 rows. Hook the edge of the lace onto the needles easing it a little to gather it. Knit 2 rows. Start pattern. Knit 128 rows tuck stitch. K 2 rows stocking stitch. Run off on WY. With pattern (tuck) facing you * replace work onto 60 needles. K 1 row. Transfer sts onto ribber as follows. 2 sts main bed. 1st on ribber throughout. T3/2. K 10 rows. Cast off 3 sts at beg of next 4 rows. Knit to R 36. Cast off.

BACK

Knit as front to *. Replace onto 48 needles. Knit 4 rows. Put 24 sts at left into H/P. K 10 rows. Cast off 5 sts at beg of next row. K to row 40. Cast off. Knit second half to match reversing the shaping.

SLEEVES (two alike)

Hook a length of lace slightly gathered onto 34 needles. Cast on by hand. Inc 1 st ev 4th row each end to 44 sts (44 rows). Cast off.

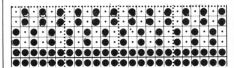

TO MAKE UP

Sew up seams. Turn up 4 rows to make hem. Run elastic through bottom of sleeves. Crochet round neck and down back opening making 3 chain loops for buttonholes – using contrast colour. Draw ribbing together to

DRESS AND PANTS

SIZE

To fit 41 cm (16 in) doll (TINY TEARS type).

MATERIALS

Approx 25 grms 2 ply acrylic. Approx 50 cms (20 ins) 1 cm (½ in) lace. We used white 2 ply and pale pink lace. Oddment of form smocking on front bodice. Sew on buttons. Thread ribbon through waist to tie at the back.

PANTS

TO KNIT (two pieces alike)

Cast on by hand 52 sts. Knit 40 rows. Dec 1 st each end of ev row 19 times. Cast off. Sew up side and crutch seams. Thread elastic through top. We used shirring elastic double. Crochet in contrast colour round legs.

CAPE

MATERIALS

Approx 30 grms 3 ply acrylic 50 cms (20 ins) baby ribbon. 3 small buttons. small length shirring elastic.

TENSION

8 sts and 11 rows measured over stocking stitch. T dial approx (6).

TO KNIT

Cast on with WY 143 sts. Knit few rows. Change to main yarn. RC 000. K 4 rows. K 1 row transferring alt sts to make picot edge. K 4 rows. Turn up picot edge. K 1 row. Remove waste yarn. K 2 rows.

Needle arrangement for pattern

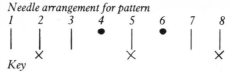

Key
● = needles not working.
x = needles tucking on rows 1-2-3.
1 = needles knitting on row 4.
Knit 140 rows in pattern. Bring all needles into WP T(7). Knit across. RC 000. Stocking stitch. K 20 rows. T(5) K 8 rows. Cast off 20 sts at each end. Run centre sts off on WY.

HOOD

Cast on 70 sts work as for cape to row 9. Work row of holes for ribbon. K 1 row. Work pattern for 80 rows. Cast off 25 sts at each side. In stocking stitch knit on centre 20 sts. Dec 1 st each end of ev 5th row to row 50. Join seams.
Replace 103 sts from WY onto machine with right side facing you. Put neck edge of hood onto same needles (wrong side facing you) T10. K 1 row. Cast off. Edge of cape will be frilled so run ribbon through and draw up so

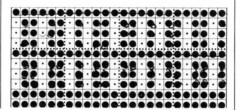

that it will lie flat. Thread elastic through neck. Crochet down plain knitting on front to make buttonholes.

DUNGAREES

MATERIALS

Approx 20 grms soft 4 ply acrylic.

TENSION

7 sts 10 rows to 2.5 cm (1 in). T dial approx (7).

TO KNIT

Cast on by hand 30 sts. K 8 rows. Inc 1 st each end of next and ev fol 6th row to 42 sts. K to row 48. RC 000. Dec 1 st each end ev 6th row to 36 sts. K to R 38. Cast off 26 sts at beg next row. Run rem sts off on WY. Knit a second piece, reversing shaping. Replace 10 sts from WY back onto machine to make bib at centre seam. Dec 1 st at each end of ev 3rd row 5 times altogether. Cast off. Sew leg seams.

STRAPS (two)

Cast on 3 sts knit approx 70 rows. Cast off.

TO MAKE UP

Thread shirring elastic through waist. Crochet round waist and bib edge. Sew straps from centre back of waist to top corners of bib.

HINTS & TIPS

A DRIVING PROBLEM

Drive lace knitting is done on the Knitmaster ribbing attachments and the instructions for it are in the ribbing attachment manual. However, here is a brief explanation. Drive lace is knitted on the ribber, so that whatever rib or hem you have started your garment, with all the stitches, must be transferred to the ribber before you start the lace. The ribber is set so that it knits normally and the main carriage is set so that it knits to the right and slips to the left (check with your instruction book if you are not sure). With the carriages on the left the 'P' carriage is taken across the ribber needles from left to right and this puts all the ribber needles up to 'C' position and ensures that they knit. Now knit from left to right. The ribber knits normally and the top bed gathers a loop on all needles. I should have said that the needle setting is full needle rib, therefore you are on half pitch. Carriages are now on the right and once again the 'P' carriage' is taken across the ribber needles from left to right. Knit to the left, the ribber knits only. Now the 'P' carriage is taken from right to left and back again across the main bed needles and this

strips the loops off forming the holes for the lace.
The whole process is then repeated. This then is the basic procedure, but of course it would not be very interesting so a punchcard is used. The card is inserted when the carriages are on the right and then the last row before the commencement of the pattern is knitted from right to left. The card is started and the whole procedure starts as just described. The purpose of the 'P' carriage (if you have not used it before you will find it in your ribber accessories) is to ensure that the ribber needles knit OK. When used on the ribber, ALWAYS from left to right only. On the main bed it is used from right to left and back again to strip the loops off the main bed needles.
When you are knitting drive lace you need a higher tension on the main bed than on the ribber so that the holes are visible.
Yarns for drive lace should be smooth and not fluffy or hairy otherwise the pattern is hidden. A shiny yarn looks well, for example bright courtelle.
For your first attempt at drive lace a plain sweater, back and front, and then make drive lace sleeves casting on the correct number of stitches for the arm-

hole width and knitting the sleeves straight and then shaping the cap in the usual way. The beginning of the sleeve can be cast on in waste yarn and then later picked up and gathered on to a cuff.

AN EASY APPROACH TO DRIVE LACE

Most knitters tackling drive lace follow the instructions to the letter to ensure success. In the process of knitting, the 'P' carriage is used to take the needles on the ribber to the 'C' position. It is easy to get carried away and inadvertently take the 'P' carriage across and back and so drop all the stitches off the machine . . . very frustrating.
The 'P' carriage can be dispensed with altogether if the tension on the ribber is loose enough for the yarn being used. Missing out on this one part of the procedure makes life very much easier and it is easy to get into a rhythm with the carriage and the 'P' carriage without the risk of losing the work.
Because lace knitting can be quite loose without detracting from the pattern, a larger stitch size does not affect the finished look of the fabric.

'Happy Christmas' stocking

For Knitmaster SK500 Electronic Machines.

MATERIALS

Any 4 ply wool. 7 20 grm balls in col 1 (red); 2 20 grm balls in col 2 (white).

TENSION

31 sts and 45 rows to 10 cms (4 ins) measured over stockinet. Tension dial at approx 7.

TO KNIT

Push 75 Ns at left and right of centre 0 to B pos. (150 Ns). Tension dial at 7. Using waste yarn, cast on and knit 7 rows. Carr at left. Row Counter 000. Using col 1, knit 1 row.

Shape Toe

* Always taking yarn round first inside N in D pos push 76 Ns at opposite end to carry to 'D' pos on next row. Push 1 N at opposite end to carr to D pos on next row. Push 1 N at opposite end to carr to D pos on next 15 rows. Push 2 Ns at opposite end to carr to D pos on next 20 rows. Push 2 inside Ns at opposite end to carr from D pos down into C pos on next 20 rows. Push 1 inside N at opposite end to carr from D pos down into C pos on next 16 rows. Push rem 75 needles at opposite end to carr from D pos down into C pos. Knit 83 rows carr at left.

Shape Heel

Foll instructions for Toe to * to *. Knit 7 rows. Inspection button on. Insert special card and set to row 1. Pattern width indicator 60. Point cams on 30 at both sides of centre 0. Needle 1 cam between Ns 30 and 31 at right of centre 0. Buttons 1 (left) and 2 (left). Knit 2 rows. Inspection button off. Insert yarn separators. Set machine for Fair Isle. With col 1 in feeder 1 and col 2 in feeder 2, knit 93 rows. Inspection button on. Remove yarn separators. Set machine for stockinet. Continue in col 1 only. Knit 87 rows. Tension dial at 5, knit 1 row. Tension dial at 7, knit 63 rows. Using col 2, knit 3 rows. Tension dial at 9, knit 1 row. Tension dial at 7, knit 4 rows. Working in stripes of 4 rows col 1 and 4 rows col 2 throughout, knit 63 rows. Tension dial at 9, knit 1 row. Tension dial at 7, knit 22 rows. Cast off.

HANGING LOOP

Using col 1, cast on by hand 10 sts. Row Counter 000. Tension dial at 7, knit 90 rows. Cast off.

TO MAKE UP

Pin out and press carefully according to manufacturers instructions. Join side and foot seam. Graft sts below waste yarn. Fold 20 cms at top to inside and catch down. Fold 15 cms to outside. Fold hanging loop in half lengthways and join seam. Fold in half to form a loop and sew to top of stocking.

CLOWN

For Knitmaster standard Punchcard and Electronic Machines.

MATERIALS

Clown

Any 4 ply wool. 3 25 grm balls in col 1 (black); 3 25 grm balls in col 2 (white); oddments in col 3 (red); kapok or foam pieces for stuffing.

Trousers

Small amounts of any double knitting wool in col 3 (red), col 4 (blue), col 5 (yellow) and col 6 (green); 2 buttons.

TENSIONS

32 sts and 35 rows to 10 cms (4 ins) measured over Fair Isle. Tension dial at approx 7. 32 sts and 42 rows to 10 cms measured over stockinet in col 2. Tension dial at approx 6. 32 sts and 38 rows to 10 cms (4 ins) measured over stockinet in col 1. Tension dial at approx 7. 26 sts and 36 rows to 10 cms (4 ins) measured over stockinet in double knitting. Tension dial at approx 9.

NOTES

Stripe Pattern

Knit 2 rows col 3, 2 rows col 4, 2 rows col 5 and 2 rows col 6.

BACK

First Leg

Push Ns 11 to 22 inclusive at left of centre 0 to B pos. (12 Ns).

Punchcard Machines

Insert card 2 and lock on row 1.

Electronic Machines

Inspection button on. Insert pattern 2, sheet 1 and set to first row. Pattern width indicator 24. Point cams on 72 at both sides of centre 0. Needle 1 cam at centre 0. Buttons 1 (left) and 2 (left).

Both Machines

With carr at left and using col 1, cast on by hand. Row Counter 000. Tension dial at 7. Knit 1 row. Cast on 3 sts at beg of next 2 rows and 2 sts at beg of next 2 rows. Inc 1 st at both ends of next and foll alt row, knit 3 rows. Inc 1 st at both ends of next and foll 6th row. 30 sts. Knit 10 rows. Dec 1 st at both ends of next and foll 6th row. 26 sts. Knit 1 row. Row Counter 036. Set machine for Fair Isle.

Punchcard Machines

Release card.

Electronic Machines

Inspection button off.

Both Machines

With col 1 in feeder 1 and col 2 in feeder 2, knit 59 rows. Carr at right. Inc 1 st at beg of next and ev foll alt row 3 times in all. 29 sts. Row Counter 100*.

Punchcard Machines

Remove card.

Electronic Machines

Inspection button on.

Both Machines

Set machine for stockinet. Using waste yarn, knit 8 rows. Release from machine.

Second Leg

Foll instructions for First Leg to * but reverse the shapings by reading right for left and vice versa. Do not reverse buttons on Electronic Machines.

Push 29 Ns at left to B pos. With purl side facing, replace sts of First Leg (Below waste yarn) onto Ns. Unravel waste yarn. 58 sts. Knit 38 rows. Carr at right.

Shape Sleeves

Inc 1 st at both ends of next and ev foll alt row 4 times in all, knit 1 row. Cast on 36 sts at beg of next 2 rows. 138 sts. Knit 4 rows. Inc 1 st at both ends of next and ev foll 5th row 3 times in all. 144 sts. Knit 3 rows. Row Counter 166. Carr at right.

Shape Shoulders

Always taking yarn round first inside N in D pos, push 11 Ns at opposite end to carr into D pos on next 4 rows. Push 12 Ns at opposite end to carr into D pos on next 6 rows. 28 sts in B pos. Break off col 1. Using nylon cord, knit 28 sts in centre by hand taking Ns down into A pos.

Punchcard Machines

Remove card.

Electronic Machines

Inspection button on.

Both Machines

Set machine for stockinet. Push 58 Ns at right from D pos down into C pos. Using waste yarn, knit 8 rows. Release from machine. Push 58 Ns at left from D pos down into C pos. Using waste yarn, knit 8 rows. Release from machine. With carr at right, unravel nylon cord, bringing Ns to B pos. Tension dial at 6.

Shape Head

Using col 2, knit 1 row. Cast on 2 sts at beg of next 2 rows. Inc 1 st at both ends of next and ev foll alt row 5 times in all, knit 3 rows. Inc 1 st at both ends of next and foll 4th row. 46 sts**. Knit 10 rows. Dec 1 st at both ends of next row, knit 3 rows. Mark centre and both edges with waste yarn for hairline. Dec 1 st at both ends of next and foll 4th row, knit 1 row. Dec 1 st at both ends of next and ev foll alt row 3 times in all. Cast off 2 sts at beg of next 6 rows and 3 sts at beg of next 4 rows. Cast off rem 10 sts.

FRONT

Foll instructions for Back to **. Knit 2 rows. Carr at right.

Shape Nose

Russel Levers I. Push all Ns except centre 2 Ns to D pos. Using col 3, knit 1 row. Taking yarn round first inside N in D pos, push 1 inside N at same side as carr to C pos on next 6 rows, knit 7 rows. Push 1 N at same side as carr to D pos on next 6 rows. Break off col 3. Russel Levers II. Continue in col 2. Knit 8 rows. Dec 1 st at both ends of next row, knit 3 rows. Mark both edges with waste yarn for hairline. Dec 1 st at both ends of next and foll 4th row, knit 1 row. Dec 1 st at both ends of next and ev foll alt row 3 times in all. Cast off 2 sts at beg of next 6 rows and 3 sts at beg of next 4 rows. Cast off rem 10 sts.

HANDS (Both alike)

Using col 2, cast on by hand 20 sts. Row Counter 000. Tension dial at 6. Knit 4 rows. Inc 1 st at both ends of next row. 22 sts. Knit 5 rows.

Shape Hand

Always taking yarn round first inside N in D pos, push 1 N at opposite end to carr to D pos on next 8 rows. Push 2 Ns at opposite end to carr to D pos on next 4 rows. Push 2 inside Ns at opposite end to carr from D pos down into C pos on next 4 rows. Push 1 inside N at opposite end to carr from D pos down into C pos on next 8 rows. Knit 5 rows. Dec 1 st at both ends of next row. 20 sts. Knit 3 rows. Cast off.

TROUSERS

First Half

Push 65 Ns to B pos. Tension dial at 9. Using waste yarn, cast on and knit 8 rows (knit 1 row extra for second half). Carr at right. Row Counter 000. Work in stripe pattern as given in notes throughout. Push 30 Ns at opposite end to carr to D pos. Mark end B pos N at left with waste yarn. Always taking yarn round first inside N in D pos, knit 2 rows. Push 3 inside Ns at opposite end to carr from D pos down into C pos, knit 2 rows. Push rem Ns at opposite end to carr from D pos down into C pos, knit 88 rows. Push 27 Ns at opposite end to carr to D pos. Always taking yarn round first inside N in D pos, knit 2 rows. Push 3 Ns at opposite end to carr to D pos, knit 1 row. Mark end B pos N at left with waste yarn. Break off yarn leaving a long end for grafting. Push all Ns from D pos down into C pos. Using waste yarn, knit 8 rows. Release from machine.

Second Half

Foll instructions for first half, noting alteration in number of rows worked and reading right for left and vice versa.

BRACES (2 alike)

Using col 3, cast on by hand 16 sts. Row Counter 000. Tension dial at 9. Working in stripe pattern as given in notes, knit 90 rows. Cast off.

TO MAKE UP

Graft shoulder. Unravel waste yarn. Join head, sleeve, side, foot and inside leg seams, leaving opening at end of sleeves. Join side seams of hands. Stuff body and hands. Sew hands into position. Make hair as for a fringe. Using a latchet tool, attach hair to back of head between markers. Embroider face features. Graft leg section of trousers together on each piece. Graft both pieces together along shaped edges. Turn in 2 sts at lower edge of legs and top of trousers to inside and catch down. Fold braces in half and join seams. Sew braces to top of trousers and attach 2 buttons on front. Place onto clown.

Pattern for the Digest dolly

MATERIALS

Any 4 ply. Approximate amounts 2 ozs (55 grms) Oatmeal, 1 oz (25 grms) white, 3 ozs (90 grms) navy, ½ oz (20 grms) brown. Some small pieces for features, ½ lb washable stuffing.

TENSION

8 sts and 12 rows to 2.5 cm (1 in). Approx tension (5).

DOLL

LEGS (both alike)

Cast on by hand 30 sts. Knit 100 rows, run off on waste yarn.
Knit second leg.
Hang both legs back onto machine with wrong side facing, start at needle 31 at left of centre 0, leave the first needle at each side of centre 0 empty. When both legs are back on the machine, increase 1 st at each side of the two pieces, 64 needles altogether.

BODY

Knit 80 rows, cast off.

FEET (both alike)

Cast on by hand 16 sts. Knit 6 rows. *Put the first needle at the opposite end to the carriage into the holding position on the next and every following row until 6 sts remain in working position.
Now put the needles back into the working position one at a time until all sts back in work. *Knit 10 rows straight. Repeat from * to *. Knit 8 rows cast off.

ARMS (both alike)

Cast on by hand 26 sts. Knit 72 rows. Dec 1 st at each end of the next 3 rows. Knit 1 row. Dec 1 st at beginning of next 10 rows. Cast off.
These decreases form the hand.

HEAD (two pieces)

Cast on by hand 18 sts. Knit 4 rows.
Inc 1 st at the beginning of every row 18 times (36 sts). Knit straight for 10 rows. Dec 1 st at beg of next 18 rows. 18 sts remain. Knit 4 rows straight, cast off.

TO MAKE UP

Stuff legs and body firmly. Join feet to legs and sew onto body. Make up head and arms likewise.
Hair
Take strands of yarn approx 16 ins long. You will need just enough to make it the thickness you require (we had about 300 strands). Tie the ends into bunches or plaits.
Sew the hair up the centre back of the head with a neat backstitch.
Cut a few strands for fringe if you wish.
Mark features on face as preferred . . . please keep face cheerful!

DOLL'S CLOTHES

MATERIALS

2 ozs (55 grms) navy, 1 oz (25 grms) white. Small length of elastic.

SKIRT

Bring 100 needles to the working position and push back every 4th needle leaving 75 needles in the working position. Cast on by hand over these needles. Knit 80 rows, cast off.

Sew side seam and carefully turn up bottom hem depth of 8 rows. Turn down smaller hem at waist, thread elastic.

JUMPER

BACK

Cast on with waste yarn 48 sts, knit a few rows. Join navy yarn* knit 12 rows, turn up hem.

Knit 28 rows straight. Cast off 10 sts at beg of next 2 rows*.

Knit 25 rows, cast off.

FRONT

Knit as for back from * to *.

Carriage at the right. Put all sts at left of centre 0 into the holding position.

Knit on 14 remaining sts.

Dec 1 st at the neck edge every 3rd row 8 times. K 1 row. Cast off. Return H/P needle to WP and knit as for right reversing shaping.

Join shoulders. Pick up 36 stitches for the sleeves between 10 cast off stitches of armholes. Knit 64 rows and cast off.

Sew side and sleeve seams.

SHOES

Heel

Cast on by hand 16 sts. Knit 10 rows. *Put 1 st into the holding position (opposite end to carriage) each row until 6 sts remain. Now knit putting each stitch back into the working position one at a time*. Knit 10 rows.

Toe

Work as for heel from * to *.

Knit 6 rows straight. Cast off the centre 8 sts leaving 6 sts each side, put one set of 6 sts into the holding position and work on the other side. Knit 10 rows and cast off. Bring the second set of sts back to the working position and knit 10 rows. Cast off.

These sts form the side of the shoe. Stitch side seams and sew cast off sts to back of heel.

COLLAR

Cast on 28 sts by hand. K 26 rows. Carriage at the right. Put 21 needles at opposite end of carriage into the holding position, leaving 7 sts working.

Knit 4 rows, dec 1 st at the neck edge, repeat 3 more times leaving 3 sts. Knit on these 3 sts for 10 rows. Fasten off.

Cast off 14 sts in the centre then work on the remaining 7 sts and knit as for first half.

Take a small length of navy yarn, make a chain stitch round the outer edge of the collar and then a second chain two stitches in from the first chain.

Using white yarn make a short cord to tie into a bow. Sew to end of collar.

PANTS

Cast on by hand 34 sts. Knit 12 rows. Dec 1 st each end of every row to the last 6 sts. K 2 rows. Inc 1 st each end of every row until 34 sts. Cast off.

Sew side seams and thread elastic if necessary.

HAT

Crown

Cast on 8 sts by hand. K 1 row. Inc 1 st at each end of the next and every following row 14 times. 36 sts. Knit 18 rows.

Dec 1 st each end of the next and every following row 14 times. 8 sts remain. Cast off.

Brim

Cast on 84 sts. Knit 24 rows, cast off. Gather in crown to fit brim and turn up the hem.

HINTS & TIPS

ANOTHER NEAT HEM

For a neat hem, put a pattern card into the pattern panel and lock it in position on a row that is punched for pattern about every 6th stitch. For the last two rows of the hem (this is a single bed turned up hem) put the cam lever to slip and this will then slip every 6th stitch, leaving you with a nice big loop to use for sewing down the hem.

WASHING THE PIECES

With yarns such as Shetland we must wash the tension swatches to gain an accurate measurement for the knitting. It is a mistake to wash the garment pieces before you sew them up because the thread with which you then assemble the pieces will always be one wash behind the piece and it will not sit together properly, in fact it will most likely be badly distorted.

RIBBER CAST ON WITH DIFFICULT YARNS

Casting on with the ribber can be difficult, especially with a difficult yarn or if you need to go straight into a pattern stitch or unusual needle setting. The cast on combs damage fragile yarns and a great deal of time and patience can be spent on those first few crucial rows. To save this hassle, try casting on with an easy yarn, knit 20 or 30 rows and let the combs and weights fall well away from the machine. Then join in the main yarn with everything set to cast on all over again. The first row of knitting will be over a row of waste yarn and not over the comb and the edge will be neat. It is a bit of a fiddle undoing the waste yarn from the main yarn because you need to take care not to pull it but it is well worth the effort for a tight, neat edge to your knitting.

SINGLE BED CAST ON ROW

For an open edge cast on, on the single bed your instructions will tell you to knit one row and then place the nylon or ravel cord over the first row and hold it down while you knit the next row. This is fine on just a small number of needles, but when you have 30 or more stitches on you will find that the cord bobs up in the middle, especially on a springy yarn, and the next row will produce a hit and miss effect. This can be avoided by pulling a couple of needles at each end and one or two along the row at regular intervals over the cord to hold it down. Now you will be able to knit the row without any trouble. A tension of 4 or looser is desirable.

NOTES ON PLASTIC CARDS

Often we need to mark our punch cards, either with colour changes or pattern changes, and it is difficult to mark on the plastic surface. A projection pen solves this problem. It will mark easily, will not smudge, but can be wiped off if necessary. Again, this is available from large stationery shops.

PILLOW CASES

Machine washing garments can be a disaster when several items become entangled, the chances are they will emerge from the machine several inches longer than they were when they went in. Put your knitteds into an old pillow case before you throw them into the machine. They will keep themselves to themselves and *not* grow in the wash.

Last minute Christmas presents

TEDDY

MATERIALS

Scraps fawn, red and blue 4 ply.

TENSION

Set tension dial to T6.

LEGS

Cast on 9 sts fawn. K 8 rows. Change to blue. K 10 rows increasing beginning of rows 9 and 13. Put needles into holding. K 2nd leg on right of 1st leg leaving gap of 2 needles and reverse shaping.
K across 22 sts k 10 rows. Dec 1 st each end on next 3 rows (16 sts). Change to red. K 3 rows. Cast on 6 sts at beginning of next 2 rows. K 8 rows.
Cast off 7 sts beginning next 2 rows. K 1 row. Change to fawn. K 1 row. Inc 1 at beginning of next 8 rows.
K 10 rows. Dec 1 each end of next 8 rows. Cast off. K 2nd piece to match.

EARS

Cast on 8 sts. K 3 rows. Dec 1 each end alt rows to 4 sts. K 1 row Inc 1 each end alt rows to 8 sts. K 1 row. Cast off.

NOSE

Cast on 16 sts. K 4 rows. Dec 1 each end next 3 rows.
Draw end through stitches and sew up seam.

TO MAKE UP

Sew together all round leaving opening at top of head for stuffing. Stuff and sew up hole. Fold ear pieces in half and sew together on right side. Stuff nose and sew on, embroider nose and eyes. Run thread round neck to draw in to shape. Finished height approx 7 ins.

KNITTED TIE

Use Jones Card 2, Knitmaster Card 7

MATERIAL

2 x 2/30 Acyllic or Bright Acrylic

TO KNIT

T dial 2 cast on by hand 30 sts – knit 16 Rows SS.
RC000. Set to TUCK in one direction.
Set to KNIT in other direction. Knit 400 Rows.
RC000. Set to PLAIN T dial 1··
Dec 1 st each end – knit 10 rows.
Dec 1 st each end – knit 10 rows
Dec 1 st each end – knit to row 200
RC000. T dial 2. Set to TUCK + knit as before.

Inc F f 1 st each end – knit 10 rows.
Inc F f 1 st each end knit to row 240.
Set to PLAIN – knit 16 rows stocking stitch.
T dial 10 knit 1 row – latch off.

TO MAKE UP

Use *plain* side as *right* side hand stitch seam making as flat as possible. Leave about 2 ins open to allow for pulling through to right side.
Machine or back-stitch across ends about ½ in from the last row of pattern. Turn to right side and finish off seam neatly.

WOVEN BAG

SIZE

Approx 35 cm (14 in) x 49 cm (19 in).

MATERIALS

Approx 5 ozs (120 grms) 3 ply for main 'A'.
Approx 4 ozs (105 grms) depending on thickness of weaving yarn 'B'.
2 wooden or plastic handles 12 ins. Lining optional.

TENSION

We used (6··) for the main tension throughout.

BAG (knitted in one piece)

Card 14 from the basic Knitmaster set was used but any weaving card is suitable.
Insert card and lock on row one.
Cast on with WY 124 sts and knit a few rows.
Join in main 'A' yarn RC 000. Knit 4 rows.
RC 000. Set machine for weaving and start pattern, weave 338 rows.
Lock the card and knit 4 rows main yarn only. Run off on WY.
To avoid too much bulk on the handles the sts must be reduced by picking up sts from WY and putting them back on the machine as follows:—
1 st onto the first 6 needles. 2 sts onto the next 56 needles and 1 st onto the last 6 needles. Reduce the tension to (6·) and knit 20 rows. Cast off.
Do the same at the other end.

TO MAKE UP

If you wish to line the bag lay it flat and cut a piece of strong material, (curtain lining is ideal) the same size as the bag. Put in a small pocket 8 ins x 5 ins and sew to bag whilst flat. Sew side seams from bottom but leave 3 ½ ins at top opening i.e. from weaving, sew on handles by making hem through handle, bringing the cast off edge down to the weaving and sew.
Square off the bottom corners by sewing across the seam.

LEG WARMERS

For keep fit, Jogging, Disco Dancing, keeping warm or a quick to knit present.

MATERIALS

Passap. 2 strands of 2/30 yarn – adult size. Knitmaster, Jones machines with ribbers. Small, Medium, Adult 4 ply – Argyll Ferntex 2.

TO KNIT

Passap
Cast on with racking T4/4 40 sts on each bed. Handle down orange strippers.
K 40 rows K/K stitch size 3 ½/3 ½.
K 350 rows N/Ex stitch size 4/4.
K 40 rows K/K stitch size 3 ½/3 ½.
Loose cast off.
Set up so that the K/K rows make a cuff top and bottom.
Knitmaster, Jones machines with ribbers
In 1x1 set up push into WP on machine bed 30 (35, 35) needles.
Push up to correspond on the ribber.
K 30 (40, 40) rows 1x1 rib stitch size 3/3.
Set for fishermans rib.
K 210 (280, 320) rows stitch size 4/4.
Change back to 1x1 rib.
K 30 (40, 40) rows stitch size 3/3.
K the last row T10 both beds transfer to the main bed latch off.

TO MAKE UP

Sew up so that the 1x1 rib forms a cuff top and bottom. Add a strand of glitter for sparkle.

FISH

MATERIALS

D K Random.

TENSION

Set tension dial to T9.

BODY

Cast on 18 sts. K 1 row. Inc 1 each end alt rows to 34 sts. K 14 rows. Dec 1 each end alt rows to 18 sts. Cast off.
Seam together leaving opening for stuffing. Sew on features.

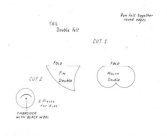

Toys

Samantha Tortoise

MATERIALS

A few oddments of soft 4 ply yarn in 3 colours. Some small pieces of felt for the eyes and eyelashes and a metre of ribbon for the shell edge and hat trim. (Stuffing for the insides . . . washable).

TENSION

Not vital . . . the bigger the stitch the bigger the tortoise but ours was 7 sts and 10 rows per inch. We used a soft 4 ply.

BASE

Cast on by hand 12 sts. Main T(7) K 1 row.
Inc 2 sts at beg of each row to 42 sts. *
Inc 1 st each end on rows 19 and 25. Knit 12 rows.
Dec 1 st each end on the next row and row 38.
Dec 2 sts at beg of each row to 12 sts. Cast off.

BODY

Cast on 12 sts k 1 row work as for base to *.
Inc 1 st each end on rows 22, 24, 26 and 28. Knit 6 rows.
Carriage on the right.
Bring 4 sts on left to H/P. K 1 row. Bring 4 sts on right to H/P. K 1 row.
Repeat these two rows twice. Carriage on the right.
Push 4 needles on the left back to the WP. K 1 row. Push 4 needles on right to WP. K 1 row. Repeat these two rows twice. K 6 rows.
Dec 1 st each end of next row. K 1 row. Repeat these 2 rows three times more.
Cast off 2 sts at beg of each row to 12 sts. K 1 row. Cast off.

FEET

4 feet . . . 8 pieces.
Cast on by hand 9 sts knit 2 rows. Inc 1 st each end of alt rows to 17 sts.
K 7 rows.
Dec 1 st each end of every 3rd row to 7 sts. Cast off.

HEAD (2 pieces)

Cast on by hand 21 sts. K 2 rows. Row 3 dec on the carriage side 1st and inc on the opposite side 1 st on alternate rows 10 times. Knit 14 rows.
Dec 1 st each end on every row to 7 sts. Cast off.
Knit the second piece reversing the shapings so that the pieces face. Sew body to base leaving an opening for stuffing . . . fill the body and join the opening. Do the same with the feet and sew them to the body.
Join the head leaving the bottom (cast on edge) open. Stuff and sew on to body 1/3 onto base and 2/3 onto body. Sew on felt eyes and embroider nose and mouth with red wool. Sew a fringe or lace round the base and back of the neck.

HAT

Cast on by hand 6 sts. 1 row. Inc 1 st each end on rows 2, 5, 8 and 11 and 14. K 9 rows.
Dec 1 st each end on rows 24, 27, 30, 33 and 36. K 1 row. Cast off.
Sew lace round edge. Run thread of wool round 3/8 in from the edge of the cap (not counting the lace) draw up and sew onto head.

Penguin

MATERIALS

Oddments. 4 ply wool. We used Black, White and Gold Acrylic Stuffing.

TENSION

Approximately (6.)

BODY

Start with Black.
Cast on 10 sts.
Knit 3 rows. (inc 1 st each end next row, k 2 rows) twice.
Inc 1 st each end of next row. K 21 rows.
Dec 1 st each end of next row. K 3 rows.
Dec 1 st each end of next row. K 4 rows.
Change to white wool. K 4 rows.
Inc 1 st each end of next row.
K 3 rows.
Inc 1 st each end of next row.
K 21 rows. (Dec 1 st each end next row. K 2 rows) three times.
Cast off.
Sew up sides, leave top open for stuffing, sew up opening.

HEAD

In Black.
Cast on 8 sts.
K 2 rows. (Inc 1 st each end of next row) twice.
K 9 rows. (Dec 1 st each end of next row) twice.
K 6 rows. (Inc 1 st each end next row) twice.
K 9 rows. (Dec 1 st each end next row) twice.
K 2 rows. Cast off.
Sew up sides and stuff, sew up opening and sew on to body.

FLIPPERS

(2 Pieces) in Black.
Cast on 5 sts.
Knit 24 rows, increasing one st each end in rows 3 and 10 and dec one st each end on rows 17 and 21.
At row 25 change to white wool.
Knit 49 rows, increasing one st each end of rows 29 and 33 and dec one st each end of rows 40 and 47.
Cast off on row 49.
Sew up side seams and stuff lightly. Sew to body.

BEAK

In Gold.
Cast on 3 sts. K 3 rows (inc 1 st each end of next row) twice.
Cast off.
Sew up seams on right side, stuffing lightly as you join up.

FEET

(2 Pieces) in Gold.
Cast on 6 sts.
K 4 rows.
Inc 1 st each end of next row.
K 3 rows.
Inc 1 st each end of next row.
K 5 rows.
Dec 1 st each end of next row.
K 3 rows.
Dec 1 st each end of next row.
K 2 rows.
Cast off.
Sew up on right side stuffing lightly.
Make eyes with white and black wool.

Mouse

MATERIALS

Oddments of DK (T8) approx.
Small piece of cardboard, cut to suitable size, for base and small piece of felt for ears.

BODY

Cast on 3 sts. K 1 row. (Cast on 2 beg next row k 1 row). Repeat to 11 rows. (K 3 rows, Dec 1 st at right side). Repeat to 7 sts. K 2 rows. Inc 1 st right next row. K 3 rows. Dec 1 st right side every row to 1 st. Cast off. Make 2nd piece to face by casting on from left to right.

BASE

Cast on 2 st. Inc 1 st each end on every other row to 12 sts.
Dec 1 st each end every 4th row to 2 sts. Cast off.
Sew back seam of body. Sew base to body leaving opening for stuffing at tail end. Make cord for tail and sew on to seam. Put in piece of card before stuffing. Sew up opening.
Make ears of double felt.
Embroider eyes.

Doggy coat

Suitable for any machine capable of Fair Isle but could be knitted in stocking stitch on any machine.

SIZE

Finished length — head to tail — approx 44 cm 17½ ins. Width at widest part of chest 42 cms (16½ ins).

MATERIALS

Two colours of any soft 4 ply. The finished coat weighs 70 grms.

TENSION

7 sts and 10 rows per inch measured over Fair Isle. T dial approx (7). Any small Fair Isle pattern can be used. We used a 4 stitch – 6 row check.

TO KNIT

Cast on in main yarn 24 sts. Work in stocking stitch. K 2 rows. Cast on 3 sts at beginning of next 4 rows. Start Fair Isle. Cast on 3 sts at beg of next 8 rows (60 sts). Cast on 2 sts at beg of next 20 rows and 1 st at beg of next 10 rows (110 sts). Inc 1 st every 4th and 5th row 16 times (142 sts). Carriage on the right. Put 114 Ns at opp end to carr into H/P. * Change to stocking stitch – main tension and knit on the rem 28 sts. Keep right edge straight. Dec 1 st at left edge on the next and ev foll 4th row 12 times. Knit 8 rows *. Break off the yarn and run the remaining 16 sts onto WY. Push next 86 sts into WP. In Fair Isle dec 1 st each end of the next and ev foll 4th row 12 times. Knit 8 rows. Run off on WY. Work remaining sts as from * to *. Reversing the shaping. Replace the stitches of the centre and right hand side onto the machine (wrong side of work facing you). K 2 rows.

Ribbers and double bed machines
Transfer sts to 1x1 rib. Rib tension but not too tight.
Knit 8 rows main col.
Knit 6 rows contrast.
Knit 6 rows main.
Knit 6 rows contrast.
Knit 6 rows main.
Cast off loosely.

Single bed machines
Transfer sts to 1x1 mock rib and knit the colour sequence through twice and pick up the hem. Cast off loosely.

TO MAKE UP

Sew seam from cast off on rib and 5½ ins of plain knitting. Crochet 2 rows of double crochet round leg holes and all round the edge.

OPTIONAL EXTRA

On the second row of crochet make a chain 3½ ins long starting 1 in before and finishing 1 in after the centre back. (For the tail!)

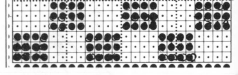